INSTITUTIONS TAKING ROOT

NEW FRONTIERS OF SOCIAL POLICY

Institutions Taking Root

Building State Capacity in Challenging Contexts

Naazneen H. Barma, Elisabeth Huybens, and
Lorena Viñuela, Editors

WORLD BANK GROUP

ISBN (paper): 978-1-4648-0269-0
ISBN (electronic): 978-1-4648-0270-6
DOI: 10.1596/978-1-4648-0269-0

Cover image is from the World Bank art program.
Cover design: Critical Stages

Library of Congress Cataloging-in-Publication Data
Institutions taking root : building state capacity in challenging contexts / edited by Naazneen H. Barma, Elisabeth Huybens, and Lorena Viñuela.
     pages cm. — (New frontiers of social policy)
Includes bibliographical references and index.
ISBN 978-1-4648-0269-0 (alk. paper) — ISBN 978-1-4648-0270-6 (electronic : alk. paper)
1. Institution   building—Developing   countries. 2. Institutional   economics—Developing countries. I. Barma, Naazneen. II. Huybens, Elisabeth. III. Viñuela, Lorena. IV. World Bank.
   JF60.I555 2014
   338.9172'4—dc23   2014026061

NEW FRONTIERS OF SOCIAL POLICY

In many developing countries, the mixed record of state effectiveness, market imperfections, and persistent structural inequities has undermined the effectiveness of social policy. To overcome these constraints, social policy needs to move beyond conventional social service approaches toward development's goals of equitable opportunity and social justice. This series has been created to promote debate among the development community, policy makers, and academia, and to broaden understanding of social policy challenges in developing country contexts.

The books in the series are linked to the World Bank's Social Development Strategy. The strategy is aimed at empowering people by transforming institutions to make them more inclusive, responsive, and accountable. This involves the transformation of subjects and beneficiaries into citizens with rights and responsibilities. Themes in this series include equity and development, assets and livelihoods, citizenship and rights-based social policy, and the social dimensions of infrastructure and climate change.

Titles in the series:

CONTENTS

Boxes

Figures

Map

Tables

I have been associated with the Institutions Taking Root project from its inception, providing advice and participating in the many discussions that were organized around the review of these case studies. It has been a privilege and an enriching learning experience.

Addressing the dynamics of poor governance and accountability, ineffective institutions, repeated political crises, and continuous cycles of violence—known collectively under the generic term "fragile situations"—is critical for reducing world poverty. It is estimated that by 2030, 40 percent of poor people will live in countries that are currently classified by the World Bank as fragile. If situations of extreme violence and active conflict in middle-income countries are added, that percentage jumps to nearly 75 percent. At the same time, global phenomena such as climate change, increased internal and cross border migration, illicit trade, and rising inequality create additional stresses.

An increasing number of studies address issues of fragility, conflict, and violence, but the literature is still very focused on understanding the drivers of fragility, as well as its impact on social and economic development. Relatively little is known about how countries and societies have managed to exit fragility. Examples of positive transformation, especially of public agencies that manage macroeconomic and fiscal policy or deliver frontline social services, are not being sufficiently studied.

Institutions Taking Root: Building State Capacity in Challenging Contexts is one exception to that trend: This study has disentangled how nine selected institutions across four fragile and conflict-affected countries have managed to improve their capacity in very challenging environments. This volume was born from a simple idea: Study public organizations that have improved their capacity and get a better understanding of how these changes actually happened. The authors of the case studies in this volume have taken a deep dive into the internal workings of nine public agencies. They looked at a comprehensive set of issues from institutional management practices to relationships with clients, and more broadly to the authorizing environment and the agencies' connections with country elites. The authors emerged from this exercise with extremely valuable insights on institutional development in fragile environments.

One insight that caught my attention is the fundamental importance of agencies' ability to carefully manage their relationship with elites. In fragile environments, these elites often operate outside predictable frameworks, and they respond to incentives created by the local sociopolitical context, which has little to do with the Weberian concept of the State. The study also reveals three common pathways that managers of the public agencies have used to handle the elites' authorizing environment. The similarity of these pathways across continents, and in very different situations, is surprising and provides a useful insight for policy makers.

Another interesting finding is that many of the internal reforms undertaken by public agencies were very similar to "good practice" management techniques from the western world. This implies that not everything has to be done differently in a fragile environment. Organizational leadership can manage the very challenging external environment, while internally applying some of the more *universal* public management innovations to improve capacity and performance.

Institutions Taking Root also highlights recommendations that stand in stark contrast to the traditional "best practices" of capacity building, which donor partners have applied routinely across varying contexts for many years. Rather than parachute solutions in from the outside, this book proposes that development partners accompany domestic agency managers and staff in their own efforts to reorient institutions. This insight implies a very different role for development partners in providing support to agencies as they handle internal and external constituencies than in traditional capacity building projects. It implies staying engaged in the very long term. And it implies finding creative mechanisms for shaping public agencies' internal culture.

Institutions Taking Root: Building State Capacity in Challenging Contexts is an important contribution to the literature on fragility; I hope that it will challenge many of the existing models of capacity building in fragile environments.

Alexandre Marc
Chief Specialist
Fragility, Conflict, and Violence
The World Bank

ACKNOWLEDGMENTS

This research was conducted by staff and consultants of The World Bank, and it was supported by the Bank–Netherlands Reform Program and the Governance Partnership Facility. The editors gratefully acknowledge the contributions of the authors and co-authors of the case studies conducted for this project—Helle M. Alvesson, Catherine Anderson, Ousman Barrie, Brendan Glynn, Marco Larizza, and Stéphanie Robert Oksen—as well as the inputs of Afri Consult, Emanic Consulting, Indochina Research Limited Laos, Josh Trindade, Fidelis Magalhanes, and Matias Saldanha.

We are extremely grateful to the leadership, staff, and clients of the nine agencies examined in the case studies. This volume could not have been written without their generosity and thoughtful insights, and its publication would not have been possible without them. The nine agencies are the Ministry of Basic and Secondary Education of The Gambia, the Ministry of Finance and Economic Affairs of The Gambia, Électricité du Laos, the Ministry of Public Works and Transport of Lao PDR, the Ministry of Finance and Economic Development of Sierra Leone, the Ministry of Local Government and Rural Development of Sierra Leone, the Ministry of Health of Timor-Leste, the Ministry of Social Solidarity of Timor-Leste, and the Central Bank of Timor-Leste.

The editors are also grateful for the inputs on the project concept and research design, as well as on the interpretation and framing of findings, from Derick Brinkerhoff, Pilar Domingo, Bernard Harborne, David Leonard, Nick Manning, Alexandre Marc, Willy McCourt, Alastair McKechnie, Mick Moore, Stephen Ndegwa, Doug Porter, Randi Ryterman, Graham Teskey, Jennifer Widner, and Yongmei Zhou. The comments and guidance from Hans Anand Beck, Genevieve F. Boyreau, Carlos Calvancatti, Luis Constantino, Pamela Dale, Habib Fetini, Nathalie Lahire, Keiko Miwa, Vera Songwe, and Sombath Southivong were also essential for completing the various case studies. Drafts of the work underpinning this volume were presented at workshops hosted at World Bank headquarters in Washington, DC, on July 18–19, 2012, and May 1–3, 2013.

The authors are obliged to the many academics, practitioners, and government counterparts who participated in these workshops and whose excellent comments and thoughtful suggestions have informed this final version of the volume.

The authors thank Cyprian Fisiy for his steady support of this work. In addition we are indebted to Rachel Ort, without whose steady and diligent stewardship this volume would not have been possible. Elizabeth Acul, Joyce Y. Chinsen, and Anju Sachdeva supplied important administrative support. We also received logistical support from The World Bank's staff in its Banjul, Dili, Freetown, and Vientiane offices. In particular, Allan Cole, Maria Isabel Alda Da Silva, Leila Maria Gusmao dos Reis Martins, Badara Alieu Joof, Warrah Mansaray, and Thalavanh Vongsonephet supported the team during the extended fieldwork.

Editors

Naazneen H. Barma is Assistant Professor of National Security Affairs at the Naval Postgraduate School in Monterey, California. Her research and teaching focus on the political economy of development, natural resource governance, and international interventions in postconflict states, with a regional specialization in East Asia and Pacific. She has published books, chapters, and journal articles on these topics. Ms. Barma previously worked at the World Bank on governance and institutional reform. She received both her PhD and MA in Political Science from the University of California, Berkeley, and her MA in International Policy Studies and BA in International Relations and Economics from Stanford University.

Elisabeth Huybens is the Practice Manager for the Social, Urban, Rural, and Resilience Global Practice in the Europe and Central Asia Region of the World Bank. The Global Practice offers advisory and operational support, research, and innovative thinking in social sustainability, focusing on what makes societies cohesive, inclusive, resilient, and accountable. Ms. Huybens also leads research on successful public institutions in fragile and conflict-affected situations. Ms. Huybens joined the World Bank in 2000 as an Economist in the Africa Region and has since held various positions, including that of Country Economist for Chad, Country Manager for Timor-Leste, Lead Country Operations Officer for South East Europe, and Sector Manager for Social Development in the Sustainable Development Vice-presidency. Ms. Huybens has a PhD in Economics from Cornell University.

Lorena Viñuela is a Public Sector Specialist with the World Bank's Governance Global Practice. Her work and research relate to the political economy of public policy reform, fiscal policy, intergovernmental relations, and comparative politics. Prior to joining the World Bank, she worked at the Maxwell School of Public Affairs of Syracuse University, the Institute for Qualitative and Multi-method Research, and the Inter-American Development Bank. She is the co-author of the book *Rents to Riches: Political Economy of Natural Resource-Led Development*, and numerous articles and book chapters related to decentralization, public finance, and political economy.

Authors

Helle M. Alvesson is a medical anthropologist and international consultant whose work and research has focused on the interface between community- and central-level practices in health and social protection. Her work elucidates how people define, experience, and cope with health and education concerns, and how people respond to public programs that promote improved human development. She holds a PhD in Public Health from Karolinska Institutet, Sweden, and an MA in Anthropology from the University of Copenhagen.

Catherine Anderson is a Public Sector Governance Specialist who has worked with the East Asia and Pacific and Africa regions of the World Bank. Her predominant experience is in extractive industries governance, public sector reform, and institutional governance in fragile and postconflict countries. She holds a Masters of Law, Development and Governance from the School of Oriental and African Studies at the University of London and a Bachelor of Arts in Political Science from Victoria University, Wellington, New Zealand.

Ousman Barrie is the Director of Saadia Consulting (Sierra Leone). He served formerly as the Deputy Commissioner General of the National Revenue Authority of Sierra Leone.

Brendan Glynn has three decades of experience as an analyst, consultant, and trainer in Public Sector Reform (PSR) and Institutional Strengthening (IS) with regional specialization in Africa and the transforming Eastern European economies. He graduated from the National University of Ireland and has a MSc in Economics from the London School of Economics. In recent years he worked as a PSR specialist at the World Bank Country Office in Sierra Leone and on projects in Burundi and Tanzania. Since

August 2013 he has been a Project Manager and Lead Expert under an IS component of the Bank-funded Zanzibar Urban Services Project.

Marco Larizza is a Governance and Senior Public Sector Specialist in the Governance Global Practice of the World Bank, and a nonresident Visiting Fellow at the Institute for Democracy and Conflict Resolution, University of Essex. His most recent work focuses on the interactions between political institutions and the provision of public goods and services in fragile and postconflict countries. He has published peer-review articles, book chapters, and policy reports related to the political economy of public service reforms, decentralization, and comparative democratization. He holds a PhD in Political Science from the University of Essex and an MA degree in Development Economics from the University of Bologna.

Stephanie R. Oksen is a social scientist based in Jakarta, Indonesia. During her four-year stay in Lao PDR she worked on energy policy and planning. She has also been engaged in monitoring socio-economic changes in communities impacted by large mining operations. She holds a PhD in International Development Studies from Roskilde University, Denmark. Her PhD investigated the state-building process in Lao PDR, through an analysis of institutions and power relations within the electricity sector. She taught Institutional Economics at the Copenhagen Business School with an emphasis on management practices within different cultural contexts, institutional development in Africa, and corporate social responsibility.

ADB	Asian Development Bank
AfDB	African Development Bank
AFPRC	Armed Forces Provisional Ruling Council
AFRC	Armed Forces Revolutionary Council
AFRC/RUF	Armed Forces Revolutionary Council/Revolutionary United Front
AG	Auditor General
AGD	Accountant General's Department
AMRC	Assets Management and Recovery Corporation
AO	Accounting Officer
APC	All People's Congress
APRC	Alliance for Patriotic Reorientation and Construction
ASEAN	Association of Southeast Asian Nations
BCC	Bo City Council
BDM	Bolsa da Mãe
BESPOR	Basic Education Support for Poverty Reduction
BIS	Bank of International Settlements
BOOT	build-own-operate-and-transfer
BPA	Banking and Payments Authority
BSL	Bank of Sierra Leone
BTL	below the line (accounts)
CA	chief administrator
CB	Central Bank of Timor-Leste
CBEMP	Capacity Building and Economic Management Project
CBOs	community-based organizations
CCM	Coordinating Committee Meetings
CFA	Central Fiscal Authority
CFAA	Country Financial Accountability Assessment
CFET	Consolidated Fund for East Timor
CFFA	Country Financial Accountability Assessment
CGD	Central Fiscal Authority

CHC	Community Health Center
CLoGPAS	Comprehensive Local Government Performance Assessment System
CNRT	National Council for Timorese Resistance
CoM	Conselho do Ministros
CPAR	Country Procurement Assessment Report
CPIA	Country Policy and Institutional Assessment
CPO	Central Payments Office
CRIS	Credit Registry Information System
CSDMRS	Commonwealth Secretariat Debt Management and Recording System
CTAP	Chiefdom and Tribal Administration Policy
DACO	Development Assistance Co-ordination Office
DC	District Council
Dec-Sec	Decentralization Secretariat
DfID	Department for International Development
DFP	Directorate of Finance and Planning
DFS	Deputy Financial Secretary
DNSS	National Directorate for Social Security
DNT	Directorate of the National Treasury
DNTP	Direcção Nacional de Terra e Propriedade
DO	district officer
DOE	Department of Electricity
DOSFEA	Department of State for Finance and Economic Affairs
DPs	development partners
DPWT	Department of Public Works and Transport
DRNS	National Directorate for Social Reinsertion
DSDP	Decentralized Service Delivery Project
EC/EU	European Commission/European Union
ECOMOG	Economic Community of West African States Monitoring Group
ECOWAS	Economic Community of West African States
ECU	Expenditure Control Unit
EDL	Électricité du Laos
EDL-GEN	Électricité du Laos Generation
EFA	Education for All
EGRA	Early Grade Reading Assessment
EITI	Extractive Industries Transparency Initiative
EMIS	Education Management Information System

EMOC	Emergency Management of Obstetric Care
EMPU	Economic Management and Policy Unit
EPRU	Economic Policy and Research Unit
ERP	Economic Recovery Program
ESI	Estimated Sustainable Income
EU	European Union
FCS	fragile and conflict-affected situations
FGD	focus group discussion
FGP	focus group participant
FMAS	Financial Management Accounting System
FRETILIN	Revolutionary Front for an Independent East Timor
FRP	financial recovery program
FS	Financial Secretary
FTI	Fast Track Initiative
GAMTEL	Gambia Telecommunications
GBA-Act	Government Budgeting and Accountability Act
GBoS	Gambia Bureau of Statistics
GDA	Gambia Divestiture Agency
GDP	gross domestic product
GGC	Gambia Groundnut Corporation
GoSL	Government of Sierra Leone
GoTL	Government of Timor-Leste
GPPA	Gambia Public Procurement Authority
GRA	Gambia Revenue Authority
GRS	Governance Reform Secretariat
GTZ	German Agency for Cooperation
HHF	Hamutuk Hari'i Futuru
HIPC	Heavily Indebted Poor Countries
HRM	human resource management
HRMO	Human Resource Management Office
HSP	health service provider
IAD	Internal Audit Department/Division
ICGR	International Crisis Group Report
ICT	information communications technology
IDA	International Development Association
IDP	internally displaced persons
IFMIS	Integrated Financial Management Information System
IHA	Interim Health Authority
ILO	International Labour Organization

IMCI	Integrated Management of Childhood Illnesses
IMF	International Monetary Fund
IMFTL	Institucao de Microfinancas de Timor-Leste
INGO	international nongovernmental organization
INTERFET	United Nations International Force for East Timor
IPP	independent power producer
I-PRSP	Interim Poverty Reduction Strategy Paper
IRCBP	Institutional Reform and Capacity Building Project
JAM	Joint Assessment Mission
JICA	Japan International Cooperation Agency
KAK	Anti-Corruption Commission
Lao PDR	Lao People's Democratic Republic
LC	local council
LGA	Local Government Act
LGFC	Local Government Finance Committee
LGFD	Local Government Finance Department
LGSC	Local Government Services Commission
LHSE	Lao Holding State Enterprise
LPRP	Lao People's Revolutionary Party
LTA	local technical assistant
LVTS	Large Value Transfer System
MCTPC	Ministry of Communication, Transport, Post, and Construction
MDAs	ministries, department, and agencies
MDGs	Millennium Development Goals
MDR	multilateral debt relief
MDTF	Multi-Donor Trust Fund
MEM	Ministry of Energy and Mines
MEPID	Ministry of Economic Planning and Industrial Development
MFR	Management and Functional Review
MLGRD	Ministry of Local Government and Rural Development
MLRC	Ministry for Labour and Community Reinsertion
MoBSE	Ministry of Basic and Secondary Education
MoDEP	Ministry of Development and Economic Planning
MoE	Ministry of Education
MoF	Ministry of Finance
MoFEA	Ministry of Finance and Economic Affairs

MoFED	Ministry of Finance and Economic Development of Sierra Leone
MoH	Ministry of Health of Timor-Leste
MoI	Ministry of Infrastructure
MoJ	Ministry of Justice
MP	Member of Parliament
MPI	Ministry of Planning and Investment
MPWT	Ministry of Public Works and Transport
MSS	Ministry of Social Solidarity
MTEF	Medium Term Expenditure Framework
NaCSA	National Commission for Social Action
NAO	National Audit Office
NAWEC	National Water and Electricity Company
NCC	National Consultative Committee
NDP	National Decentralisation Policy
NEC	National Electoral Commission
NEFCOM	National Emergency Fiscal Committee
NEM	New Economic Mechanism
NGO	nongovernmental organization
NHSSP	National Health Sector Support Program
NHSSP-SP	National Health Sector Strategic Plan–Support Project
NPC	National Planning Commission
NPL	nonperforming loan
NPP	National Priority Program
NPRC	National Provisional Ruling Council
NPS	National Public Service Survey
NRA	National Revenue Authority
NRS	National Recovery Strategy
NSEDP	National Socio-Economic Development Plan
ODA	Official Development Assistance
ODI	Overseas Development Institute
OPWT	Office of Public Works and Transport
P2P	Power to the Poor
PAC	Public Accounts Committee
PAGE	Program for Accelerated Growth and Employment
PBU	Peacebuilding Unit
PC	paramount chief
PCC	Provincial Coordinating Committee

PCU	Project Coordination Unit
PDD I	Programa Dezenvolvimento Decentralisado I
PDD II	Programa Dezenvolvimento Decentralisado II
PDFS	Principal Deputy Financial Secretary
PDHJ	Provedore for Justice and Human Rights and Justice
PDMU	Public Debt Management Unit
PEFA	Public Expenditure and Financial Accountability
PER	Public Expenditure Review
PETS	Public Expenditure Tracking Survey
PF	Petroleum Fund
PFM	Public Financial Management
PFMRU	Public Finance Management Unit
PIU	Project Implementation Unit
PMDC	People's Movement for Democratic Change
PMO	Personnel Management Office
PMS	Performance Management System
PNTL	Policia National de Timor-Leste
PPP	People's Progressive Party
PRGF	Poverty Reduction and Growth Facility
PRSP	Poverty Reduction Strategy Paper
PS	Provincial Secretary
PSF	Promotores Saude Familia (Family Health Promoters)
PSMSP	Public Sector Management Support Project
PTA	parent-teacher association
PURA	Public Utilities Regulatory Agency
RENETIL	Resistencia Nacional Dos Estudantes De Timor-Leste
RMF	Road Maintenance Fund
RTF	Resident Technical Facilitator
RUF	Revolutionary United Front
SAMES	Autonomous Medical Supply System
SDP	Social Dialogue Program
SDT	Social Dialogue Team
SEACEN	South East Asian Central Banks
SIDA	Swedish International Development Agency
SIGRH	Human Resource Management Integrated System
SISCA	Integrated Community Health System
SLPP	Sierra Leone People's Party
SLRA	Sierra Leone Road Authority
SMC	School Management Committee

SMD	single-member district
SMEs	small and medium enterprises
SMT	Senior Management Team
SOE	state-owned enterprise
SSA	Sub-Saharan Africa
SSLRC	Secretary of State for Labour and Community Reinsertion
SSLS	Secretary of State for Labour and Solidarity
TAs	tribal authorities
TFET	Trust Fund for East Timor
TLDHS	Timor-Leste Demographic Health Survey
TSP	Transition Support Team
TTL	task team leader
UNDP	United Nations Development Programme
UNFPA	United Nations Population Fund
UNICEF	United Nations Fund for Children
UNIFEM	United Nations Development Fund for Women
UNMISET	United Nations Mission in Timor-Leste
UNMIT	United Nations Integrated Mission in Timor-Leste
UNOTIL	United Nations Office in Timor-Leste
UNTAET	United Nations Transitional Administration of East Timor
UNTL	National University of Timor-Leste
USAID	U.S. Agency for International Development
VAT	value-added tax
VSO	Voluntary Service Overseas program
WAEMU	West African Economic and Monetary Union
WAMZ	West African Monetary Zone
WDC	Ward Development Committee
WDR	World Development Report
WFP	World Food Programme
WHO	World Health Organization

Institutions Taking Root: Building State Capacity in Challenging Contexts

Lorena Viñuela, Naazneen H. Barma, and Elisabeth Huybens

Building and operating successful public institutions is a perennial and long-term challenge for governments, even under ideal circumstances. The complexity of this challenge is compounded by the volatile conditions found in fragile and conflict-affected settings (FCS), where human security, social cohesion, political stability, and economic activity have been dislocated. The academic and practitioner literature on FCS is replete with instances of institution-building challenges, obstacles, and—ultimately—failures. Yet, despite the daunting odds, some public institutions in FCS do manage to take root and effectively deliver results and core services, earn legitimacy in the eyes of the citizenry, and forge resilience in an otherwise tumultuous operational context. This observation is the analytical puzzle motivating this study. We concentrate on a sample of these success stories in order to illuminate the shared causal factors underlying success and thereby isolate the institutional practices and processes that underpin capable public institutions in inhospitable settings. The findings contribute to filling a critical gap in the literature on FCS and provide guidance for policy makers engaged in public sector institution-building efforts in countries with weak institutional capacity.[1]

Institution building is a lengthy and complex undertaking anywhere, yet in FCS the challenges that must be navigated are especially daunting. FCS are marked by salient, often long-standing, societal, political, and geographical cleavages. The sociopolitical landscape is often fluid and subject to large and unpredictable sways. Usually the state has a light footprint beyond the capital and informal institutions are more present in citizens' lives than formal ones. Patronage and widespread rent-seeking and corruption are common. The state has little legitimacy in the eyes of the citizenry and the state-society compact is weak at best. Development partners are inconsistent in their responses to these situations: on the one hand, they often disengage from situations that are broadly dysfunctional, while, on the other hand, they pour abundant and often poorly coordinated resources into the immediate aftermath of violent conflict.

We find that institutions succeed in these inhospitable environments when they are able to construct strategies of deft management—through a shared repertoire of tools and reforms—and concurrently employ tactics to navigate the broader sociopolitical environment in which they are embedded. In our sample, there are no clear predictors of which institutions or sectors will be successful. Sector institutions that are succeeding in one country are failing in other FCS. Yet one clear pattern emerges from our study: by focusing on delivering results and generating legitimacy at the same time, successful organizations develop internal efficiency and create the external constituencies needed to secure political support. They cumulatively build resilience and the ability to sustain gains in what can be rapidly shifting political-economic environments. Broad social support makes it politically attractive for principals to support reforms and can help restrain excessive political interference. In all of the cases, a network of technical leaders and practitioners ignites and sustains the successful trajectory.

The agencies in this study display different patterns in the manner in which they connect their micro-organizational strategies to the broader macro-sociopolitical environment. Some institutions succeed on the basis of a positive cycle driven by strong elite commitment to their particular policy area. Other successful institutions seize on a window of opportunity to lock in reforms and build a measure of operational autonomy before the political equilibrium shifts. Still other agencies succeed by more actively cultivating broad support from clients and key stakeholders, sometimes in the face of an adverse political environment, working under the radar to implement reforms and achieve results, later mobilizing some support from political principals. The distinction between these three pathways to institutional success is in the degree to which institutional success emanates from political incentives and imperatives or the institution's own ability to build a case for its political significance. Yet all of these profiles combine macropolitical and microinstitutional strategies in ways that enable institutions to take root and succeed. Notably, the repertoire of strategies these agencies deploy is remarkably similar across the different pathways.

We build our argument as follows. First, we frame the pursuit of state capacity in challenging environments as an undertaking at the intersection of macropolitical context and opportunities and microinstitutional choices and strategies. Second, we define institutional success, outline the structured, focused case comparative methodology employed in the study, and discuss our sample of successful agencies. Next we turn to the empirical findings emerging from case studies of nine successful public agencies in The Gambia, the Lao People's Democratic Republic, Sierra Leone, and Timor-Leste. Third, we describe three alternative pathways to institutional success. Fourth, we briefly catalog the core institutional repertoire of tools and strategies underpinning success across the variety of agencies in our study. And fifth, we present the policy implications emerging from our study. The conclusion briefly revisits our key findings and suggests further research possibilities on this topic.

Literature Review: Building State Capacity in Challenging Contexts

The development community has converged on the consensus that the challenges facing fragile states lie in the extreme degree to which they lack institutional capacity. Elites in FCS must develop two dimensions of institutional capacity to be able to effectively deliver on any form of state-society compact. The first dimension of state capacity is the "Weberian" element of intensive capacity, which rests on the internal organization and autonomy of public agencies (World Bank 1997). The second dimension of institutional capacity is the "Tocquevillian" element of extensive capacity, focused on the state's connections to society.[2] In short, successful public agencies require the internal organization to define and act on their mandate and they must manage their external relationships to deliver on societal needs and successfully navigate the sociopolitical context.

Macro Side: Fit with the Sociopolitical Context

Institutional capacity-building and reform initiatives, to be tractable, durable, and legitimate, must resonate with a country's social and political fabric, aligning with the incentives of the makers and implementers of policy and taking into account the social context in which the broader population lives. *World Development Report 2011* advances such a good-fit, incentive-compatible philosophy, arguing that institutional reforms in FCS do not need to be technically perfect; rather, they should be adapted to the political context and incentives in place at any given point in time.

Some have argued, in this vein, that successful institution building must necessarily be aligned with the negotiation and composition of the state-society compact.[3] The ability of public institutions to deliver on the state's compact with society depends on their interaction with many sets of stakeholders—including their political and bureaucratic principals, their donors and implementation partners (public and private), and their service clients. Leonard (2010) points out that organizational effectiveness depends, in part, on the benefits the agency generates for politically power-ful groups.[4] Manor (2007) argues on the basis of detailed empirical case studies that organizations in FCS are more likely to be successful if they design programs and adapt implementation based on close consultation with local-level stakeholders.

Similarly, the ability of an institution to take root is embedded in political processes and power structures, both formal and informal, and the country's historical trajectory.[5] Some elements of fragility are deeply ingrained in societal dynamics and relationships, and a core dimension of institutional capacity concerns the extent to which the agencies of the state are able to help mediate social conflict and assist in repairing and building the sociopolitical fabric.[6]

In fragile states, with low institutional capacity, these political forces and macro social cleavages can be fluid and sometimes subject to surprisingly swift—and easily reversible—change. In a practical sense, organizational effectiveness is contingent on the broader political context and institutions that shape what is operationally feasible.[7] In some cases, the overarching elite political bargain will serve developmental goals; in other cases, the interests of the political elite may give it a particular interest in a specific sector or category of public services for an important part of society.

Micro Dimensions: Institutional Strategies for Success

Scholars and development practitioners have found that internal and exter-nal dimensions are relevant in explaining successful institution building in challenging contexts; and, moreover, they tend to argue that the two dimensions interact.[8] In surveying the literature, Leonard (2010) observes that one major strand of hypotheses on organizational effectiveness holds that it is determined in large part by how an organization's management structures it to achieve its tasks. Grindle (1997), for example, highlights four characteristics that enable public sector organizations to perform relatively well in otherwise unfavorable developing country contexts. Successful organizations develop an organizational mystique, or an internalized sense of mission; have flexible managers who are problem-solving and teamwork oriented; have clearly defined performance expectations; and have some autonomy in personnel management.

The focus on how an agency's functions can affect performance is akin to Israel's (1987) landmark theory of "specificity" in institutional development, whereby organizations that perform more highly technical and specialized functions (e.g., central banks, compared with education ministries) are more likely to be high performers.[9] Fukuyama (2004) narrows the concept of specificity to suggest that state-building and institutional reform efforts are most successful in agencies where tasks are highly specific and the volume of transactions is low, because these are the organizations in which monitoring outputs and accountability is most possible.

Moving away from the recourse to first-best reform dictums, the development community has come to agree on the concept of "good enough governance," first articulated by Grindle (2004, 2007). The notion centers on "good-fit" approaches, or contextually grounded and feasible institutional arrangements that achieve a de minimus degree of quality sufficient to enable a country to fulfill its developmental goals. In a similar vein, institutions are more likely to be successful in fragile contexts when they carefully identify, tap into, and build on preexisting capacity—whether this capacity is situated in the agency, other public institutions, or nongovernmental or civic groups. Teskey (2005), for example, emphasizes the importance of aligning individual staff competence, the organization, and institutional context in the pursuit of sustained capacity building. As mechanisms for doing so, he underlines the importance of precisely defining the institutional challenge and the interests involved, as well as constructing a targeted approach to the scope of organizational reform.

Often, public sector agencies that pursue certain functions adopt similar institutional forms across countries, especially in response to donor preferences and programs that emphasize certain normative models of organization—for example, ministries of finance tend to resemble each other quite closely.[10] Isomorphic mimicry can prove an important strategy for successful institutions to garner financial resources and other forms of donor support. Yet, as Pritchett, Woolcock, and Andrews (2013) assert, this focus on institutional form can often mask a lack of functional development activity and create a "capability trap" instead of enhancing capacity. In practice, the institutional form of public sector agencies can and should vary in their pursuit of specific functions.[11]

Research Design: Explaining Institutional Success

Many advances have been made in recent years in defining and measuring public sector institutional capacity writ large.[12] Yet relatively little causal thinking has been devoted to assessing what elements of institutional design and operation actually contribute to success. This study seeks to understand the underpinnings of successful institution building by focusing on those public organizations in which success has been achieved. In choosing to study only successful institutions, we are deliberately selecting on the dependent variable. The approach of focusing on success stories to understand organizational effectiveness in developing countries has a demonstrated intellectual lineage. Leonard (2010, 94) points out a small, yet influential, group of scholars—including himself, Norman Uphoff, Judith Tendler, and Samuel Paul—who have studied successful development interventions on the premise that "it is dangerous to derive development prescriptions only from data that are largely dominated by failures." This includes the research project Institutions for Successful Societies led by Jennifer Widner, at Princeton University, that investigates and chronicles how reformers build effective government institutions.

We define an institution as successful if, at a minimum, it achieves three core sets of outcomes: results, legitimacy, and durability.[13] An institution is considered to achieve results if it exhibits sustained, measurable improvements in key agency outputs and outcomes. In measuring legitimacy, we focus on the population's sentiments regarding the agency's performance, including whether an institution has achieved results across any cleavages (e.g., rural-urban, between ethnic groups, and so forth) that may exist.[14] Finally, a resilient institution is durable, sustaining and enhancing results over time, even in the face of changing leadership and exogenous shocks. These three dimensions of success are, of course, interwoven—an organization's legitimacy depends at least partly on its results; an institution that is seen as legitimate is more likely to be resilient; and, in turn, a more resilient institution has a greater opportunity to earn legitimacy and achieve results.

We considered for analysis any public institution in a country on the World Bank's FCS list in 2009 that met the defined criteria of success as long as it can be reasonably seen as a permanent instrument of the state. The public institution could thus be a finance ministry, a service delivery institution, or even a state-owned enterprise—but not a project implementation unit or donor-funded program. We use the term "institution" colloquially, that is, interchangeably with "agency" or "organization," rather than hewing to the new institutional economics definition of institutions (see North 1990) as "rules of the game" or "established social practices" that are distinct from organizations.

A pool of potential case study institutions was created by soliciting from FCS practitioners at the World Bank examples of institutions that appeared to meet the three defined criteria of success. The success of each institution proposed through this process was subsequently corroborated through secondary research and a round of narrative-based interviews with individuals with firsthand experience with the institutions. Three criteria were then applied to this sample of successful institutions to select a subset of cases for intensive study. First, we narrowed the list of countries to those in which two or more successful institutions were identified, thus enhancing analytical leverage of the study by enabling each country case to encompass at least two units of observation. Second, we selected countries to cover a broadly categorized spectrum of institutional capacity in FCS, ranging as follows: (a) generally disintegrating institutional capacity; (b) weak institutional capacity with some pockets of effectiveness; (c) broadly improving institutional capacity, with some serious deficiencies; and (d) strengthening institutional capacity across the board.[15] Finally, we aimed for some degree of cross-regional coverage for the purpose of global knowledge building and sharing.

Applying these three selection criteria, the study covers nine varied public organizations in four countries: in The Gambia, the Ministry of Basic and Secondary Education (MoBSE) and the Ministry of Finance and Economic Affairs (MoFEA); in the Lao PDR, the Ministry of Public Works and Transport (MPWT) and Électricité du Laos (EDL); in Sierra Leone, the Ministry of Finance and Economic Development (MoFED) and Local Councils; and in Timor-Leste, the Ministry of Health (MoH), the Central Bank (formerly the Banking and Payments Authority or BPA), and the Ministry of Social Solidarity (MSS). The analysis of each organization's evolution extends over one or two decades, thus covering periods of fragility or conflict as well as the ensuing developments. The contrast between the selected institutions and the overall quality of public administration is particularly stark in countries with low overall institutional capacity.

But the cases are also positive outliers even in countries in which overall institutional quality has markedly improved in recent years. Although the four countries vary in their level of overall state capacity, they all are at the lower end of global capacity and fragility scales.[16] The four countries in the sample are all relatively small, and generalizing findings demands caution; nevertheless, the study's methodological approach enables the drawing of contextualized insights that will be relevant to the FCS universe.

The selected institutions were examined through a structured, focused comparison across cases to shed light on the shared causal underpinnings of success, along with process-tracing within cases to bolster our understanding of how the various causal mechanisms are sequenced and combine to produce observed outcomes. The method is "structured" in that the case study guide was grounded in a set of questions reflecting the research objective and hypotheses; and the method is "focused" in that it deals only with certain aspects of the historical cases examined. Overall, this methodology is well suited to identifying causal mechanisms and to building theoretical generalizations on the relatively small universe of cases of institutional success in FCS. Use of the case study guide to standardize data collection enables a systematic comparison of the cases and also allows for future research on additional cases to test and strengthen the findings.[17]

The core causal expectations shaping the inquiry covered three concentric circles of internal institutional workings, external operating environment, and broader sociopolitical context. Field research on the basis of the case study guide was conducted through a combination of in-depth elite interviews and focus group discussions with agency officials, staff, stakeholders, and clients; these were complemented through secondary survey sources where possible. Interviews and focus groups were sequenced in a manner both outside-in (focusing on external stakeholders and clients first before moving to agency staff) and bottom-up (beginning with frontline service providers before moving to agency management and political leaders), so as to ensure that typically less dominant viewpoints were represented.

The following two empirical sections present the key findings emerging from this research program. First, we map three broad pathways along which successful agencies navigate the evolving sociopolitical context in which they are embedded, emphasizing how they do so by introducing internal management reforms while increasing their engagement with clients and stakeholders. Second, we catalog the core institutional repertoire of tools and strategies underpinning success across the agencies in our study.

Pathways to Institutional Success: Navigating the Evolving Sociopolitical Context

This section synthesizes the experiences of the nine studied institutions by describing three alternative pathways along which the agencies interact with their evolving sociopolitical context.[18] These three pathways represent stylized descriptions of the dynamic—often nonlinear—manner in which micro-organizational-level strategies and reforms connect with the macro-sociopolitical environment in the context of FCS. These three pathways are neither country- nor institution-specific. Different institutions may be situated along different pathways in the same country. And the same institution may switch pathways over time as it finds itself in a shifting macro-political environment.

The first pathway is one in which the institution's objectives are closely and consistently aligned with elite incentives, which facilitates the introduction of wide-ranging reforms in a relatively short time span and generates a positive cycle of better results and more political support. The second route is one in which the institution takes advantage of an initial alignment between the organization's goals and elite incentives, quickly implementing and locking in reforms before the prevailing political equilibrium changes. The third trajectory is one in which a public organization works with no active support from political principals and may in fact face adversity from them. Yet the institution uses its results and connections with a broader set of stakeholders to build credibility and, ultimately, mobilize support from elites to reinforce existing gains.

We find that the concurrence of an organization's goals with the incentives of the political elite is important and can help achieve results quickly, but it is neither a necessary nor a sufficient condition for institutional success. First, all the nine institutions we examine deploy, to a remarkably similar degree, a micro-institutional repertoire of management tools and reforms which we catalog in the next section. This repertoire appears to be important for institution building in all three trajectories regardless of the level of elite support. Second, agencies build connections with clients, other stakeholders and donors to shield the institution from adverse elite influence or to secure elite support. This is particularly important when the institution's goals are not aligned with those of the broader political elite. In other words, institutions that achieve momentum for reform and legitimacy can influence their macropolitical environment rather than merely being subject to it. In our description of the three pathways, we therefore emphasize the organization's relationship to not only its political principals, but also its clients and other stakeholders, including its external donors.

In a comparative snapshot, it can be difficult to differentiate those institutions that have always relied on elite support from those that have had to build such support more actively. Because of that, it may erroneously be concluded that an institution invariably has to count on elite support to succeed. Looking at institutional trajectories over time reveals changes in elite behavior toward the institution and sheds light on the strategies institutions have deployed to affect elite views and support. A longitudinal approach also highlights the importance of organizational inertia and path dependence, illustrating how institutions that achieve results in a period of elite support build resilience toward times of waning elite support, especially when they have built bridges to other stakeholders.

Positive Cycle of Strong Elite Commitment and Results

The first pathway captures those cases in which the objectives of elites and those of a public agency are aligned. This agreement creates a virtuous cycle of results and legitimacy that reinforces support for the agency by the political elite. In some cases, this virtuous cycle generates legitimacy well beyond the confines of the agency itself and strengthens the legitimacy of the state as a whole.

Elite support can initially be motivated by factors that range from development aspirations to badly needed donor resources, or even a genuine existential threat. Because of the support from elites, the agency enjoys the resources and space to manage its affairs based on technocratic grounds. Elite support can also help mobilize informal institutions and actors to reinforce reforms and remove spoilers or roadblocks to implementation. All this yields visible results that generate legitimacy for the institution among citizens. Elites can exhibit these results to domestic and external audiences, which in turn helps sustain their interest and support for the agency. Over time, the positive cycle translates into the scaling-up of services and increasingly sophisticated internal management systems.

Early reforms and results also make the agency an attractive partner for development organizations and bilateral donors, which see the institution as an entry point in an otherwise difficult environment and a place where their assistance can generate returns. Organizations on this pathway become progressively more capable of coordinating and integrating aid programs and driving the dialogue with external partners. The financial and technical support of development partners amplifies elite commitment and provides the institution with additional resources to continue its reform program.

The trajectories of Lao PDR's EDL (Barma and Robert -Osken in this volume) and MPWT (Barma and Robert Osken in this volume) as well as Sierra Leone's MoFED (Viñuela and Barrie in this volume) exemplify this pathway. We briefly illustrate the pathway with the case of MPWT; details on all three cases can be found in the respective case studies.

At the end of Lao PDR's violent conflict in 1975, the Lao People's Revolutionary Party was greatly preoccupied with solidifying the territorial integrity of the young country. This concern underpinned initial elite support for the transport sector. The state has thus devoted a substantive portion of domestic resources to expanding the road network, with MPWT for its part focusing on results and the efficiency of its investments. A small but consistent set of bilateral and multilateral donors has supported the sector for more than 30 years, and MPWT benefited from early bilateral support centered on planning, human resource management, and financial management. Donors adopted a division of labor on the basis of geography. Having demonstrated strong financial management practices, MPWT was able to resist the practice of donor-specific project implementation units and instead mainstreamed the administration of donor-financed programs, enabling the in-housing of this institutional capacity. Once the reach and density of the road network had been expanded, MPWT progressively shifted part of its efforts to maintenance and introduced a more advanced evidence-based performance management system to determine the frequency and level of capital allocations needed to preserve existing roads.

Opportunity to Lock in Reforms

The second pathway captures those cases where the political landscape temporarily allows for locking in reforms. The reforms may be part of a peace settlement or seen as necessary to prevent a relapse into conflict or fragility. Over time, the political commitment fades as the sense of urgency diminishes or because politics shift. Foreseeing the possibility of such a reversal and trying to maximize the momentum for reform, leaders of agencies on this pathway push for rapid changes and fast-track reform programs before the window of opportunity closes. Such reform efforts may focus on human resource gaps, financial systems, or legal provisions, but—most importantly—they also put substantial effort into translating these initial reforms into rapid and visible results that earn the agency legitimacy with clients.

In the medium term, the agencies on this second pathway are able to sustain the gains made, thanks to the institutional capacity harnessed during the years of intensive investment. In some cases, the autonomy of the institution has been "locked-in" by a legal framework or resourcing provisions that cannot be changed easily. As part of the strategy to make reform policies stick, agencies on this pathway mobilize a wide range of domestic and external stakeholders and engage clients in frequent dialogue to disseminate information about programs and their results, get feedback to adjust interventions, and promote trust in the institution. Visible and documented results and stakeholder appreciation provide some shield to the organization for when political priorities change and act to restrain elites from more actively intervening or clawing back resources and autonomy.

Along with clients, development partners value the achievements made by agencies on this pathway. This backing serves as important capital for the organization and, at times, a crucial counterweight when the political elite withdraw their support for the agency. Development partners can reinforce their support to the sector through additional resources, by sharing its results widely, or by actively advocating for the agency and its autonomy.

The Sierra Leone Local Councils (Glynn and Larizza in this volume) and the Timor-Leste MoH (Anderson in this volume) and BPA (Viñuela in this volume) exemplify this second pathway. We illustrate this pathway by briefly describing the histories of the local councils and the BPA. Details for these two cases as well as MoH can be found in the respective case studies.

Even before the conflict in Sierra Leone ended in 2002, there was widespread agreement among political leaders and development partners that addressing the root causes of conflict would require not only improving security and control over the territory, but also rapidly delivering services to regions long neglected by the central government. One of the main groups that could have opposed the restoration of local councils—the traditional chiefs—had little collective action capacity at the time since they had been a prominent target for rebels. To lock in the decentralization reform, a law creating local councils was rapidly approved, before the formal decentralization policy was adopted. The first round of local elections was held in 2004—a year before the national elections, which ultimately led to a change in ruling party. Once established, local councils were given a block grant and asked to deliver a first round of small capital projects in the first 100 days of their mandate. This strategy helped the councils to acquire visibility rapidly and engage with citizens. Six years later, a 2010 survey showed that a greater percentage of Sierra Leone's citizens trust local government than central government. A central government that seeks reelection may thus refrain from reneging on the popular decentralization agenda, at least publicly. Nonetheless, the incumbent party, which has strong links with traditional authorities and has historically used them as its political operators, has shifted some important revenue sources to the chiefdoms, eroding the revenue base of the local councils.

Another example of the second pathway is Timor-Leste's quasi central bank, BPA. During the early years of independence, the Timorese elite prioritized the legal underpinnings of the state and created a lean government, including laying the foundations for an independent central bank and for the transparent and conservative management of revenues from the then nascent oil sector. BPA quickly adopted a roadmap for institutional development and supported the preparation and passing of key pieces of legislation (including the Petroleum Law), the capitalization of the institution, and the adoption of a separate human resource policy and pay scale. BPA early on established an outreach strategy for citizens, along with regular press conferences and releases of data for civil society organizations, parliamentarians, and other stakeholders. The autonomy BPA had gained by 2006 helped the agency to manage the transition toward a government that favored the immediate use of petroleum revenues, undermining the institution's efforts for maintaining price stability and the transparency of petroleum revenue management. Although the government has not decreased the autonomy or independence of BPA and has even passed an organic law to establish it as the Central Bank, a new Petroleum Law has drastically limited the institution's influence over the management of oil revenues. Strictly sticking to its mandate, the Central Bank has used its considerable institutional and outreach capacity to inform decision makers and the public at large of the risks associated with the revised policies.

Results to Mobilize Support from the Ground Up

The third pathway captures those organizations that lack explicit support from the political elite because the institution's objectives run contrary to elite interests or do not make the list of their priorities. These institutions have had to actively mobilize support from their principals and advocate for their organizational goals.

Initially, these institutions may not be shielded from direct and frequent unwanted interventions from principals. They work under the radar to implement internal reforms and achieve early results and mobilize domestic and external assistance to scale up programs. They try to shield critical areas from frequent political interference by parsing functions and introducing legal autonomy. The leaders of agencies on this pathway are active advocates for their sector and dynamically mobilize political support. In particular, they reach out to clients and build coalitions that are able to act as a counterweight to the ruling elite. They display results to convince principals of the importance of their policy area and the potential returns to increasing investment in their organizations. Demonstrations of external recognition (good scores in international rankings or assessments, progress against international goals, prizes and mentions, among others) may also help elevate the sector on the national policy agenda.

This set of successful agencies offers an attractive opportunity for domestic elites and external donors to add support and by doing so, receive some credit for the achievements. The results that emerge from internal reforms, along with the increasing flows of external aid and recognition, help them to increase the attention and interest of leaders in their policy area and, in turn, cement their own successes. In a very real sense, the organization contributes to the transformation of its external operational environment. Tangible results enhance the position of the state in society more broadly. Increasing client satisfaction reflects positively on the legitimacy of the regime and thereby creates a positive feedback effect that triggers the favor of political principals. A positive cycle ensues and allows the institution to introduce more sophisticated internal management systems and make further gains in terms of results.

Development partners working in these situations can deploy resources and technical assistance to support internal changes and help expand the space for reforms. At times, they actively help shield the sector's resources from political interventions by channeling support through ring-fenced mechanisms, or through projects, resources, or the suspension of programs to aid sector officials and dissuade the elite from interfering in technical decisions.

The Gambia's MoBSE and MoFEA (Viñuela and Alvesson in this volume) as well as Timor-Leste's MSS (Anderson in this volume) exemplify this pathway. We illustrate this pathway by briefly describing the journeys of MoBSE and MSS. Details are available in the respective case studies.

In The Gambia, expanding access to education in rural areas and increasing the participation of girls and minorities was a not a high priority in the public agenda until recently. Nonetheless, from the early 1990s, MoBSE, partnering with several domestic and external organizations, began making consistent gains in school enrollment that accelerated after 2000. It was only then that President Jammeh started to highlight the sector in his public addresses and launched a program to support girls' education. Having made significant progress on enrollment, MoBSE has now turned its attention to improving the quality of education and expanding the number of qualified teachers.

Another example is the case of MSS in Timor-Leste. The country's social protection agenda was hampered by the first independent government's strong dislike of the subsidies and cash transfers used under Indonesian rule. Building on the experience and credibility of administering programs for veterans and internally displaced populations and managing disaster relief, the organization slowly introduced several initiatives for other groups, including mothers and children, the elderly, and disabled individuals. As these programs proved effective and valued by citizens and district and traditional authorities, the government started to support their scale-up. With new external support, MSS is now focused on increasing its efficiency to deliver cash transfers and monitor their effectiveness and is scaling up a program of community mediation.

Core Institutional Repertoire: Shared Underpinnings of Success

Each of the organizations in our sample has resourcefully navigated the sociopolitical context in which it is embedded. Each of the organizations has achieved results and expanded the scope and coverage of the services it provides, making special efforts to ensure services for hard-to-reach populations and across societal cleavages. Each of the institutions has built relationships with its clients and other stakeholders, enabling them to establish legitimacy and manage shocks and changing conditions. The institutions have commonly resorted to formal and informal partnerships to augment the scope, legitimacy, and stability of their mandates.

Our research shows that the agencies deploy a repertoire of organizational tools in achieving these outcomes that is remarkably similar across the sample. The repertoire includes making strategic choices; adapting administrative architecture and processes to the mission; managing people; building organizational identity; relying on leadership beyond individuals; fostering learning and self-evaluation; and cultivating relationships with clients and other stakeholders. Table O.1 summarizes the strategies observed across the cases. Grindle (1997) identifies many of the elements of these strategies as contributors to organizational success in developing countries; the elements also represent the conventional wisdom in organizational management theory more generally. The study confirms that these earlier conclusions and generalizations are applicable to FCS and should be given more weight in operational approaches to supporting FCS.

Making Strategic Choices

Reorienting the mission and focusing on results, identifying the agency's most immediate needs and ways to neutralize spoilers, making effective use of change management, and constant messaging of priorities are all common strategies used by the well-performing organizations we study. Clearly targeted and implementable goals, along with an early focus on implementation, have been an important building block of organizational effectiveness. In most examples, institutions have developed strategic and mid-term plans through participatory means, which have ensured that the mission can easily be identified by staff at all levels, by clients, and by relevant stakeholders. Raising awareness about the organization's mission and targets has had the added benefit of creating a constituency for change and establishing external accountability.

Adapting Administrative Architecture and Processes to Mission

Following an incremental or building block approach in developing organizational structure and functions has helped several of the studied agencies to deploy existing resources and capacities more effectively and build on them to expand the mission's scope gradually. Restructuring has been used to flatten organograms and delegate decision making to middle managers who are located closer to the front line of service provision. As services expand and the number of clients grows, these agencies have streamlined processes and systems to adapt to the new scale and complexity. Timor-Leste's BPA, for example, started out simply handling payments for the administration and gradually added other functions, always making sure adequately trained staff were in place before the new function was activated. In other organizations, especially in the case of central finance agencies, insulation was used to shield several functions from political interference by granting semiautonomous status to various units.

Managing People

A common characteristic of the analyzed institutions is that they pay a great deal of attention to the agency's staff. They mobilize and build on existing skills (or "organizational survivors"), competitively recruit senior and middle management staff, train new employees, and retain staff in the medium and long term. Access to continued training as well as international exposure have been important in attracting and retaining staff. Électricité du Laos and Timor-Leste's Central Bank and MoH, for example, have implemented long-term capacity-building initiatives with foresight. Timor-Leste's MoH temporarily subcontracted services to international nongovernmental organizations (NGOs) while sending staff to be trained abroad, offering them a guaranteed position on return. After fully resuming the responsibility for health services, it absorbed the well-trained local personnel of the international NGOs and those that had worked for the Indonesian government.

The ability to retain staff has often been a function of remuneration and benefits. The more autonomous agencies, such as the Central Bank of Timor-Leste and Électricité du Laos, offer salaries that are much more competitive than those of other public entities. In other cases, above-average remuneration has been introduced through ad hoc systems or project-funded positions. More flexibility in pay schemes, whether through a different pay scale or the use of special allowances, has permitted these agencies to deploy skilled staff closer to their clients, which in turn has helped institutions to understand and meet their needs.

Many of the public agencies in the sample have instituted processes to motivate people to improve their performance. Such efforts range from fairly sophisticated 360-degree performance evaluation to much simpler appraisal mechanisms, but all link the attainment of certain goals to rewards (cash payments and in kind) and career advancement opportunities. In these agencies, the evaluation of work programs has provided a basis for planning and implementing service improvements and has provided staff with information on their performance and an understanding of how they fit in the organization.

Building Organizational Identity

The institutions in our sample have deliberately cultivated an organizational identity. Organizational success, and the external recognition that

Table O1. Repertoire of Practices

Practice	Local councils (SL)	MoFED (SL)	MoBSE (TG)	MoFEA (TG)	BPA/CB (TL)	MoH (TL)	MSS (TL)	EDL (LPDR)	MPWT (LPDR)
Strategic choices									
• Reorienting the mission and focusing on results	Yes	Yes	Yes	Yes	Yes	Yes	Yes	Yes	Yes
• Focusing on most immediate needs	Yes	Yes	Yes	Yes	Yes	Yes	Yes	Yes	Yes
• Changing management and messaging	Yes	Yes	Yes	Yes	Yes	No	No	Yes	Yes
Administrative architecture and processes									
• Building-block approach to institution building	Yes	No	Yes	No	Yes	Yes	No	No	Yes
• Deconcentration of decision making	Yes	Yes	Yes	Yes	No	Yes	No	No	Yes
• Building implementation partnerships	No	Yes	Yes	Yes	Yes	Yes	Yes	Yes	Yes
• Streamlining of processes	Yes	Yes	Yes	Yes	Yes	Yes	Yes	Yes	Yes
• Insulation of functions	No	Yes	No	Yes	Yes	No	No	Yes	No
Managing people									
• Competitive recruitment	Yes	Yes	Yes	Yes	Yes	Yes	Yes	Yes	Yes
• Competitive compensation	Yes	Partially	No	No	Yes	Yes	No	Yes	No
• Performance review	Yes	Partially	Yes	No	Yes	Yes	No	Yes	Yes
• Performance rewards	No	No	No	No	Yes	No	No	Yes	No
• Restructuring of individual work processes	No	Yes	Yes	Yes	Yes	No	No	Yes	Yes
• Limiting external consultants and project personnel	No	No	Yes	No	Yes	No	No	No	Yes
• Promoting staff within the institution (including top leadership)	Yes	Yes	Yes	Yes	Yes	Yes	No	Yes	Yes
• Identifying, attracting, and deploying skilled staff close to clients	Yes	Yes	Yes	Yes	No	Yes	Yes	Yes	Yes
• Mobilize and build on existing skills	Yes	Yes	Yes	Yes	Yes	Yes	Yes	Yes	Yes
• Longer tenure of senior and middle managers	No	Yes	Yes	No	Yes	No	No	Yes	Yes
Building organizational identity									
• Emphasizing institutional values	Yes	Yes	Yes	Yes	Yes	Yes	Yes	Yes	Yes
• Leadership and role modeling	No	Yes	Yes	No	Yes	No	Yes	No	Yes
• Internal communication	Yes	Yes	Yes	No	Yes	No	Yes	Yes	Yes

Leadership beyond individuals

Core group of senior technical staff and managers helped maintain a consistent approach in the institution's development	Yes	Yes	Yes	Yes	Yes	Yes	Yes	Yes
Senior organizational leaders rose through the ranks of the institution	Partially	Yes	Yes	Partially	No	Yes	Yes	Yes

Learning and self-evaluation (information)

Early introduction of monitoring tools and development of self-evaluation skills	Yes	Yes	Yes	Yes	Yes	No	Yes	Yes
Customizing data collection to needs and capacities	Yes	Yes	Yes	Yes	Yes	No	Yes	Yes
Information collection linked to planning and policy development	Partially	Yes	Yes	Yes	Partially	No	Yes	Yes

Relationship with clients and stakeholders (coalition building)

Consulting and listening to clients and stakeholders	Yes	Yes	Yes	No	No	Yes	Yes	No
Adapting policies to informal institutions and cultural practices	No	No	Yes	No	Yes	No	No	No
Displaying results and advocacy	Yes	Yes	Yes	Yes	Yes	Yes	Yes	Yes
Signaling competence by adopting international standards and systems	No	Yes	Yes	Yes	Yes	No	Yes	No
Facilitating/demanding informal and formal donor coordination	Yes	Yes	Yes	No	Yes	No	Yes	Yes

Note: SL = Sierra Leone; TG = The Gambia; TL = Timor-Leste; LPDR = Lao PDR; MoFED = Ministry of Finance and Economic Development of Sierra Leone; MoBSE = Ministry of Basic and Secondary Education of The Gambia; MoFEA = Ministry of Finance and Economic Affairs of The Gambia; BPA/CB = Banks and Payments Authority of Timor-Leste/Central Bank of Timor-Leste; MoH = Ministry of Health of Timor-Leste; MSS = Ministry of Social Solidarity of Timor-Leste; EDL = Électricité du Laos; MPWT = Ministry of Public Works and Transport of Lao PDR.

it entails, is a significant part of the culture and narratives that prevail in the studied organizations. The sense of collective accomplishment has contributed to reinforcing an esprit de corps and the strong identification of staff with the organization. Organizational culture and professional values have been an important factor in driving success. Deliberate efforts to model, articulate, and encourage values by political and technical managers have played a significant role in shaping organizational culture. In most cases, organizational leaders have been central in the move from relatively rigid and control-oriented organizations to more participatory and entrepreneurial organizations. At the same time, they have empowered and collaborated with career civil servants in senior management positions to promote more durable change.

Improving internal communication, information sharing, and employee participation has been a core element of building corporate identity and improving performance. By actively involving employees, organizations are also tapping their explicit and implicit knowledge, skills, and commitment. Newsletters, posters, training, and other means are often used to complement face-to-face communication. Front line staff and other levels of civil servants interviewed for the study cited better communication as having been important for improving their morale and understanding of programs, as well as for giving them the opportunity to voice their concerns to senior management. Some agencies also deploy symbolic features to strengthen institutional identity. The blue-shirt uniforms of Électricité du Laos staff, for example, make staff instantly recognizable as belonging to a cherished institution and are thus a source of respect and pride.

Relying on Leadership Beyond Individuals

Although institutional success is often attributed to charismatic leadership, our case studies highlight that leadership is not exercised by a single individual even if some individuals stand out. In all the cases we examined, a core group of senior technical staff and managers have been crucial in delivering results and building legitimacy and resilience. In the moments of greatest turmoil, these leaders have been essential in ensuring the continuity of service delivery and maintaining the institutional memory of their agencies, sometimes in the face of a severe shortage of staff and widespread physical destruction of facilities and systems. Beyond crisis situations, these networks of leaders have ignited and sustained a successful trajectory for their institutions.

Even after the Sierra Leone civil conflict reached the capital in 1998–99 and MoFED's main building was destroyed, for example, the ministry continued to function thanks to a core group of staff and local consultants. They remained in the capital, exercised key functions, and preserved critical records. After Timor-Leste's independence, a small group of leaders became instrumental in designing the organizational structure and service protocols for MoH. These were built around the pool of qualified nurses and doctors who had been trained and employed by the Indonesian health services and by religious organizations, and who continued to provide services, either privately or through NGOs after much of the health infrastructure was destroyed in the violence unleashed by the country's vote for independence from Indonesia. The Gambia's MoBSE relied on a network of committed education specialists who, in the late 1980s and early 1990s, were trained and deployed as part of its policy planning unit. This was essential in keeping a consistent approach and sustaining the organization along its trajectory. This pool of individuals, moving in and out of MoBSE as a result of political interventions in top-level staffing, led a number of reform initiatives in various corners of the institution and provided the human assets to fill the most senior positions in the ministry and partner organizations. They were instrumental in maintaining a consistent approach along the institution's trajectory.

Across the case studies, leaders have employed deliberate efforts to communicate, model, and encourage values that actively shape organizational culture. The leaders of the Lao MPWT have been committed to excellence in service delivery and have emphasized a hands-on, learning-by-doing, problem-solving approach to the ministry's work. Their credibility with the ministry's personnel is enhanced a great deal by the fact that they have risen up through the ranks of the organization. In addition, agency leaders effectively used rhetoric and coalition-building strategies in the service of institutional change and reforms. In The Gambia, for example, MoBSE leadership has played a significant role in advocating for the sector, moving education to a higher position on the political agenda, and building internal and external coalitions to support sector goals. They have consistently fostered a culture of learning and self-evaluation.

The majority of leaders rose through the ranks of public service, and they often combine technical competencies with social and political capital. In Timor-Leste, for example, leaders often hail from the resistance movement and have strong ties to traditional leadership structures, augmenting their legitimacy in the eyes of the public. The leaders we encountered in our case studies are astute politicians who understand that achieving results can be a platform for their subsequent political and professional careers, and importantly, they can effectively translate technical issues into the political language of their principals. They sometimes move in and out of the public agency supporting the sector alternately from within and beyond. They are also well networked through their educational and professional experiences, internally and abroad.

Fostering Learning and Self-Evaluation

The early introduction of monitoring tools and development of analytical skills for self-evaluation is an important organizational feature across the cases in the sample. The Gambia's MoBSE, for example, introduced a process to measure and record student and teacher performance. Although systems vary in their degree of complexity and sophistication, they all collect information about outcomes, and some measure client satisfaction. The most successful systems have been those that are customized to the specific needs and capacities of a given institution; hence, they are often not very sophisticated. Beyond putting in place information systems, these organizations have actually linked the collection of information with their planning and policy development processes to improve services and adapt strategies. At the same time, giving employees opportunities for participation, learning, and change has improved employee morale and motivation even when facing disappointing results. Information systems have contributed to better targeting of resources, developing standards, and improving efficiency in service delivery. Realistically assessing human, financial, and institutional constraints has helped managers develop approaches for dealing with them.

Cultivating Relationships with Clients and Other Stakeholders

The institutions in our sample have built durable relations and coalitions that help them deliver on their mandates and mobilize support for their programs. These include a strategic attention to consultative mechanisms with service clients; an emphasis on displaying results, with a particular emphasis on signaling competence; innovative implementation partnerships with private and public sector organizations; policies adapted to informal institutions; and promotion of, and assistance with, donor coordination.

The organizations in the sample have reached out to clients to assess their needs and consult with them on strategies and alternatives to prioritize them or to seek feedback on the quality of services. Increasing accountability and bottom-up communication with end users appears to have had beneficial effects on program effectiveness and afforded the institutions a better understanding of clients' preferences. A remarkable example is provided by The Gambia's MoBSE, which introduced a Coordinating Committee in the late 1990s that met every two months with directors of all regions and included visits to front line staff and inspections by senior management. This has been a remarkable mechanism in a political context where open debate is extremely limited. Over the next decade, the committee was expanded to include teachers, principals, partner NGOs and donors, as well as other relevant stakeholders. Électricité du Laos has a hotline where consumers can report issues, and these are almost invariably attended to within days.

Building Implementation Partnerships

The service delivery agencies in our sample have cultivated and relied on innovative partnerships with other public agencies, the private sector, and informal institutions. One example is the social dialogue program managed by Timor-Leste's MSS. The program was initially created to facilitate the return of displaced populations after the 2006 crisis. It also focused on mitigating conflict risks, dealing with violence between martial arts groups, and mediating land and cultural disputes. Innovatively, the social dialogue model works in partnership with community leaders and uses traditional dispute resolution methods. The use of these familiar mechanisms has allowed MSS to realize significant achievements in a short period of time and to secure the trust of the population.

In the Lao power sector, the push to reach 90 percent electrification by 2020, has prompted EDL in concert with provincial governments to contract small and medium private companies to extend the grid to remote areas, through a build-operate-transfer model. In the aftermath of Timor-Leste's 1999 independence vote, the MoH's ability to restore services was the result of its partnership with international civil society and religious organizations. Since the early 1990s, road sector development in Lao PDR has emphasized the building of private sector capacity. In the delegated MPWT system, project management (including budgeting, planning, and quality control) was shifted to the provincial level, and implementation was contracted out to a nascent private sector at the provincial and district levels.

Signaling Capacity to Mobilize External Resources

All of the studied organizations have been successful in mobilizing financial resources to fund their mandates and, under some circumstances, to expand the number of activities that they undertake. The ability to signal effectiveness, report results, and obtain external recognition has been a critical aspect of that effort. Most organizations have at least basic monitoring and data collection systems that allow them to document their activities and achievements and show decision makers that financial resources are being well spent.

In addition, the case studies offer multiple examples of how organizations have adopted similar models as organizations in the same sector in other countries. Whether adopting these models has contributed to greater effectiveness is difficult to determine with this sample size. Nonetheless, it is clear that adopting certain organizational forms has constituted an important signal for development partners and, in many cases, has been driven by the need to conform to requirements to access funding or external assistance. This has led in some cases to disruptive changes that have not furthered institutional interests or effectiveness. In many cases, isomorphic pressures are the result of the specialization of international agencies providing technical assistance in a given area, as well as of the professional norms shared.

Policy Implications

One of the explicit goals of this study has been to understand the shared causal factors underlying successful institution building in FCS to provide the basis for targeted operational insights for policies and programs concerning institutional reform. The detailed empirical discussion above has identified a number of specific lessons in terms of the institutional underpinnings that public agencies should attempt to pursue and that development partners would be well advised to support. Although our sample size is small, our robust methodology allows us to offer some additional operational lessons. We start by discussing how our findings help to provide evidence on a piece of relatively established conventional wisdom on institution building. Then we elaborate a series of more actionable lessons for FCS policy makers and their development partners.

Designing Good Fit IS Best Practice

Our research confirms that good-fit institutional strategies are essential, a point we are not alone in emphasizing.[19] Nevertheless, our work reveals a subtle point about institutional fit, in that it must be achieved in two dimensions—micro-organizational strategies must be chosen and supported on the basis of their ultimate function, *and* they must be implemented in light of the macro-sociopolitical context in which public agencies are embedded. We have emphasized, in this regard, the importance of viewing institutional development and success as a nonlinear, dynamic, evolving process. The pathways to institutional success illustrate a self-reinforcing dynamic such that the causality between institutional repertoire and the sociopolitical context works both ways. Better understanding the history of institutions and how their makeup of individuals, programs, and policies has evolved is critical to designing better interventions and programs for institutional strengthening. A better grasp of how institutions forge domestic and external coalitions for change can also inform more comprehensive external support to aid those efforts.

A focus on institutional form is hence only warranted by context, never ex ante. Isomorphic mimicry can sometimes be positive in helping agencies to signal competence, but it should not be pushed beyond the pursuit of very specific functions. Normative approaches to best practice only make sense if they fit with the political economy context; and their implementation must be tailored to the existing capacity of agencies. In terms of the scripts of institutional reform, donor coordination is crucial—especially to mitigate fragmentary and contradictory advice—although many successful institutions take care of this themselves.

Suggestions for Policy Makers

Implement a Building-Block Strategy. Public institutions, with the support of their development partners, should follow a building-block approach to developing their mandate that combines short- and long-term objective-setting on the basis of clearly defined targets. Agencies should focus on scoring early, monitorable, and reportable successes that can be used to generate further support, leverage resources, and build morale and momentum. Where possible, functions should be added in step with the development of the necessary capacity. Alternatively, institutions can outsource functions to NGOs or the private sector either temporarily or permanently, while focusing on providing the policy and regulatory framework, setting standards, monitoring outcomes, evaluating programs, and identifying course corrections.

Emphasize Constant Learning and Use Evidence Wisely to Implement Course Corrections. Institutions achieve and sustain success with an

emphasis on continuous organizational learning and evidence-based decision making. Information itself is not enough; the key is what is done with
the information—how it is used to validate successful strategies, scale up
experiments and pilots that have gone well, close down initiatives that
have shown lesser results, and continuously correct the institution's course.
Client surveys and feedback can be used to shape changes in service delivery goals and processes; and systems to collect basic and real-time data on
service provision can be used to make incremental as well as more serious
adjustments to reforms.

Give Staff and Clients a Stake in the Institution's Success. Often institutions and donors focus too much on the very top leadership of the agency
and their connections with the outside world—and too little on building
and encouraging leadership qualities in the broader management team
that are more internally focused. Middle and senior managers can sty-
mie otherwise well-designed reforms, or they can be essential in determining and successfully implementing an agency's mandate. Enabling
some measure of autonomy in financial and human resource management is important, along with greater managerial flexibility to give them
a stake in success. For technical staff and frontline service providers,
a similar pride and stake in the organization can be cultivated through
tangible performance incentives and more intangible corporate culture
and practices.

Clients can be a potent source of political leverage for an institution,
and yet they are often an overlooked stakeholder. Client participation and
feedback is important for optimizing services, but also because social forces
can be the most dramatic and supportive of stakeholders. How, then, can
institutions better connect with their clients and mobilize this force? The
act of closer communication with clients gives them a deeper stake in the
institution's success and thereby builds a constituency for sustained change.
A further step to empowering that constituency—and building broader
state legitimacy in the eyes of society—is to integrate client consultation
and participation into decision-making processes. If the essence of fragility
is the disintegration of the state and social fabrics, then their mutual regen-
eration is a crucial element in overcoming it.

Reflections for Development Partners
Revisiting "Country Ownership." Our research confirms the general consensus that donor support contributes to results when agency counterparts

are firmly in the driver's seat. Yet donors must be nuanced in "respecting country ownership." The political landscape rarely produces unequivocal support for reforms, and agencies sometimes face considerable hostility and interference from political elites. In this context, donors can help to shape the immediate operating environment of an agency by helping it to connect to a broader set of stakeholders internally and abroad. In so doing, donors can help the institution buffer itself to some degree against unwanted political interference.

Support Networks of Leaders. We have highlighted the importance of the networks of leaders that ignite and sustain institutional success, usually heads of agencies and a cadre of managers and technical staff around them, sometimes reaching into the private and nongovernmental sectors. Donors can support these local networks by expanding their ability to connect across borders and learn from each other. Donors can reward effective leadership through initiatives like the Ibrahim Prize for Achievement in African Leadership and by offering other avenues for international recognition.

Be in It for the Long Haul. The one certain good that donors can provide to their counterparts is a greater degree of stability and continuity in programming and staffing, along with more hands-on and continued engagement from the donor side. Institution building is a dynamic, nonlinear process that moves in fits and starts and is often reversible. To embrace the reality of institutional change, development partners must be prepared to recognize these facts and work flexibly to add momentum to salutary change and help protect agencies against adverse change. Nimble, opportunistic pursuit of reform moments and champions has its place—but must be accompanied by sustained, incremental partnerships for long-term success and lasting change.

There Is No Such Thing as a Blank Slate. This study emphasizes, above all, that micro-institutional strategies must be consonant with the macro-sociopolitical context if organizations are to succeed. To state that donors must understand the political economy of reforms has become a truism; but the development community is still a long way from putting that wisdom in practice. The sine qua non of good program design is a deep and nuanced understanding of the sociopolitical context in which institutions are embedded, combined with an accurate assessment of organizational capacity, appreciating at least a measure of the historical trajectory shaping both. Understanding who the leaders are in a sector within and outside the public agency and how they fit in the broader sociopolitical context is particularly important. For development assistance to work, it must be undertaken in the context of the particular conditions agencies face. One concrete way of thinking about this is that the three pathways to success articulated above suggest different opportunities and entry points for donors to act on in addition to the elements of support that will make sense no matter what. Furthermore, the specific methodology we have developed and employed in conducting this study serves as a concrete tool for undertaking adequate upstream due diligence and thereby maximizing the potential for donors to support institutional success in FCS.

Conclusion

This volume describes how institutions in fragile and conflict-affected states succeed when they are able to construct strategies of deft internal management and astute external connections to negotiate the broader sociopolitical environment in which they are embedded. Successful institutions share a core institutional repertoire in so doing; and the agencies in our study display different patterns in the manner in which they connect these microorganizational strategies to the broader macro-sociopolitical environment.

The comparative method employed in this study has enabled us to more systematically test some of the hypotheses and causal expectations that individual case studies and more theoretical scholarship have pointed to before. It offers the potential, as well, for further research to test, refine, and expand on our findings. Most of our cases studies concern central agencies and service delivery organizations. This work could usefully be complemented by an examination of success in other areas that are considered critical in FCS, such as security services and judicial institutions. A dedicated analysis of successful decentralization would also be useful. Another promising avenue for research would be to focus more narrowly on how development partners have specifically aided the agencies in our study, along with careful process-tracing of how significant those elements of support were in achieving success.

We have endeavored not to project successful sequences as necessarily being the product of a series of conscious choices—sometimes luck intervenes, in the form of a particular political moment. We have emphasized the importance of looking at institutional development as a long-term process.

Institutional success is a nonlinear and dynamic process; the governance puzzles that must be solved on the route to success evolve constantly and are sharper at some moments and more opaque at others. A better understanding of the context in which institutions are embedded, their own particular trajectory in connecting to that context, and the internal resources, human and otherwise, of those institutions is essential for designing better interventions and programs for institutional strengthening.

In presenting our findings, we believe that we have moved the study of institution building in FCS beyond the high-order contextual factors often analyzed, such as overarching questions of political stability and systemic institutional strength in cross-cutting governance functions such as public financial management or civil service capacity. Holding such factors constant in their often low equilibria, we still observe islands of success—such public institutions manage to operate successfully despite the overwhelming odds against them. Hence we see some institutional successes in otherwise stalemated or even highly conflictual political environments. We also see specific achievements in institution building even when systemic public sector capacity-building initiatives have stalled. Sometimes, as the agencies in our sample display, the success of individual institutions can even have a positive feedback effect on the broader (re)construction of state legitimacy and the institutional landscape.

Notes

1. The study is intended to make a contribution to the broad dialogue on fragile state engagement; for example, OECD (2008); LSE et al. (2008); Jones et al. (2008); OECD (2010); ECDPM (2008); NORAD (2009); IPPG (2010); Cox and Hemon (2009).
2. Evans, Rueschemeyer, and Skocpol (1985); Migdal (1988).
3. Jones et al. (2008); World Bank (2012). See also Bates (2008); Hickey (2012); North et al. (2007); (North, Wallis, and Weingast (2009); Slater (2010); Vom Hau (2012); and Waldner (1999).
4. Some institutions are more likely to sustain good performance if they are accountable to multiple principals, such as a legislative body or to the public, particularly if these multiple channels of accountability offer agencies alternative tactical options. By contrast, if agencies are dependent on satisfying *all* of these multiple, competing principals, they can get tied up in process-oriented knots.
5. IPPG (2010); OECD (2010), World Bank (2011).

6. The World Bank's *Societal Dynamics and Fragility* study (World Bank 2012) examines these societal dimensions of fragility and state-building on the basis of detailed empirical work.

7. Mahoney and Thelen (2010) offer a complementary perspective on institutions as vehicles through which sociopolitical power is expressed and shaped.

8. In an important research agenda-setting piece, Leonard (2010) examines "pockets" of institutional effectiveness in countries with poor governance and weak administrative records. He reviews the literature on this subject to generate five meta-hypotheses—two of which are internal and three external—and discusses how they may interact.

9. On specificity, see also Hirschman (1967) and Wilson (1989).

10. A large institutionalist literature addresses the causes of isomorphism in organizations. See, in particular, Meyer and Rowan (1977), DiMaggio and Powell (1983), and Meyer et al. (1997). For an explicit treatment of institutional isomorphism in public sector agencies, see Frumkin and Galaskiewicz (2004). Pritchett and de Weijer (2010) also discuss institutional mimicry and its consequences for de jure form versus de facto function in building institutional capacity in fragile states.

11. Rodrik (2007) has emphasized the value and significance of focusing on institutional function, with locally rooted innovation, over institutional form.

12. World Bank (2011); IPPG (2010); Fukuyama (2004); and Pritchett and de Weijer (2010).

13. Barma (2011) and Barma, Huybens, and Viñuela (2012) detail the research design of the study, including a fuller definition of the outcomes studied, the process by which cases were selected, and the case-centered methodology.

14. See Lamb (2005), Weatherford (1992), and Bellina et al. (2009) on measuring legitimacy.

15. The notion of institutional capacity improving first in pockets and then more broadly fits with the notion that there is a "virtuous cycle" element to successful institution building whereby stronger institutions are better able to mediate internal and external stressors to stability, and also that enclaves of good governance can accrete to a dynamic process of institutional improvement. See, respectively, World Bank (2011) and North et al. (2007).

16. Lao PDR and The Gambia experienced stagnation and fragility during the 1990s, while Sierra Leone and Timor-Leste emerged from protracted conflicts in the early 2000s. Lao PDR and The Gambia graduated from the World Bank list of fragile situations in 2010 as their Country Policy and Institutional Assessment scores improved.

17. Case-centered methodological insights are adapted from George and Bennett (2005). Barma (2011) provides more details on the study's research design, including a discussion of the potential limitations of the research design and

ways in which these were mitigated, along with the structured, focused inquiry comprising the case study guide.

18. Other cases might reveal additional pathways, but it is beyond the scope of this study to speculate on these.

19. Grindle's (2004, 2007) concept of "good enough governance" is foundational on this point. See Pritchett, Woolcock, and Andrews (2013) for the most recent discussion of this issue; other citations are in the literature review above.

References

Barma, Naazneen H. 2011. "Institutions Taking Root: Project Description and Case Study Guide." Unpublished manuscript. World Bank, Washington, DC.

Barma, Naazneen H., Elisabeth Huybens, and Lorena Viñuela. 2012. "Institutions Taking Root: Building State Capacity in Challenging Contexts." Paper presented at the International Research Society for Public Management XVI Conference. Rome, April 11–13, 2012.

Bates, Robert. 2008. *When Things Fell Apart: State Failure in Late-Century Africa.* New York: Cambridge University Press.

Bellina, S., D. Darbon, S.S. Eriksen, and O.J. Sending. 2009. "The Legitimacy of the State in Fragile Situations." OECD DAC International Network on Conflict and Fragility. OECD, Paris.

Cox, Marcus, and Kristina Hemon. 2009. "Engagement in Fragile Situations: Preliminary Lessons from Donor Experience." DFID Evaluation Report EV699. DFID, London.

DiMaggio, Paul J., and Walter W. Powell. 1983. "The Iron Cage Revisited: Institutional Isomorphism and Collective Rationality in Organizational Fields." *American Sociological Review* 48(2): 147–60.

ECDPM (European Centre for Development Policy Management). 2008. "Capacity Change and Performance: Insights and Implications for Development Cooperation." Policy Management Brief No. 21. ECDPM, Maastricht.

Evans, P. B., D. Rueschemeyer, and T. Skocpol, eds. 1985. *Bringing the State Back In.* Cambridge: Cambridge University Press.

Frumkin, Peter, and Joseph Galaskiewicz. 2004. "Institutional Isomorphism and Public Sector Organizations." *Journal of Public Administration Research and Theory* 14(3): 283–307. doi: 10.1093/jopart/muh028.

Fukuyama, Francis. 2004. *State-Building: Governance and World Order in the 21st Century.* Ithaca: Cornell University Press.

George, Alexander L., and Andrew Bennett. 2005. *Case Studies and Theory Development in the Social Sciences.* Cambridge: MIT Press.

Grindle, Merilee S. 1997. "Divergent Cultures? When Public Organizations Perform Well in Developing Countries." *World Development* 25(4): 481–95.

———. 2004. "Good Enough Governance: Poverty Reduction and Reform in Developing Countries." *Governance* 17(4): 525–48. doi: 10.1016/ S0305-750X(96)00123-4.

———. 2007. "Good Enough Governance Revisited." *Development Policy Review* 25(5): 553–74.

Hickey, Sam. 2012. "Turning Governance Thinking Upside-Down? Insights from 'the Politics of What Works.'" *Third World Quarterly* 33(7): 1231–47. doi:10. 1080/01436597.2012.695516.

Hirschman, Albert O. 1967. *Development Projects Observed.* Washington, DC: The Brookings Institution.

IPPG (Improving Institutions for Pro-Poor Growth). 2010. "Beyond Institutions: Institutions and Organizations in the Politics and Economics of Growth and Poverty Reduction—A Thematic Synthesis of Research Evidence." DFID-funded Research Programme Consortium on Improving Institutions for Pro-Poor Growth (IPPG), London.

Israel, Arturo. 1987. *Institutional Development: Incentives to Performance.* Baltimore: Johns Hopkins University Press.

Jones, Bruce, et al. 2008. "From Fragility to Resilience: Concepts and Dilemmas of State Building in Fragile Situations." Joint study by the Center on International Cooperation at New York University and the International Peace Academy, prepared for OECD DAC Fragile States Group.

Lamb, Robert D. 2005. "Measuring Legitimacy in Weak States." Center for International and Security Studies at Maryland, College Park, Md.

Leonard, David K. 2010. "Pockets of Effective Agencies in Weak Governance States: Where are They Likely and Why Does it Matter?" *Public Administration and Development* 30: 91–101.

LSE et al. (London school of Economics and Pricewaterhouse Coopers, LLP). 2008. "State-building in Fragile Situations: How Can Donors 'Do No Harm' and Maximize Their Positive Impact." Joint study by the London School of Economics and Pricewaterhouse Coopers, LLP (prepared for OECD DAC Fragile States Group).

Mahoney, James, and Kathleen Thelen, eds. 2010. *Explaining Institutional Change: Ambiguity, Agency, and Power.* Cambridge: Cambridge University Press.

Manor, James, ed. 2007. *Aid That Works: Successful Development in Fragile States.* Washington, DC: World Bank.

Meyer, John W., John Boli, G.M. Thomas, and F.O. Ramirez. 1997. "World Society and the Nation-State." *American Journal of Sociology* 103(1): 144–81.

Meyer, John W., and Brian Rowan. 1977. "Institutionalized Organizations: Formal Structure as Myth and Ceremony." *American Journal of Sociology* 83(2): 340–63.

Migdal, Joel S. 1988. *Strong Societies and Weak States: State-Society Relations and State Capabilities in the Third World.* Princeton: Princeton University Press.

NORAD. 2009. *The Legitimacy of the State in Fragile Situations.* NORAD Report 20/2009 Discussion. Oslo: NORAD.

North, Douglass C. 1990. *Institutions, Institutional Change and Economic Performance*. Cambridge: Cambridge University Press.

North, Douglass C., et al. 2007. "Limited Access Orders in the Developing World: A New Approach to the Problems of Development." Policy Research Working Paper 4359. World Bank, Washington, DC.

North, Douglass C., John J. Wallis, and Barry R. Weingast. 2009. *Violence and Social Orders: A Conceptual Framework for Interpreting Recorded Human History*. New York: Cambridge University Press.

OECD (Organisation for Economic Co-operation and Development). 2010. *Do No Harm: International Support for State-Building*. Paris: OECD.

Pritchett, Lant, and Frauke de Weijer. 2010. "Fragile States: Stuck in a Capability Trap?" Background paper for the World Development Report 2011, World Bank, Washington, DC.

Pritchett, Lant, Michael Woolcock, and Matt Andrews. 2013. "Looking Like a State: Techniques of Persistent Failure in State Capability for Implementation." *Journal of Development Studies* 49(1): 1–18.

Rodrik, Dani. 2007. *One Economics, Many Recipes*. Princeton, NJ: Princeton University Press.

Slater, Dan. 2010. *Ordering Power: Contentious Politics and Authoritarian Leviathans in Southeast Asia*. New York: Cambridge University Press.

Teskey, Graham. 2005. "Capacity Development and State Building: Issues, Evidence and Implications for DFID." Department for International Development (DFID), London.

Vom Hau, Matthias. 2012. "State Capacity and Inclusive Development: New Challenges and Directions." Working Paper No. 2, Effective States and Inclusive Development Research Center, University of Manchester, United Kingdom.

Waldner, David. 1999. *State Building and Late Development*. Ithaca: Cornell University Press.

Weatherford, M. Stephen. 1992. "Measuring Political Legitimacy." *The American Political Science Review* 86(1): 149–66.

Wilson, James Q. 1989. *Bureaucracy: What Government Agencies Do and Why They Do It*. New York: Basic Books.

World Bank. 1997. *World Development Report 1997: The State in a Changing World*. Oxford: Oxford University Press.

———. 2011. *World Development Report 2011: Conflict, Security, and Development*. Washington, DC: World Bank.

———. 2012. *Societal Dynamics and Fragility: Engaging Societies in Responding to Fragile Situations*. Washington, DC: World Bank.

PART I

THE GAMBIA

CHAPTER 1

The Gambia: Balancing Structural Constraints and Hegemonic Politics

Lorena Viñuela

As a small country, surrounded by Senegal, with little natural resources and high dependence on official development assistance,[1] The Gambia is exposed to external shocks and deeply concerned with preserving its independence. The Gambia faces challenges in generating sufficient revenues to cover annual expenses and more broadly address its vast developmental needs. Of its population of 1.7 million, 58 percent live in poverty. Agriculture, mainly related to the production of peanuts and subsistence, employs two-thirds of the population and represents a quarter of gross domestic product, while the service sector, including tourism, accounts for the rest. Agriculture is frequently affected by extreme climatic events.

The Gambia became independent from England in 1965 and converted into a republic in 1971, emerging as one of a handful of multiparty democracies in Africa. Although freely contested elections were held every five years, the People's Progressive Party (PPP) dominated politics for the next three decades. President Sir Dawda Kairaba Jawara, who was the leader of the independence movement and had a strong base of support in the Mandinka rural population, was reelected five consecutive times and ruled until a coup d'état ousted him and banned his party from electoral competition.[2] The three opposition parties represented largely the interest of urban centers, whose leadership came primarily from the Wolof/Aku ethnic groups. Although coexistence of different groups has been mostly peaceful, politics have often taken ethnic undertones, and there have been sporadic events of violence.

In the 1970s, as many other countries in West Africa, The Gambia pursued a policy of industrial substitution that channeled the surplus from agricultural exports into industrial ventures in urban centers. Part of the substitution policy involved subsidies for the population of Kanifing and Banjul and reinforced some of the long-standing biases in favor of the metropolitan area. A parastatal, the Gambia Oilseeds Marketing Board, controlled the exports of the main cash crop, groundnuts. Yet, in response to the government's taxation policies, peanut producers changed crops or resorted to smuggling products to Senegal in search of better prices. In time, this, together with the failure of many of the import substitution initiatives, led to a sharp drop in public revenue and gave rise to a parallel market that diverted much of the foreign exchange from the formal system. At the same time that the government experimented with industrialization, the minute state apparatus left in place by the British expanded rapidly. The number of civil servants grew geometrically with the creation of 4,500 new posts and soon the financial situation of the state deteriorated.

By 1980, the country began having problems serving its debt obligations and the Central Bank's reserves dwindled. Rising unemployment and food prices led to increasing social unrest and an eventual coup attempt by a group of Jola paramilitary in 1981 that was stopped by the intervention of the Senegalese army. The intervention led to widespread violence. In reaction to the instability, a Senegambia Confederation was established in 1982, and for the first time, a national army was created. In addition to providing for common security, the goal of the Confederation was to coordinate foreign affairs and economic policies.

In the late 1980s, the plunging international price of groundnuts, population growth, dwindling external assistance, and climatic hardships led to a deep economic crisis as attempts by the government to adjust fiscal policies intensified the downturn. The IMF/World Bank-financed Economic Recovery Program (ERP) sought to curtail inflation, privatize state-owned companies, and liberalize agricultural prices, but did not succeed in boosting economic growth. The prolonged nature of the economic stagnation eventually resulted in wide discontent. In 1989, fearing the loss of lucrative indirect taxes if a custom union was established, The Gambia withdrew from the Senegambia Confederation.

As relations with Senegal grew strained, President Jawara became increasingly isolated politically. In 1994, unrest developed in the Gambian army after the government signed a defense agreement that allowed Nigerian officers to head the army. In July, Lieutenant Yahya Jammeh succeeded in overthrowing the government and banned the PPP from participating in electoral contests for seven years. The United Kingdom, Denmark, and Sweden, in particular, warned their citizens against traveling to The Gambia, which in turn led to an estimated loss of 25 percent of tourist industry employment, while other countries suspended direct support.

Responding to pressure for a return to civilian rule, Jammeh's Armed Forces Provisional Ruling Council (AFPRC) established a National Consultative Committee (NCC) to draft a new constitution. The new constitution, approved two years later, granted additional prerogatives to the presidency over the unicameral legislature and the judiciary. A presidential election gave an ample victory to President Jammeh and his party, the Alliance for Patriotic Reorientation and Construction (APRC) in 1996. Since then, Jammeh has won three consecutive elections.

Slowly after the transition to civilian rule, relations with donors normalized despite the restricted level of political and civilian liberties. In July 2001, the ban on the PPP was lifted. Nonetheless, the opposition is weak and divided, and it is widely considered to have no real chance of gaining power, with the APRC controlling the majority in the 53-seat National Assembly since 1996 (of which five members are directly appointed by the president). Over the years, the regime has increasingly limited press liberty and arrested various journalists and opposition leaders.[3] Local nongovernmental organizations (NGOs) are generally weak, with a few exceptions, and independent media is very limited. Governance reached one of its lowest points in 2002–03, when irregularities in economic management and monetary policy led to a severe crisis.

Notes

1. As a former British colony, The Gambia maintains strong links with the United Kingdom and other Commonwealth countries in West Africa, such as Sierra Leone, Ghana, and Nigeria. Among emerging partners, Taiwan, China, remains the most important, followed by Cuba and República Bolivariana de Venezuela, while Kuwait exerts a growing influence. Libya was an important association between 1995 and 2011. However, traditional development partners, including the World Bank, the International Monetary Fund (IMF), and the African Development Bank (AfDB), retain important roles.

2. It is important to note that until 1996 The Gambia had an unusual voting system in which voters deposited marbles into a steel drum marked with the candidate of their choice.

3. Eight of the detainees were sentenced to death and executed for their part in an alleged coup plot in 2010.

CHAPTER 2

The Gambia Case Study: Ministry of Finance and Economic Affairs

Lorena Viñuela and Helle M. Alvesson

The Gambia's recent history has been marked by economic shocks and low political inclusiveness that have had negatively affected the country's development. Fragility has been the result of weakening state institutions, increasing centralization of power in the executive, and the deteriorating socioeconomic conditions that reached a critical point in 2003. The Ministry of Finance and Economic Affairs (MoFEA) has been directly influenced by the political context and was at the center of the economic crisis and the subsequent recovery.

As in many low-income countries, the ministry faces significant challenges in pursuing more effective and transparent public financial management and prudent fiscal policies. These difficulties are compounded by volatile economic conditions and the nature of the political regime. The country is heavily dependent on external assistance, and this gives international finance institutions and other development partners providing programmatic support some influence in the institution's operational environment. As a small but open economy, the impact of fiscal policies and external economic shocks are felt rapidly, and this constitutes an important stress factor.

There have been two important turning points in the development of the institution that have contributed to giving greater autonomy (or dissuaded principals from actively intervening in internal matters), at least in some areas of public financial management. On the one hand, the 2002–03 monetary crisis acted as a strong focusing event to renew development partners' support and technical assistance to the Central Bank and MoFEA.

The crisis demonstrated the risks that manipulating the exchange rate and rising domestic debt can have in an economy of the size of The Gambia and created a wide consensus on the need to consistently invest in the capacity and credibility of the Central Bank and the central finance agency. On the other hand, the Heavily Indebted Poor Country (HIPC) and the Multilateral Debt Relief (MDR) mechanisms offered significant incentives for reform, allowing the country to cut external debt by half and access critical technical assistance. At the same time, greater coordination among donors has facilitated dialogue with the institution. Advances in the various dimensions of fiscal policy have had positive feedback effects in motivating additional reforms, attracting new talent and resources, and mobilizing budget support.

Domestic coalitions and constituencies for economic stability have played a critical role in the response to the crisis and in helping to mitigate ongoing challenges emerging from political interference in the allocation of funds and pushing for greater transparency in public accounts. The close collaboration with the Central Bank, which enjoys greater autonomy, has allowed the ministry to access local technical capacity and resources. In addition, the private sector has been a strong and influential advocate of macroeconomic sustainability.

Internally, the institution has undergone major restructuring and modernizing of processes since 2004. These changes have been accompanied by considerable updating of the budget legal and regulatory frameworks. In recent years, greater attention has been paid to the staffing of middle management positions and attracting new professional staff. Nevertheless, a core group of technical staff and individuals that remained or returned to the institution have played an important role in conserving the institutional memory and helping the institution navigate a turbulent political and economic environment. Notably, the introduction of a new financial management system has acted as a major catalyst for process modernization and improving the coordination and communication with spending ministries. Having real-time information on spending and revenues proved critical during the international financial crisis of 2008–09 and allowed the ministry to rapidly react and contain the impact on The Gambian economy.

The ministry has managed the challenging political context by maintaining a "technocratic front," while at the same time, providing maximal political discretion to the president to remove ministers frequently. This strategy has, to some extent, removed civil service appointments from direct political interference. This arrangement has offered several advantages, including opening space for broad reforms, such as the implementation of transformational projects like the new integrated financial management information system and the clearing of the backlog of financial statements, as well as facilitating the working relationship with development agencies. It has fallen short, however, from ensuring the continuity of these reforms, especially when economic and political circumstances lead to a shortage in funds from development agencies.

Institutional Success

Emerging from the 2002–03 crisis, MoFEA has set a path toward its capability to deliver on its core mandate and address demands from clients and various stakeholders. Within a constrained environment, in economic and political terms, MoFEA has undergone a significant transformation. Many challenges lie ahead in the institutional evolution of MoFEA, and the description of the institutional success should be considered in that context and with the necessary caveats.

In the mid-2000s, the ministry was affected by a host of problems and relied on structures and systems that were glaringly inadequate for managing public resources effectively. The regulatory framework for fiscal policy dated from colonial times, there was a multiplicity of information systems that had been built on an ad hoc basis that did not communicate with each other, and most of the accounting and transactions were still being processed manually. The plethora of problems included poor debt recording, low credibility of budgeting practices, use of unreliable data and models to forecast revenues, inadequate public accounting practices, and a decade-long delay in producing general ledgers and financial statements (World Bank 2005b). Moreover, there were large discrepancies between payroll and personnel data, below-the-line accounts were opaque, and accounts had not been audited for many years. Large arrears had accumulated and domestic revenue mobilization was low in comparison with other low-income countries.

Since then, a wide array of reforms in the organization's structure and processes have had tangible results and helped to build MoFEA's credibility. New processes have improved communication flows and coordination with line ministries and counterparts, allowing for more effective and efficient public expenditure management. In addition, the country has managed to maintain macroeconomic stability in the face of external shocks during 2008 caused by high food and fuel prices, as well as abrupt reduction in official assistance and tourism revenues in 2009–10.

Results

MoFEA has exhibited measurable and gradually improving results in several areas. The Gambia has made important progress in public financial management and toward achieving debt sustainability. The positive trajectory has been reflected in improving Country Policy and Institutional Assessment (CPIA) indicators. Since 2005, The Gambia has received higher scores in key areas related to the ministry's mandate (see figure 2.1 and table 2.1), including macroeconomic management, fiscal policy, and the quality of budgeting and financial management. A more modest improvement has been achieved in debt policy, mainly because of concerns about rising domestic debt during 2009 and 2010.

Many elements of public expenditure management have consistently improved in the past seven years, including an update of the legal and regulatory framework, improvements in the timeliness of financial reporting with an introduction of an integrated financial management information system, and a more organized budget process. The backlog of accounts has been cleared and sent to the National Assembly and presently there is

Figure 2.1. Performance of Key CPIA Indicators, 2005–10

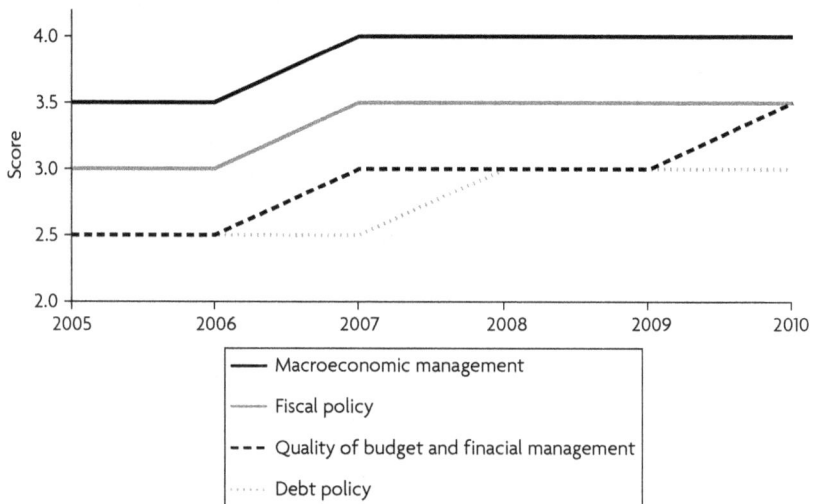

Source: World Bank Indicators, 2013.
Note: CPIA = Country Policy and Institutional Assessment.

Table 2.1. CPIA Scores

	The Gambia		IDA average	
Indicator	2005	2010	2005	2010
1. Macroeconomic management	3.5	4.0	3.8	3.7
2. Fiscal policy	3.0	3.5	3.4	3.5
3. Debt policy	2.5	3.0	3.4	3.4
13. Quality of budget and financial management	2.5	3.5	3.2	3.3
14. Efficiency of revenue mobilization	3.5	3.5	3.4	3.5
16. Transparency, accountability, and corruption in the public sector	3.0	3.0	2.9	2.9

Source: World Bank Indicators, 2013.
Note: IDA = International Development Association.

within-year reporting. These improvements in public financial management are reflected in the Public Expenditure and Financial Accountability (PEFA) performance scores (see annex). The Gambia has obtained above average marks in the aggregate expenditure and revenue outputs, budget classification and comprehensiveness of budget information, and orderliness and participation in the budget process, as well as account reporting (World Bank 2010b).

Although efforts to reduce domestic debt have been curtailed by various economic shocks, the ministry has taken important steps to improve the quality of debt management systems and data, and it has successfully taken advantage of debt reduction facilities that translated into sizable reductions of external debt levels. Some of the improvements included adopting a medium-term debt management strategy and a new recording system, establishing a dedicated unit for debt management, improving coordination and sharing of data with the Central Bank, carrying out regular debt sustainability analyses. In turn, and in the context of global relief initiatives including HIPC and the MDR mechanism, The Gambia was able to halve external debt. In parallel, between 2003 and 2008, the Central Bank's financing was significantly reduced (see figure 2.2), whereas the overall deficit as a share of gross domestic product (GDP) improved from 2005 to 2007 (see figure 2.3). However, domestic debt levels have since risen. The government made use of treasury bills as a short-term strategy to bridge the widening gap between domestic revenues and expenditures in 2009 and 2010.

Another dimension of public financial management in which the country has made considerable advances is revenue mobilization. Greater efficiency in tax administration resulting from the merging of the two major tax collection agencies has translated into a steady increase in domestic revenue. Between 2004 and 2010, tax revenue increased an

Figure 2.2. Central Bank Financing as a Share of the Previous Year's Tax Revenue, 2001–10

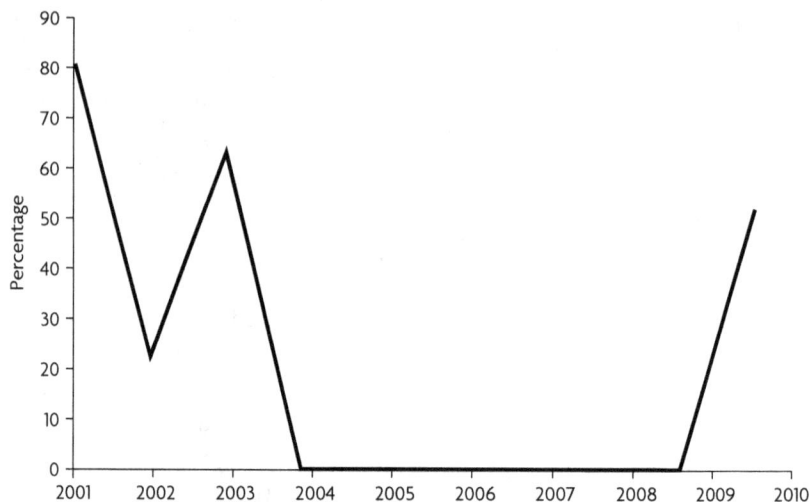

Source: ECOMAC, 2013 (http://www.wami-imao.org/ecomac/english/Statistics/macro.htm).

Figure 2.3. Overall Deficit as a Share of GDP, 2001–10

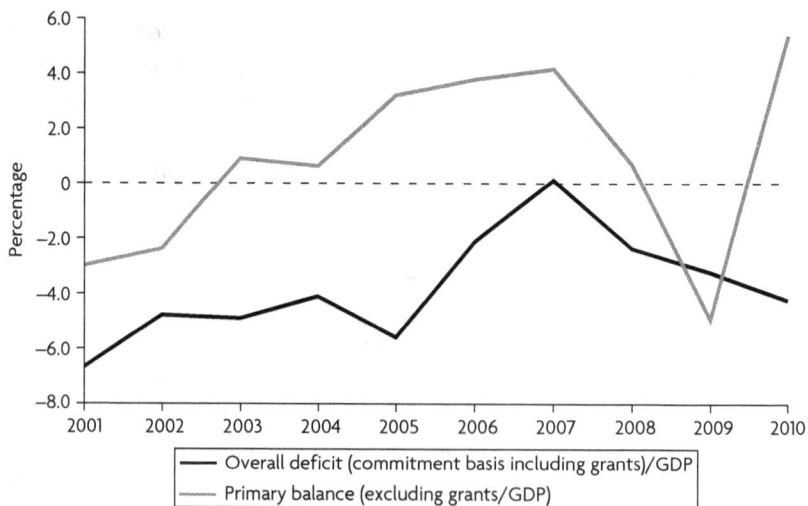

Source: ECOMAC, 2013.

Figure 2.4. Tax Revenue, 2001–10

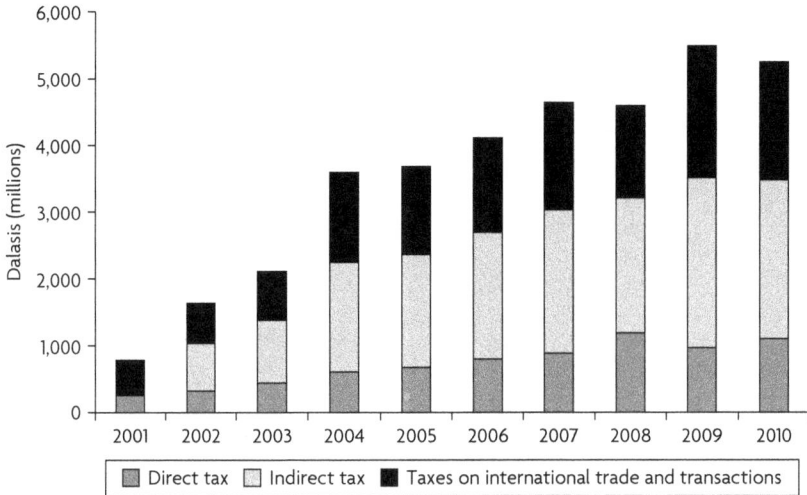

Source: ECOMAC, 2013.

average of 17 percent per year (see figure 2.4). Domestic revenue has also risen as a share of GDP, reaching 21 percent in 2007 and then falling again (figure 2.5). The government planned to replace sales taxes with a value-added tax (VAT) by January 2013, which is expected to further increase public revenues. However, the prevalent informality in the economy continues to be a major obstacle to broadening the tax base and is yet to be addressed.

Legitimacy

The output legitimacy, or the outward performance, of the ministry is high across clients and external stakeholders. The institution's perceived effectiveness has improved as a result of institutional changes and the streamlining of processes related to budgeting and account recording. In particular, the deployment of budget officers and accountants in line ministries has led to more frequent and effective interactions with them in the daily management of financial resources. Clients were mostly positive about the cash management system and the financial management information system, as well as training opportunities that came with the latter. Others referred to the support received from the ministry in contractual and technical matters in positive terms.

Figure 2.5. Domestic Revenue, 2001–10

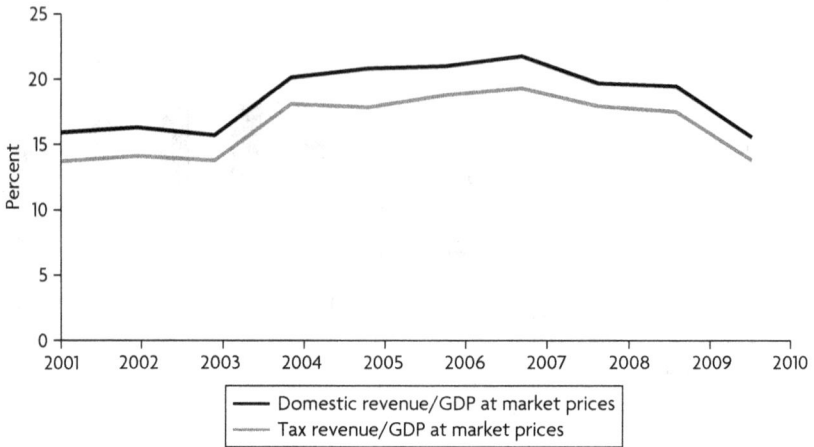

Source: ECOMAC, 2013.

Conversely, the procedural legitimacy appears weaker. Some observers have reported that MoFEA has limited engagement with other economic agencies. The ministry is sometimes perceived as paying limited attention to the preferences of clients. Although there are some formal consultations, for example through the budget forum and hearings in the National Assembly, clients do not see them as having a significant impact on the decision-making process. Many of the public agencies interviewed also expressed their concerns about the scarcity of funding and how cash constraints affect their program component, but they also recognized that such factors were beyond the control of the ministry.

Despite these persisting challenges, the ministry has consistently gained credibility and legitimacy vis-à-vis external and domestic stakeholders. The improving trust in its capacity to manage funds has been reflected in the recovering level of external assistance. Reforms on public expenditure management have been extremely important in allowing The Gambia to mobilize more development assistance, including budget support. As figure 2.6 and figure 2.7 show, after an sizable drop in 2002–03 (a drop of approximately a third), official development aid more than doubled and reached US$130 million by 2009, or 19 percent of GDP.

Figure 2.6. Net ODA and Official Aid Received, 2000–10

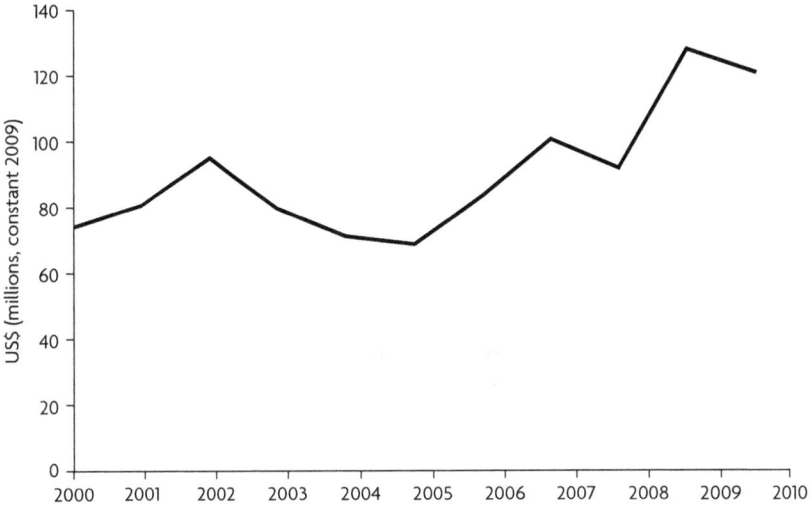

Source: World Bank Indicators, 2013.

Figure 2.7. Net ODA Received, 2000–10

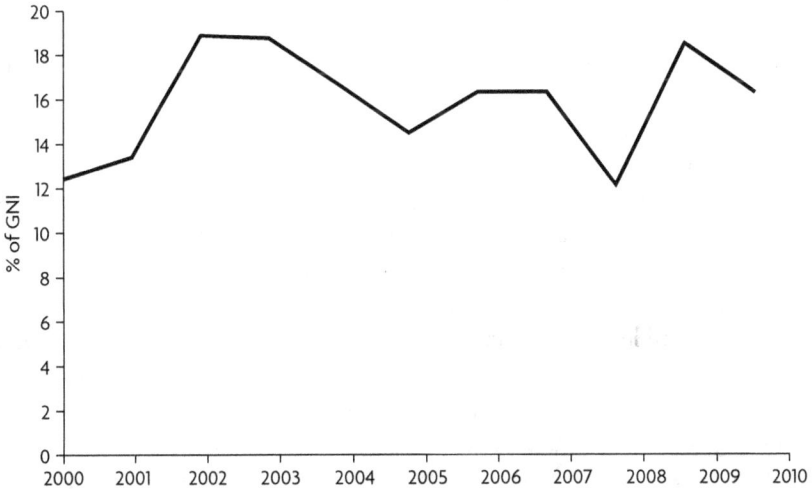

Source: World Bank Indicators, 2013.
Note: ODA = Official Development Assistance; GNI = gross national income.

Resilience

The resilience of MoFEA, or its ability to sustain and enhance results over time, has been tested in several ways. First, the improvement in results has been maintained despite a high turnover of ministers and personnel. Second, The Gambia has weathered the 2008 food price crisis and downturn in the international financial system.

Improved information management—particularly related to accounting, forecasting, and debt management—and a closer collaboration with the Central Bank have allowed the ministry to adjust policies and spending rapidly to changing macroeconomic circumstances. MoFEA resorted to cash rationing during 2008 and 2009 to cope with the food crisis and the rising prices of fuel. In 2010, the ministry was able to manage a large shock generated by the suspension of the European Union's contribution to budget support.

Sociopolitical and Historical Context

The high concentration of power in the presidency and the Alliance for Patriotic Reorientation and Construction (APRC) has been accompanied by an increasingly discretionary treatment of civil servants. State capacity has been severely undermined by the politicization of the civil service and deterioration of public salaries, as evidenced in the high turnover of personnel at all levels. In practice, civil servants no longer enjoy stability in their positions and can be summarily dismissed. At the same time, there is a centralization of decisions at the highest levels of authority over policy, managerial, and personnel issues. For example, the president is also the Minister of Agriculture and in the recent past has simultaneously held the position of Minister of Higher Education.

Frequent changes and reshuffles in the cabinet have been a common feature of contemporary The Gambia. The turnover also reaches senior civil servants, permanent secretaries and deputy permanent secretaries, and almost all levels of the civil service. This level of insecurity has driven qualified staff to seek employment in international and civil society organizations, donor programs, and the growing service sector, in particular banking. The trend was especially acute during the 2002 crisis.

During 2002–03, expansionary fiscal policy, accommodating monetary policy, and a drought led to a deep economic crisis. Inflation rose from 5 percent to 17 percent in two years; the national currency, the dalasi, depreciated by 55 percent; and gross national income plunged (see figure 2.8). The large increase in government domestic borrowing to cover current expenditures had destabilizing effects. During this period, civil servants' salaries were severely eroded (see figure 2.9). The IMF Poverty Reduction and Growth Facility loan and other international assistance programs were suspended because of concern about various irregularities in reporting and the lack of compliance with macroeconomic goals.

In the then Department of State Finance (now MoFEA), this episode was marked with the appointment of a minister, who did not count with a technical background, and an exodus of technical staff—including some that are now back in the institution. Nevertheless, the crisis acted as a strong catalyst for renewed external support to the ministry. The assistance focused on improving fiscal discipline and increasing coordination between the ministry and the Central Bank.

The crisis helped to create better awareness of the implications that expansionary fiscal policies and rising domestic debt can have on an economy of the size of The Gambia. It also contributed to create a wide consensus on the need to invest in the skills of the Central Bank and the Ministry of Finance. Since the crisis, and after a steep and prolonged decline in state

Figure 2.8. GNI per Capita, Atlas, 1980–2010

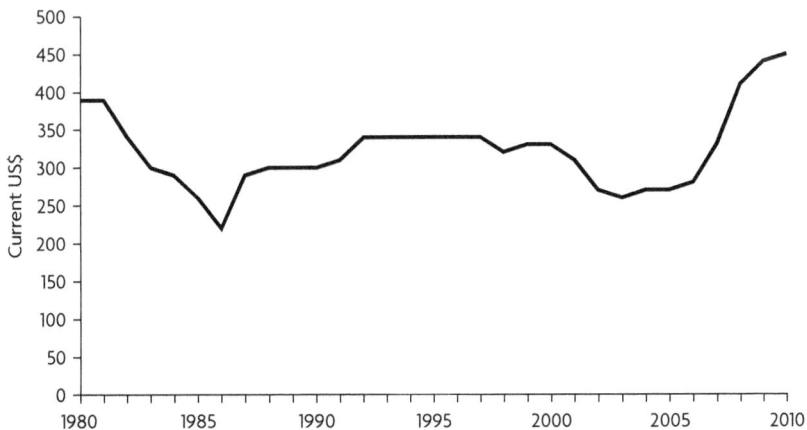

Source: World Bank Indicators, 2011.
Note: GNI = gross national income.

Figure 2.9. Wages and Salaries as a Share of Domestic Revenues, 2001–10

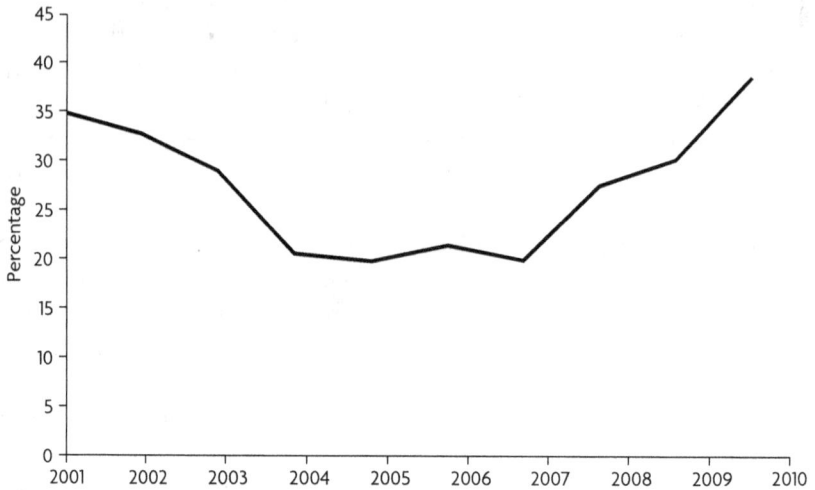

Source: MoFEA, 2012.

capacity,[1] The Gambia has started moving toward strengthening its institutional capacity and improving the conditions of public employment again. The country graduated from the list of fragile and conflict-affected situations in 2011, and its overall CPIA score has consistently increased since 2005. Although the overall quality of public administration is comparable to that of other International Development Association (IDA) countries, the country's Macroeconomic Management and Quality of Budgeting and Financial Management scores are above the average. The areas in which The Gambia lags are Transparency, Accountability, and Corruption in the Public Sector and Debt Policy. Similarly, The Gambia scores below the median in most of the Worldwide Governance Indicators, except for political stability.

External Operational Environment

In a challenging sociopolitical context, the operational environment of MoFEA has been marked by the increasing politicization of public financial management since the mid-1990s. As a critical arena of politics, fiscal policy has been exposed to interference and political pressures to allocate resources according to short-term priorities. The ministry is less insulated from the political economy context than the Central Bank. In practice, this has meant that ministers' tenure depends on their relation with the executive and that they are likely to be removed or transferred to another government entity when it changes. Yet, despite the lack of continuity in political leadership, there has been relative stability in senior and middle management positions, especially in the Treasury and the heads of semiautonomous agencies.[2] Under pressure from donors, the ministry has increased the number of partially autonomous agencies as a way to shield certain strategic functions, such as revenue administration and procurement.

In addition, the ability of the ministry to deliver on its core mandate is affected by its high exposure to external shocks and dependency on external aid. Disruptions and uneasy relations with traditional donors have often resulted in shortfalls in project financing and budget support. More recently, high energy and food prices pose an important challenge to the continuation of economic reforms. At the same time, the global economic downturn in countries during 2008–11 negatively impacted two of the main sources of foreign receipts, tourism and official aid, and remittances decreased.

However, the ministry benefits from being one of the main interlocutors of international finance institutions and development partners and having access to resources and technical assistance. In recent years, donor coordination has improved and two key donors, the African Development Bank and the World Bank, adopted a Joint Assistance Strategy. Moreover, the introduction of budget support as an assistance tool has provided a clearer framework for engaging development partners and reducing transaction costs for the institution. However, the ministry has been subjected to sometimes contradictory pressures and priorities from donors.

Another source of motivation for policy reform is The Gambia's membership in the West African Monetary Zone (WAMZ) along with five other countries. They plan to introduce a common currency, the eco, by the year 2015. This commitment to regional integration has helped the country to set objectives and goals and has provided a monitoring and peer review mechanism.

Domestically, MoFEA's partnership with the Central Bank, which has rebuilt its own capacity, has been critical in advocating for the need of attracting and retaining trained individuals and communicating key messages to the leadership around fiscal sustainability. Foreign and domestic investors in the hospitality and service sectors have also been important constituents of sound fiscal policy, debt management, and regulatory reform.

Reestablishing Coordination with the Central Bank

The Central Bank is an important domestic stakeholder. Having gained greater autonomy in recent years, it is in a stronger position to demand actions from MoFEA, and to offer technical support in key areas. The Central Bank vocally advocates for more prudent fiscal policy and for reducing domestic debt and the use of treasury bills. In the words of the governor, "An understanding was reached that the Central Bank alone cannot achieve price stability … we are doing this together." Thus, the agency has been a strong backer of the introduction of the Integrated Financial Management Information System (IFMIS) and worked closely with the Debt Management Unit to improve its recording and forecasting systems, as well as seconded a senior staff to lead the Budget Department.

In addition, the two institutions have formalized their channels of communication and set up a number of joint committees to monitor common targets. Three new committees have been fundamental for harmonizing the fiscal and monetary policies by bringing together the two institutions, but also creating a clear reporting framework. These include the Treasury Bills, Liquidity, and Monetary Coordination committees. Their meetings are often attended by donors and other technical assistants. This interagency partnership has been instrumental in communicating to key decision makers the potential consequences of pursuing expansive fiscal policies and has increased the stability of their programs. The introduction of various data collection systems (debt recording, accounting, and forecasting) in the Ministry of Finance has allowed better and timelier coordination between the two institutions, and provided clearer targets and an accountability mechanism.

Navigating Disruptive Isomorphic Influences

Isomorphic influences are visible in the structure and systems of the ministry. In order to conform to international best practices and requirements from donors, the organization and processes of the ministry have been revised numerous times. Subsequent reforms have introduced new functions and transformed several departments into semiautonomous agencies. Major landmarks in this process were the passage of the Government Budget Management Accountability Act (2004), the Procurement Act (2004), and the Revenue Authority Act of 2005. The Public Utilities Regulatory Agency (PURA) had been created in 2001.

Most of the changes have been made to meet the triggers of various funding projects or in direct response to recommendations from the World Bank or the International Monetary Fund (IMF). As one senior official of the ministry described it, "project performance is a key driver of the development of the organization." By adopting models that are widely considered good practice, the government has signaled its commitment to certain objectives, such as improving debt management, increasing domestic revenue mobilization, and improving budgeting and reporting practices. However, at times, isomorphic pressures have proven often difficult to manage. The not always consistent nature of technical advice and assistance has been evidenced in the creation and dismantling of the Ministry of Planning and Industrial Policy within the same year in 2010.

In addition, isomorphic pressures emerge from the specialization or division of labor between donors. Systems and structures in some areas are comparable to those of other countries in the region where these development partners have also provided technical assistance. For example, the Debt Management Unit has introduced the Commonwealth's Debt Recording and Management System that is used in other English-speaking countries of the region. The defunct National Planning Commission, and later the Ministry Planning, had a structure similar to institutions supported by the African Development Bank and the United Nations Development Programme (UNDP) in other countries in the region. Similarly, the setup of the IFMIS, which was financed by the World Bank, has incorporated lessons from the implementation of financial systems in Tanzania and Rwanda, and the project counted with the same experts that assisted those countries.

However, the dissemination of ideas, through the training staff members receive and the professional circles they belong to, has contributed to normative isomorphism. As a department head put it, "The Ministry is all about its people." There is a relatively small pool of Gambians, living in the country, with the qualifications to undertake the technical tasks that most positions in the ministry require. The large majority of those individuals studied abroad, in either other English-speaking West African countries or the United Kingdom, and in many cases, they were classmates. In turn, only a small number of high schools have traditionally provided students access to scholarships and opportunities to study abroad. Most professionals in the ministry attended one of these and many personal relationships and networks were forged during those early years. Furthermore, once recruited, staffers are sent to the same institutions to receive further training, including in the IMF Institute and summer programs in universities in the United States, which have contributed to reinforce certain professional norms and views on the role of a finance agency. Likewise, the consultants and experts that advise the ministry tend to bring with them practices and models from other developed and developing countries where they were trained or had a professional career.

Internal Institutional Workings

Mirroring the changes in the sociopolitical context and external operational environment, MoFEA has gone through a cycle of institutional strengthening in the 1990s, deterioration of technical capacity and outflow of professionals during the early 2000s, and rebuilding since 2004–05. The more recent efforts to improve the institution's internal workings have been made possible by the renewed interest and support from development partners and domestic constituents.

Although some of the building blocks for the establishment of more efficient and transparent public financial management were put in place in the late 1990s, it was only after the so-called Gambian crisis that the reform agenda gained momentum. Once the high-level commitment to improving the functioning of the institution and the necessary resources were secured, a rapid succession of changes followed. The main transformations related to attracting qualified professionals to key units, rebuilding the capacity of the ministry to collect and analyze data, introducing information management systems to support core functions, and improving support to and collaboration with line ministries and other public agencies.

Because the institution's setup and systems were so dated, large gains in efficiency were achieved in a span of five years through the introduction of automated information systems, process reengineering, and the restructuring of the most important areas, including treasury, budgeting, revenue administration, and debt management. In turn, these rapid and sizable gains helped reinforce the internal commitment to institutional development and the real-time information that the new systems produced allowed the ministry to more effectively handle economic turbulence thus demonstrating to its principals the value of maintaining such investments.

Prioritizing Public Financial Management and Circumscribing the Mandate

The reform effort departed from updating and confining the institution's mandate to a set of specific macroeconomic and public financial management tasks through a new legal framework and strategic plan.[3] Furthermore, in 2010, MoFEA, along with nine other government agencies, received support from the UNDP/Spanish Schematic Trust Fund to develop a strategic plan.

The new mandate and strategic objectives provide a clear monitoring framework against which to measure the organization's performance. At the same time, the mission and mandate, as currently defined, include elements of governance change that are beyond the control of the institution. Although the leadership, senior management, and staff clearly articulate the mandate, they are conscious of the constraints that the institution faces in achieving this mission, especially regarding objectives on accountability and fiscal discipline. Consequently, the focus has been placed on improving the effectiveness and efficiency of public finance management and making marginal gains in the areas of transparency and accountability.

Restructuring and Insulation of Functions

Concomitantly, the institution underwent a major reorganization. The majority of changes aimed at insulating and protecting from political interference functions that were seen as critical to improving the mobilization of resources and the allocation of public resources. From 2001 to 2007, following the passage of various pieces of legislation, six semiautonomous agencies were created—including the Public Utilities Regulatory Agency, the Revenue Authority, the Public Procurement Authority, the Bureau of Statistics, and the Divesture Agency. The new revenue administration agency merged two previously independent tax collection agencies, the Department of Domestic Taxes and the Department of Customs and Excise. Yet, these agencies exhibit considerable variation in their capacity and effectiveness largely because of differences in their ability to mobilize own revenues and the amount of technical assistance they have received. Conversely, the previously independent Accountant General's office was transformed into the Directorate of Treasury, which now reports to the minister directly.

Achieving Rapid Efficiency Gains through Information Management Modernization

Some of the most important changes in the internal workings of the ministry relate to improvements in its management practices (table 2.2). In particular, upgrading of information systems and streamlining budget

Table 2.2. Milestones of the Ministry of Finance and Economic Affairs

Year	Sociopolitical context	External operating environment	Internal institutional workings
1994	Jawara ousted in coup led by Lieutenant Yahya Jammeh		
1996	Vision 2020 adopted[a] New constitution promulgated Jammeh elected President		
2000	Ban is lifted on the political parties		
2001	Jammeh wins a second term	Gambia Public Procurement Authority Act Public Utilities Regulatory Act	Public Utilities Regulatory Agency (PURA) began operating
2002	APRC wins parliamentary elections Drought		
2003	Economic Crisis	PRSP I Suspension of IMF Poverty Reduction and Growth Facility	Gambia Public Procurement Authority began operating
2004		Normalization of relations with donors and IFIs Government Budget Management Accountability Act Procurement Act	
2005	Ministers and civil servants are dismissed and more than 30 senior officials are arrested over corruption allegations	Revenue Authority Act Statistics Act Central Bank Bill enacted to guarantee the operational independence of the Central Bank	
2006	National elections		IFMIS implementation began The Gambia Bureau of Statistics replaced the former Central Statistics Department The National Planning Commission is created
2007		PRSP II Memorandum of Understanding with the Central Bank HIPC process initiation	The Gambia Revenue Authority began operating The Gambia Bureau of Statistics began operating Debt Management department was created Revenue Authority began operating

(continued next page)

Table 2.2. Milestones of the Ministry of Finance and Economic Affairs (*continued*)

Year	Sociopolitical context	External operating environment	Internal institutional workings
2008	Food and Fuel Crisis		Accountant General's office is transformed into the National Treasury Directorate
2009	International Financial Crisis		
2010	Eight men, including a former army chief, are sentenced to death for their part in an alleged coup plot in 2009	Budget support negotiations start The National Planning Commission is transformed into the Ministry of Economic Planning and Industrial Development, which is later closed Government-wide pay reform	The Department of State of Finance is transformed into MoFEA and merged with the planning Ministry IFMIS rollout
2011	President Jammeh wins another term Severe drought	European Union cancels planned budget support	
2012	Ruling party wins parliamentarypolls boycotted by the opposition	PAGE[b] European Union approves 10 million euros in budget support	

Note: IMF = International Monetary Fund; IFI = international financial institution; HIPC = Heavily Indebted Poor Countries; IFMIS = Integrated Financial Management Information System; PAGE = Programme for Accelerated Growth and Employment; PRSP = Poverty Reduction Strategy Paper.
a. A long-term development framework for economic development.
b. Based on Vision 2020 and various past strategies and the government's long-term vision.

process have been highlighted by staff and clients as one of the most important building blocks of the gains in performance observed since 2005–06. Notably, the introduction of an IFMIS has led to improvements across the board in the capacity of the ministry and in particular of the Directorate of Treasury (see box 2.1). As well, the project has provided for training and deployed specialists in all major public agencies and line ministries. As expected, the implementation of IFMIS has implied improvements in information communications technology services and significant gains in the efficiency of the ministry's work. It has also meant that ad hoc systems have been unified, and there is now a sizeable group of staff with proficiency in the system. Before 2008, for example, there was one individual who had the capability to use the payroll utility in the entire government, and many other transactions were still done manually. Simultaneously,

---

BOX 2.1

The IFMIS Project

The Integrated Financial Management Information System (IFMIS) Project, which became effective in August 2010, builds on the initial introduction of the Integrated Financial Management System in The Gambia under the preceding Capacity Building for Economic Management Project (CBEMP), which closed in December 2008. The Gambia's IFMIS is an enterprise resource planning software application that bundles budget preparation, budget execution, accounting, payroll, financial management, and reporting activities. In the first phase of the establishment of the application in The Gambia (supported through CBEMP), the setup of the system was accompanied by organizational restructuring, reengineering of operational procedures, and extensive training of staff. The system is now processing all central government transactions and producing the annual accounts and monthly fiscal reports in a timely manner. IFMIS has helped reduce the substantial backlog of annual audits dating back to the early 1990s. With the improved reporting and better documentation provided by the system, IFMIS is expected to facilitate the more timely preparation of future audits.

In the second phase, IFMIS has been rolled out to 39 additional government ministries and agencies and is expected to be rolled out to the Central Bank later this year, which will enable sector resources to be managed better thanks to access to real-time information on the status of their budgets. The project also aims at ensuring that the government will be able to operate and maintain IFMIS in the future without external support, in order to sustain beyond the duration of the project the gains that have arisen from the establishment of the system.

Source: World Bank 2010c.

---

special skill and IFMIS allowances have been used to motivate employees to use the system and attract a new cohort of professionals.

Through the various reorganizations and process updates, the structuring of individual tasks has become clearer and more specific overtime. In addition, a number of measures have been taken to improve internal communication. There are regular staff meetings, newsletters, and some of the agencies have an intranet that makes collaboration easier. The ministry has appointed focal points for each of the semiautonomous agencies that represent the institution in each of the respective boards.

Staffing Key Units and Dealing with Pay Challenges

In recent years, the institution has actively taken steps to attract qualified individuals for middle and senior management positions from other institutions, such as the Central Bank, and former employees, Gambians that have pursued higher education abroad, and the private sector. These efforts have encompassed the management and technical positions of projects that now are almost exclusively staffed by nationals. MoFEA, as part of a broader public service reform, has increased salaries and stipends, introduced special skills allowances and incentives for participating in regular trainings, and provided opportunities for continuing education in The Gambia and abroad.[4] Access to on-the-job learning, training, and networking opportunities were consistently cited by the interviewed staff as the main features that attract professionals to the ministry.

Senior positions, such as the director of aid coordination and the director of budget, were filled with professionals recruited from the private sector and the Central Bank to improve the profiles of these offices. There is an emphasis on learning and increasing the speed of the response to external economic shocks and improving the efficiency of debt and cash management. Technical assistants and external consultants are routinely paired with civil servants to facilitate knowledge transfer. Unlike most fragile and conflict-affected countries, the number of externally funded technical assistants is relatively low, and emphasis has been placed on improving the training and remuneration of civil servants.

Nonetheless, relatively uncompetitive salaries remain a hindrance for retaining personnel in the long term. Institutional autonomy in personnel management and pay scales has empowered semiautonomous agencies to attract qualified personnel at all levels and, thereby, enhanced their performance. In some cases, the agencies have brought in staff from the core directorates to the detriment of the ministry's capacity. Performance appraisal has been introduced and used to promote individuals, but the general lack of stability in public employment undermines the benefits.

The ministry is governed by the civil service pay scale and has relatively little room to compete with the private sector, semiautonomous government agencies, and donor-funded project management units. In this context, externally funded workshops and travel are highly valued for their per diems, as well as long-term training abroad. Fuel and cars, access to laptops, as well as food items, housing, and responsibility allowances have been widely used to compensate staff. Allowances are on average

38 percent of the total compensation that public employees received (World Bank 2010b). The downside of this approach has been that employees and managers are regularly taken away from their jobs, affecting the implementation of programs and the performance of the departments.

Coping with Leadership Turnover

Being at the center of economic and political turbulence, MoFEA has experienced frequent changes in its top leadership, ministers, and permanent secretaries, much like most institutions in The Gambia. Removals and cabinet reshuffles have been a frequent occurrence since 1994. Since then, there have been 11 ministers,[5] three of which were appointed during successive reshuffles in 2010. The result is often a loss of institutional memory and delays in implementation, as new ministers need to become aware of the policy issues and programs.

Ministers are acutely aware that their position is of a short-term nature. This has inspired some of them to try to make the most of their time. A former senior civil servant compared it to a track race, stating

> It looks like a relay in a track race which may not take long because the runners are very fast, and yet those runners become so motivated to make the best of this short time by making sure that each runs their distances the fastest they can, that the race is won even before spectators are able to identify them; but knowing that afterwards they will become the hot topics of discussions and admiration by the same spectators until another similar race is run.... Each race won moves the team much closer to the goal and this is the way, in which each incremental effectiveness and efficiency in the MoFEA leans to every Minister and/or Permanent Secretary that served it even if for just a day.

The pervasiveness change at the top, however, discourages interactions with the technical staff. A former civil servant stated: "We live with it. We look in the newspaper every morning to read who has been fired....so the lesson is 'Don't deal with PS and Ministers'—they will leave!"

The leadership positions of various government agencies, especially the more specialized ones, such as Trade and Finance, commonly rotate among a relatively small number of individuals, given the constraints in skills in the country. The level of technical competency of ministers and permanent secretaries has been for the most part generally high. In fact, the large majority of senior and middle managers started their careers at the ministry as cadet economists or budget officers and benefited from access to long- and short-term training and on-the-job learning. The Economic

Management and Planning Unit is where most of the senior civil servants (including the minister, the permanent secretary, and the deputy permanent secretary) began their careers. Many left the institutions temporarily and later returned to more senior positions; others rose through the institution's ranks. The Ministry of Trade, sometimes referred to as "the other half of the Ministry of Finance," has overlapping interests with MoFEA, for example on the development of local industries and attracting foreign investment. The mobility of staff at all levels is unsurprisingly high between the two institutions.

But, despite the excessively high turnover of political heads, the stability in the technical and administrative management has been greater and, to some extent, this has mitigated the negative consequences of the continuous turnover in the leadership. The experience of the Central Bank is similar in that mobility among young economists should be expected—likewise at the top—but it is important to maintain staff at the director level. In general terms, the more specialized the unit and the more specific the skills, the greater the stability in their management and the efforts to retain personnel has been. Examples of this are the Budget Unit and the Treasury, which have typically enjoyed greater stability than their counterparts in aid coordination and debt management.

In addition, individuals who belong to the ministry, as well as those who at some point of their career were staff members,[6] strongly identify with the institution and its professional norms. The esprit de corps is visible. Nonetheless, uncertainty over job security and the general political context have taken a toll on the internal culture and motivation of individuals.

Rebuilding Relationships with Clients

The ministry has not had a strong tradition of consulting clients, although it has sporadically held consultations with clients, for example, when it developed its current strategy or through the IFMIS project. Nonetheless, more recently, the institution has taken additional steps to improve its outreach to various stakeholders, including the National Assembly and non-state actors. The ministry is recognized as vital for the operation of sector ministries, but its interactions with line ministries is mainly associated with the budgetary process.

Clients recognize the limitations of the Gambian economy and that the ministry has to respond to challenging circumstances on the ground and make difficult choices when allocating resources. At the same time, there is an understanding that some of these decisions are not necessarily made by the ministry but respond to political preferences. The space of the ministry to navigate between these choices is perceived to be limited. Frustration with the damaging effects that governance problems have on national growth is at times directly coined on behalf of the MoFEA, as in the words of a former official:

> On the one side you have [economic growth] and might conclude that the President is doing well. At the same time they (MoFEA) experience that when two journalists are thrown in prison then the country loses 2% of the GDP.

The ministry is seen as benefitting from its direct contact with donors and the international financial community. This contact is perceived as creating opportunities that the officials of other agencies do not necessarily have. Travels abroad to headquarters of international organizations or to countries for diplomatic or business-related exchanges carry several monetary and nonmonetary connotations.

MoFEA is recognized by the main stakeholders to have improved several fundamental structures in recent years, but the improvements started at a low level with the implication that the ministry still has a long way to go. It is widely acknowledged that budget processes have improved over the past two or three years. The bilateral budget negotiations are now well prepared, and the ministry provides line ministries with updated information on budget flows and is requesting performance targets.

However, the actual allocation of the budget provided to line ministries is perceived to be a top-down decision and sector ministries have to accept the suggested budget. As one senior staff summarized: "We receive what we are told is available." Whereas the allocated budget is transferred in a timely manner throughout the year, the tranches are consistently smaller than anticipated (about 70 percent). The ministry is generally not perceived to be responsible for the latter, and it is generally stated that "they allocate what they have." With the rollout of IFMIS and the improvements in the budget process, there have been some spillover effects. One manager clarified:

> IFMIS is very helpful in general, but also during negotiations [with MoFEA] because it helps us to see how effectively we are using our funds. If we have not utilized them, the Ministry will identify it and ask us why we have not used the allocations. The introduction of IFMIS really has

helped the MoFEA to be more efficient. They are also more open to us now ... access to information is key to me—previously it was difficult to track payments.

The budgetary procedures have improved and the communications surrounding them are more professionalized; however, it is the nonbudgetary interactions that are described as scarce in scope. A general comment is that there is limited outreach to clients to be consulted on macroeconomic discussions related to their sector. Some clients also pointed out that ministries or agencies that generate revenues or have other sources of funding are in a better position to negotiate with MoFEA. The clients who depend solely on domestic funding report facing more difficulties in getting attention from the ministry on their work program and having discussions about how it links to other sectors.

External clients expressed few opinions or insights on the internal workings of the institution. This may have been because they were reluctant to share information with the team, but it may also reflect a limited communication and visibility strategy beyond the interactions related to budget preparations, allocations, and activities related to IFMIS. An exception was on the side of the Central Bank, which more closely interacts with several of MoFEA's departments. Several department heads in that institution pointed out the progress achieved on various fronts, while recognizing the areas in which more work needs to be done. The general dissemination of fiscal and monetary information to citizens from MoFEA is limited. MoFEA supports a website with features, but more direct methods of communication are rarely used.

Challenges

MoFEA has made important strides to improve its functioning, promote economic growth, and sustain gains despite the challenging political and economic context. Nonetheless, there are still significant risks related to the high domestic indebtedness and concerns about extra-budgetary spending. This trend has raised concerns among external observers and domestic stakeholders because it is setting the country on a nonsustainable path that could undermine the gains made on other fronts.

In 2009–10, the country resorted to treasury bills to finance its current expenditure, although by 2011, domestic borrowing had been curbed. That year, net borrowing was only slightly above the budget and strict cash budgeting was used to limit spending, although it was an election year. While poverty-reducing programs in education, health, and agriculture have continued to be funded, the level of spending is still relatively low, and considerable resources go to finance fuel subsidies and extra-budgetary expenditures. The other important challenge is expanding the revenue base.

There are additional concerns about the sustainability of the IFMIS program and the long-term ability of MoFEA to retain technical staff. The still frequent political influence in internal decisions and the high turnover of senior officials are some other challenges that are unlikely to be resolved without broader change.

The combination of the elevated economic vulnerability to external shocks and the high turnover of leadership highlights the need for a new paradigm of capacity building for MoFEA. Specifically, the government and its development partners should move from a narrow focus on organizational, technocratic, and public management approaches to a broader perspective that incorporates the political dynamics and the institutional rules of the game within which public organizations operate.

Conclusions

The case of The Gambia's MoFEA underscores that even in restricted political environments, internal constituencies can play a significant role in economic growth and stability and lead to marginal gains in areas such as transparency and efficiency of public spending. Moderation that comes from trade openness and aid dependence can be used to further promote policy reform.

The experience of MoFEA illustrates the importance of pursuing reforms in a comprehensive manner and the synergy of supporting concurrently the central finance agency and the Central Bank. In addition, other capable institutions in the country can not only advocate for change but also provide resources.

The case of MoFEA is one in which drivers of change have predominantly emerged from the external operational environment. The size of the economy, scarce natural resources, and the consequent long-term dependence on external assistance have all given development partners strong leverage to press for institutional reform. An environment of increasing donor coordination and more consistent engagement has created conducive conditions for dialogue. Nevertheless, external dependence has also led to sometimes contradictory changes and imposed taxing reporting requirements on the institution. In addition, there are domestic constituents for economic and price stability, in particular in the tourism and banking sectors, that are important sources of foreign exchange.

The 2002–03 crisis put macroeconomic management at the top of the political agenda, motivated learning, increased attention to middle management, and brought recognition that technical skills are critical. The successful reform of the Central Bank also provided an example of how effective institution building could be achieved. The positive handling of more recent financial turbulence has reinforced the commitment by development partners.

Since 2005, a relative reduction in political interference in the functioning of the institution has allowed for the return of many civil servants that were rotated into other positions or that left to work in other sectors. The greater attention paid to the staffing of middle management positions and the training of technical staff has had positive impacts in the performance of the organization. The introduction of new systems and technology has increased the efficiency of internal processes and allowed for a much more rapid response to external changes. Throughout this process, a core group of technical staff and individuals that remained or returned to the institution have been important in conserving the institutional memory and helping the institution navigate a turbulent political and economic environment.

PEFA Complete Indicator Set

A. PFM OUT-TURNS: Credibility of the budget		Score
PI-1	Aggregate expenditure out-turn compared with original approved budget	B
PI-2	Composition of expenditure out-turn compared with original approved budget	C
PI-3	Aggregate revenue out-turn compared with original approved budget	B
PI-4	Stock and monitoring of expenditure payment arrears	NS
B. KEY CROSS-CUTTING ISSUES: Comprehensiveness and transparency		**Score**
PI-5	Classification of the budget	B
PI-6	Comprehensiveness of information included in budget documentation	B
PI-7	Extent of unreported government operations	D+
PI-8	Transparency of intergovernmental fiscal relations	D
PI-9	Oversight of aggregate fiscal risk from other public sector entities	D+
PI-10	Public access to key fiscal information	D

(continued next page)

(continued)

C. BUDGET CYCLE		Score
C(i) Policy-Based Budgeting		
PI-11	Orderliness and participation in the annual budget process	B
PI-12	Multiyear perspective in fiscal planning, expenditure policy, and budgeting	D+
C(ii) Predictability and Control in Budget Execution		
PI-13	Transparency of taxpayer obligations and liabilities	C
PI-14	Effectiveness of measures for taxpayer registration and tax assessment	C
PI-15	Effectiveness in collection of tax payments	NS
PI-16	Predictability in the availability of funds for commitment of expenditures	C
PI-17	Recording and management of cash balances, debt, and guarantees	B
PI-18	Effectiveness of payroll controls	C+
PI-19	Competition, value for money, and controls in procurement	NS
PI-20	Effectiveness of internal controls for nonsalary expenditure	C+
PI-21	Effectiveness of internal audit	D
C(iii) Accounting, Recording, and Reporting		
PI-22	Timeliness and regularity of accounts reconciliation	C
PI-23	Availability of information on resources received by service delivery units	D
PI-24	Quality and timeliness of in-year budget reports	B+
PI-25	Quality and timeliness of annual financial statements	D+
C(iv) External Scrutiny and Audit		
PI-26	Scope, nature, and follow-up of external audit	D+
PI-27	Legislative scrutiny of the annual budget law	C+
PI-28	Legislative scrutiny of external audit reports	D+
D. DONOR PRACTICES		Score
D-1	Predictability of Direct Budget Support	NS
D-2	Financial information provided by donors for budgeting and reporting on project and program aid	NS
D-3	Proportion of aid that is managed by use of national procedures	NS

Source: CFAA Report, World Bank (2009).
Note: NS = not scored. CFAA = Country Financial Accountability Assessment.

Notes

1. The downward trajectory in the competence of the civil services had started in the mid-1970s and was driven by the overexpansion of the staff, patronage hiring, corruption, informality, and the drain of professional and technical skills (World Bank 2010a). Nonetheless, serious deficiencies are still unaddressed, including the politicization of the civil service, low pay, and the disruptive nature of senior and middle management rotation.
2. These agencies have powers of self-government within a larger organization or structure.
3. The Government Budget and Management Act of 2004 established that the ministry's mandate would include (a) developing the government's

macrofiscal policy and the medium-term revenue and expenditure framework for budget preparation; (b) managing the budget preparation process; (c) coordinating the management of external grants and loans; (d) carrying out budget execution and internal auditing, cash management and current-year financial planning, management of government banking arrangements, management of government accounting and reporting, and management of public debt; (e) promoting fiscal transparency and effective management in respect of revenues, expenditures, and assets and liabilities of the government; (f) exercising control over the implementation of the government budget, including any adjustments to the current-year budget; (g) publishing, where appropriate, the progress of budget execution; (h) inspecting the financial operations and proper management of budget agencies; and (i) preparing and submitting annual statements of government accounts to the Auditor General and publishing them for the interest of the general public.

4. The institution has a bonding system in place to ensure that individuals return and apply their skills.

5. Secretaries of State Darboe, Jahumpa, Mendy, Jatta, Colley, Foon, and Gaye and Ministers Keita, Ngum, and Njie.

6. Many of the leadership or senior management positions in other ministries, civil society organizations, and local teams of development partners are occupied by former employees of the ministry.

References

World Bank. 2005a. "Fragile States—Good Practice in Country Assistance Strategies. Operations Policy and Country Services." World Bank, Washington, DC.

———. 2005b. *Poverty Reduction Strategy Paper-Annual Progress Report Joint Staff Advisory Note.* Africa Region Report No. 32009-GM. World Bank, Washington, DC.

———. 2009. "Republic of the Gambia: Country Financial Accountability Assessment." World Bank, Washington, DC.

———. 2010a. "Debt Management Performance Assessment (DeMPA)." World Bank, Washington, DC.

———. 2010b. *The Gambia: Improving Civil Service Performance.* Vols. I and II. Report No. 51655-GM. World Bank, Washington, DC.

———. 2010c. *The Gambia: 2010 Public Expenditure Review Update.* Report No. 59309-GM. World Bank, Washington, DC.

CHAPTER 3

The Gambia Case Study: Ministry of Basic and Secondary Education

Helle M. Alvesson and Lorena Viñuela

Despite facing formidable political, economic, and capacity challenges, The Gambia has recorded sizable advances in the education sector in a relatively short time frame. Since 2000, enrollment has more than doubled in secondary schools, while the number of students enrolled in basic education has increased by 40 percent, with notable growth in the *madrassas* schools. Gender equality and completion rates in basic education have continued to improve across the board and surpass the regional averages. Simultaneously, the number of teachers formally trained and the number of students enrolled in the Teachers' College has grown considerably since 2005.

These gains are directly linked to the scaled-up investment in the sector, which has translated into a greater number of schools, larger number of qualified teachers and monitors, and the introduction of innovative programs catering to hard-to-reach groups. In turn, these achievements have been made possible by the organizational and management changes introduced by the Ministry of Basic and Secondary Education (MoBSE) and its ability to remain focused on a small set of goals, report results, and mobilize domestic and external support to realize them, while generating and renewing its leadership cadre. To achieve this, the institution has had to navigate and solve numerous challenges in its internal organization and in the governance environment.

MoBSE has benefitted from significant and increasing technical and financial assistance for more than two decades. In parallel, the share of the national budget allocated to the sector has increased over time. Initiatives such as Education for All and the Millennium Development Goals created a favorable environment for prioritizing universal access to basic education. The institution's leadership has played an important role in advocating for the sector, moving education to a higher position in the political agenda, and building internal and external coalitions to support MoBSE's goals. In doing so, the minister has shielded the institution from frequent senior management turnover and created a more stable operating environment, which is rare in the Gambian context.

Continuity of senior management and middle management has allowed the institution to lock in capacity gains made through various assistance and training programs. Notably, a core group of staff that were trained and mentored in the Policy, Planning, and Budgeting Unit in the late 1980s and early 1990s has been instrumental in realizing a wide-ranging reform program over two decades, with three ministers and two permanent secretaries coming from this unit. Staff stability has enabled skill development and the establishment of a culture of organizational learning. In addition, the longer tenure of senior and middle managers has contributed to better implementation of reform programs and allowed for greater accountability. At the same time, the use of monitoring tools and development of analytical skills for self-evaluation have been critical. The introduction of the Education Management Information System (EMIS) database, the Early Grade Reading Assessment (EGRA), and other assessment tools has allowed MoBSE to not only measure outcomes but also to plan more effectively and allocate resources.

Internally, MoBSE has crafted its internal communication to reinforce organizational goals and strategies. Changes in structure and communication strategies have been carefully coordinated to impact organizational culture. In parallel, organizational success and the external recognition that it has generated have contributed significantly to the prevalent culture and narratives of the ministry and staff about the organization's evolution. Recently, the ministry introduced a sophisticated performance management system.

The institution stands out in the Gambian context because of its level of openness and accessibility to stakeholders and clients. Some notable examples of how the ministry interacts with its stakeholders include holding bimonthly visits from senior management to districts, a community scorecard on education outcomes, and an integrated school management system. As part of this system, parent-teacher associations and mother circles comprise part of school managing boards and oversee the finances and the implementation of the curricula. Moreover, MoBSE has collaborated closely with religious and community organizations in tailoring basic education curricula, introducing Arabic and local languages, and using the *madrassa* system to include its system hard-to-reach groups. The organization has relied on local community leaders and women's groups to identify children, especially girls, not enrolled in the system.

To fully appreciate the progress made in the education sector, it is important to consider the backdrop against which the ministry operates. Although it is a small country, with 1.7 million inhabitants, The Gambia is a diverse society in terms of ethnic, linguistic, and religious affiliations. This introduces special challenges related to reaching and catering to the preferences of distinct groups. With few natural resources and relatively low agricultural productivity, poverty is endemic and two-thirds of the population lives under the poverty line.

Poverty continues to be the main constraint preventing children from attending school. However, there are other obstacles, including the direct and indirect costs of education, the relatively low perceived relevance of education, fear of erosion of traditional values—and for girls more specifically, early marriage and pregnancy.[1] Over half of the adult population has no formal education, illustrating the long-standing biases in access to public services that until recently negatively affected rural and female children. For most of the country's history, access to and quality of education have been uneven across its territory and across genders.

Institutional Success

The dire initial conditions of enrollment levels, gender inequality, and low completion rates have gradually improved over the past two decades, and today, the sector is recognized as having turned into a well-performing sector.

Results

The results that categorize MoBSE as a success are related to access, equity, and teacher training.[2] The Gambia is among the most advanced countries in the region in terms of enrollment and completion rates at all levels. School enrollment has risen significantly, particularly among girls.

Between 2000 and 2009, enrollment increased 25 percent in lower basic education, 85 percent in upper basic education, and 20 percent at the secondary school level (see figures 3.1 to 3.4). Toward a goal of 90 percent enrollment, upward of 75 percent of all school-age children (7–15 years old) are currently enrolled in basic and secondary school (World Bank 2011).

Concerted efforts to increase access to education in the interior of the country have resulted in enrollment gains in all regions. The gross enrollment ratio in basic education levels is greater than 60 percent in 30 of 37 districts, and greater than 80 percent in 20 districts

Figure 3.1. Enrollment in Lower Basic Education, 2000–09

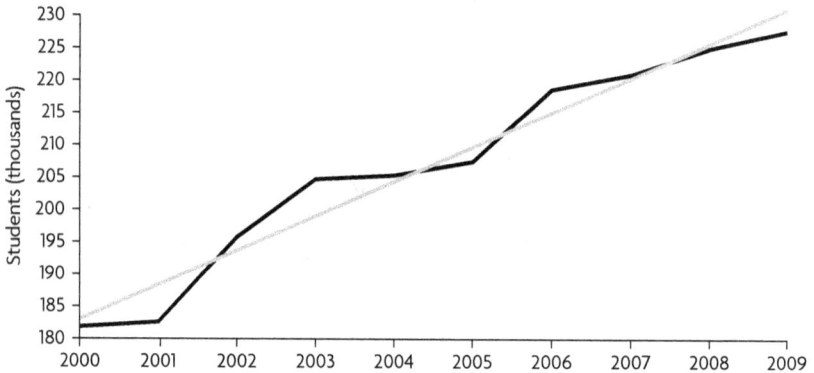

Source: World Bank (2011).

Figure 3.2. Enrollment in Upper Basic Education, 2000–09

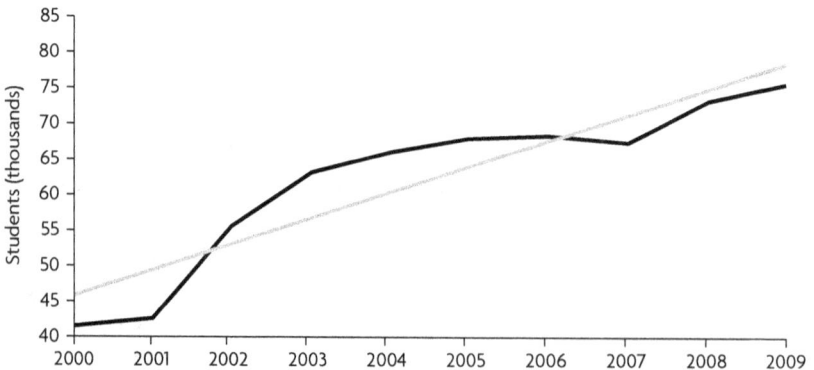

Source: World Bank (2011).

Figure 3.3. Enrollment in Secondary School, 2004–09

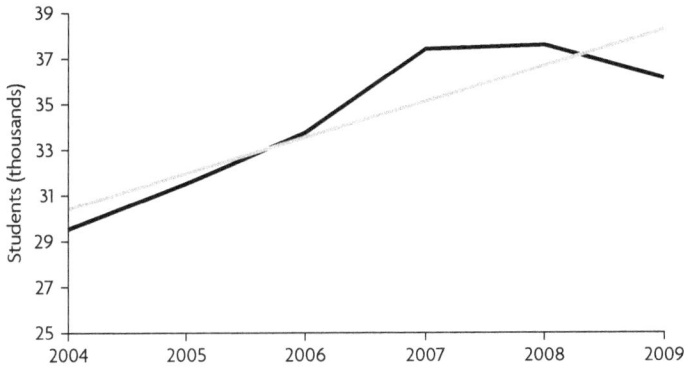

Source: World Bank (2011).

Figure 3.4. Enrollment in Higher Education, 2004–09

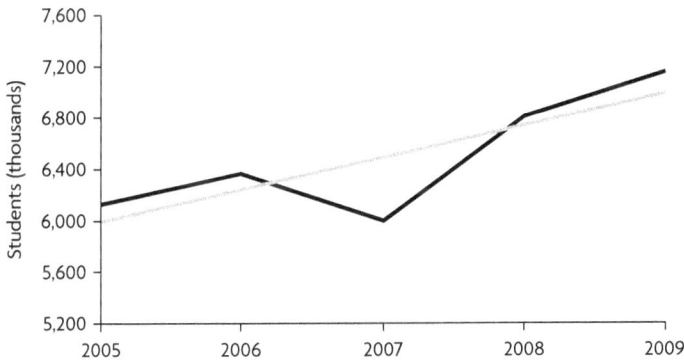

Source: World Bank (2011).

(see map 3.1). Moreover, thanks to substantial investments in infrastructure and teacher training, only 6 percent of students are attending incomplete schools, or schools that do not offer all grades (compared with 21 percent in Chad and 38 percent in Guinea) (World Bank 2011).

The Gambia has the second highest completion rate in the region for basic and secondary education. School expectancy, or the number of years of education that a Gambian child would receive, is 7.8 on average. This figure is higher than the average 6.9 years for other countries in the region at a comparable gross domestic product (GDP) per capita

(World Bank 2011) (see figure 3.5). Female completion rates have grown as well, from 34 percent to 71 percent (see figure 3.6). In this category, The Gambia surpasses other countries in the region by more than 10 percentage points.

The Gambia has made important strides in increasing gender equality in basic education and secondary education. In a decade, the country went from 73 percent of girls to boys to equal numbers by 2010, and from being below the regional average to surpassing it by 10 percentage points (see figure 3.7). The percentage of girls graduating from basic education and progressing to secondary school is going up, but at a slower pace (figure 3.8). Nevertheless, the improvement is extensive when the current 82 percent rate is compared with the 38 percent in 1992.

Map 3.1. Gross Enrollment Ratio, Basic Education, 2009–10

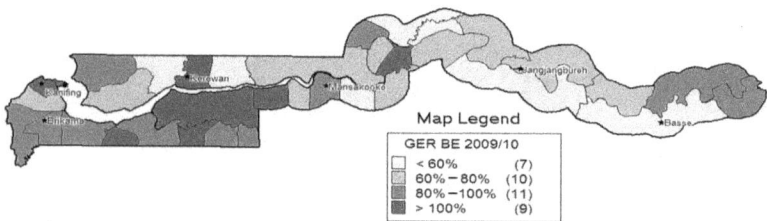

Map Legend

GER BE 2009/10

☐	< 60%	(7)
	60% – 80%	(10)
	80% –100%	(11)
	> 100%	(9)

Source: MoBSE (2011).

Figure 3.5. Primary School Completion Rate, Total, 1992–2010

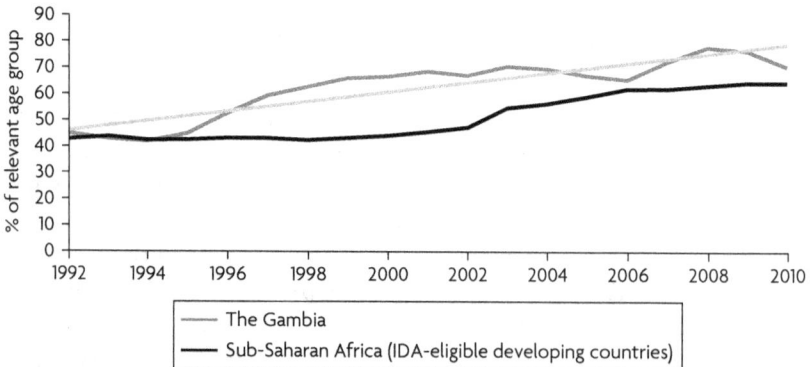

The Gambia

Sub-Saharan Africa (IDA-eligible developing countries)

Source: World Bank (2011).

Figure 3.6. Primary School Completion Rate, Female, 1992–2010

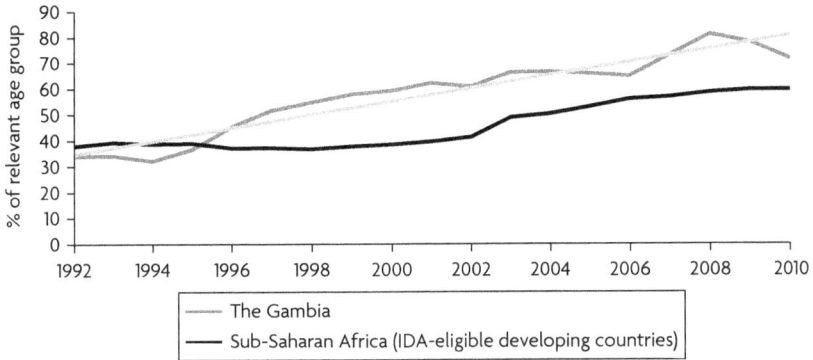

Source: World Bank (2011).

Figure 3.7. Ratio of Girls to Boys in Primary and Secondary Education, 2000 and 2010

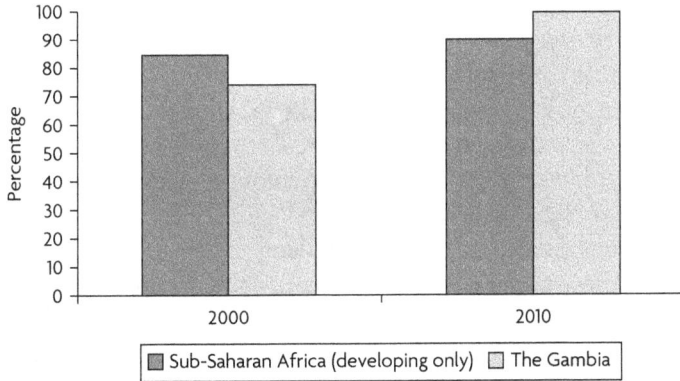

Source: World Bank (2011).

Another dimension in which the ministry has introduced important innovations is in the integration of Koranic schools. The Gambian school system permits the establishment of private and religious schools in addition to public schools. During the past five years, the ministry has intensified its collaboration with religious schools, in particular the Koranic *madrassas* as well as the preschool *daras*. The main goal is

Figure 3.8. Progression to Secondary School, Female, 2000–10

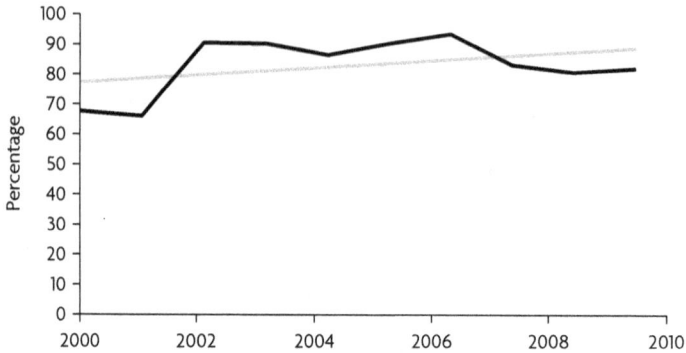

Source: World Bank (2011).

to increase the enrollment rate of hard-to-reach children through this collaboration.

Although efforts to include and cater to the Muslim population are not new—for example, Koranic classes have been offered in conventional schools since the 1970s—in recent years, the ministry has radically revised its approach to working with Islamic schools. MoBSE has developed Islamic and Arabic trainings and special tracks for teachers through The Gambia College and translated text books and other materials into that language. *Madrassas* now have the option to adopt a special curriculum that is aligned with the official one, but in which subjects are taught in Arabic. A harmonized curriculum allows students to transition more easily into upper basic and secondary schools once they graduate without having to repeat grades in the conventional system. The ministry also provides *madrassas* with English teachers and other resources, such as text books, furniture, and the construction of additional classrooms and other civil works. The *madrassas* that collaborate with the ministry are supervised by the respective regional directorates and the Secretariat for Arabic Education. Recently, the School Management Manual has been translated into Arabic. But the institutionalization of *madrassas* at a larger scale is only starting to emerge. Not all school supervisors, or cluster monitors, are fluent in Arabic and, therefore, there are limitations in their supervision. To address this shortcoming, there is an initiative to introduce focal persons for *madrassas* in each region and thus far two have been appointed.

Legitimacy

The ministry enjoys increasing legitimacy among the majority of its clients and stakeholders. As the improved enrollment numbers demonstrate, the mobilization and sensitization of students have been successful. The ministry is largely attributed with this impact, although nongovernmental organizations (NGOs), supported by the United Nations Children's Fund (UNICEF) Mothers' Clubs, and the World Food Programme (WFP) School Feeding Program, are other sources of influence. One parent in a focus group expresses the importance ascribed to education this way:

> *Although we [most parents] have not gone to school; we have seen the benefit of education either through our children or from other people. As such, we will continue to make every effort to ensure that we promote education in our community.*

Despite the fact that gains in access have not been accompanied with equal progress in terms of quality, the majority of citizens are satisfied with the quality of education and the construction of schools in their communities. In the most recent household survey, only 13.4 percent of household heads responded that the quality of education was poor (see figure 3.9).

Nevertheless, the results of the citizen scorecards suggest that there may be considerable differences in perceptions between rural and urban locations (figure 3.10). In 2005, the government conducted a pilot on community score cards as part of a process to improve accountability and participatory monitoring and evaluation. The pilot involved 59 public

Figure 3.9. Perceptions of Household Heads on the Quality of Public Education, 2007

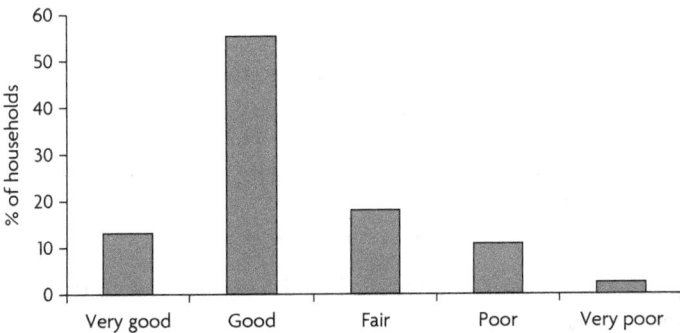

Source: Gambia Bureau of Statistics 2007.

Figure 3.10. Satisfaction with Primary Education Services in the Six Regions

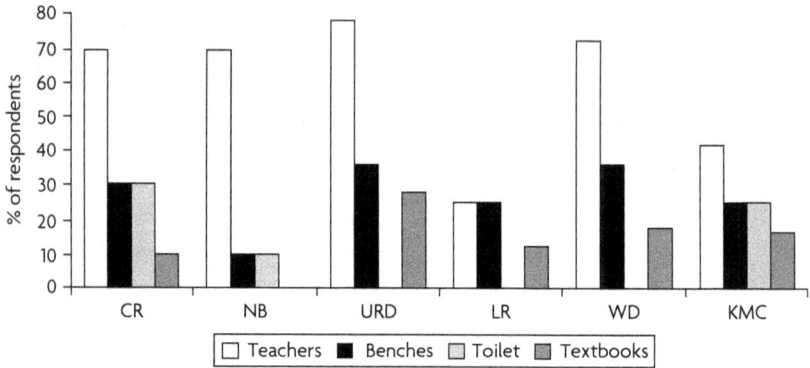

Source: MoBSE 2011.

schools and 15 health services. The pilot indicated large differences in the overall performance of schools across the six regions. The approval rating for teachers was more than 70 percent for all regions, except Kanifig, which is the largest urban area in the country. The results from this exercise suggest that satisfaction with school facilities and textbooks is much lower and varied across regions.

Yet in the context of the focus group consultations, many participants expressed that they had better quality teachers in the new classrooms. Schools seem to have lowered learning outcomes as access has expanded, in particular after grade 6. There is some recognition that the ministry is aware of the quality gap, in particular in regions 1 and 2 where principals and cluster monitors appear most informed about the ongoing discussions in the ministry. A principal of a school participating in a focus group discussion in an urban area highlighted:

> Thank God that there is a very good team in the Ministry and they have realized and accepted that quality is dropping and they are also doing something about it. An example is the introduction of EGRA. By the time those in grade 1, 2 and 3 get to grade 6, they would be able to write any letter and also be able to read well. Quality will come back to the level it was. However, I am worried as to whether it is going to be sustained.

In the regions outside the capital area, the information flow to the principals and the schools did not appear as dense and concern about quality was linked instead to deteriorating discipline and motivation of students, which the ongoing reforms were not perceived to address. For schools that still have unmet need for classrooms or auditoriums, more infrastructure investment is a priority. The ministry has created high expectations for the capacity to deliver classrooms. However, the general picture is that many communities have received a school or an additional classroom and that teacher absenteeism has decreased. This earns the ministry significant legitimacy in these areas.

MoBSE has for more than a decade demonstrated to development partners its ability to plan strategically, disburse funding, and achieve the main results agreed in relation to improving access to education in primary and basic schools. The perceived effectiveness related to output is strong and stable. With the support of the donor community, about five years ago, the ministry initiated a major effort to improve the performance of teachers so as to achieve better learning outcomes. In this process, the institution and its senior management have acted with openness in identifying and acknowledging the poor level of content knowledge of teachers. This honesty and self-examining attitude has been commended by the largest donors. The critique of the delay in systematically approaching the complex area of improving quality of education derives mostly from nongovernmental stakeholders and clients.

Trained teachers with classroom experience make for a large proportion of the management in the ministry. This is a highly respected platform for policy makers in the ministry and, in particular, is recognized by nongovernmental stakeholders and local agencies. The homogeneity in the career path is shared, in fact, by stakeholders and, apart from being a strong identifying marker, it is perceived as making collaboration more directed at solving well-known problems in the sector.

In procedural terms, the ministry earns substantial legitimacy from all partners involved in this study. The ministry has actively consulted with communities on how to solve problems and reach more children. One development partner explains:

So they took some of those suggestions from the communities for the development of the new program. It could be something as basic as, okay the young kids they have to walk a long way to go to the schools, what do we do with those kids? So we should show that they actually attend school. So they had something very simple, but you might not think about this having the donkey with the carriage. So now they go with the donkey on the carriage. And the fact that we now need to procure those donkeys is very unique.

The regular visits of the Coordinating Committee Meetings (CCMs) appear also to have ascribed more authority from local leaders. Ward councilors or governors are reported to join CCM when it passes their region and the initial fear has largely been replaced with appreciation. Misuse of CCM to report on teachers or particular schools is still a concern among principals, and the fact that the leadership still reminds participants about the focus of improving performance and not blaming each other are indications of the big normative changes the ministry is trying to achieve. However, the conclusion about CCM is that it is respected for its fine adjustment to the regional and local contexts and its applicability for schools and regional cluster monitors.

CCM is powerful because it includes not only people from the ministry, but all stakeholders, including donors. Current or future donors are thus potential observers during the school inspections, and it is within the mandate of the permanent secretary to close down a school if it does not live up to the requirements. The visibility of the leadership in the CCMs makes these points clear to schools, which in turn helps the supervisors in their daily work.

During the past four years, the president has publicly expressed his support to the ministry. He has encouraged other sectors to learn from MoBSE, for example, from its performance management system and focus on strategic planning.

Durability

MoBSE has sustained its performance during more than a decade. There are several elements in this resilience. The Senior Management Team (SMT) comprises a group of five or six persons with extensive experience in education reform who have worked together more than 10 years. There is a strong sense of purpose in the group to improve the sector, good training, and a diversity of operational experiences. There is peer pressure to perform at the same time as social and informal interaction is intertwined with delivering results. The shared values of leading the country out of poverty with professionalism through education and of empowering girls have contributed to building a strong SMT.

The ministry has resorted to two main learning sources, quantitative data through EMIS and field observations through CCM. The ministry has institutionalized CCM as an accountability measure that provides the opportunity for regional and national clients and stakeholders to participate in the ongoing supervision of the ministry. CCM provides SMT, including the minister, regional visibility and learning opportunities to strengthen the links between policy and practice. The EMIS was introduced in the late 1990s, and the ministry currently uses the data to make decisions and explore alternatives to improve quality. There has been a high focus on data related to access, while indicators of retention and quality have received less attention. Data related to access have fed back into the formulation of the policy for a number of years, while is it only recently that the content knowledge of teachers and the reading skills of students have begun to be systematically monitored.

Solutions for Governance Challenges

Since the 1970s, the ministry has benefitted from substantial external financial and technical support, which has contributed to strengthening its capacity and coverage. In addition, the ministry has been spared from senior and middle management rotations and has retained qualified staff at the same time as new professional staff has been recruited. The snapshot of the evolution of the sector in the following section will highlight long-term and strategic investments in the education sector.

The role of education as a driver out of poverty and out of dependence on the former British colonial power was emphasized after independence in 1965. Previously, access to education was restricted to the capital area of Banjul and left children in the rural areas with limited opportunities. The estimated enrollment rates in primary schools were less than 20 percent in the late 1960s (World Bank 1969).

The country embarked on a long-term sensitization program to engage the population in the benefits of schooling for young children, and by 1974 the enrollment rate had increased to approximately 24 percent (World Bank 1975). The British Overseas Development Ministry provided financial support to the education sector, and a few other international donors considered investing in the education sector in the early 1970s. In a working plan covering 1976–86, the government's policy objectives for education included improving the quality of education, particularly at the primary and secondary levels, improving access for the rural population, and aligning education and training with employment needs (World Bank 1978).

During the late 1970s, the government received financial support through newly initiated education projects—among them the first

World Bank–financed project (World Bank 1978). The objective of the first US$6.5 million investment was to alleviate the shortage of managerial skills through building learning institutes and centers, upgrading secondary education, and improving educational planning and administration. One of the conditions for obtaining the credit was to set up a planning unit. The first task of the unit was to draw a school map and a detailed plan for expanding primary education in rural areas. Other major donors initiating their support in the 1970s included the African Development Bank, the Islamic Development Fund, the European Economic Community, and the Overseas Development Ministry (United Kingdom). The latter provided technical assistance through teacher trainings and curriculum development. NGOs were still few, but the United Kingdom–based Voluntary Service Overseas Program was also established early on and provided low-cost technical assistance to the education sector.

The expansion of primary schools was secured through the construction of government schools, the start-up of self-help schools, and establishment of parent-teacher associations (PTAs) to mobilize the communities and channel technical and financial support from international NGOs to the sector. ActionAid became, for example, instrumental in setting up community schools and providing teachers in rural districts where no government schools were available. The light state footprint in the eastern regions that was inherited from the colonial period was still reflected in higher percentages of children out of school (more than 20 percent) in the northeastern areas than in the western areas of the country. The first steps toward improving access to schools were later capitalized in the 1988–2003 Education Policy, which was prepared with the assistance of the World Bank.

The 1988–2003 Education Policy, sometimes referred to as the "access policy," highlighted the need of prioritizing the physical infrastructure and basic school supplies to an even higher extent. The number of children was fast increasing at the time, and the coverage in rural areas was still very low. Generating access was the uncontested priority until the preparations of the New Education Policy (2004) were initiated.

Already in the late 1970s, external support was seen as essential for moving the sector forward. International Development Association (IDA) investment became the first of an uninterrupted series of World Bank education projects, which are still active and currently on the Third Education Project–Phase II. United Nations agencies, such as UNICEF and WFP, have continuously supported the education sector as well. The more recent Education for All–Fast Track Initiative is currently providing substantive financial support to the sector. The Department for International Development (DFID) has been a major bilateral player, most recently with the Basic Education Support for Poverty Reduction (BESPOR) Program, which has influenced the managerial and organizational changes in the ministry directly. However, DFID phased out its support to The Gambia in 2011.

Table 3.1 lists the key events since 1978. The events signify important policy and programmatic decisions that have contributed to the institution building of the ministry. Some of the events have had major financial impact, such as membership in the "Education for All" movement, while others have resulted in major programmatic shifts in approach and priority, such as the inclusion of regional directors on the SMT.

The school system in The Gambia has historically consisted of a mix of schools, notably private mission and Koranic schools, in addition to public schools. Children of the local elites have attended a few well-established mission schools in the capital. With nongovernmental boards, market-based tuition, and competitive salaries for teachers, mission schools have secured the availability of good schools for the wealthiest households in the capital. Several Catholic mission schools are so-called grant-aided schools, which are governed by their own board but receive government-paid teachers in return for maintaining the regulated tuition levels agreed with MoBSE.

With the investment in rural schools since the late 1980s, a portion of the urban-rural inequality in access to education has increasingly been addressed. The early establishment of PTAs provided an entry point for engaged parents and politically or financially strong representatives to gain some influence in the running of the local schools. The role of the PTA was redefined in 2008 to revitalize community participation in school management.

Already in the later 1970s, the first building blocks in strengthening the planning capacity of the ministry were defined, and this process was continued during the preparation of the second IDA credit in 1990. A reorganization and reinforcement of the educational planning and management capacity was one of the key objectives of the project. These early investments, including technical assistance in statistics, contributed to the launching of EMIS in 2000.

In 2003, The Gambia became an official member of the Education for All (EFA) movement as a Fast Track Initiative (FTI) participant based on

Table 3.1. Timeline of Key Events in the Ministry of Basic and Secondary Education

Year	Sociopolitical context	External operating environment	Internal institutional workings
1978		World Bank Education Project (US$5.5 million)	
1988		Education Policy 1988–2003	
1990		World Bank Education Sector Project (US$21.2 million)	
1994	Jawara ousted in coup led by Lieutenant Yahya Jammeh		
1995			
1996	Vision 2020 adopted[a] New constitution promulgated Jammeh elected President		Abolition of the Primary School Leaving Certificate Examinations Introduction of the Joint Coordinating Committee Meeting
1997		Local Government Act	Guidelines for Provision of Government Assistance to the Madrassa
1998		World Bank Third Education Project (US$51.3 million)	
2000	Ban is lifted on the political parties	Reaffirm commitment to Education For All in Dakar Presidential Fund for Girls' Education	Establishment of the Education Management Information System
2001	Jammeh wins second term		
2002	APRC wins parliamentary elections Drought		
2003	Economic Crisis	Joined the Education for All—Fast Track Initiative Partnership Sectorwide approach	Abolition of entrance examinations at the end of grades 6 and 9
2004		New Education Policy (2004–15) (Key areas: access to basic education; quality of teaching and learning; teaching and learning materials; nonformal education; and skills training in appropriate technology) President's Empowerment of Girls Project	Establishment of the National Training Authority through a public-private partnership Regional Directorates to monitor the decentralization process and the takeover of schools Establishment of the Senior Management Team(s) Restructuring of the Joint Coordinating Committee Meeting Girl-Friendly School Initiative Scholarship Trust Fund for Girls
2005	Ministers and civil servants are dismissed and more than 30 senior officials are arrested over corruption allegations	Children's Act established compulsory basic education BESPOR Program begins	Girls' Education Unit renamed "Gender Education Unit" Introduction of education in Gambian language in grades 1 to 3 and from grade 4 on as a subject Participatory Performance Monitoring

(continued next page)

Table 3.1. Timeline of Key Events in the Ministry of Basic and Secondary Education
(*continued*)

Year	Sociopolitical context	External operating environment	Internal institutional workings
2006	National elections	World Bank Third Education Project - Phase II (US$77.2 million)	First Public Expenditure Review of the Education Sector Education Sector Strategic Plan 2006–15
2007	Ten ex-army officers are sentenced to prison for plotting a coup		School Management Manual School Review Manual Early Grade Reading Assessment The Department of State for Education is divided into the Department of State for Tertiary and Higher Education, Research and Scientific Technology, and the Department of Basic and Secondary Education Introduction of the Cluster Monitors Schools develop mission and vision statements
2008	Food and fuel crisis		First National Assessment Test (and then annually) Medium-Term Plan (2008–11) Restructuring of the Coordinating Committee Meetings New PTA Constitution Second Public Expenditure Review of the Education Sector
2009	International financial crisis	The Gambia EFA-FTI Catalytic Fund 2009–11 (US$28 million)	Adoption of Minimal Standards for Basic School Management
2010	Eight men, including a former army chief, are sentenced to death for their part in an alleged coup plot in 2009		
2011	President Jammeh wins another term Severe drought	DFID phases out support and BESPOR program ends	Introduction of the School Improvement Program
2012	Ruling party wins parliamentary polls boycotted by the opposition		

Source: Authors' compilation, based on materials from the Ministry of Basic and Secondary Education, and interviews.
Note: BESPOR = Basic Education Support for Poverty Reduction; EFA-FTI = Education for All–Fast-Track Initiative; DFID = Department for International Development, United Kingdom; PTA = parent-teacher association.
a. A long-term development framework for economic development.

its successful mobilization of financial and political capital to reach universal education by 2015.[3] This membership provided opportunities for international and national advocacy for education, which in turn made the country eligible for technical and financial support for the ministry and civil society. EFA membership became a key turning point for the ministry. It also led to the establishment of the EFA network of NGOs in 2003.

Although the ministry has benefitted from stable leadership—changing ministers and permanent secretaries only twice since 1999, which for the Gambian context is a low number—the shift in ministers at the end of 2004 and the internal turbulence that preceded it led to the loss of several senior staff. One of the elements of the internal crisis was the stark deterioration of salaries across the civil service because of the 2002–03 economic crisis, increased politicization, and interference in the everyday management of the ministry. The senior management staffs that left the ministry continued their careers in education, but in the civil society. The instability in the management group negatively affected the working environment, especially at the central level, but the policy review and EFA membership were completed in time.

Paradoxically, the internal instability occurred during this productive period of several important and lasting outputs. The education sector policy review that resulted in the New Education Policy (2004–15) was the first policy to be prepared in a broadly participatory manner in which stakeholders at the regional and central levels were consulted. The processes are recounted at the central level as groundbreaking in method and results. In 2005 a new senior management team led by new Minister Fatou L. Faye initiated the implementation of this comprehensive new policy, which, in addition to access, highlighted quality and relevance in education. In parallel, the BESPOR project financed by DFID was launched. BESPOR provided technical assistance to adopt a sectorwide approach in education and more specifically to develop the quality of teachers and education outputs—and became another new and energized partner in education.

Notwithstanding the autocratic character of the current regime, improving access to education became a goal compatible with President Jammeh's priorities. During the past decade, education has climbed to the top of the political agenda. External funding of the education sector was already substantive when President Jammeh took power and enrollment rates were improving. The president initiated a fund in 2000 to boost girls' enrollment in schools and has actively supported the fast-tracking of girls' education.

The education sector has made important advances in increasing its overall funding and, most important, the amount of domestic resources dedicated to this area. Education represents 22 percent of recurrent expenditure (see figure 3.11) and 18 percent of total government expenditure, the highest allocation among all public sector services and above average for Sub-Saharan Africa. Yet, public spending on education in 2010 equaled about 5 percent of GDP, which is relatively low though still above average for Sub-Saharan Africa (see figure 3.12). Government spending on education over the past eight years has grown slowly but steadily. Lower basic education accounts for 51 percent of overall MoBSE expenditure.

External Operational Environment

MoBSE has actively worked to mobilize support from its principals and other stakeholders. Although education was congruent with the goals of both presidents, it only became a priority in the past decade, to some extent as a result of prior achievements. As donors ramped up funding for the sector, thanks to the good performance of the ministry and international initiatives to support the commitments for Education for All and the education Millennium Development Goals that generated

Figure 3.11. Public Spending on Education, Total, 2010

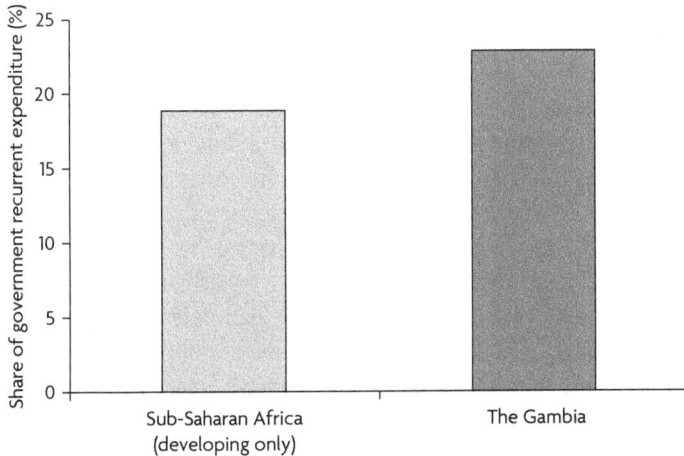

Source: World Bank 2011.

Figure 3.12. Public Spending on Education, Total, 2000 and 2010

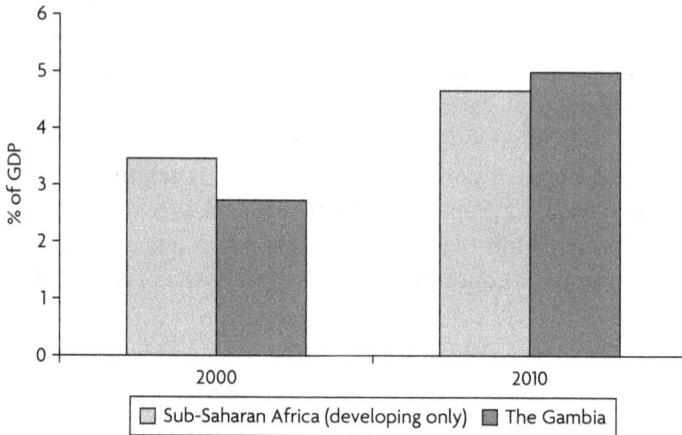

Source: World Bank 2011.

strong momentum, the government has also increased domestic funding for the sector.

The long-term commitment to education, from the ministry and the donor community, has critically contributed to the formal and informal coordination of activities. This is one of the crucial elements underpinning the positive outcomes of the sector, together with the scale-up of investment. The institution has actively reached out to clients and has built critical coalitions of stakeholders that offer some counterweight to the ruling elite.

Displaying results has been critical to convince principals and stakeholders to show not only the importance of the policy area, but also the potential returns of increasing investment in their organization. External recognition—in particular, progress against international goals, prizes and mentions, among others—has also helped raise the sector in the domestic policy agenda and mobilize own-source resources to sustain and expand the gains achieved. Moreover, improvements in access to education have supported the position of the state in society more broadly as citizen' satisfaction has increased, reflecting positively on the legitimacy of the regime. Thus, there is a feedback effect triggering the favor of political principals.

Presently, President Jammeh frequently expresses his support of the education sector, and the ministry has gradually become surrounded with a long list of engaged supporters, from the vice president to local communities. During the past three years, the president has in his public speeches made direct reference to innovations in the ministry. National-level stakeholders emphasize the leadership of the ministry as driving the change; the stability of the minister and the permanent secretary is therefore perceived as essential for continued success, and people are worried about the consequences if they were to leave. The ministry is viewed as a high-performing and respected institution that echoes the views of the president.

As a maturing institution that is in a position to drive the agenda of the sector or policy area and the dialogue with internal and external stakeholders, the additional support provided by the country's top leadership has helped amplify some of the gains. A positive cycle has ensued and is allowing the institution to introduce ever more sophisticated internal management systems and to make further gains in terms of results.

Achieving External Accountability Through Collaborative Mechanisms

The ministry is ultimately accountable to the president and the cabinet and, because of blurred lines between the executive and the legislative, rapport with the president is essential. This places great weight on the capacity of the minister to establish and maintain a working relationship with the president and vice president. Apart from the informal entry points, there are formal meetings in the cabinet during which the minister reports or answers to specific issues on education.

The ministry is also formally accountable to the National Assembly and, since a few years back, reports annually to the Assembly on progress and future work. The Select Committee on Education within the National Assembly has become increasingly involved and informed about developments in education, and the ministry has adopted participatory and testimonial approaches to engage the parliamentarians since the formulation of the Education Policy in 2003 and 2004. For example, committee members have been taken on school visits and confronted with students being excluded from school. These approaches have been described as innovative and effective eye-openers for the committee to understand the challenges the ministry faces. One stakeholder explains:

> The Select Committee in the National Assembly—they visited schools. It became a wake-up-call in their own constituencies, in their own schools. When they went and visited to see for themselves ..., making schools is one thing but—even before the CCMs—they went out to the schools.

This was in collaboration with ProPAC.[4] Maybe the whole idea of the CCM has originated from that... I don't know. In 2004–2005 they made the first visit and it was eye-opening. They saw things that really needed to be addressed.

The methods signify a shift in prioritizing strategic advocacy activities targeting the broader political representatives and not only the cabinet.

The most recent and innovative accountability measure is CCM. Over the course of the past three to four years, CCM has evolved into a wide-ranging forum where the main stakeholders of education are members. This includes Gambia Teacher Union, international and national NGOs active in education, development partners, and local government representatives (ward councilors or the governor) from the region in which CCM is held. Although SMT is responsible for decisions related to policy, CCM has developed into a coordinating body for decisions related to implementation and for recommendations to SMT on policy changes. CCM has by all national and regional stakeholders been described as an innovative accountability measure.

The transformation of CCM emerged as a part of the development of the Performance Management System (see box 3.1). "We have a crisis in the system" was one of the clear conclusions in 2005 after the realization that reading levels were very low. This ignited a long process of strengthening the reporting and monitoring systems in the technical and administrative directorates as well as the schools. The BESPOR Project was instrumental in this process. As an integral part of the performance system, CCM—with its ambition of creating a space for openly discussing problems and achievements—has been adopted by the sector. In a public speech, the president encouraged other ministries to replicate this performance management system. Through financial support from DFID and other donors, it has become possible for the ministry to finance these events. The direct and open discussion of identified problems in an otherwise politically sensitive climate has been framed as a tool of performance management.

Mobilizing and Consulting Clients

Given its distribution and large number of core clients, the ministry applies various strategies to reach families. The strategies include local discussion forums, mass media campaigns, and dissemination of education messages through NGOs. In practice, the most frequently applied channel of

---

BOX 3.1

The Innovations of the Coordinating Committee Meetings

In 2008, the Coordination Committee Meeting (CCM) was transformed into a bimonthly, rotational monitoring and supervision forum with the purpose of tracking progress on targets in the Strategic Plan and the Medium-Term Plan. The mandate of CCM was changed to a forum where decisions for implementation can be made. Prior to 2008, CCMs were composed of managers in the ministry, and the meetings were held in the capital and were characterized more as a forum of information sharing.

On-site participatory inspections of 15 schools in one Regional Directorate at a time feeds directly into the monitoring system and anchors the following two days of discussions on implementation progress and challenges. In each of the 15 schools, CCM members visit one day and make observations on the extent to which minimum standards of the school environment are followed. The observations are reported to all CCM participants and identified issues are discussed, and when possible solved during the meeting. The plenary format is mentioned as a strength in terms of addressing the gaps immediately, although they also can imply highly engaged discussions. During the data collection for this study, CCM identified several unregistered schools in the region under observation that indicated a severe gap between the collaboration between the regional directorate and the central-level planning directorate. The severity of the identified problems was referred to by several stakeholders throughout the data collection for this study.

With the expansion of participants to include representatives from civil society, district and ward authorities, donors, and other ministries, CCM has become a strong internal and external accountability measure. Teachers have mentioned the fact that CCM can bring the minister into their classroom as a very strong motivating factor for improvements.

With the change of mandate into making decisions related to implementation, the direct observations, discussions, and conclusions provide new space for external stakeholders and mid-level managers in the ministry to take an active part in the review of the region in which they work.

---

information is the local school, through the teachers, which has the benefit of contextualizing the information.

The perceived performance trend of the ministry is positive. A substantial increase in the number of school buildings, available learning materials, and teachers are the visible improvements most frequently mentioned.

The improved access to schooling for young children is described as an essential community platform for the future and an intervention that directly addresses a need in rural as well as urban neighborhoods. The steep expansion of schools has improved access. The long walks of primary school children or the need for accommodation of secondary school students in capital cities in the rural regions have been reduced considerably, which is seen as a fundamental improvement. Closeness to a school was described as the single most important indicator of a child entering primary or continuing secondary school.

School management practice is an area of prioritized reforms by the ministry. The reform includes a broadening of the management group at each school, the development of a school management manual and the implementation of minimum standards of school management. The principal has traditionally been in charge of the management of the individual school. The management is now suggested to be shared between the principal and the School Management Committee (SMC), which consists of PTA representatives, mother's clubs, and head teachers. The implementation is ongoing; it requires normative changes and implies a long-term process.

One of the new tasks of SMC is to develop annual and five-year work plans for the school. The suggested activities and improvements should be differentiated by level of costs. Although all the focus group discussions agreed on the benefits of restructuring school management practices, the implementation was reported to vary. The level of activity in the SMC was reported to vary considerably among schools. The seats in the SMC that are filled by representatives from the community are selected through election every four years. This is a recent and important change from the traditional long-term or life-long service of PTA chairs and members. In schools with positive experiences of raising additional funds, there was consensus that the requirement of a maximum number of years of service in the PTA was important in order to reduce capture by the most influential persons in the community.

However, it was also found that the goal of having informed, engaged parents and communities is not as easy to achieve in poorer areas with lower enrollment levels. In these settings, there are many challenges related to sensitizing families on the importance of education for boys and girls. The parallel, rather than sequenced, mobilization of parents to send children to school—at the same time as they were invited to participate in the SMC was perceived as less effective by PTAs and teachers. The challenge involved two elements. First, in rural areas where about every fifth child is out of school, the sensitization of parents involves economic and social considerations that relate not only to the supply of schooling, but also to the demand for schooling. Second, the recent democratization of SMC implies sociocultural changes to include parents with no prior tradition of participating in management groups.

The development of a school management manual and the identification of minimum standards of school management have been received positively by principals and teachers. The manual was reportedly available in the SMCs included in the study. The minimum standards were commended for being operational and relevant, except in cases when changes implied high investment costs, such as the construction of additional gender-separate bathrooms. The low- or no-cost improvements in the schools are emphasized as being designed as a mitigating measure for poorer communities, but clients expressed limited support for this strategy in resource-poor communities. The mothers' clubs were instead mentioned as instrumental in sensitizing communities through locally appropriate means to prioritize education of their children. The communities have experienced that resources are available for infrastructure improvement and for those schools that still lack classrooms or auditoriums for national examinations; the low- or no-cost alternatives were not well received.

Some of the identified challenges between the ministry and the local schools are the abolition of the middle school entrance exam and of physical punishment in schools. The preferences of the clients are not overlapping with the policy changes in these respects. The abolition of physical punishment is perceived to be one of the causes of disruptive classes. The ministry has developed tools for alternative disciplinary methods, but perceptions about corporal punishment will take time to change. The gap between policy and client preference should be understood in the broader context of child discipline. Over 84 percent of children aged 2 to 14 were subjected to at least one form of psychological or physical punishment by their mothers, caretakers, or other household members according to a household survey (GBoS 2007). And 21.5 percent of children were exposed to severe physical punishment, strongly indicating the gap between practices in the homes and in the schools.

The second challenge identified was a concern about the abolition of the middle school entrance exam in grade 6. The exam was associated with selectivity of the academically strong students, but more important, it was a direct motivator for students to perform well on the test. With the loss of the exam, parents and teachers report experiencing a dilution of concentration at an age where academic achievement should advance. Members in the senior management group disagreed on these views and explained that children who have low reading skills are the students who prior to the school reform would not have passed the entrance exam. Principals agreed to a large extent, but nuanced the situation by adding that the new emphasis was on ensuring that children learn to read during the first years of schooling through emphasizing phonetics. In schools that have implemented the early grade reading program, it is found that children in grade 3 are better readers than students in grade 6. EGRA is presented as the solution for the new students, but is not applicable for the children at the end of their schooling.

The traditional public discussion forum *Bantabar* is a popular venue for addressing current social and cultural issues in society. The ministry has adjusted this tradition of public discussion forums to the opportunities of national television and is weekly broadcasting a *Bantabar* on a selected topic related to education, such as reading skills improvements. An increasing number of especially urban households have access to television. Local community radio programs reach a broader segment of the population, according to clients.

Managing Isomorphic Influences

The ministry has received technical and financial support since the late 1970s, and a substantial part of this support has been directed as capacity building and improving the managerial aspects of the ministry. In particular, during the past 15 years, the development partners, which have been the main source of financial support, have redefined their roles and responsibilities. The capacity of the government to receive support has improved. Initially donors coordinated projects to ensure the continuation of funding and technical support through the sequencing of various projects. Post-Paris declaration, more formal mechanisms were introduced, such as regular Joint Donor Review meetings, participation in the bimonthly Joint Coordinating Committee Meeting, and the Fast Track Initiative–funding mechanism.

Defining the source of influence is a composite task in tightknit collaborations. Task team leaders (TTLs) and technical advisors from multilateral and bilateral development partners have worked in close coordination with the SMT for more than a decade. The turnover of

TTLs and advisors has been low in multilateral and bilateral organizations, as has the turnover in SMT. This stability has contributed to deeper engagement.

In asking one of the TTLs if a particular process was led by the international organization, the answer was that it is not this simple. "We came in together" is one of the opening explanations of how the close collaboration between a main donor and the leadership were established. The sense of urgency in strengthening the sector was shared. Another representative from the donor community explained the normative isomorphism through the same training opportunities and access to the academic literature on education reforms:

> They look at the literature; they have consultants who come quite often and they have discussions with us all the time. So these are things that filter through the literature. It's nothing really purely [donor-specific] in the country.

The SMT and donor group was explained to share the same understanding of development in Gambian education, which implies there is a short distance from identified need or problem to solution. This is an indication of the strategic capacity of the ministry to manage development partners and mobilize a long-term interest in education in The Gambia. Close relationships have been established with TTLs of the main donors, which have resulted in direct operational assistance from TTLs, as when the first Public Expenditure Review (PER) in 1998 was prepared. From the point of view of the ministry, it was expressed that results, and more specifically documented results, are essential in securing this engagement. When this is accomplished, the donors are able to help the ministry in identifying new sources of support. For example, donors have advocated on behalf of the ministry for additional resources from the Treasury, and they have communicated concerns when potential changes in senior management were seen as endangering previous achievements and the reform agenda. The common drive for better results among donors and the ministry has created a strategic space where each partner speaks to the other's expectations.

The composition of development partners has resulted in different responses by the ministry. Since 2005, the ministry has benefited from substantial financial and technical support from FTI, the World Bank, and DFID. BESPOR, a DFID-funded program, opted for placing a senior technical assistant in the ministry who was accepted to join the SMT. The ministry has expanded the collaboration with NGOs in particular since the EFA membership and financial support, which included a requirement to include civil society in the movement. Because of the increased volume of financial support for constructing schools, the Project Implementation Unit (PIU) was transformed into a Project Coordinating Unit (PCU). This transformation is in line with international best practice.

EFA-FTI resources made it possible to expand primary school education radically so children would have to travel less than three kilometers to a school. The ministry had already reformed the school structure and introduced nine years of schooling followed by three years of secondary schooling in accordance with international recommendations. In 2005, when the Child Act was signed, schooling became mandatory.

The Performance Management System (PMS) was introduced, with BESPOR's support, at a time when the ministry had realized that many children per class were not able to read after several years of schooling. "We have a crisis in the system" framed the following five to seven years of improving performance of teachers and administrative and technical staff. In developing the PMS, it was explicitly recognized that the systems had been developed in high-income, Western settings. Examples of PMS implementation in other African countries were discussed, and apart from a few initial international consultants, the consultants who had performed assessments and studies related to PMS were locally recruited in an attempt to adjust the system to the local context. PMS is complemented with a program in which retired teachers provide in-service training to teachers to create incentives to perform better.

Several new functions in MoBSE have been developed over time, in addition to the transition from a PIU to a PCU and the development of EMIS, which is a unit under the Directorate of Planning. A Monitoring and Evaluation Unit was established under the Directorate of Planning to strengthen the evidence base of education policy rather than the individual projects. Science and mathematics have been weak in the curriculum, and the capacity to design a program was recognized as challenging and expensive. A new directorate of science was established to increase focus on this area. The director and staff were recruited externally with the task to sensitize the population to science through private-public partnerships. Although the need is in line with international best practices, the method in gaining momentum appears homegrown.

Internal Institutional Workings

The current structure of the ministry is the result of a major reorganization in 1998. The restructuring became a turning point for capacity building of the ministry. The 1988–2003 policy was reviewed at mid-term in 1995, and one of the main findings was to transform the ministry into a directorate model to fit better with the increasing number of functions in the ministry. During the restructuring, the number of directorates doubled. The Directorate of Information Technology and Human Resources was established. The Directorate of Planning gained more importance with the creation of EMIS and in the development of the budget. The regional offices were upgraded to Regional Education Directorates in an effort to adjust better and support implementation at the local level. It took a few years before all the directorates were in place; for example, the Directorate of Science and Technology Education was first established in 2001.

The SMT was also revised in 1998, and two management committees were given the responsibility for effective management and coordination of policy implementation, respectively. SMT is comprised of the directors, the permanent secretary, and two deputy permanent secretaries and chaired by the minister. The CCM became the second management forum and was originally composed of directors, principal education officers, managers or deputy managers, and deputy permanent secretaries and chaired by the permanent secretary. CCM was conceptualized in the beginning of the 1990s, but it was with the restructuring in 1998 that CCMs became functional and were used to strengthen the central-regional relationship. Over the years, CCM suffered some setbacks caused by lack of regularity and some challenges in living up to the principle of collective accountability measures since 2005. In 2008 CCM was expanded to include political and nongovernmental stakeholders. It is now more institutionalized; regular meetings are held in the regions, and the principle of making CCM decisions during the meetings is respected and identified as one of the most important aspects of the ministry.

In 2007 the Ministry of Higher Education and Research was created as a response to the need to strengthen tertiary education in the country. The Directorate of Tertiary Education was transferred to the new ministry. With the increased number of students completing secondary schooling, the need for tertiary education has increased. The opening of the University of The Gambia indicates the ambitions of strengthening tertiary education and research. The new ministry was tasked with increasing funding for these plans and thus reflects an adjustment to the local context.

Renewing the Seeds of Leadership

MoBSE has been the most stable ministry in terms of leadership since the coup in 1994. The ministry has been led by only three ministers and seven permanent secretaries over this period. The former ministers had similar backgrounds in education and moved on to work in international education. The current minister came into office in 2005. The institutional memory in SMT is strong, with several directors having served the ministry since the early 1990s. A group of five to six professionals entered the planning office, worked in the ranks, and eventually became members in SMT (see box 3.2). The Directorate of Planning has been given a central role in emphasizing the need for monitoring implementation. Production and dissemination of education data have gradually been used as a tool to advocate the importance of impact in education. As a former senior member of the Planning Directorate concluded:

> If you don't have data you are not moving. But data has to feed into policy process; if it does not feed into policy—data does not help you.

The ministry has benefitted from substantial capacity building since the 1990s, and the proportion of staff with a master's degree is reportedly the highest in the country. The need for capacity building was emphasized in the first PER, and the donors have since then contributed funding for capacity building. Many of the current SMT members came into the ministry as young teachers, benefited from training abroad, and were able to rise quickly in the system. This is replicated in the current mid-level management (heads of units).

This aspect is described as unique for the ministry. The traditional model in civil service is described as hierarchical, where even directors are expected to clear initiatives with the permanent secretary before moving ahead. The internal working environment is ascribed high importance by staff and managers, and the current leadership is attributed to have created a conducive environment in which technocracy is the main guiding principle.

The leadership is almost exclusively composed of teachers who have made a career in the ministry and now are members of SMT. From the minister to the regional education officers, the majority of staff initiated their employment as teaches and refer to this experience as essential for their performance in the ministry today. It is associated with a comprehensive list of

---

BOX 3.2

Building the Directorate of Planning

The function of a planning unit was already established in 1978, but it was not until 1995–96 that the office was able to present data of fair quality and provide feedback to the management and to schools. Around 1998, Coordinating Committee Meetings became one of the new venues for presenting and discussing data. The Directorate of Planning had strengthened its capacity and was able to improve data collection, coverage, and timely reporting and to produce annual statistics. The team was built through two main mechanisms. The African Development Bank supported the government with planning units in selected sectors of which education was a part (others included the Ministry of Health, Ministry of Agriculture, and Women's Bureau). As technical assistance, the ministry received funding for one statistician and one economist, and the ministry was successful in retaining staff from schools and other areas of the administration to work to the planning office. A highly qualified group of staff was formed and has largely stayed in the ministry since then. The influence of this group is well recognized internally and externally. Over the years, the directorate has benefited from several short- and long-term training opportunities, which have had great importance in improving the quality of data and reporting.

---

social skills, an operational approach to management, hard work and dedication, and joy in improving the results of education. Identification as an "educationalist" is very strong. It is mentioned with pride and is the most inclusive fundamental of the esprit du corps. However, this is changing as professionals entering the middle to high positions tend to have a master's degree in education rather than teaching experience. The generational gap is only slowly becoming visible.

The ministry internally emphasizes the priority of listening to the grassroots. Inclusive leadership is described as an important source of inspiration and linked to the fact that several members in SMT left the ministry in the early 2000s, worked for NGOs, and returned to the ministry in 2005. An internal narrative on the leadership emphasizes "the aggressive leadership." It is positively framed and implies boldness, directness, and dedication to achieve results. It also describes confrontational strategies for when problems need difficult solutions. These characteristics constitute the reasons why the ministry perceives itself as a trendsetter, not only nationally, but also internationally.

Implementing Performance Management and Improving Internal Communication to Build Morale

The ministry presents itself as a learning institution, and its management practices are seen as reinforcing this strategic principle. One senior staff member specified the meaning of this principle when stating, "We are managing change to our limits," implying the high ambitions but also the sociopolitical restrictions of change in the country.

The broader management practices of MoBSE include the structuring of individual tasks that have been the focus of attention, especially since the startup of the DFID-supported project in 2005. There has been a strong push to assess current practices and identify solutions to the problems and gaps that to some degree has consumed SMT. An earlier attempt to introduce an appraisal system failed, and the new Performance Management System (PMS) took these lessons into account by directly addressing the identified management problems and taking a more holistic and developmental approach (Petersen 2010). The PMS was built gradually, but the current challenge is to link all the elements into a holistic system. The management reforms initiated in April 2005 are extensive and touch traditions, such as autocratic management styles and high-power distances within the ministry.

In contextualizing the reforms, it is clear that the transformation of promotion from seniority to promotion based on performance requires time and targeted sensitization. This is one of the areas in which the ministry emphasizes ongoing learning. There are examples of senior staff that were initially against PMS but now are ambassadors for the system. And there are examples of staff that have accepted that their current position did not fit well with their qualifications and therefore were transferred to another post. The meeting is normally opened by the permanent secretary reminding participants that CCM is a social accountability measure. The leap in management practice is off to a very positive start, but sustainability of the system is not fully developed.

The motivation of individuals has been targeted through PMS over the past couple years, and positive improvements have been reported at the mid-level staff level and at the regional directorate level and among teachers in schools reporting fewer days of absenteeism. Training opportunities are highly valued and attractive for staff at all levels in the institution, and have been mentioned as a factor where the civil service outcompetes opportunities in the private sector. Through external funding and close collaboration with The Gambia College, the ministry has developed several new training programs for principals, teachers, and unqualified teachers. The upgrading of technical skills of qualified and unqualified teachers has been identified as a priority that serves as a strong individual motivator as well. The volume of training opportunities at low- and mid-levels has increased, which is highly appreciated by staff. Linked to the program of improving the conditions for teachers more in the rural areas, teachers' living quarters are being built. The provision of housing is a strong motivator for teachers to accept a rural appointment and for staying in the job. In particular for unmarried women, these facilities are important.

The ministry has built a reputation as a large and relatively stable employer and recruitment of young professionals with master's degrees is a developing trend. Although the ministry is bound by the civil servant payroll levels, a special skill allowance for mid-to-high-level staff, and a remote location allowance for teachers and principals have been introduced. These allowances provide a substantial increase to the very low salary level. Staff that has been trained in IFMIS benefit from an additional allowance. In addition, the ministry has benefited from some flexibility in recruiting new staff with particular profiles. For example, the staff at the newly established Directorate of Science and Technology was recruited externally to fill the positions with specialized skills.

The ministry produces a monthly newsletter in addition to reports on the bimonthly CCMs. Each directorate holds staff meetings, but the level of delegation of decision-making processes is directly dependent of the director in place. The communication of the policy and implementation changes between the central level and local schools has been substantially improved through the introduction of cluster monitors (replacing school inspectors). Cluster monitors belong organizationally to Regional Education (RED). A cluster monitor is the contact person for a geographical area consisting of five to fifteen schools and has quickly become an appreciated link between RED and principals. Interviewed principals were very appreciative of the direct contact with cluster monitors. But in spite of the improvement brought by the cluster monitors, some concern has been expressed about the excessive workload of the cluster monitors.

Challenges

MoBSE needs to address several challenges. As the strong push to expand the number of schools slows down, the ministry is shifting its attention to the more challenging task of improving quality outcomes, particularly in remote areas. Related to this, there is also a need to improve the training of teachers and include more female teachers in the workforce. In 2009–10, the teaching force was estimated at around 7,600 teachers, of which 6,360 were working in government and grant-aided schools. More than 25 percent were not qualified teachers. Similarly, the share of female teachers was less than a third of the total number. Female representation also decreases with the level of education, from 33 percent at basic education schools to 9 percent at the secondary level.

Another important task at hand is to continue to promote leadership within the institution so that when the current senior managers change, there is enough internal capacity to take on senior positions and enough technical and political capital to navigate the country environment.

Similarly, many factors remain outside the control of the ministry, such as determining the salaries of teachers. In many ways, mobilizing resources to build infrastructure has been easier than financing recurrent expenditures or investing in improving human capital. The Gambia is likely to remain vulnerable to economic shocks, and economic conditions will continue to constrain families in sending boys and girls to school, while important cultural barriers will change slowly. Retention of girls, particularly at the higher levels of the educational ladder, poses serious challenges, especially in some ethnic and geographic regions. The remaining percentage of children out of school will likely be more difficult to reach than those that have already become part of the system.

Conclusion

In The Gambia, expanding access to education in rural areas and increasing the participation of girls and minorities was not a high priority in the public agenda until recently. Nonetheless, since the early 1990s, MoBSE, partnering with several domestic and external organizations, has made consistent gains in school enrollment, which accelerated after 2000 and gained political recognition.

The ministry relied on a network of committed education specialists who, in the late 1980s and early 1990s, were trained and deployed as part of its policy planning unit. This was essential in keeping a consistent approach and sustaining the organization along its trajectory. This pool of individuals, moving in and out of MoBSE as a result of political interventions in top-level staffing, led several reform initiatives in various corners of the institution and provided the human assets to fill the most senior positions in the ministry and its partner organizations. They were instrumental in maintaining a consistent approach to institutional development.

The organizational reform of MoBSE strengthened the role and responsibility of the regional directorates. Building these regional structures has contributed to an intensified focus on implementation. A strong project and financial unit has responded to all donors' needs for monitoring and reporting, providing a platform for the scaling-up of external financing.

The introduction of the CCM has provided the ministry with a situational flat organizational setup for decisions related to implementation. CCM provides the opportunity to shortcut the bureaucratic processes and makes on-the-spot decisions. This drives the focus on addressing gaps immediately when they occur. As an external accountability measure, CCM retains important stakeholders to their long-term commitments. Direct access to the minister and permanent secretary gives CCM its high profile and perceived effectiveness.

The ministry has benefited from an increasing proportion of the national budget. The government has decided to reach the international goal of spending 20 percent of the national budget on education by 2015. The ministry has been able to monitor, analyze, and present results-based documents in the budgetary negotiations and thus provided MoFEA with strategic documentation of the impact of investing in education, which has not been the case with other sector ministries.

Leadership has played a significant role in advocating for the sector, moving education to a higher position on the political agenda, and building internal and external coalitions to support sector goals. Leadership has also consistently fostered a culture of learning and self-evaluation. The accessibility of the leadership was a recurrent theme in interviews with stakeholders at the central level, and it is clear that the ministry is perceived to have well-developed formal and informal strategies.

Annex 3A

Table 3A.1. The Gambia: National and Regional Study Sample, 2011

Location	Focus group participants and in-depth interviews	Number of focus groups (number of participants)	Number of in-depth interviews
Banjul (national study)	Interviews with senior staff and the leadership in the MoBSE, political and nongovernmental stakeholder, development partners		25
RED1-6 (regional study)	In each region, two mixed focus groups comprised of parents, teachers, and ward councilors from each region	12 (100)	
	In two regions, two focus groups with principals	2 (12)	
	In two regions, two focus groups with cluster monitors	2 (11)	
	Interviews with regional directors in five regions; interviews with one cluster monitor and one principal in each of six regions		16
Total		16 (123)	41

Source: Authors' compilation.

Table 3A.2. Focus Group Discussants for the Regional Study

Category	Focus group discussions						
	Cluster monitors	Teachers	Principals	PTAs	Mothers' club representatives	Ward councilors	Total
Women	0	14	3	1	8	0	26
Men	11	63	9	13	0	1	97
Age group	35–45	35–45	45–55	50–60	30–40	40–50	35–45
Subtotal	11	77	12	14	8	1	123

Source: Authors' compilation.

Table 3A.3. Interviewees for the Regional Study

Category	Individual interviewees			
	Cluster monitors	Regional directors	Principals	Total
Women	0	1	1	2
Men	6	3	5	14
Age group	40–50	45–55	45–55	45–55
Subtotal	6	4	6	16
Total	17	81	18	139

Source: Authors' compilation.

Notes

1. Of students who never attended school, half say it was because of religious reasons and half say it was too expensive. Children from the poorest 20 percent of households are 3.8 times more likely to be out of school than those from the wealthiest 20 percent. Those from urban areas are 2.4 times less likely to be out of school than those from rural areas (World Bank 2011). As many as 49 percent of women are married before the age of 18, and of these, around 10 percent are married before they have turned 15.
2. However, the quality of education still lags considerably. In a recent sample of 25 4th graders, only 10 percent and 6.7 percent of the students met the achievement goals in English and mathematics, respectively (World Bank 2011).
3. The international community met in Dakar in 2000 to reenergize the EFA initiative, but it was not until three years later that the action plans were funded.
4. The current permanent secretary was director of Plateforme Sous-Régionale des Organisations Paysannes d'Afrique Centrale (ProPAC) at the time.

References

Gambia Bureau of Statistics (GBoS). 2007. *The Gambia Multiple Indicator Cluster Survey. 2005/2006*. Report. Banjul.

Ministry of Basic and Secondary Education (MoBSE). 2011. "The Gambia: Journey towards Improving Learning for All." Presentation at the World Bank, Washington, DC.

Petersen, Erling. 2010. PhD thesis.

World Bank. 1969. "The Gambian Economy." World Bank, Washington, DC.

———. 1975. *The Economy of The Gambia*. Report No. 907-GM. Western Africa Region, Country Programs II, World Bank, Washington, DC.

———. 1978. *Gambia—Education Project*. Washington, DC: World Bank.

———. 2011. "The Gambia. Education Country Status Report." World Bank, Washington, DC.

PART II

LAO PEOPLE'S DEMOCRATIC REPUBLIC

CHAPTER 4

The Institution-Building Context in Lao PDR

Naazneen H. Barma and Stephanie Robert Oksen

The Lao People's Democratic Republic is a small, landlocked, geographically diverse country, populated sparsely with 6.5 million multiethnic peoples. Lao PDR is one of the poorest countries in the East Asia and the Pacific region, but it has enjoyed more than two decades of rapid economic development. The country's overall level of institutional capacity has risen steadily over the past 20 years—in tandem with growth and as a result of a concerted program of economic and administrative reforms. This brief introduction contextualizes the political economy environment and imperatives that have enabled and shaped two particular cases of successful institutional development in Lao PDR—the Ministry of Public Works and Transport (MPWT) in the roads sector and Électricité du Laos (EDL) in the power sector.

Lao PDR is a one-party, socialist republic governed by the Lao People's Revolutionary Party (LPRP), which came to power in 1975. LPRP is the first contemporary authority to govern the whole country, and the centralization and legitimization of authority have been the crucial challenges of nation- and state-building in the modern, post-independence period.[1] These challenges have been compounded by the country's diverse and difficult geography, its very low population density, and the sociopolitical and economic divisions in Lao PDR—including those among the lowland Lao of the Mekong valley, the highland Lao of the plains in the country's north and east, and the diverse ethnic peoples of Lao PDR, many of whom dwell in remote, mountainous areas.[2] Political and administrative governance decisions at all levels—from the macro-level trajectory set for economic reform and modernization, to the micro-institutional questions of government agencies' mandates and modes of organization—should be viewed in the context of the overarching sociopolitical and economic challenges associated with nation- and state-building.

Traditional Fragmentation and the Socialist Revolution

The traditional Lao sociopolitical structure was one of hereditary, decentralized governance units, linked together in a hierarchy of personal loyalties best conceptualized as concentric circles. Scholars describe this concentric structure of power as a *mandala* system—a multitude of clan-based settlements (*meaung*) with similar internal organization, positioned in a hierarchy where larger centers functioning more as principalities extract tribute from smaller ones and power relationships are variable and constantly shifting (Stuart-Fox 1997, 7). The territory known as modern Lao PDR was always organized in three main divisions, North, Central, and South—each linked, at various times, more closely with neighboring countries and peoples than with each other. For most of the country's centuries-long history, these three regions were governed independently of each other; this was also the case, in practice, even under the nominally national unity governments of post-independence Lao PDR (Stuart-Fox 2004). Colonial French administrators and post-colonial Lao elites found that the notion of the nation-state—a centrally administered territory with agreed-upon boundaries—faced tensions when confronted with the Southeast Asian *mandala*-centered traditional model of power.

Political culture and organization in Laos has remained rooted in regional clans, with powerful families enmeshed in regional and personal rivalries continuing to exert hereditary political and economic influence through patronage and marital ties, as well as through regional business networks (Stuart-Fox 1997, 60; Soukamneuth 2006, 62–64). The core LPRP leadership cadre originally comprised socialist revolutionaries with few traditional sources of power. Many of them came from disenfranchised tribal and mountainous groups and were elevated on the basis of their military prowess and international socialist ties, particularly with the Vietnamese regime. Yet, both the LPRP and the government bureaucracy have incorporated and become more beholden to the traditionally powerful, regionally based clans, although the armed forces, a small revolutionary cadre, and overseas-educated technocrats serve as counterweights within the state apparatus.[3] These regional clans occupy high-level ranks in the Party's all-powerful Central Committee, which governs the country from Vientiane. They also exercise a great deal of influence through their placement in and connections with provincial governor's offices, which remain extremely powerful in the country's overall political equilibrium. The Party has pursued centralizing reforms, particularly in pursuit of creating a genuinely national economy and taking the reins of economic and fiscal governance (Soukamneuth 2006, 71, 187–90). Nonetheless, the marketization reforms initiated in 1986 have cemented the concentrated and interlocking political-economic dominance of the powerful Lao clans (Stuart-Fox 2004, 8). Because of the political nature of the bureaucracy and state apparatus, decision making in Lao PDR is concentrated in the hands of very high-level officials—in particular those in the LPRP's Central Committee, which includes key ministers and provincial governors.

State Building and Multifaceted Reform

A series of initial obstacles notwithstanding, LPRP has essentially succeeded in extending its governing authority across the country, binding the nation itself together, and building a national economy and administrative infrastructure. The party has governed the Lao PDR with a great deal of overall stability since 1975 under the socialist principle of democratic centralism. In the early years of the Lao PDR, the Soviet Union and communist Eastern Europe provided the country with 60 percent of its military aid, and advisors from the Communist bloc were prominent in Lao PDR. Vietnam played an even more direct role in the country's governance, with advisers placed at all key levels in the administration working closely with LPRP cadres.[4]

Guided by a blueprint for socialist economic modernization at the outset, the LPRP identified crucial sectors for investment and capacity building, including the power and roads sectors. Yet LPRP's attempts at more radical socialist economic methods, such as agricultural collectivization, nationalization of large businesses, and a centrally planned economy, were recognized as failures relatively early, prompting market-oriented reforms in the 1980s (Evans 2002, 195). A crucial turning point in the country's development trajectory was the government's 1986 decision to embark on the New Economic Mechanism (NEM), a program of market-oriented economic reforms accompanied by significant administrative reforms. Although the

Lao state continues to be involved in a great deal of economic activity, NEM reforms have transformed the country's political economy over the past three decades.

Lao PDR has been characterized by recurrent patterns of decentralization and recentralization. Under NEM, the government officially devolved control over revenues and budgetary expenditures, as well as some measure of autonomy on civil service management, to provincial authorities. Because of a combination of weaker government capacity and parochial political imperatives at the provincial level, the reform led to fiscal imbalances and macroeconomic instability, which in turn led to a marked deterioration in public service delivery. At the end of the 1980s, as marketization reforms picked up steam, the party recognized the inefficiency of the administrative system, which had become heavily bureaucratic and faced a dearth of skilled engineers and administrative staff at the local level.[5] As a result, the government embarked on an attempt at administrative centralization, formulated first in the 1991 Lao Constitution, which called for a centralization of revenues and reaffirmed "democratic centralism" as the management principle guiding public administration. Through the 1990s, line ministries regained more direct control over their provincial technical branches. Yet provincial governors, holding high ranks in the LPRP, remained politically powerful—and defended their autonomy in the management of their localities.

The Lao government maintains its vision of a centralized state and its principle of democratic centralism, while still pursuing a measure of devolution. Government elites—supported and advised by development partners—are progressively building a centralized state apparatus to enforce national policies and integration, while devolving day-to-day management and implementation to the provincial authorities. Thus, the Ministry of Planning and Investment and the Ministry of Finance have retained their prerogative as the agencies charged, respectively, with defining socioeconomic development priorities and centralizing all revenues and reallocating them on the basis of a bottom-up planning system. At the same time, in the early 2000s, the provinces were officially handed back some measure of fiscal and administrative functional autonomy—with the goal of building the provinces as the strategic, decision-making units, and the districts as the planning, budgeting, and implementation units. Today, Lao PDR is often characterized as a deconcentrated system with powerful governors, an administrative result that matches the country's political imperatives.

Economic Objectives and Institutional Capacity

Lao PDR remains today one of the poorest countries in the East Asia and Pacific region—with poverty rates still particularly high among ethnic minorities and remote rural populations. From 1990 onward, however—as the market-oriented reforms took hold—Lao PDR has enjoyed a period of robust economic development and poverty reduction. Over the past two decades, the economy has grown at an average of 6.5 percent per year, and per capita incomes tripled to US$1,260 in 2012. The number of poor households fell from 46 percent in 1992–93 to 27 percent in 2007–08.

An overarching development imperative for the Lao government has been its focus on moving out of least-developed country status and joining regional neighbors in the ranks of middle-income countries.[6] The original LPRP leadership cohort recognized relatively early that growth and development would be central to their legitimacy and to the long-term stability of the country under their rule. A common refrain today is that Lao PDR wants to be like its Association of Southeast Asian Nations (ASEAN) neighbors in terms of economic development and social modernization. LPRP has guided the country's economic liberalization while retaining political and administrative control, explicitly following the examples of China and Vietnam. At the same time, the role of multilateral development banks and bilateral donors was enhanced with the initiation of reforms in the mid-1980s.

Lao PDR has made steady improvements in its level of institutional capacity, graduating from the ranks of the fragile and conflict-affected situations (FCS) in the early 2000s. Its current governance structures have both strengths and weaknesses. The country is situated in a propitious neighborhood of economies with high growth potential and in which elites generally have a strong developmental orientation, albeit with varying systems of government. Yet, while Lao PDR compares favorably with other developing countries in East Asia and the Pacific and FCS in terms of political stability, it underperforms regional and FCS comparators on other key governance dimensions (see figures 4.1a and 4.1b). Significant areas of overall weakness include accountability and regulatory quality, although the single-party political system with strongly centralized accountability appears to have evolved somewhat in recent years. In particular, the role of the 100-plus member National Assembly in policy making continues to strengthen, and the State Audit Office has been expanded and now reports

Figure 4.1. Governance in Lao PDR in Comparison with the Average

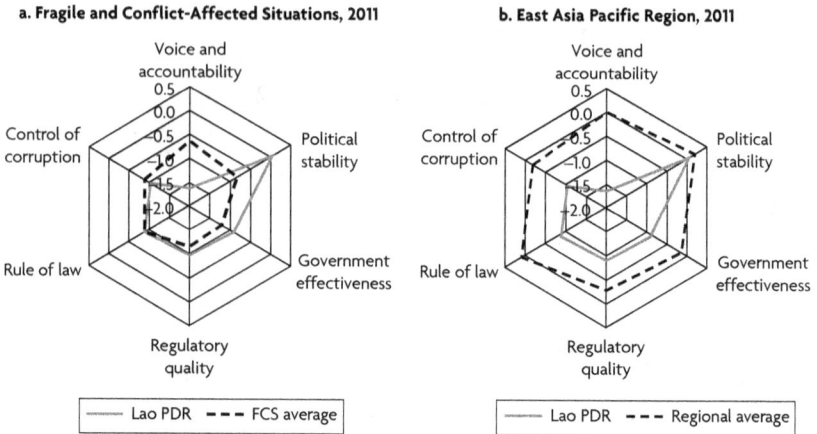

a. Fragile and Conflict-Affected Situations, 2011

b. East Asia Pacific Region, 2011

Source: Worldwide Governance Indicators, World Bank Institute.
Note: Data are available at http://info.worldbank.org/governance/wgi/index.asp. The six governance indicators shown are aggregated from a series of underlying indices and scored from −2.5 to 2.5 for each country in the data set. These data should be treated with caution, but they provide a reasonable "at-a-glance" snapshot of a country's governance context in comparative perspective. See also Kaufmann, Kraay, Mastruzzi (2010). FCS = fragile and conflict-affected situations; EAP = East Asia Pacific.

to the National Assembly rather than the government. Accountability pressures appear to be building overall; for example, a new hotline was established for the expression of citizens' grievances to the National Assembly. Lao people are much more exposed to different systems of governance through connections with regional neighbors and, in particular, Thai television. The growing private sector, with international involvement, also raises accountability demands on government.

Government effectiveness and the rule of law are also challenges for Lao PDR. Governance and public administration reforms were introduced to support economic reforms, yet administrative capacity and efficiency remain a major constraint in both central and line ministries. Anecdotal evidence suggests that corruption—in the form of state capture as well as administrative rent-seeking—is common and increasingly problematic, but a lack of public opinion or enterprise surveys has hampered meaningful assessment of the issue. Legal reform has been pursued with a view to establishing the rule of law more firmly and numerous new laws have been enacted; but these remain little understood and, consequently, poorly and inconsistently implemented.[7] On the plus side—even as it continues to face weaknesses in accountability, regulatory quality, and government effectiveness—the government has made important advances over the past five years in strengthening its public financial management system and improving internal oversight mechanisms, thus improving the overall level of public sector institutional quality.

Notes

1. LPRP has developed a nationalist historiography that casts itself as the heir to the Kingdom of Lan Xang, which, centered in the ancient capital of Luang Prabang was the only other authority that governed most of contemporary Lao PDR.
2. Almost three-quarters of the Lao population live in rural areas. The population is made up of 49 recognized ethnic groups with 160 subcategories. The ethnic Lao make up the largest group, at 55 percent of the population, and predominantly live in the Mekong lowland areas; the ethnic minorities that comprise the rest of the population live mostly in the highland and mountainous regions of the country (Lao Department of Statistics 2008).
3. Today's core Party leadership, as represented in the Politburo, retains members from the original revolutionary group, with a strengthened role for the military (Stuart-Fox 2004, 207).
4. China, for regional geopolitical reasons (especially the conflict over Cambodia), was essentially frozen out of establishing close relations with LPRP by the Vietnamese; the Lao-China relationship only became stronger and more important from the mid-1990s onward (Evans 2002, 189–91).
5. 5th Party Resolution, 1988.
6. The Lao government's oft-stated goals in this area are to reduce the country's poverty level to 10 percent, achieve the Millennium Development Goals by 2015, and graduate from least-developed country status by 2020.
7. See Stuart-Fox (2004) for a deeper discussion of legal reforms, along with an analysis of the evolving politics of reform in Lao PDR.

References

Evans, Grant. 2002. *A Short History of Laos: The Land In-Between*. Chiang Mai: Silkworm Books.

Kaufmann, Dani, Aart Kraay, and Massimo Mastruzzi. 2010. "The Worldwide Governance Indicators: Methodology and Analytical Issues." Policy Research Working Paper. 5430. World Bank, Washington, DC.

Lao Department of Statistics. 2008. *Socioeconomic Atlas of the Lao PDR*.

Soukamneuth, Bounlonh. 2006. "The Political Economy of Transition in Laos: From Peripheral Socialism to the Margins of Global Capital." PhD thesis, Cornell University.

Stuart-Fox, Martin. 1997. *A History of Laos*. Cambridge: Cambridge University Press.

———. 2004. "Politics and Reform in the Lao People's Democratic Republic." Working Paper No. 1, Political Economy of Development Series, College of William & Mary.

CHAPTER 5

Lao PDR Case Study: Électricité du Laos

Naazneen H. Barma and Stephanie Robert Oksen

Électricité du Laos (EDL), the public electricity utility of the Lao People's Democratic Republic, has achieved remarkable institutional success over the past two decades, particularly in terms of the gains in rural electrification it has achieved in the country. EDL has distributed electricity to a steadily increasing proportion of the Lao population, with improving levels of service consistency and technical efficiency. Through the expansion of the electricity grid to remote areas and the poorest elements of the Lao population, EDL has built legitimacy for itself in the eyes of its clients and stakeholders across the country and, in turn, played an important part in building the legitimacy of the state. Its successes have, moreover, proven durable over almost four decades, across several changes in leadership and in the face of setbacks. EDL's mandate includes the essential business of electricity generation, a dimension that has provided essential financial and institutional resources to the Government of Lao PDR and has become even more crucial as the country has modernized.

This chapter examines how and why, in the otherwise challenging context of a low-income and relatively low-capacity country, EDL has been able to achieve these successes. It describes how the core underpinnings

The authors are grateful to colleagues in Vientiane, Lao PDR, and Washington, DC, for their comments and guidance on this case study. The authors are indebted, in particular, to H.E. Soulivong Daravong, William Rex, Indochina Research Limited (Laos), and the officials from Électricité du Laos, the Ministry of Energy and Mines, and other government agencies and partners who generously spoke with the team over the course of this research.

of this institutional success emerge in the three concentric circles constituting EDL's operating environment—the sociopolitical context in which
it is positioned, its more immediate external operational relationships,
and its internal institutional workings. This introduction provides some
key highlights of the causal argument, with subsequent sections delivering more detail.

The sociopolitical context in which EDL is situated has enabled and laid
the conditions for the agency's success (Barma and Robert Oksen chapter 4,
this volume). EDL plays a unique, symbolic role in Lao PDR. It was formed
before the Lao People's Revolutionary Party (LPRP) and, in the first decades
after LPRP came to power in 1975, was a crucial source of revenue and
foreign exchange for the government. EDL was accordingly granted a privileged status among the various organs of the new state. The Government of
Lao PDR identified the electricity sector as a spearhead and crucial mechanism of socialist modernization—viewing it as essential to enabling heavy
industrialization and rural livelihoods.[1] In addition to these economic goals,
the power sector has played a major sociopolitical role, serving the government and LPRP as a crucial nation-building mechanism by physically binding together the nation with a geographically expanding electricity grid.

Likewise, the state-building function served by EDL has been crucial. For
many Lao citizens, their access to the electricity grid and their interaction
with EDL employees serve as their primary, and sometimes sole, tangible
connection to the state. EDL's rural electrification program continues to
serve these nation- and state-building imperatives, as the government uses
the lure of connection to the public electricity grid to encourage remote villages to resettle and form into clusters. More recently, Lao PDR has become
increasingly poised to take its place in the regional economy as the "battery
of Southeast Asia," based on its tremendous hydropower potential. The
electricity sector has thus taken on even more significance, with EDL at the
helm of the government's work in this area. Electricity thus continues to be an
important symbol of Lao PDR's economic development and national identity, as well as an instrument for the achievement of these goals of modernity.

EDL has been adept at capitalizing on the crucial symbolic and practical roles assigned to the electricity sector. In turn, it has delivered important results for the Lao governing elite in terms of its goals of nation- and
state-building as well as economic modernization. In the context of EDL's
priority status, its leaders have carved out a sphere of operational independence for the agency in an otherwise tightly circumscribed and controlled
governance environment, managing to insulate the agency from external

governance pressures in part by making the services it delivers invaluable to LPRP leadership. This relative operational autonomy has enabled EDL to pursue internal management strategies that are singularly focused on achieving ambitious and ever-expanding service delivery mandates.

As a state-owned enterprise, EDL enjoys relative autonomy in the manner in which it recruits, compensates, and deploys staff. Remuneration levels are high, and EDL is able to attract the country's most highly skilled and motivated workers. The organizational ethic is one that emphasizes professionalism and technical excellence. Furthermore, although the company operates in a hierarchical, bureaucratic fashion that eclipses true flexibility further down the ranks, its management systems and organizational culture are such that those workers feel themselves valued members of the institution. Such practices range from a transparent annual performance bonus system to the utility's widely respected blue-shirt uniform for all staff, including management. EDL emphasizes technical efficiency in a manner that relies on constant data usage, using a service standards manual for field operatives, operating 24-hour service hotlines for all clients, and ensuring electricity losses are minimized. The utility's considerable financial and human resources are thus marshaled toward delivering public services in a manner that bolsters EDL's and the government's connection with the Lao people and builds state legitimacy in their eyes.

The manner in which EDL has operated vis-à-vis its external partners and context complements its management of its human and financial resources, further enabling it to achieve continued success. While leveraging its relative autonomy, EDL is nonetheless adept at managing its relationships with the various stakeholders that serve as its principals and implementation partners—including donors and small and medium enterprises in the power sector—and prioritizes a close connection with its clients. The Ministry of Energy and Mines (MEM) is responsible for overall strategy and policy making in the power sector. Yet, despite its de jure agent status, EDL has a wide operational scope in the electricity sector. MEM grants EDL a great deal of functional autonomy in practice; the relationship is smoothed by the revolving door for top officials between the two institutions. MEM is represented on EDL's board of directors, along with several other important principals, such as the Ministry of Finance (MOF), and the board serves as a consensus-building mechanism such that any internal divisions are not apparent outside the agency. EDL senior management is also well-positioned in the party hierarchy and able to represent the agency's best interests in the political arena. EDL has benefitted a great deal from the government's consistent prioritization of, and long-term strategic vision for, the development of the power sector. In particular, the policy environment put in place to position Lao PDR in the regional energy market has been conducive to EDL's success, especially since the agency has been able to adapt itself well to evolving needs and objectives.

Related in part to the organizational narrative that it is providing a crucial public service, EDL has an exceptionally strong focus on the end users of electricity, including households, commercial and industrial entities, and government agencies. EDL's targets are framed in terms of the rate of rural household electrification, and its deconcentrated planning and implementation systems are structured in pursuit of those goals. Furthermore, EDL has successfully deployed development partner assistance while remaining in the driver's seat. An early vision of the role of the power sector in Lao PDR's development trajectory was developed by its first cohort of revolutionary leaders in the 1970s and has been used as a blueprint to guide sector development over the past four decades. Subsequently, however, the contemporary power sector strategy was developed in the early 1990s in concert with donors' institutional development programs after the country embarked on economic and administrative reforms. The government has managed donor involvement accordingly, relying on multilateral development banks for assistance with infrastructure development and the rural electrification program (the Asian Development Bank in the north of the country and the World Bank in the south) and on bilateral donors, including the Soviet Union and France, for policy guidance and technical assistance.

Institutional Success

EDL was founded in 1961, before the formation of the Lao PDR in 1975. It is the state-owned public utility that manages Lao PDR's electricity generation, transmission, and distribution assets across the country, as well as the import and export of electricity with neighboring countries. The EDL Decree of 1986 established EDL as a national company, requiring the progressive integration of what had been provincial public utility companies under the supervision and leadership of EDL Vientiane. EDL is officially under the management of the Ministry of Energy and Mines, which sets sector policy; in practice, EDL has a great deal of operational autonomy in terms of planning and implementing its service delivery mandate. This case study of successful institution building focuses on EDL's electricity distribution, or electrification, function, which constitutes its major public service and developmental role, rather than its power generation business, which is more commercially oriented.[2] EDL has demonstrated success across the three criteria of results, legitimacy, and resilience, as is reflected in objective measures and interviewee responses.

Results

EDL has achieved several tangible successes in terms of its major objective of expanding reliable access to electricity throughout the country. First and foremost is the remarkable growth in the country's electrification rates through extension of the electricity grid and household connections to it, especially across rural areas. The Lao government and EDL have emphasized distributing electricity to rural areas for more than 20 years, setting target electrification ratios over time and coordinating donor support to achieve improvements in rural access to electricity. In 1995 the Minister of Energy and Mines declared electrification targets of 70 percent by 2010 and 90 percent by 2020. EDL has steadily worked toward achieving these targets and, as a result of this concerted effort, Lao PDR's electrification ratio has increased an average 4 percent annually since 1995. Over 15 years, the number of household connections more than quadrupled from about 120,000 households (15 percent) in 1995 to more than 700,000 households (almost 70 percent) in 2009 (World Bank 2012). Access to electricity increased especially rapidly in the latter part of the past decade, with the ratio of households connected to the EDL grid climbing from 45 percent in 2005 to 72 percent in 2010. Currently, over 80 percent of households have access to electricity (including off-grid solutions) and the government is well on the way to meeting its 90 percent target (see table 5.1). Remarkably, Lao PDR has achieved its electrification ratio at a relatively low level of per capita income and at a more rapid pace of implementation in comparison with other countries that have also carried out successful electrification programs (World Bank 2012, vii).

Table 5.1. Household Electrification Ratio, 1995–2010
Percentage of all households

	1995	2000	2005	2010
Electrification ratio (households with access to EDL system)	12	33	46	73
Electrification ratio (households with access to any system)	15	36	48	80

Source: Robert Oksen (2012), derived from MEM Statistical Yearbooks.

Most recently, in support of the goal of 90 percent electrification by 2020, EDL has implemented the Power to the Poor (P2P) Program in partnership with donors. P2P is intended to provide access to the poorest households that have remained off the grid because they cannot afford grid connection fees. The program provides an interest-free credit to poor households for the connection fee (averaging 700,000–850,000 kip), which the households then pay back to EDL in small installments as part of their monthly electricity bill over three years.[3] The monthly payments are roughly equivalent to what poor households would be spending monthly on inferior energy sources, such as batteries or diesel lamps.

In addition to improving the nation's electrification ratio, EDL has also improved the quality of the electricity supply. It has managed to reduce its technical losses over the past 20 years (figure 5.1) through improvements in the utility's technical capacity and knowledge. Households and corporate clients agree that the reliability and quality of the electricity supplied to clients has improved, with the frequency of blackouts decreasing and EDL being able to restore interrupted power supply more quickly. Many clients noted satisfaction with EDL's service responsiveness (especially its 24-hour service hotline) and the professionalism of the billing and service staff.

Figure 5.1. Historical Records of EDL Losses, 1991–2010

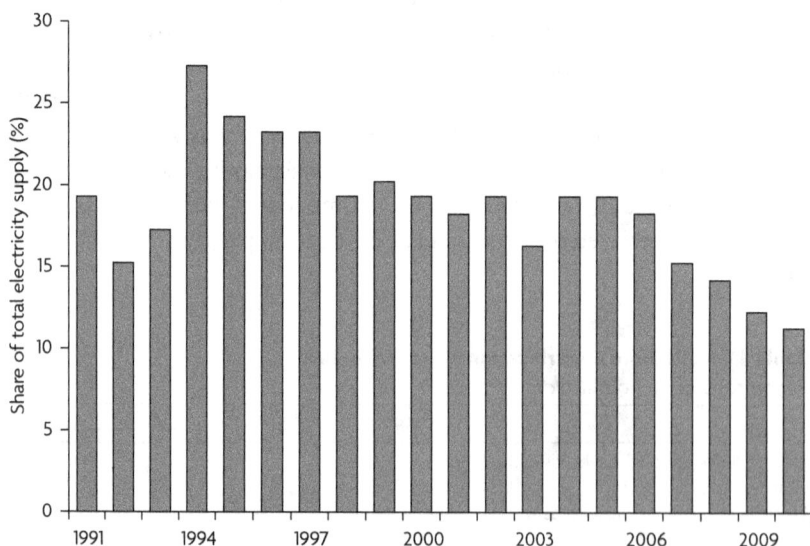

Source: Robert Oksen (2012), derived from EDL Annual Reports.

Some clients noted, however, that voltage drops during peak periods are common in the villages and power shortages are still a problem.

EDL has grown, almost doubling the employee roll from 1,983 to 3,522 over the past 15 years. And it has increased the efficiency with which it provides electricity services, with the number of clients per employee and the electricity sales per employee increasing fourfold over 15 years (figure 5.2). As it has achieved these results, EDL has moved toward adopting international standards for a public electricity utility—for example, recently being granted ISO certification 9001 in recognition of the "International Standard Quality Management Systems" of EDL and its general efforts in aligning with international practices.

EDL has also demonstrated results in terms of its generation capacity, playing a crucial role in increasing Lao PDR's electricity generation by an average of 3 percent per year since the early 1990s.[4] Because of the significant and steady increase in domestic electricity consumption (which increased by a factor of 14 over those 20 years), EDL's electricity exports have fallen an average of 3 percent and Lao PDR's electricity imports have increased to reach 45 percent of domestic electricity consumption. The import of electricity is a sensitive issue in Lao PDR, since there are varying views even within government on the relative merits of EDL continuing to export electricity versus ensuring the country's power self-sufficiency.

Figure 5.2. EDL Efficiency Gains, 1995–2010

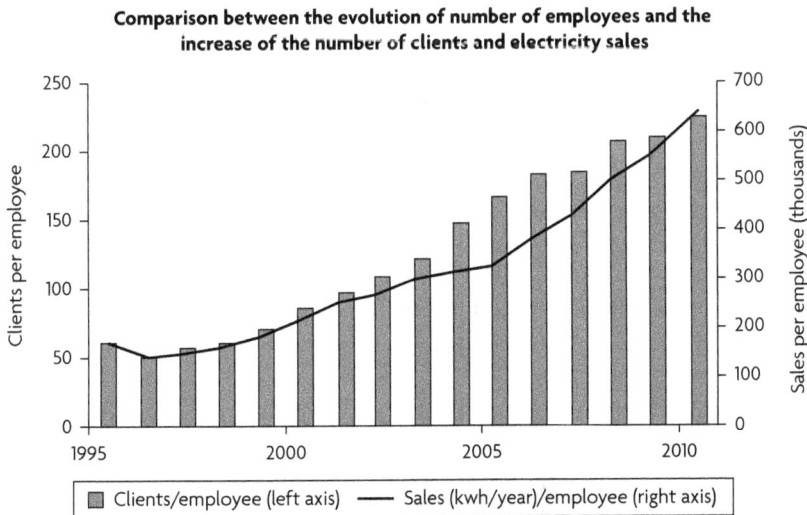

Comparison between the evolution of number of employees and the increase of the number of clients and electricity sales

Source: Robert Oksen (2012), derived from EDL Annual Reports.

Power imports are, in part, a geographical necessity. The power transmission lines from the country's main generation plants are oriented toward export to neighboring countries, and electricity must be imported into other regions of the country. There are also advantages to an export orientation: it brings benefits, such as foreign investment, technical assistance, skills, and technology that have assisted EDL in its goal of becoming a state-of-the-art electricity company. EDL's mandate has always incorporated electricity generation but donor recommendations in the early 1990s, as well as the regional power sector context, contributed to the dissociation of electricity generation and distribution, along with an overall trend toward the privatization of power generation in Lao PDR. While EDL remains the main agency charged with the rural electrification mandate, the responsibility for power generation and export is shared among other power sectors stakeholders, such as the Lao Holding State Enterprise, MEM, and independent power producers that are typically joint ventures between Lao and other regional interests.

Legitimacy

By increasing the Lao population's access to electricity, EDL plays a crucial role in serving the government's overall socioeconomic development objectives. In turn, EDL enjoys a high degree of legitimacy in the eyes of the population and contributes to building the overall legitimacy of the state. For many Lao people, access to the public electricity grid is one, if not the only, tangible way in which they interface with the state. In turn, their interactions with EDL employees on grid connection, billing, and service calls are a major aspect of how they experience the state in their lives. EDL benefits from a certain aura in the eyes of the population, delivering as it does the essential public service of electricity. Users typically perceive EDL as "a company serving the development of the nation" and as "a service provider."[5] A large measure of EDL's legitimacy arises from its particular mandate to fulfill the government's pledge of electricity access to all villages. Delivering on this mandate is enabled by unique operational factors, such as EDL's monopoly in service provision as well as the public subsidies that maintain low electricity prices and facilitate household connections to the grid even in remote areas.

The level of public trust in EDL is relatively high. A majority of electricity users in focus groups report their overall level of trust in EDL as *medium* and evaluate the institution's technical capacities and equity in service delivery as *trustworthy*. One area of lower trust is in EDL's ability to supply stable and high-quality power. The results on trust are corroborated by levels of reported client satisfaction. A majority of users rate EDL services and communication as highly satisfactory; but five focus groups of twelve rated their satisfaction as medium-low, demanding a higher-quality power supply even as they recognized that capacity was being stretched because of new users.

Resilience

EDL predates the formation of the Lao PDR and it has been adept at navigating and adapting to sociopolitical changes, macroeconomic and institutional reforms, and even financial crisis. Throughout its more than 50-year history, it has been recognized by the Lao people as an important service provider and by the government as a crucial symbol of modernization and vehicle for economic development. Its role as a central revenue source for government, through the generation of hydropower, has contributed to its durable institutional success.

EDL has been headed by several managing directors over time and handled leadership transitions well. Top management at EDL typically rises through the organization's ranks and provides important continuity. In addition, the revolving door in top management between EDL and MEM along with EDL's board structure, comprising representatives from all major ministries, contributes to its sustained role as a major, well-resourced state agency that provides an essential public service in close coordination with other government entities.

EDL has also survived a recent crisis, albeit with the financial intervention of the government. Between 1997 and 2001, EDL's financial performance was significantly affected by the depreciation of the kip (a result of the Asian Financial Crisis) because the company was borrowing almost all its debt in foreign currency. The International Monetary Fund's structural adjustment evaluation underlined that EDL had generated nonperforming loans to such an extent that its restructuring was unavoidable. In essence, MOF "recapitalized" EDL to prevent its bankruptcy. The government signed a financial recovery program that committed EDL to restoring its financial viability and improving its capacity to generate funds to meet future investment needs. EDL also signed a performance contract with two key principals, MOF and the Ministry of Industry and Handicraft (MEM's precursor). The contract established targets for EDL's technical, commercial, and financial performance; reorganized the utility into profit centers; and instituted formal audit practices and accountability mechanisms

(Government of Lao PDR 2001). These reforms subsequently positioned EDL to recover its operational successes.

Institutional Sociopolitical Context: Electricity as a Leading Edge of Modernization

The power sector has consistently been strategically emphasized as an important symbol, major priority, and crucial tool of the Lao socialist modernization and development trajectory. Current development of the hydropower sector still follows components of the Mekong Committee's development projects in the 1950s as well as a national assessment first completed in the 1960s (Robert Oksen 2009). The power sector was seen as central to the country's push to industrialize and to take its geographic place as a crossroads for trade. EDL, which was formed in 1961 well before the LPRP came to power, serves as an important symbolic role in the country's modernization. Furthermore, in the first decades after the declaration of the Lao PDR in 1975, EDL was a central source of revenue and foreign exchange for the government, which faced acute current account and budget deficits, and was granted a privileged status accordingly. EDL, in turn, has benefitted from its state-granted monopoly over the production and supply of electricity. It has taken advantage of the opportunities offered by economic reform and increasing regional interconnectedness, in particular through building a cohort of skilled managers and engineers who rely on their international network to focus the EDL mission on professional standards.

Governing Elites and the Power Sector

EDL was established as a state-owned enterprise in 1961 in the context of a broader vision placing the power sector as central to Southeast Asia's push to industrialize and identifying Lao PDR, with its rich hydropower potential, as a key electricity supplier for the region. EDL thus received the early support of nations from both Cold War blocs to install the first Lao power plants and to develop the power transmission network. During its early years, EDL was a microcosm of wider political rivalries (Robert Oksen 2009). For example, although the utility's director was a core member of the neutralist faction of the Royal Lao government, EDL managers and technical staff formed a labor union supporting the revolutionary Pathet Lao. This period endowed EDL with a pool of skilled engineers and managers, educated in the colonial era and through key power develop-ment projects (mainly the Nam Ngum Dam). These skilled EDL engineers earned the trust of the leaders of the LPRP as a result of their support during the revolution. The engineers also offered the country's new politi-cal elite the crucial technical and administrative skills necessary to deliver electricity and the financial resources that came with the country's early investment in the power sector (Robert Oksen 2009).

EDL was, crucially, able to generate revenue and foreign exchange for the government until the late 1980s. It was thus essential in helping the new LPRP regime to establish its legitimacy and ability to govern and was granted a privileged status accordingly. In addition, electricity has served LPRP and the Government of Lao PDR as a nation-building mechanism, physically binding together what has been in its contemporary history a regionally, ethnically, and geographically fractured country (Barma and Robert Oksen chapter 4, this volume). The rural electrification program continues to serve this nation-building imperative, encouraging village clusters to form to take advantage of power infrastructure and speeding the relocation of remote villagers in mountainous areas (where many tribal and ethnic minorities continue to live) to more densely populated areas in the lowlands.

Furthermore, the power sector was envisioned by the revolution-ary leadership as a tool for development, providing electricity supply to households and enterprises; and it was seen as a core industry itself, driving and representing Lao developmental achievements. The original LPRP leadership recognized relatively early that growth and develop-ment would be central to their legitimacy and the long-term stability of the country under their rule. A common refrain today is that Lao PDR wants to be like its Association of Southeast Asian Nations (ASEAN) neighbors in terms of economic development and social modernization. Electricity continues to be used as both a symbol of this development and a crucial vehicle for its achievement. In addition, the delivery of pro-poor public services such as electricity is a central element of LPRP's strategy for retaining popular support and solidarity with the Party. EDL itself was embedded in an integrated vision of sector development in the earli-est days of the Lao PDR (Robert Oksen 2009, 2012; Larsen 2001). It has, in turn, benefitted from its state-granted monopoly over the production and supply of electricity, notwithstanding the structural reforms toward privatization of the electricity market since the mid-1990s. In addition, the government has resourced the sector, in financial and human terms, in line with its importance.

Reform and New Opportunities

An important turning point in Lao PDR's development trajectory was the government's 1986 decision to embark on the New Economic Mechanism (NEM), a program of market-oriented economic reforms accompanied by significant administrative reforms (Barma and Robert Oksen chapter 4, this volume). Several interviewees identified this reform program as central to the subsequent success of the power sector—not least because it was under this set of reforms that state enterprises, including EDL, were granted operational autonomy and market accountability. In addition to providing greater autonomy to EDL in terms of its management, this reform opened the way for skilled engineers and managers educated abroad to reintegrate into the company. These reforms, in turn, made it possible for EDL to enter the regional electricity market as a supplier of affordable hydropower (Robert Oksen 2009).

The EDL Decree promulgated with the 1986 NEM reforms aimed to rebuild EDL as a national company, requiring the progressive integration of the provincial public utility companies under the supervision and leadership of EDL Vientiane (Robert Oksen 2012). This centralization process illustrates many of the core underpinnings of EDL's continued success. The policy proved difficult to implement at first but became easier from the 1990s onward, as provincial power systems (beginning with Luang Prabang) were connected to the central (Nam Ngum) grid. The support of development partners in transmission and distribution projects was essential in the centralization of the various existing electricity systems.

A new generation of power sector managers was trained in the first crop of international, independent power projects in Lao PDR, such as Nam Ngum, Xeset, Houay Ho, and Theun Hinboun. The leadership of this cohort was crucial in integrating and managing the new national company. They facilitated the process of centralization and the standardization of procedures in the new, national, state-owned enterprise (SOE) through effective delegation of their authority to an increased number of deputies across technical departments, with an emphasis on professional standards. This deconcentration of implementation capacity—whereby departments, branches, offices, and projects were responsible for day-to-day tasks—also contributed to EDL's increasing reach and ability to deliver services to local communities.

Structural adjustment triggers in the 1980s, as well as the regional trend toward privatization of the electricity sector in the 1990s, pursued an emphasis on increasing transparency in the financial relationships between SOEs, including EDL, and the government. In turn, these reforms improved the operating efficiency and financial footing of many SOEs and put them on a gradual path toward increased commercialization. EDL was no exception and was reorganized as a commercial enterprise in the late 1990s, with the introduction of a board of directors and a managing director. This major structural change coincided with the increased influence of a newer generation of managers, many professionally trained by, and networked into, projects funded by international investors and development partners.[6]

More recently, the government's emphasis on the power sector has continued with a slightly different cast, as Lao PDR is becoming more deeply integrated into the Mekong subregion. Electricity remains central to developing the country's trade connections, in particular with Thailand, Vietnam, and China, which in turn have delivered large financial flows and numerous advantages in terms of economic development. This is evidenced by the impressive growth of the provinces most closely connected economically with neighboring countries, especially Champassak and Phongsaly. Representatives of the power sector expressed a conscious pride in their role in facilitating economic livelihoods and trade, powering other sectors, and being a key to economic development. Furthermore, Lao PDR has become increasingly poised to take its place as the "battery of Southeast Asia," based on its tremendous hydropower potential. The electricity sector has taken on even more significance, especially as large international power producers have struck major power deals with the government, supported by development partners (such as the Nam Theun II hydropower project).

EDL has demonstrated over more than five decades the ability to retain its core mandates and position as a leading edge of Lao socioeconomic development and modernization. To that effect, the capacity to adapt its organizational structure to its sociopolitical context as well as proactive responses to emerging opportunities have been essential. Moreover, it has protected itself from demands for state-owned enterprise reform as the Lao economy has become increasingly marketized and globally connected. This adaptiveness is a hallmark of the institution's durability and resilience. Its institutional success in terms of delivering results and earning legitimacy rest on two sets of core underpinnings. One is a high degree of operational autonomy that enables an emphasis on technical and practical choices geared toward achieving its service delivery targets.

The other is the astute management of its connections with Lao stakeholders, EDL's end-user clients, and its implementation and development partners. The next two sections discuss each of these sets of causal explanations of success in turn.

Results through Operational Autonomy

Électricité du Laos has built its institutional success by capitalizing on its priority sector status and resourcing privileges to carve out a high degree of operational autonomy for itself. In turn, it has channeled this autonomy into a focus on achieving its service delivery mandate through astute management. It has pursued strategic and balanced sector planning in the context of the broader socialist planning system; cultivated a strong corporate and professional identity along with a service-oriented work ethic and organizational culture; built a reliance on data and cutting-edge technical standards to aid organizational performance; and emphasized professional and technical standards through relative autonomy in and attention to personnel management. In turn, its cumulative success in delivering various forms of results for the Lao political elite has garnered the agency even more operational autonomy over time.

Sector Prioritization and Planning

The overall stability of the Lao governing regime, along with the sustained emphasis it has placed over time on the power sector and rural electrification, were identified across the board as core contributors to EDL's success. The government's prioritization of the power sector and its clear and consistent policies for the sector are signaled by the steady support (financial and nonfinancial) provided to EDL and by the important position the agency occupies within the power structure of government. In turn, EDL's success in delivering electricity throughout the country has contributed to the government's cumulative legitimacy. EDL's success has thus been built on the layered combination of political resolve to provide national electrification as a public good, clear targets for electricity access, the necessary policy and financial commitment to achieve the goals set, and the establishment of positive and long-standing relationships with regional power sector stakeholders and international donors (World Bank 2012, 7).

The power sector's priority status is not necessarily reflected in direct resourcing by the government. Since 2000, government spending on the combined mining and power sector has been between 1 percent and 5 percent of total public expenditures.[7] The government contributed more direct funds to EDL in the 1990s—including a great deal of public investment in the power sector and loans from development partners to build high-capacity transmission lines. Today, EDL can and does turn to commercial sources of funding, especially for hydropower generation and transmission. The rural electrification program, however, remains publicly funded and is reliant on the support of donors.[8]

The government's nonfinancial support of EDL, by contrast, has been consistent and essential. From a policy environment perspective, the government has acted to protect the company from demands for structural changes and to create favorable conditions for the nascent electricity market. In particular, government policy was crucial in creating the favorable conditions for foreign direct investment and the technological transfers that came with it. Massive investments were required for Lao PDR to become the "Battery of Asia" that neither the government nor EDL itself, on the basis of its own revenue stream in a limited market, could afford. Sector reforms in the 1990s focused on the privatization of power generation with the proclamation of the Electricity Law (1997) and the amended Investment Law (1994), which endorsed the build-own-operate-and-transfer model for independent power producers. The government maintained its participation in the new hydropower plants through EDL. Several interviewees noted that the government views the energy sector as serving as a demonstration effect for international investors, showing that it is not too risky to invest in the country.

The National Socio-Economic Development Plan, the government's five-year planning system, and the annual planning mechanisms are crucial in terms of overall sector strategy, resourcing, and operational targets for any government agency. The annual planning process is facilitated by the Ministry of Planning and Investment. The process begins bottom-up, with needs articulated at the district level, collated at the provincial level with the supervision of the provincial governor's office, and passed up the vertical line to the agency in question. Prioritization takes place at the top level, with discussions over strategy conducted at the highest level of government. Resources are then allocated through the ministries to the provincial and district levels. As an SOE, EDL's interests in the planning system are represented by its principals, MOF and MEM, which directly allocate resources to EDL headquarters. EDL is then responsible for resourcing each of its branches according to their plans. De jure, nothing can be implemented without being incorporated into the plan; de facto, this means that the plan is amended throughout implementation to incorporate new projects that are developed when new sources of funding emerge. For example, if a village raises funding for a grid connection in collaboration with a private sector provider, permission to establish the connection must be granted at EDL headquarters and reported in the revised provincial-level plan.

A problematic aspect of the centralized planning process is that although, in theory, inter-ministry coordination is supposed to occur bottom-up through the local development plan, in practice there is little coordination at the provincial level between the technical staff or even the middle management of various government agencies. A core advantage of the planning system, nevertheless, is that EDL's annual operational targets are extremely clear, and the organization can and does work toward them in a focused manner. Furthermore, the lack of inter-ministry coordination and of human and financial resources at the local level has created space for EDL to progressively gain autonomy in its management. Committed to achieving the overall sector targets as defined by the party and the state administration, EDL relies on a data-based system to define priority areas of intervention. For example, the rural electrification planning process has become a multiyear expansion plan running alongside the broader plan system: "It takes into account the financial and economic viability of every investment and incorporates a project selection methodology that prioritizes areas and villages to be electrified to maximize social impact, within the constraints of available resources." (World Bank 2012, 10)

Data-Based Organizational Performance and Cutting-Edge Standards

EDL maintains a thorough data collection and analysis system, with operational decisions made on the basis of these relatively sophisticated tools. In other words, the agency practices evidence-based decision making and emphasizes the institutionalization of systematic tools for effective management. This behavior is illustrated by Champassak province's success in addressing its electricity losses, which fell from 26 percent in 2006 (then the highest level of provincial losses by far) to 5 percent in 2011 (the lowest level of losses by far). The root of this dramatic success in dealing with the technical problem was a concerted strategy implemented throughout the EDL hierarchy in the province. Data analysis revealed that sources of electricity losses were faulty conductors and equipment, inadequate switching stations, and stealing of electricity through unauthorized connections to the grid. A meeting of all district branches within the province was held to discuss these reasons and elaborate on a strategy for addressing them. The necessary equipment was purchased from neighboring countries; a training manual was developed for service-unit technical staff to assist them with equipment maintenance; and a new system of checking client usage against billing records was established. Moreover, implementation of the strategy was concerted—district branches drew up their own plans of action, the management team at the branch office handled prioritization and supervision of the strategy, and EDL headquarters assisted as necessary with training.[9]

Other signs of a data-enabled focus on performance exist. EDL frontline service providers work with a service manual, with precise instructions on steps to take for conducting assessments, equipment installation, maintenance, and so forth, as well as a protocol for when decisions need to be elevated up the chain or when assistance is required. EDL also functions on the basis of service standards and maintains detailed logs of all service calls, recording the request, the action taken, and the response time. At headquarters, data records are everywhere in evidence and by all accounts thoroughly used to improve the organization's technical efficiency and service standards. Whether EDL is a "learning" organization is a bit more difficult to say. A true learning organization would likely be more flexible in adapting to incoming information than EDL, which does seem to have relatively rigid, albeit efficient, channels for response.

Several senior officials at EDL and MEM observed that the nature of the power sector—more specifically, the need to be competitive in order to attract international investment—simply demands cutting-edge technology and an emphasis on standards. As a result, EDL is at the vanguard of technology, including administrative techniques, within government. Interviewees pointed out that this emphasis on standards includes the imperative for staff to be up-to-date in their education. The fact that EDL was recently granted ISO certification 9001 in recognition of its "International Standard Quality Management Systems" demonstrates that EDL emphasizes and has moved toward international standards for a public electricity utility.

The efficiency and financial sustainability of EDL operations are key motivating factors, as indicated by the strong commitment to reducing technical losses and improving bill collection and recovering arrears. Individual performance is measured in addition to that of the organization through a personnel performance evaluation system. On that basis, EDL also has a performance-based incentive system where work teams are financially rewarded if they reach their targets and individuals receive annual bonuses on the basis of performance. Weekly meetings are organized at the district branch level to monitor the achievements of front line staff, and monthly meetings are held between managers at the provincial branch to report challenges and discuss performance.

Corporate Identity and Service-Oriented Organizational Culture

EDL exhibits a strong corporate identity.[10] The utility's employees, all the way up to the managerial ranks, wear a distinctive blue shirt uniform, which is reported to bring instant respect and status for EDL employees in the field. Professionals in the organization, as well as across the energy sector, share training backgrounds and a strong professional identity as power sector engineers, which contributes to an organizational mystique and sense of belonging. EDL emphasizes the importance of skilled professionals with formal engineering training and, from its founding, served as an incubator of Lao capacity and technical knowledge in the power sector. Today's senior officials in EDL and MEM's Department of Electricity (DOE) come from an original cohort of engineers trained in the Soviet Union and Eastern Europe that was later joined by engineers trained in Japan and Western Europe. In addition, many current EDL and MEM managers come from the cohort that worked on the Nam Ngum Hydropower Project, the first major power generation project in Lao PDR. Some members of these engineering cohorts are now on the private industry side, and DOE officials observed that their continuing professional association with their colleagues was an important source of new, innovative engineering systems and principles of competition and efficiency.

The organization is imbued with a shared sense of purpose that is well-understood and absorbed throughout the hierarchy. EDL does not appear to have a clearly articulated mandate in a typical form, but employees quite far down the ranks are able to recite the core goals and objectives of the organization and share a sense of pride and commitment to the mission—with a clear emphasis on accountability for collectively achieving results. In interviews, that mission was phrased as "delivering socioeconomic development," "bringing civilization," and "delivering the government's message in remote areas." Staff across EDL pointed to rural electrification and grid extension as a core EDL goal, emphasizing the importance of "providing services to the client" and "supplying quality, affordable, and reliable power" for industrialization and modernization, as well as "exporting electricity to generate state revenues."[11] To stimulate an esprit de corps, EDL rewards staff performance and commitment through financial bonuses, promotions, and training, along with annual recreational events focused on team building.

EDL is a relatively centralized agency, with traditional, hierarchical implementation systems. Provincial and district units essentially function as frontline service delivery providers, responsible for implementing the precise plans established at the central level in concert with DOE. The district units are crucial, representing EDL at the local level and functioning as service centers. The district units work with clients to monitor payment and provide service (24-hour response), installation, and maintenance. Regular management meetings are held throughout the organization to ensure that goals are shared across the hierarchy, including weekly meetings of technical unit heads at the district level and monthly meetings of district unit heads at the provincial branch level. Provincial EDL branches are responsible for the implementation of electrification targets, improvements in customer service, and reduction of technical losses. Branch offices are empowered with the systems and management to achieve these tasks, along with a "highly professional and motivated staff, who take pride in their mission and mandate" (World Bank 2012, 10). The organizational structure thus reinforces the emphasis on accountability for results generated by the corporate culture.

Autonomy in Personnel Management

EDL handles its own personnel management, as is its statutory right as a state-owned enterprise. It has developed a competitive and systematic recruitment process that includes centrally administered technical entrance exams, in-house and field-based training, and probation procedures for new hires. The Central Committee of the Lao People's Revolutionary Party appears to be encouraging a general reorientation in the civil service and senior managerial ranks toward more technocratic, professionalized cadres. EDL has emphasized more meritocratic recruitment and career advancement for some time, and is often mentioned as a model for the public sector as a whole.

Interviewees at all levels expressed trust in the institution's practice of career advancement on the basis of merit, with respondents confident that anyone can take their career to the management level.[12] Long-time Managing Director Khammany Inthirath (who was promoted to vice-minister of MEM in 2012) worked his way up through the organizational ranks from more junior field-based and management positions. More generally, the majority of senior staff is reported to have done grassroots work, essential for "understanding people's needs, and the organization's roots."[13] The institution deploys its staff with attention to local-level cultural and linguistic issues. In particular, native-language speakers are used in remote, tribal, and ethnic areas—and typically district and provincial branches—are staffed with individuals from those localities. EDL employees have access to continued support in terms of education, training, and capacity building and, as with all other government employees, EDL staff receive political training, organized by provincial and district MEM units.

EDL maintains a salary scale different from that of the Lao civil service, with higher salaries for all ranks of employees, although EDL remains within the government system. In practice, this means that EDL employees are among the best-paid workers in Lao PDR, and jobs in the company are extremely sought after.[14] This relatively high level of remuneration is seen as central to attracting and motivating top-quality employees, as well as to building a sense of organizational pride and legitimacy in external eyes.

EDL has an annual performance bonus system that is handled at the provincial level, whereby all employees receive a one-time bonus of at least 50 percent of their monthly salary, and the top performers in the most successful provinces can receive a bonus of up to 200 percent of their monthly salary.[15] Human resource management is structured on the basis of team assignments to specific tasks, within the context of the hierarchical organization. Each head of department, branch, office, and project is responsible for implementing strategy by supervising and allocating tasks and resources to teams. Individual motivation on the basis of performance bonuses is important; but team work, solidarity, and equality are core values in the organization.

Mandate Implementation through Partnerships

Although EDL has created and benefited from a high degree of operational autonomy, it has also prioritized its relationships with clients, implementation partners, and stakeholders in building its successes. It has carefully managed its relationships with its principals and peers in government, placed a singular operational emphasis on concerted attention to client needs and levels of satisfaction, and built coordinated service delivery partnerships with donors and the private sector.

Relationships with Government Stakeholders

EDL is officially under MEM management, yet in practice it has a great deal of operational autonomy. Many interviewees pointed to a functional working relationship between EDL and MEM as the sine qua non of EDL's success. The Minister of Energy and Mines himself employed a telling analogy in describing the relationship, noting that he held a string connecting EDL to the ministry but that he gave that string a great deal of slack, empowering EDL to manage itself in delivering on its mandate.[16]

EDL must cooperate closely with MEM's Department of Energy for all aspects of its operation; this relationship is delicate but not contentious. DOE was established as part of institutional reforms in the power sector in the late 1990s, staffed and managed by Lao engineers who had returned from overseas training.[17] One particular DOE division was assigned responsibility for rural off-grid electrification, marking the significance of this part of the mandate. DOE takes on key strategic roles related to the power sector—overall sector policy, planning, and regulation; coordinating with donors; and communicating sector strategy to the government and national assembly. Senior DOE officials noted that this enables EDL to focus exclusively on the quality and efficiency of day-to-day operations and service delivery without needing to worry about long-run strategy. Thus, although EDL does not have policy autonomy and is in this respect an agent of MEM, it has successfully maneuvered for itself a great deal of scope in terms of operational autonomy.

Close cooperation between EDL and DOE has been facilitated by transfers of senior officials between the two agencies. For example, the DOE director-general at the time of research was a member of EDL's board of directors and had previously been EDL's managing director. EDL's board has also been an important mechanism of close interagency collaboration, with the current board comprising senior officials from MEM and the Ministry of Finance. A strategic approach to overall staffing across the power sector also emerges because each of these senior individuals, as is typical across government, is nominated by the prime minister and vetted by the Party's Central Committee.

A senior DOE official remarked that the power sector needs an "interpreter" to talk to politicians, a function the minister serves well because he knows the technical and political contexts. This communication is especially important because there is sometimes a tension between the interests of DOE and those of the party as represented in the higher government ranks. Party officials, for example, are typically more interested in energy self-sufficiency, and do not understand the practice of exporting electricity from some locations and importing it at higher rates from others. The minister is thus a crucial champion of EDL in the broader government. EDL and MEM are headed by individuals who are increasingly senior members of the party's Central Committee, a reflection of their individual success as well as the significance placed by the party on the power sector.[18] Observers noted that leaders in the sector have been adept, over time, at building just the right degree of momentum for innovation and reform without running into political constraints. This ability is facilitated, in part, by the connections of power sector leaders to the technical network of the broader regional and international power sector. For example, retired EDL leaders have joined independent power producers as advisors while maintaining their ability to lobby in the Lao political arena, emphasizing their technical expertise and support from their external network to influence government decision making.

Staff revolves between EDL and MEM constantly, including at the uppermost echelons of management. MEM and EDL share one Party Secretariat, an important factor in a country in which the party exercises political and administrative control. Yet this close cooperation appears to break down somewhat below the central levels. Several power sector stakeholders expressed the sense that coordination between EDL and DOE is weak at the provincial and district levels. For example, the two agencies sometimes have different lists or maps of which villages are electrified; and there are often delays (up to six months to a year) in when data transmitted to Vientiane by one agency are shared at higher levels with the other. Provincial-level EDL and MEM branches share political training through the horizontal connection to the provincial administration, but the management of EDL's provincial branches and district service centers is centralized under EDL headquarters. Provincial EDL units follow direction from this vertical line, which manifests as a high degree of EDL operational autonomy at the subnational level.

Client Connection

Related in part to the organizational narrative that it is providing a crucial public service, EDL has an exceptionally strong focus on the end users of electricity, including households, commercial and industrial entities, and government agencies. The target of 90 percent electrification by 2020 is expressed in terms of households connected, which means in turn, that a great deal of attention is paid to satisfying the energy needs of the population. The district branch of EDL serves as the crucial point of interface with the population, essentially functioning as a service center.[19] District branches represent EDL at the local level, conducting billing, carrying out maintenance of transmission lines, and working with clients on service requests, including installation and repairs. Each EDL district branch staffs a 24-hour service hotline, which focus group respondents pointed to as a crucial recent improvement in client responsiveness.

EDL pays particular attention to its relationships with its clients, ensuring that households understand the principles of its contracting system. Staff often mentioned the time dedicated to explaining to clients matters such as billing details and how to save energy. EDL employs an interesting billing model at the village level, outsourcing the collection of household payments to local people, such as students or villagers, who get paid 1,500 kip per bill collected. This has enhanced payment levels and would seem to represent an important mechanism through which EDL ensures sensitivity to local cultural practices and language in its client relationships.

Two aspects of the Lao electricity tariff structure are of particular note (see table 5.2, which breaks down the major categories of electricity users and illustrates how tariffs have evolved in recent years). First, residential electricity is heavily subsidized by the government, with the poorest households (consuming the least electricity) subsidized the most; and irrigation, an important service for subsistence agriculture, is also heavily subsidized.[20] In practice, the poorest consumers of electricity in Lao PDR have been subsidized by other customer segments (World Bank 2012, 19). Second, during 2005–10, electricity tariffs remained relatively stable (with only the heaviest subsidies being reduced slightly), even as the Lao hydropower sector began to take off. This will likely change since, under the planned gradual tariff adjustment process, most customers will be paying tariffs that exceed the marginal cost of supply (World Bank 2012, 19).

Although EDL works with MEM to build strategic plans for grid rollout based on viability studies, provincial governors and their administrations serve, in practice, as an intermediary for village households and hence represent an important group of principals that EDL must work with effectively. EDL's budget is allocated by headquarters, on a negotiated basis between MOF, MEM, and EDL, yet strategic decisions about geographic locations for grid extension, which EDL must then implement, are coordinated by MEM and the provincial governors' offices. EDL appears to play this agent role effectively, coordinating with provincial and district

Table 5.2. Electricity Tariffs, 2005–10

Electricity prices (Kip/kWh)	2005	2006	2007	2008	2009	2010
Residential						
0–25 kWh	114	132	152	177	203	269
26–150 kWh	265	273	281	293	301	320
> 150 kWh	765	765	765	773	773	773
Embassies and international organizations						
Low voltage	990	1066	1066	1077	1077	1077
Entertainment businesses						
Low voltage	1095	1095	1095	1106	1106	1106
Agriculture and irrigation						
Low voltage	295	310	325	345	362	399
Medium voltage	251	263	276	293	308	340
Industry						
Low voltage	636	627	618	616	607	591
Medium voltage	541	533	526	524	516	502
Commercial businesses and services						
Low voltage	826	826	826	835	835	835
Medium voltage	702	702	702	709	709	709
Government offices						
Low voltage	706	696	686	684	674	656
Medium voltage	600	592	583	581	573	557

Source: Robert Oksen (2012), derived from EDL Annual Reports, 2005–10.

administrations where necessary, but essentially retaining a focus on implementation rather than negotiating on strategy. EDL's relative autonomy notwithstanding, its provincial and district units sometimes work closely with local authorities to build good relationships with the client. EDL can rely on its financial resources as well as the company's aura to build good relationships with villages; at the same time, EDL relies on advice from local authorities to tailor service appropriately.

Implementation Partnerships with Donors and the Private Sector

The Lao power sector, and EDL in particular, have benefited from early and sustained partnerships with donors. Many observers noted that donor commitment to rural electrification was a major factor in delivering successes in this area. The Asian Development Bank (ADB) and the World Bank initiated their project portfolios in the Lao power sector at the beginning of the 1980s. Aid to the power sector represented about 15 percent of total overseas development assistance to Lao PDR from the late 1990s to the mid-2000s and has since declined to about 6 percent.

The World Bank estimates the total cost of the rural grid extension rollout from 1987 to 2009 as costing about US$600 million, about 75 percent of which was financed by concessionary loans and grants from multilateral and bilateral agencies and the balance predominantly from EDL's hydropower export revenues (World Bank 2012, 15).

Until relatively recently, however, only a few international partners were engaged in the power sector and, in an interesting twist on donor harmonization, their contributions were geographically bounded and dedicated to specific objectives. The delimitation of donor support was largely based on the donors' regional and country strategies, but the Government of Lao PDR appears to have played a coordinating role as well. ADB has typically prioritized power generation projects for export, with a geographic focus on developing the Greater Mekong Subregion to the north. The World Bank has focused its support on building mechanisms for the efficiency and sustainability of EDL as well as more generally reforming the power sector. Hence, ADB primarily concentrated its interventions in the North, while the World Bank (along with the Swedish International Development Cooperation Agency) principally supported rural electrification in the South. De facto, then, aid was relatively coordinated and efficiently allocated in the sector in that there was little overlap between key donors. Smaller donors and international nongovernmental organizations have also been central in assisting EDL and DOE in expanding access to electricity, especially via off-grid and pico (small-scale) solutions, and thereby accelerating the pace of rural electrification. Of today's 70 percent national coverage, about 2.5 percent of households receive access through off-grid solutions.

Donor representatives concur that the government's ownership of power projects and energy sector strategy is high. In part, this has been maintained through continuity in staffing key donor counterparts on the Lao side. Since the party supervises the careers of senior officials, they can remain designated counterparts even when moving across positions in the sector (e.g., from MEM to EDL or vice versa). In addition, the government has demonstrated a long time horizon and strategic vision in defining and remaining committed to its core goals in the power sector. All government agencies attract investments and support in alignment with the strategic objectives defined by the party, and the government has demonstrated that it will delay reforms that are not in line with strategic goals. The Power Development Plans and the recent Rural Electrification Master Plan clearly demonstrate this coordinating vision in the sense that they are actually built as a list of potential projects. Nevertheless, projects at the local level are sometimes competing and overlapping, even if the national-level coordination of development partners appears strong. The overlap is especially acute between EDL's grid extension projects, and the off-grid projects supported by DOE and local authorities, reflecting the relative lack of on-the-ground coordination and cooperation between these agencies.

EDL has been oriented toward electricity exports to Thailand since the 1980s, when approximately 75 percent of the country's hydropower production, mainly from the Nam Ngum plant, was being exported to Thailand. During this time, electricity exports made up more than 50 percent of Lao PDR's exports and served as crucial revenues for the government. In the 1990s, Thailand's sustained economic growth and increasing electricity consumption, particularly for industrial development, helped make Lao electricity exports even more successful (Robert Oksen 2012). Although electricity generation and export are beyond the scope of this study, it is crucial to note that the Thai power sector was privatized during this period, having a major demonstration effect on the structure of the Lao electricity sector and the operations of EDL itself.

The role of regional bilateral partners, especially the Chinese government, has become increasingly significant since the mid-2000s. There are no detailed records of this support, but interviewees reported, for example, that the Chinese government provides grants and soft loans to the power sector, principally for the expansion of transmission and distribution. In the specific area of hydropower project development, Chinese contractors are increasingly competing with Thai investors. The Chinese government has recently invested a great deal in EDL itself, assisting with the building of EDL's new headquarters building and, as did Thailand earlier, influencing the way in which EDL does business.

Thus, there appear to be isomorphic influences in the power sector, driven by the advice of development partners and market-oriented models and, more recently, by newly important regional bilateral donors, especially China. Lao PDR aims to position itself strategically in the regional energy market and, therefore, needs to align its policies, regulatory framework, and operations with international practice, especially on the generation and transmission side. One senior DOE official stated that the "nature of the industry pushed us to do things right from the beginning;" it was not necessarily that government officials and EDL managers were "so clever." Because important stakeholders in the sector—from Nordic partners, to Thailand, to China—have had such diverse practices, EDL's adoption of varied practices has also meant, interestingly, that there has been continuous experimentation with organizational models in the sector.[21] Thus, the government has been able to test EDL's evolving structure against its development objectives, choosing to stick with practices that serve its developmental and political objectives and jettisoning those that are less aligned.

Private sector partners have also been crucial in the Lao power sector. Independent power producers (IPPs) play a dominant role in electricity generation and transmission and are crucial revenue sources for the state in terms of taxes, royalties, and dividends from the government share of concessions. IPPs have been central in setting financial as well as social and environmental standards in the sector.[22] In terms of the rural electrification side of EDL on which this chapter focuses, IPPs have played a crucial role in training a large proportion of EDL and MEM managers, many of whom began their careers in the power sector working on early IPP installations, such as Nam Ngum, Xeset, Houay Ho, and Theun Hinboun.

Small and medium enterprises (SMEs) have been more significant on the electricity distribution side, at least since the early 2000s. For example, a World Bank program encouraged the creation of small local companies to install solar home systems. These companies do not work directly with EDL but as contractors and implementing partners of DOE projects. DOE has an established pre-electrification strategy, in which connection to an off-grid system presents an opportunity to test villagers' ability to pay for electricity services before EDL invests in grid extension. In this sense, the public-private partnership between DOE and the SMEs in the sector supports EDL in achieving its mandate to increase access to electricity in remote areas.

In a relatively new aspect of electricity distribution prompted by the push to reach 90 percent electrification by 2020, provincial governments have begun contracting private companies to extend the grid to remote areas. Companies install and operate these systems for five years, at which time the infrastructure reverts to government ownership upon repayment of the investment along with a reasonable return. Although these partnerships represent increased participation of the private sector in power distribution, especially in remote rural areas, the electricity law states that all electrical systems shall be handed over and administered by the provincial government even if they were built by MEM. Moreover, although these partnerships have provided access to electricity in remote areas, SME development and expansion in the power sector has potentially been undermined by a bias—in terms of policy as well as in client preferences—in favor of public grid extension and thereby access to subsidized electricity tariffs. In this respect, the state monopoly over the domestic production, transmission, and distribution of electricity is being preserved.

Challenges

EDL's record in achieving results has enabled it to build institutional legitimacy. Yet, this may be challenged by the growing expectations of high-quality services, the meeting of which in turn rests on the company's ability to generate the resources necessary to meet the growing demand for electricity. Several senior managers and principals of the utility stated that the lack of self-sufficiency in power generation is constraining EDL's commercial development. The interviewees drew attention to the need to increase technical capacities in power generation. EDL's development plan for 2011–17 is thus strongly focused on increasing its generation capacity, at an estimated cost of US$3.3 billion (Électricité du Laos 2010).

Over the course of its history, EDL has managed a complicated, bifurcated mandate—on the one hand, electrification (distribution); on the other hand, generation and transmission (or production and export), which also entails acting as the government representative for international power projects. A recent major institutional change for EDL was the separation in 2010 of its electricity distribution functions (retained in EDL) from its generation functions (now listed separately as EDL-GEN). Two interrelated reasons were mentioned to explain this split. One was the increasing commercialization of the utility and power sector management writ large and the government's (and key partners') desire for Lao PDR to position itself more astutely in the context of the evolving regional energy landscape and increasing demand for energy. The second reason was financial viability. A recurrent concern for the government and its development partners has been that the institution's debt has been a major challenge to the sustained commercialization of EDL. The split enabled the debt to be contained in one agency, with EDL-GEN then being poised to become a profitable commercial entity, albeit one that is still owned by the state.

Many are concerned that the split weakens the ability of EDL itself to deliver on rural electrification. Electricity tariffs do not cover the costs of electricity generation and supply to the country's rural areas. In the past, EDL was able to employ a cross-subsidy model with funds from generation to plow back into and subsidize electrification. The strategy was encouraged by donors and international power purchasers. In other words, large hydro-generation projects for export that generate sizeable, predictable, and sustainable cash streams were the key to successful rural electrification over time, along with international development financing. Yet, this model worked best when electrification rates were low and there were easy-access distribution decisions to be made that did not hurt EDL's bottom-line profitability as much.[23] The final push on electrification is much more expensive at the margin—the average cost per grid connection almost doubled from about 4.2 million kip (US$500) in 2005 to about 7.7 million kip (US$900) in 2012—and more difficult for EDL to finance now that the split has occurred. Achieving the target of 90 percent household electricity access by 2020 will require at least a threefold increase in access provided by off-grid solutions and will be a central implementation challenge going forward.

Conclusion

The power sector and hence EDL itself have been consistently prioritized and supported by LPRP and the government, as a spearhead and symbol of the Lao modernization and development trajectory. EDL has been adept at capitalizing on the crucial roles, symbolic and practical, assigned to the electricity sector. In turn, EDL has delivered important results for the Lao governing elite in terms of nation building and economic modernization goals. The significance of the power sector and the reigning model for its development and expansion have evolved over time—from a revolutionary-era blueprint to more donor- and private sector–oriented norms and practices—and EDL itself has transformed accordingly.

In the context of the agency's priority status, EDL leaders have carved out a sphere of operational independence for the agency in an otherwise tightly controlled governance environment, managing to insulate the agency from external governance pressures in part by making the services it delivers invaluable to elites. This relative operational autonomy has enabled EDL to make operational choices and pursue internal management strategies that are singularly focused on achieving ambitious and ever-expanding service delivery targets. The institution enjoys relative autonomy in the manner in which it recruits, compensates, and deploys staff, and it is imbued with an organizational philosophy that emphasizes corporate professionalism and technical excellence. EDL thus marshals its financial and human resources to deliver the public service of electricity to the population in a manner that bolsters EDL's and the government's connection with the Lao people and builds state legitimacy in their eyes.

The astute manner in which EDL has operated vis-à-vis its Lao stakeholders, clients, and donor and private sector implementation partners complements its service-oriented organizational culture and structure, further enabling it to achieve continued success. Related in part to the organizational narrative that it is providing a crucial public service, EDL has an exceptionally strong focus on the end users of electricity. In achieving its electrification targets, the institution has successfully deployed development partner assistance while remaining in the driver's seat. Over time, EDL has experimented with diverse organizational models and practices, retaining those practices that serve its developmental and political objectives and jettisoning those that are less aligned.

Notes

1. The other four sectors LPRP viewed as pillars of socialist modernization, to which all villages should have access, were roads, health, education, and water.
2. Although we do not examine the results of the EDL generation function, we do explore the role this mandate played in the power sector's early priority status.
3. For more details about P2P, see World Bank (2012, 20–26).
4. This is outside the explanatory scope of this chapter, which focuses on the electrification (distribution) side of EDL's business, but worth highlighting as part of this brief snapshot of EDL's success as an institution.
5. The quotes are from focus groups of EDL clients conducted on behalf of the study by Indochina Research Limited (Laos).
6. Robert Oksen (2012) notes that these new managers were still appointed by the party, signaling that the Party was gradually introducing more autonomy and commercial orientation in EDL's activities, as well as pushing to attract greater foreign investment through managers more conversant with regional and international power sector stakeholders.
7. A comprehensive record of government expenditures is only available from 2000/01 onward.
8. Program evaluations by development partners have consistently underlined the lack of transparency in the flow of funds between the government and EDL, providing additional justification for separating generation from transmission and distribution activities.

9. Group interview with leadership of the Champassak Province EDL office.
10. See also World Bank (2012, 9–10).
11. The quotes are from EDL and MEM officials and EDL frontline staff.
12. As with all other government agencies, promotion to managerial levels (deputy division head and above) is overseen by the Party.
13. EDL official.
14. Civil service compensation is on par with private sector pay in the country and additional benefits—pensions, health insurance, job stability, prestige—associated with government employment make it extremely attractive. See World Bank (2010).
15. By contrast, the provincial departments of MEM have certificates of appreciation for top performers but cannot afford financial rewards.
16. Interview with H.E. Mr. Soulivong Daravong, Minister of Energy and Mines, February 9, 2012.
17. DOE was established as the Hydropower Office in 1997 and reorganized later into today's Department of Electricity.
18. The relevant minister has, over time, always been in the top half of the Central Committee's ranks.
19. Interviews with EDL provincial and district branch officials, Champassak and Xekong provinces, February 2, 2012.
20. There is a significant difference between the average Lao electricity generation price (about 240 kip per kilowatt-hour) and the average price of electricity purchase from Thailand (about 560 kip per kilowatt-hour); the latter is the price at which 60 percent of domestic usage is provided. Subsidies for poorer households are not high in relation to the Lao generation price, but they are in terms of the import price.
21. Robert Oksen (2012) points out that these varied organizational models have come with diverse developmental visions for the sector (on the part of international stakeholders and Lao power sector players), which have competed with each other over time.
22. These IPPs are outside the scope of this report. They are nonpublic entities that own facilities to generate power for sale to the public utility (EDL) and other end users (e.g., the Electricity Generating Authority of Thailand). An important example (and an unusual one, because it is not wholly privately owned) is the Nam Theun Power Company, a joint-venture IPP that was granted the concession to build-operate-and-transfer the major Nam Theun 2 Hydropower Project. The project has served as a major driver of momentum in the Lao power sector because it formalized and standardized procedures for foreign direct investment, with development partners, including the World Bank and ADB, playing crucial roles in providing risk guarantees to investors and securing some measure of social and environmental responsibility through project safeguards.

23. This cross-subsidy model along with the challenges associated with the increasing marginal cost of grid expansion are described in more detail in World Bank (2012, ix, 8, 15–16, 30).

References

Électricité du Laos. 2010. *Power Development Plan: 2010–2020.* Vientiane: Électricité du Laos.

Government of Lao PDR. 2001. *Power Sector Policy Statement.* Vientiane: Government of Lao PDR.

Larsen, Morten. 2001. *Large Investment in Small States: Analyzing Governance Capacities in the Hydropower Sector in Lao PDR.* Master's thesis, Development Studies and International Business Management, Copenhagen Business School, Copenhagen.

Robert Oksen, Stephanie. 2009. "L'électricité et ses reseaux au Laos des annees 1950 aux annees 2000." PhD thesis, IDS Roskilde University / Universite Paris7 / ADEME / UNEP Risoe Center.

———. 2012. "Aide Memoire on Électricité du Laos (EDL): ESW Exercise on Institutions Taking Root in Fragile States." Unpublished manuscript.

Stuart-Fox, Martin. 2004. "Politics and Reform in the Lao People's Democratic Republic." Working Paper No. 1, Political Economy of Development Series, College of William & Mary. Williamsburg, VA.

World Bank. 2010. *Lao PDR: Civil Service Pay and Compensation Review: Attracting and Motivating Civil Servants.* Report 58018-LA, East Asia and Pacific Region Poverty Reduction and Economic Management Unit, World Bank, Washington, DC.

———. 2012. *Lao PDR—Power to the People: Twenty Years of National Electrification.* Asia Sustainable and Alternative Energy Program. World Bank: Washington, DC.

CHAPTER 6

Lao PDR Case Study: Ministry of Public Works and Transport

Naazneen H. Barma and Stephanie Robert Oksen

The Ministry of Public Works and Transport (MPWT) of the Lao People's Democratic Republic has achieved a great deal of institutional success in the road sector over the past 30 years. The ministry has led the construction and expansion of the road network and, in turn, dramatically improved transport times and access to economic opportunities for Lao households and enterprises. MPWT has generated legitimacy in the eyes of the Lao people for both itself and the Government of the Lao PDR writ large, in particular by improving access to markets and public services across the country and by helping to physically knit the country together. It has slowly expanded its mandate in the road sector and served as a crucial incubator of commercial enterprise in the Lao construction sector. Moreover, the ministry has continued operations through several changes in leadership and demonstrated resilience in the face of crises.

This chapter examines how and why, in the otherwise challenging context of a low-income and relatively low-capacity country, MPWT has been able to achieve these successes. It describes how the core underpinnings of this institutional success have emerged in the three concentric circles constituting MPWT's operating environment: the sociopolitical context in which MPWT is positioned, MPWT's more immediate external operational

The authors are grateful to numerous colleagues in Vientiane, Lao PDR, and Washington, DC, for their comments and guidance on this case study. The authors are indebted, in particular, to H. E. Sommad Pholsena, Sombath Southivong, Indochina Research Limited (Laos), and officials at the Ministry of Public Works and Transport and other government agencies and partners who generously spoke with the team over the course of this research.

relationships, and MPWT's internal institutional workings. This introduction provides some key highlights of the causal argument, with subsequent sections delivering more detail.

The sociopolitical context in which MPWT is situated has enabled and laid the conditions for the agency's success (Barma and Robert Oksen chapter 4, this volume). The road sector plays an important symbolic role in Lao PDR, serving as a crucial mechanism of national identity building. The road network is metaphorically and literally the backbone of the nation, physically binding together in the post-revolutionary period what had been a decentralized country comprised of disparate groups over a complicated geographical terrain. Moreover, roads have connected Lao PDR with its neighbors and hence its major markets, and have improved the access of almost all Lao citizens to economic opportunities. Roads have thus served as the crucial arteries through which commerce and people can flow, and have been essential to the country's modernization and socio-economic development, especially after its 1986 economic liberalization reforms. The Lao People's Revolutionary Party (LPRP), recognizing the sociopolitical and economic benefits of road building, has prioritized the sector from the inception of Lao PDR in 1975.

Capitalizing on this mandate and the resources that have come with it, MPWT has delivered on the Lao political elite's crucial state-building and modernization goals. The agency stands out for its ability to negotiate the constraints and embrace the facilitating factors in its external and internal environments in a manner that has enabled it to resolve creatively the governance challenges facing the agency and the political elite to which it must be responsive. MPWT has built institutional success by capitalizing on its priority sector status and the government's planning system; successfully introducing a commercialized and decentralized approach to construction and maintenance of the road network in the context of the New Economic Mechanism (NEM) and broader governance reforms; carefully managing stakeholder relations in the context of macro power structures and relationships in the country; and building an organizational esprit de corps that emphasizes the agency's central role in the pursuit of Lao socio-economic modernization.

MPWT has managed various factors in its external and internal environment in ways that have enhanced its ability to deliver on its institutional mandate. In particular, MPWT's and the government's emphasis on building physical infrastructure has aligned with the goals of Lao PDR's development partners. These goals include state building though public service delivery, institutional strengthening and capacity building, technical criteria for decision making in line ministries, and a trend toward deconcentration and commercialization of road construction and maintenance. The agency has carefully managed its relationships with donors, emphasizing that the ministry is in the driver's seat, handling aid harmonization, and insisting on in-house capacity building rather than relying on project management units. As a government ministry, MPWT is subject to public sector recruitment and compensation rules and regulations. Within those constraints, nevertheless, MPWT has consistently emphasized strategically building the human resource capacity of the ministry and has developed its own personnel management system to ensure a focus on performance, complete with incentives for high performers. Moreover, MPWT is a learning organization that builds on a leadership that has, from the top down, instituted and supported a work ethic and systems oriented toward problem solving and a reliance on data to aid organizational performance and sector management.

Institutional Success

MPWT is the government agency tasked with the country's roads, its other transportation systems (including civil aviation, urban transport systems, and river transport), and other public works, including water and sanitation.[1] This chapter focuses on MPWT's road sector operations, where the ministry has demonstrated success across the three criteria of results, legitimacy, and resilience, according to objective measures and interviewee responses.

Results

The road sector in Lao PDR faces three major challenges. First, building a road network in a landlocked country that relies on road transport for internal economic activity and external trade links is a complex undertaking. Second, it is extremely costly to deliver rural road connections to the national road network for a low-density population. Third, adequate maintenance is crucial to ensure that existing assets do not deteriorate even as new construction continues apace.[2] There is a clear consensus across MPWT management, employees, clients, and other stakeholders that the institution has achieved sustained and impressive results on all three fronts.

There is a widespread perception that MPWT has expanded the Lao road network to a significant degree. In turn, this road expansion has greatly increased market access across the country, making commercial and household enterprise, as well as rural livelihoods, more viable. Frontline staff, in particular, noted that road access enables villagers to sell their products directly at a market, reducing their dependence on local traders and middlemen. On this basis, moreover, villagers began diversifying their production to meet demand, thereby enhancing livelihoods. A multivariate analysis estimates that of the 9.5 percent decline in poverty incidence in Lao PDR from 1998 to 2003, fully 13 percent of the decline in rural poverty can be attributed to improved road access alone (Warr 2010).

Increased road access reduces transaction costs and makes more forms of economic activity viable; it also facilitates access to other public services, such as health and education services, located in village, district, and provincial centers. A central measure of success, then, is a reduction in travel time. There is no systematic statistical record of this over time, yet oft-cited data on this point include a decrease in travel time, over the past two decades, from the national capital to major provincial urban centers as follows: Vientiane to Savannakhet, from two days to five hours, and Vientiane to Luang Prabang, from five days to eight hours. The interprovincial network has improved considerably, with travel time between Pakse and Xekong, for example, being reduced from two days to two hours. Today, almost all the country's districts are reachable by road, although a major limiting factor is that some are reachable only during the dry season.

In line with MPWT's stated goals, rural accessibility—access of villages to the national and provincial road network—has increased significantly over the past decade, with all-season access growing from 54 percent of villages in 2002–03 to 84 percent in 2007–08.[3] Rural road extension has grown at the fastest rate in comparison with other forms of road construction. The share of rural roads in the overall road network increased from 24 percent in 2000 to 42 percent in 2010.[4] In addition to increased road coverage across the country, improvements in the quality of the road network are a crucial measure of results. The proportion of sealed and graveled surfaces in the country's road network increased from 42 percent in 2000 to 50 percent in 2010.[5] In addition, a large road development and maintenance program implemented by MPWT between 2002 and 2006 succeeded in decreasing the proportion of rough road surfaces from 37 percent of the road network in 2002 to 4 percent in 2009 (MPWT 2009). Villagers who were interviewed noted that improvement of road quality is essential, since it reduces travel time as well as expenditures on vehicle maintenance and repair. The program overall was evaluated as delivering a medium level of service, since as it drew to a close road maintenance slowed and overall road conditions declined.

Legitimacy

MPWT plays an important role in serving the government's overall socioeconomic development objectives. In turn, it enjoys some degree of legitimacy in the eyes of the population and helps in building the overall legitimacy of the state. For many Lao citizens, access to roads is a tangible way in which they interface with the state. Road sector employees benefit from a certain aura in the eyes of the population; villagers and other road users expressed a high degree of trust in and admiration for the central and provincial levels of MPWT. Yet, these same users were more critical of the district-level branches of MPWT, typically complaining about their relative lack of capacity to manage the road extension process and supervise the construction companies involved.

MPWT appears to have gained a great deal of legitimacy and public trust from its successes in extending the road network. Now that minimal road access needs have been exceeded, however, there is an increasing sense among the public that road quality is not as good as it should be. In other words, many villagers expressed the feeling that MPWT's emphasis on the quantity of roads was negatively affecting the quality of construction. Moreover, villagers expressed dissatisfaction regarding MPWT's communication systems, pointing out that they were often left in the dark about progress on projects, because consultations during road construction involved only village authorities and not public forums.

Villagers in the focus groups viewed MPWT as a public service provider, not a business. They kept clear the distinction between the public agency itself and its various implementation partners, including private sector construction companies. In this respect, villagers are willing to contribute financing as well as labor to build and maintain village roads, although they voiced concerns about being properly compensated for losing land. Villagers tend to believe that MPWT should be responsible for systematically maintaining the quality of access roads (i.e., district, provincial, and national roads) to the village and that the villagers should not be responsible for financial contributions for road maintenance and rehabilitation.

Resilience

The quality of Lao PDR's roads and the institutional capacity of MPWT (then the Ministry of Communication, Transport, Post, and Construction) were extremely poor at the initiation of the reforms associated with the 1986 NEM.[6] From the early 1990s onward, nevertheless, MPWT has displayed a great deal of resilience in the sense of maintaining success over time and through changes in leadership. Interviewees emphasized the ministry's cohesion, stability, and ability to adapt in the context of broad socioeconomic and institutional changes in the country.

This resilience in MPWT's ability to perform successfully has persisted through and been fortified by several major structural changes in the ministry and its implementation partnerships over the past two decades. The institution has always faced the challenge of securing the high levels of funding necessary for major infrastructure projects and maintenance, yet it has been able to develop innovative new funding mechanisms over time to overcome this constraint. In particular, the agency has demonstrated a great capacity for attracting and channeling donor funds and programs while maintaining a focus on the government's agenda. In another dimension of resilience, MPWT performed well in the face of a recent crisis: after Typhoon Ketsana destroyed a full 15 percent of the road and bridge network in the Southern Lao provinces in late 2009, the ministry achieved its goal of repairing and rebuilding 60 percent of the damaged roads over the next two years (Government of the Lao PDR 2009).

Institutional Sociopolitical Context: Roads as a Crucial Modernization Vehicle

Since Lao PDR's inception, the government has strategically emphasized the road sector as a major symbol, priority, and crucial tool of the Lao socialist modernization and development trajectory. Indeed, the overarching strategic vision expressed in LPRP resolutions through the late 1990s refer to the road sector as a "spearhead sector," and this is still a common refrain of stakeholders in the sector. Heavy industrialization and rural livelihoods, in other words, were not possible without good roads.[7] The push to build a road network throughout the country, as well as to link all villages to the network, has been a central goal in the sector for more than three decades.

Although roads were identified as a strategic sector, road development prior to the mid-1990s was fragmented, with responsibilities dispersed across a range of agencies, including the Ministry of Communication and Transport, the Ministry of Agriculture, and the Ministry of the Interior.

The country's transition to the market through the 1986 NEM further underlined the importance of a functioning national road network, which was seen as crucial to economic success. The primacy of roads in the government's list of priorities after the initiation of economic and administrative reforms is apparent: the Third Five-Year Plan (1990–95) emphasized improving the country's transport network and the government's 1991–95 Public Investment Program focused on developing roads and other physical infrastructure (Barma 2002). Accompanying this greater strategic clarity, road sector management was rationalized and institutionalized in the then Ministry of Communication, Transport, Post and Construction (MCTPC).

In addition to their economic functions in terms of industrialization, the development of an agroforestry sector, and rural livelihoods, roads have served the government and LPRP as a crucial nation-building mechanism—physically binding together what has been in its contemporary history a regionally, ethnically, and geographically fractured country (Barma and Robert Oksen chapter 4, this volume). The first major route emphasized after the formation of Lao PDR in 1975 was the country's core North-South trunk road, Road 13, a project seen as essential for territorial integration and internal security. Road network building continues to serve this nation-building imperative, encouraging village clusters to form to take advantage of connections to the network and thereby, in some cases, speeding the relocation of remote villagers in mountainous areas (where many tribal and ethnic minorities continue to live) to more densely populated areas in the lowlands.

The government's early vision for Lao economic modernization saw the central role of the transport network in transforming the country's territorial identity from a landlocked country to a transit country (Pholsena and Banomyong 2007). The emphasis on connectivity to neighboring countries and to the South China Sea preceded the emphasis on rural road access, with an acute demonstration of the country's geographic vulnerabilities emerging when Thailand closed its border with Lao PDR and embargoed exports in 1976. The construction of Roads 8 and 9, connecting Lao PDR with Vietnam, was crucial in response. More recently, emphasis on the road sector has continued with a slightly different cast, as Lao PDR has become more deeply integrated into the Mekong subregion, joining the Asian Development Bank's (ADB's) Greater Mekong Subregion scheme in 1992 and the Association of Southeast Asian Nations in 1997. The sector remains central to developing the country's trade connections—in particular with Thailand,

Vietnam, and China—which in turn have delivered large financial flows and numerous advantages in terms of economic development. This is evidenced by the impressive growth of the provinces most closely connected economically with neighboring countries, especially Champassak and Phongsaly, where, not coincidentally, major public and private road-building efforts continue apace.

Sector representatives expressed conscious pride in their role in facilitating economic livelihoods and trade, transporting the inputs and products of other sectors, and being a key to economic development and the country's prosperity. For example, a provincial unit of MPWT displayed a slogan that read, "Love your nation, maintain the roads." In addition, the delivery of pro-poor public services such as road access is a central element of LPRP's strategy for retaining popular support and solidarity with the party. In short, roads continue to be used as a symbol of economic development and socialist modernization and as a crucial vehicle for their achievement.

In functioning in this sociopolitical context, MPWT has a span of control over two concentric circles of institutional function—first, the organization of the internal workings of the agency and, second, the manner in which the agency structures its partnerships and other operational mechanisms in the context of the immediate external environment in which it functions. Many of the operational decisions made by MPWT in its immediate external environment and relationships as well as its internal institutional workings can be seen as resolving, concretely, a series of governance challenges for the agency and the government and political elite it serves. In other words, some of the causal underpinnings of institutional success identified are explicit responses to the institution's role and position in the broader political and governance structures. In particular, the adoption of NEM and the series of political and governance changes around that reform actually set in motion several specific institutional strategies. Other causal underpinnings of success are, by contrast, more geared toward efficient institutional functioning than toward resolving specific political and governance conundrums. These factors serve to institutionalize MPWT in the context of the government's attempts, supported by donors, to forge a more efficient public administration. Perhaps as a consequence, the causal dimensions in this second set are more closely tied to donor advice and institutional models that are either isomorphic with international best practice or result from greater interconnectivity with neighboring countries and markets.

Institutional Strategies to Resolve Governance Challenges

MPWT has negotiated the constraints and embraced the facilitating factors in its immediate external environment and internal institutional workings in creative ways that have enabled it to resolve governance challenges facing the agency and the political elite to which it must be responsive. MPWT has built its institutional success by capitalizing on its priority sector status and the government's planning system, successfully introducing a commercialized and decentralized approach to construction and maintenance of the road network in the context of NEM and broader governance reforms, carefully managing stakeholder relations in the context of macro power structures and relationships in the country, and building an organizational esprit de corps that emphasizes the agency's central role in the pursuit of the country's socioeconomic modernization.

From Sector Prioritization to Integrated Sector Planning

The overall stability of the Lao governing regime, along with the sustained emphasis it has placed over time on the road sector, were identified across the board as core elements of MPWT's success. The government's prioritization of roads as a "spearhead" sector and its consistent policies for the sector are apparent in its relatively high resourcing of MPWT and the important position the agency occupies within the power structure of the government. In turn, MPWT's success in increasing road access throughout the country has contributed to the government's cumulative legitimacy. Indeed, increasing public access to public services, such as schools and health clinics, through better road access has been a core goal of the government's approach to road expansion in rural and remote areas. Prior to the introduction of the Road Management System, the Party prioritized road construction on the basis of broad goals, such as territorial integration and economic interconnectivity with the region. The government's broad vision also emphasized developing road access to every provincial capital, followed by district centers and large village clusters. Only later, with deeper integration with the donor-supported sector management system, did a shift emerge to prioritization of road access on the basis of population density and access to urban centers with public services, thus enabling MPWT to continue serving essential nation-building and political objectives.

The road sector's priority status has been reflected in direct resourcing by the government as well as donor funding. Public expenditure patterns over time demonstrate an extended commitment to public works and transport. Quite simply, it has long been the single largest spending sector in Lao PDR, with a share in total expenditure of 40–50 percent over the past 30 years.[8] Although this share has declined slightly in recent years, the road sector still accounts for by far the largest share of capital expenditures. This high level of resourcing was made possible by the government's endorsement of road construction and rehabilitation projects over many consecutive five-year plans.

Despite the large flow of revenues to the sector, most of the road network in the late 1990s was evaluated as being in poor condition and progressively more emphasis was placed on road maintenance (Barma 2002). This required new funding sources and an efficient, locally based planning system to track and anticipate necessary investments, as well as to plan road development in relation to the ability of central and local governments to maintain the system. In turn, this resulted in a reorganization of the planning and budget allocation system. Road construction is now financed directly by the government budget—including central expenditure, which is allocated to national road construction and rehabilitation, and provincial expenditure for the development of provincial, district, and rural access roads.[9] Road maintenance, by contrast, is provided for through the Road Maintenance Fund (RMF),[10] which was originally financed primarily by donors and is now primarily financed, with some donor support, by a fuel levy (approximately 70 percent of total RMF revenues[11]), bridge and road tolls, and fines for overloaded trucks. RMF allocates funds only to national and provincial road maintenance.[12] Local road maintenance is carried out through village financial or labor contributions; and district road maintenance is supposed to be provided for by District Development Funds, which, in turn, depend on donor contributions and household contributions based on income levels.

The National Socio-Economic Development Plan, the government's five-year planning system, and the annual planning mechanisms are crucial in terms of overall sector strategy, resourcing, and operational targets for any government agency—and MPWT is no exception. The annual planning process is facilitated by the Ministry of Planning and Investment (MPI), which centralizes and coordinates the local plans for road development. The planning process begins bottom-up, with needs articulated at the district level, collated at the provincial level with the supervision of the provincial governor's office, and passed up the vertical line to the agency in question. Prioritization takes place at this top level, with overall strategic and resourcing needs decided at the highest level of government. Resources are then allocated through the ministries to the provincial and district levels. De jure, nothing can be implemented without being reported to the central line and incorporated into the plan; de facto, this means that the plan is amended throughout implementation to incorporate new projects that are developed when new sources of funding emerge. For example, if a village raises funding for an access road in collaboration with a private sector provider, permission to construct the road must be granted at the provincial level and reflected in the revised plan.

The planning and reporting system follows two logics. On the one hand, LPRP's principle of "democratic centralism" requires plans to be established at the local level, with a bottom-up approach. On the other hand, the reporting system through the vertical line to the central ministry ensures a functioning public administration. MPWT is seen as outstanding among its central ministry peers in terms of its capability for undertaking a nationwide assessment of the sector and planning future development and maintenance requirements in an integrated manner. One problematic aspect of the centralized planning process is that, although in theory inter-ministry coordination is supposed to be a bottom-up process through the local development plan, in practice there is little coordination at the provincial level between technical staff or even middle management across different government agencies. Instead, each ministry has extremely important bilateral relationships with the provincial governor's office and the provincial units of MPI. Stakeholders noted that the provincial units of MPWT enjoy particularly close cooperative and productive relationships with both of these crucial local-level allies. A core advantage of the planning system, nevertheless, is that MPWT's annual operational targets are extremely clear and the organization can and does work toward them in a focused manner.

Delegated Implementation: Decentralization and Commercialization

The road sector and MPWT underwent a major institutional reset in the early 1990s, after the government introduced market-oriented reforms with the 1986 NEM. Prior to NEM, road sector development was handled in-house at MPWT, with an emphasis on top-down management from the central ministry and, under the "force account" system, a labor force for construction and maintenance positioned within the ministry or state-owned companies. The reform reflected the government's broader governing dilemma in defining a clear division of tasks between the political dimensions of governance, undertaken increasingly through the horizontal line across provinces, and administrative and technical line responsibilities, assigned to the ministerial vertical line. Until this reorganization of the road sector administration—which occurred in the context of more general governance reforms—road sector development was handled across the political level, with an emphasis on top-down management from the prime minister's office, the State Planning Committee, and the provincial governors.

The goal of the government's decentralization initiative was to establish provinces as the strategic (decision-making) units and districts as the implementation units.[13] MPWT, recognizing the need for improvements in efficiency and implementation quality, follows this system to its great advantage. It implemented a radical overhaul of its management, decentralizing and delegating its operations to the provincial and district levels, and accelerated the commercialization of its implementation activities through partnerships with the private sector. Project management (including budgeting, implementation, and quality control) shifted to the provincial level, with implementation contracted out to a nascent private sector at the provincial and district levels.[14] The provincial departments of MPWT have a great deal of decision-making authority and accountability. The bulk of road sector management and service delivery implementation is coordinated at the provincial level, through the Departments of Public Works and Transport (DPWT). DPWT manages and implements the sector budget for its respective province and, according to the Public Investment Law, construction bids below five billion kip are tendered at the provincial level. In terms of implementation, DPWT engineers work with the district-level Office of Public Works and Transport (OPWT) to provide on-site contract supervision and quality assurance. By 2000, almost all road sector construction and maintenance was being operated on a commercial basis and managed and contracted down the MPWT hierarchy by the provincial and district units of the ministry. The central MPWT retained responsibility for sector strategy, standards, training, monitoring and evaluation and overall sector coordination (including donor coordination and aid harmonization). In essence, MPWT went from being a direct service provider to an institution that sets policy for and manages service provision but does not really implement it directly.

Road sector development since the early 1990s has emphasized the building of private sector capacity. Road construction and maintenance depend on this partnership with the private sector. Prior to NEM, many state-owned enterprises (SOEs) were responsible for constructing and maintaining the country's road network on the basis of their workforce contributions. Each of these SOEs was tied closely to its home location and was managed directly by the provincial authorities, thus representing more a department within the provincial administration than an enterprise or an implementation agency of MCTPC. These SOEs were split into smaller, semiautonomous entities toward the end of the 1980s. Each was designated specific construction projects by the government and provided capacity-building and financial support for this contracted work.[15] After the 1986 introduction of NEM and the opening of the country to international development partners, these companies also bid for donor-supported projects and received training and technical assistance from the donors. Indeed, privatization was an explicit institutional development objective of World Bank and other donor programs in the road sector (Barma 2002).

From 1996 onward, the government ceased supporting these state-owned enterprises under the force account system. There has since been a process of winnowing out. Less successful SOEs were allowed to fail, while the more successful SOEs expanded their scope to nationwide contracting, with some of them merging together. These successful SOEs continue to be major implementation partners for MPWT, especially in remote locations and areas in which it is otherwise difficult to operate (e.g., "red zones," where unexploded ordinances or drug trafficking exist). Subcontracting with donors (in particular, the World Bank, ADB, and the Japan International Cooperation Agency) has been essential in building the capacity, equipment, and systems of the successful SOEs.

A vibrant and fast-growing private sector has thus developed around road construction, with the number of road construction companies estimated at more than 200. Yet, it is a bifurcated sector. On the one hand, there are the larger companies located in the bigger cities that focus on road construction. Many of these originally gained their foothold in the construction sector through resource concession for infrastructure deals with the government; and they often rely on joint ventures with companies from across the region for financing and capacity development. Smaller, locally run companies, on the other hand, are contracted by MPWT on three-year contracts for road maintenance work; these are constrained in terms of their capacity and equipment from taking on larger and more lucrative tasks. Interviewees reported three ways for private-sector companies and

SOEs to be awarded construction and maintenance projects: responding to an advertised bid; negotiating with the government, which under some circumstances directly chooses a company for a project; and subcontracting with donors and larger companies. Road construction enterprises at the provincial level mostly subcontract for large companies form Vientiane or neighboring countries. Across the country, however, road enterprise managers and engineers share backgrounds and training with provincial and district road sector employees, including shared SOE employment in the past. These connections and shared understanding make for good working relationships at the local level.

The decentralization and commercialization reforms discussed here have strengthened and formalized the central role of provincial governors in strategic planning in the sector, but they have not undermined the role of MPWT. On the contrary, MPWT has built its influence by emphasizing its technical skills and its reinforced position as the overall regulator in the road sector. It also offers crucial support to central and local governments in conducting integrated planning that evaluates road construction needs while conserving government assets through an evidence-based needs analysis. Moreover, MPWT's vertical line remains strong through firm leadership and an emphasis on technical skills and sector cohesion.

Stakeholder Management

MPWT must manage multiple, complicated stakeholder relationships, both formal and informal. The ministry is accountable to many principals, including the government at the central level, provincial governors, and development partners. At the same time, it is responsible for a complicated set of implementation arrangements with its own agents, including SOEs and domestic and international private contractors. MPWT appears to handle these stakeholder relationships quite well. On the principal side, the current MPWT leadership seems adept at rallying the support of elites and key stakeholders for its central programs. Provincial governors are particularly influential, so MPWT must ensure their needs are met. On the agent side, MPWT has successfully distributed implementation responsibilities to various partners, yet retains a strategic management role and ensures that it still earns plaudits itself for successful outcomes.

MPWT has worked hard to find the right balance between control of the country's road development versus flexibility in terms of actual construction and maintenance. Careful management of the policy and quality dimensions of road construction is crucial in this respect. MPWT appears to handle the policy side well but there are concerns on the quality control side. Villagers believe that the process of selection of priority areas for road development is fair and justified—expressing their faith in the centralized, top-down process of road development planning facilitated by the provincial-level DPWTs. But they also expressed the view that they do not have close enough contact with the district-level OPWTs, indicating that the institution as a whole may need to improve its communication and interface with clients.

With the devolution of road planning and construction, provincial governors' offices have become responsible for developing new road projects in their respective locations, while national and "strategic" roads have remained under the central responsibility of MPWT.[16] The overall implementation of Party directives on road access for every district and village has become the responsibility of provincial authorities and this has included the responsibility for resourcing local road projects. Thus, provincial governors' offices have become more involved in developing new road projects along with financing ideas. Champassak province has, for example, recently put together a new financing model for building a major road from the provincial capital, Pakse, to the Wat Phu monument.[17] The province successfully borrowed money from the Bank of the Lao PDR in order to finance the road construction on a build-operate-transfer basis. Once the road is constructed, tolls are charged for usage (collected by the road operators on behalf of the province) and the province later pays back the bank loan. This was reported as the first time Champassak province itself has borrowed money; and there are growing and significant reports of similar off-budget financing of road construction across the country (World Bank 2012).[18] For example, another off-budget road financing story emerged in Vientiane province regarding the building of a similar major road.[19]

The director of the provincial-level DPWT reports to the provincial governor (the horizontal line) as well as the ministry (the vertical line). In practice, DPWT works more closely with the provincial governor's office than with the central ministry and the provincial-level collaboration manages day-to-day resource implementation decisions. In part because of this decentralized system, MPWT is subject to the pressures of regional politics and the influence of provincial governors. The Minister of Public Works and Transport has recently moved to emphasize the vertical line and strengthen internal controls; it is, of course, the ministry that is accountable in terms of sector goals and responding to complaints. MPWT employees themselves are adept at satisfying both sets of goals—the political exigencies, typically articulated by provincial governors, and the integrity of public administration, represented by the central MPWT institution and its donor relations. Interviewees emphasized the strong cohesion and cooperative capacity at all levels of the MPWT hierarchy as a major factor behind the institution's success.

Organizational Esprit de Corps

MPWT employees share a remarkable esprit de corps, which is founded on their shared identity as engineering professionals and their mission of serving the public. This appears to be strongest at the provincial level, where strategic decisions are made and day-to-day management is conducted. Road sector employees reported that they are received with respect by villagers in the field, bringing them a measure of status. Many professionals within the organization—as well as in the private concerns active in the road sector—share technical training backgrounds, albeit from diverse countries, and a strong professional identity as road sector engineers that contributes to a sense of community. Integrated within this cohesive community are non-engineers, including those employees with more political or revolutionary backgrounds. Many of today's senior cohort of road engineers who are in MPWT, at state-owned enterprises, and running private contracting companies, say that they "grew up" together under donor-funded projects in the 1990s.

The organization is imbued with a shared sense of purpose that is well-understood and absorbed throughout the hierarchy. MPWT does not appear to have a clearly articulated mandate in a typical form and employees tend to equate the notion of a mandate with their own unit's terms of reference. Nevertheless, employees far down the ranks are able to recite the core goals and objectives of the organization and share a sense of pride and commitment to the mission. Indeed, that commitment—stemming from the public service and development role staff believe they are performing—was often identified as the main factor in MPWT's success. Such sentiments were expressed, illustratively, in the following ways: "We serve the people and the grassroots level;" "The road is like the blood flow;" "A song written for Public Works technical staff ... reflects that as workers we have an important role in the country's development;" "We bring civilization to the grassroots level."[20]

Institutionalization, Professionalism, and Mandate Implementation

MPWT has managed other factors in its external and internal environment in ways that have enhanced its ability to deliver on its institutional mandate. The agency has carefully managed its relationships with donors, emphasizing that the ministry itself is in the driver's seat and handling aid harmonization, and insisting on in-house capacity building rather than relying on project management units. As a government ministry, MPWT is subject to public sector recruitment and compensation rules and regulations. Within those constraints, nevertheless, MPWT has consistently emphasized the strategic building of human resource capacity within the ministry and has developed its own personnel management system to ensure a focus on performance, complete with incentives for high performers. MPWT is, moreover, a learning organization, as a result of a leadership that has, from the top-down, instituted and supported a work ethic and a system oriented toward problem solving, as well as a reliance on data to aid organizational performance and sector management.

Visionary Leadership Committed to Problem-Solving

Road sector planning and management in the 1980s and 1990s was fragmented among various government concerns. Since the mid-1990s, successive strong leaders of MCTPC and MPWT have played a central role in institutionalizing the role of MPWT as the lead agency for the sector. The 1999 Public Road Law was a crucial mechanism for consolidating MPWT's role. There has been a great deal of leadership continuity, with only three ministers overseeing the road sector over a period of 40 years. This continuity seems deliberate on the part of the political elite, as was the focused and incremental approach to national road development.

Each of the three ministers who have taken the helm of MPWT supported the Pathet Lao during the revolution and all have been high-ranking members of the Party's Central Committee. Thus, the sector has been led and driven by strong, symbolic figures who have reinforced the sector's cohesion and identity through the narratives of nationalism and service to the grassroots (Robert Oksen 2012). The first minister, Colonel Bounnaphol, an engineer educated abroad, was instrumental in leading the sector drive to open Lao PDR toward the sea and its neighbors and to increase trade interconnectivity within the country. His successor was a mastermind of the Rural Development Strategy during his mandate at the State Planning

Committee and drove forward the Rural Transport Infrastructure Strategy (Dennis 2000).

MPWT's leaders have been committed to excellence in service delivery and have emphasized a hands-on, learning-by-doing, and problem-solving approach to the ministry's work. The minister at the time of writing, H. E. Sommad Pholsena, exemplifies these values. His credibility with the ministry's personnel is enhanced a great deal by the fact that he has risen up through the ranks of the organization and combines his political acumen with his technical training and expertise. One of his constant axioms is "learning by doing," emphasizing delegation of responsibilities and building expertise via experimentation with various models.

A delegated, problem-solving approach to delivering on MPWT's goals, along with a conviction in learning-by-doing, is replicated down the institutional hierarchy. Department and division heads are delegated responsibilities, which it is then their job to ensure are carried out well. Staff throughout the organization reported having generally clear terms of reference along with relatively free reign, particularly in the Lao PDR context, to do their jobs. In turn, this ability for staff to take their own initiative was seen as an important contributor to the ministry's success. The staff's consequent respect for its leaders along with its ownership in sector projects is also crucial.

Donor Harmonization

MPWT pursued an explicit strategy of institutionalizing projects, and hence capacity-building, in the ministry itself, refusing to use project implementation units (PIUs). It was the first Lao ministry to take this approach to PIUs. A senior official emphasized that sector policy is first decided by the government and then donors are invited to join in implementation. The sector has nevertheless enjoyed high donor support and involvement in the sector—including, especially, a great deal of engagement with the ADB, the Swedish International Development Cooperation Agency (SIDA), and the World Bank—with iterated interactions and learning over time. Continuity on the donor side, including particularly the use of long-term task-team leaders with deep and extensive ties with their Lao counterparts, has contributed immeasurably to successful partnerships in the sector. Assistance is coordinated, with MPWT in the driver's seat. The minister was interested in a sector-wide approach to aid projects even before the concept of donor harmonization really took hold. When it abolished PIUs, the ministry set up instead an over-arching Project Monitoring Division, which is intended to be a one-stop shop for donors and donor coordination. Many interviewees noted that almost all key senior managers in MPWT (and in many private and state-owned enterprises active in the sector) are alumni of donor programs.

MPWT has benefited from early and sustained partnerships with donors since the 1980s. Many observers noted that donor commitment to road construction and maintenance was a major factor in delivering successes in the sector. The road sector has gained from formal and informal donor coordination. Initially, there was some regional-based division of labor among donors in the road sector: in the early 1980s, the Soviet Union was committed to road expansion to Vietnam, and Western assistance was targeted toward the country's main North-South trunk road, Road 13. In addition to geographic areas of responsibility, development partners have focused on different but complementary substantive areas—ADB on road network extension and rehabilitation, the World Bank on institutional development and maintenance, SIDA on local-level MPWT capacity-building and road improvement, other bilateral donors (e.g., Japan) on bridges, and so forth. This complementary division of labor has helped MPWT to pursue a building-block strategy in the sector, layering road maintenance and institutional systems building on top of a sustained commitment to expanding construction of the national road network.

Development partners have been engaged in road construction for almost three decades. Throughout this period, the transport sector consistently received the largest share of total official development assistance disbursements, ranging from 40 percent in the 1980s to about 20 percent since 2000. External funds still represent 75 percent of public works and transport sector spending.[21] Rural roads continue to be important components of integrated rural development projects as well as in the social sectors, since they are essential to increasing rural access to public services. Road construction remained an important part of government and donor spending in the 1990s, but attention progressively shifted to road rehabilitation needs and, consequently, the urgent need to develop a high-quality management system for the road sector that emphasized commitment to infrastructure maintenance. Two key elements of today's MPWT were thus introduced with donor support: the Road Maintenance Fund and the Road Management System, which measures system performance and serves as a planning and budget allocation tool.

In coordinating donor support over time, MPWT has institutionalized its role as a strong public institution dedicated to leading a domestically driven path of national road development. Its committed ownership of sector strategy and planning, along with the complementary division of tasks among implementation partners, are two central strengths MPWT has displayed. Although it has voluntarily integrated core components from donor programs, especially the technical approach to planning and the necessary analytical tools and methods, it has resisted and postponed other dimensions advanced by donors that were seen as not directly compatible with the sector and the national sociopolitical context.

Sophisticated Adaptations in Human Resource Management

MPWT human resource management (HRM) practices must remain aligned to the broader civil service system,[22] yet it is widely believed that—within those constraints—MPWT personnel practices are the most sophisticated in the government. The Personnel Department at the central ministry utilizes in-house software to capture demographic data and education, training, and career decisions and development for each employee. Personnel assessments are carried out annually (with a tool developed by SIDA) at the level of district performance, evaluating individual capacity as well as assessing the capacity of the unit as a whole. These assessments are then used to develop plans for staff improvement, identifying gaps and deploying and training staff as indicated.

Personnel skills within the institution have increased a great deal. Interviewees noted that most road sector personnel in Lao PDR's early days were civil servants who were teachers rather than road engineers and simply did not know what to do in terms of road development. MPWT managers at the district, provincial, and central levels noted the upgrading of skills across the institution, including the proliferation of advanced degrees. Training programs and study tours abroad through scholarships were emphasized in the 1990s.

Development partners contributed a great deal to the upgrading of staff skills at the local level, through on-the-job capacity building. Technical assistance in the road sector actually provided some measure of skills transfer to Lao counterparts.[23] Donor support was also essential in building private sector implementation skills over time: "The construction companies were the sons of donors. Each company had its donor and project. We received new equipment as well as technical and management training. When the state-owned enterprises collapsed, employees built up small new companies."[24]

Across the institution, from the minister down, there is an emphasis on on-the-job training and learning-by-doing. In turn, this necessitates the rotation of staff to field positions, since the provincial and district level is where the ministry's implementation work truly occurs: "Good field managers make good office managers ... If you are not trained in the field, you are not qualified to come to the Ministry."[25] Thus, MPWT has made a big push to decentralize personnel throughout the ranks, moving project management and other HR capacity from central to provincial or district levels.[26] Employees are, in turn, ensured good positions in the central ministry when they return; directors are rotated through the provinces and central ministry. The institution deploys its staff with attention to local-level cultural and linguistic issues, in particular using native-language speakers in remote, tribal, and ethnic areas, and also typically staffing district and provincial branches with individuals from those localities. The exception is in the poorer provinces, where the necessary skills cannot be found (e.g., Sekong district-level employees do not speak the Sekong dialects).

MPWT has deployed some of the HRM systems recommended by its development partners, particularly the use of analytical tools. Overall, however, MPWT's HRM practices seem to represent more of a hybrid that adapts donor systems to the domestic context. For example, the systems of staff rotation and local-level capacity-building HRM, achieved by placing skilled engineers and managers in the districts and provinces, are consonant with the Party's strategy of institutionalizing democratic centralism through the establishment of direct relations with the grassroots (Robert Oksen 2012).

Another important dimension of MPWT's astute human resource management is the emphasis placed on individual motivation and performance. In part this is made possible by HR performance assessments. Yet, with the exception of promotion based on the civil service system and its annual performance evaluation, there are no tangible performance incentives. Instead, the institution successfully motivates staff through training, capacity building, and weekly meetings that ensure tasks are allocated appropriately and difficulties are discussed. In addition, team work is prized and various recreational activities are organized to maintain team spirit and cohesion.

Evidence-Based Sector Management

In the 1990s, MPWT shifted its core mission to develop an emphasis on maintenance as well as construction. In turn, this organizational shift, along with the move to decentralization and commercialization, required paying attention to administrative capacity in the institution. The emphasis on maintenance necessitated data management and administrative oversight skills in addition to the engineering capacity needed for construction.

One mechanism through which MPWT has enhanced its administrative capacities is through the use of a relatively sophisticated data collection and management system for maintenance of the road network, the Road Maintenance System. This system, introduced with World Bank support, performs to international standards and has been adapted to the Lao PDR context. It is used to measure system performance as well as serve as a planning and budgeting tool and operates throughout the MPWT hierarchy. District engineers submit data to the provincial-level DPWT to update the provincial maintenance management system, which DPWT then analyzes and passes to MPWT. In turn, after further data analysis (by the Public Works and Transport Institute, which reports directly to the minister), the central MPWT then allocates road maintenance funds, in renegotiation with provincial departments.

If DPWT analysis indicates any problems or specific challenges, the relevant provincial branch itself is charged with proposing a plan of action, to be approved by the central ministry. By the same logic, the district is supposed to report problems to the province. MPWT thus shows signs of being a "learning" organization that is flexible in adapting to incoming information and adjusts policy and management accordingly. For example, provincial units are tasked with analyzing their own data and developing solutions for identified problems. In addition, in implementing major changes in the late 1990s, MPWT piloted approaches in four provinces and modified them accordingly. The quality of contracted-out road construction and maintenance is also closely supervised by the district-level OPWT, which reports to the provincial-level DPWT. Maintenance contracts with private sector enterprises are typically over three years, with their continuation and renewal predicated on measured performance.

In short, MPWT has the capacity and tools to put together, analyze, and plan and allocate resources on the basis of evidence. The Road Maintenance System analyzes road conditions, traffic volumes, and populations served. It enables the costing of development scenarios as well as the identification of maintenance needs on the basis of projected available funds. The system provides financial evidence to aid decision making between further road expansion (increasing capital assets) and road maintenance (protecting capital assets). MPWT uses evidence-based analysis to propose and bolster its plans and role within the broader political arena. The institution thus maintains a thorough data collection and analysis system, with decisions around sector strategy and implementation made on the basis of these relatively sophisticated tools. In other words, the agency practices evidence-based decision making and emphasizes the institutionalization of systematic tools for effective administrative and political management.

Challenges

MPWT appears to have gained a great deal of legitimacy and public trust from its successes in extending the road network. Now that minimal road access needs have been exceeded, however, there is an increasing sense among the public that road quality is not as good as it should be. In other words, many villagers expressed the feeling that MPWT's emphasis on the quantity of roads was negatively affecting the quality of construction.

Capacity at the provincial level was reported to have improved markedly over the past decade, through a concerted capacity-building push. Yet, observers noted that district-level capacity still requires a great deal of upgrading. Focus groups at the village level revealed that users have mixed views on district-level OPWTs. Road users respect the staff's technical capacity, but believe that OPWTs tend not to enforce quality standards strictly enough through supervision of construction companies. Interviews with frontline MPWT staff emphasized gaps in human resource and technical capacities, confirming that district-level units are undercapacitated to perform their decentralized supervision responsibilities.

New financing and construction models are emerging in the road sector. One new approach is for private sector construction companies to take on the financing liability for building new roads, with contractual commitments from the government to repay the firm upon completion in tranches over five years.[27] This model appears to be particularly popular at the provincial government level, where governors can sign off on projects below 5 billion kip. But there appears to be some concern developing at the senior level about the accumulating financial liability for government in light of this new approach to road construction. In addition to the evolving build-operate-transfer model of financing, there is a resource-for-infrastructure model emerging, whereby roads are built in exchange for natural resource concessions. For example, in Sekong Province, there appear to be agreements to compensate private sector companies upgrading provincial roads (a US$12 billion project) with coal ore and timber from the province. Provincial governors are powerful on this matter, and the government has yet to develop a systematic, country-wide strategy for such construction models.

There seem to be barriers to entry to the private sector in road construction and maintenance, in the sense that those companies most well-connected to Party leaders are those that will most likely succeed in any meaningful way. The military is involved in some major construction companies and is especially likely to have a role in road construction and maintenance contracts associated with natural resource concessions. Increasingly, too, bids are tendered under international competitive bidding, which means they are usually won by Vietnamese and Chinese companies instead of Lao companies. Lao subcontractors on these projects get squeezed, as the foreign companies retain the bulk of the profits. This was identified as problematic from the point of view of trying to build local enterprises with appropriate capacity.

With the exception of reporting to donors, the ministry seems to employ relatively limited forms of external accountability. For example, it neither uses client hotlines or systematic grievance processes; nor does it appear to canvass the public regularly to determine citizens' demand for road services. Villagers expressed dissatisfaction regarding MPWT's communication systems, pointing out that they were often left in the dark about progress on projects, since consultations during road construction involved only village authorities and not public forums. This indicates that the institution may need to improve its communication and interface with clients throughout the hierarchy. Yet, the provincial units of MPWT work in close collaboration with provincial governors' offices, potentially reducing the need for direct client consultation.

Conclusion

The road sector has been crucial to Lao PDR's modernization and socio-economic development, especially after the country embarked on economic liberalization reforms in 1986. LPRP, recognizing the sociopolitical and economic benefits of road building, has prioritized the sector from the inception of the Lao PDR in 1975. The MPWT has built its institutional success on the basis of this mandate and the resources that have come with it. The agency has demonstrated a remarkable ability to operate within its immediate external environment and manage its internal institutional workings in creative ways that meet two meta-level objectives. First, MPWT has proven adept, even indispensable, in ensuring that the Lao political elite's goals of state building and modernization can be met. Second, the agency has astutely managed other elements of its external and internal environment in ways that have enhanced its ability to deliver on its institutional mandate.

In meeting these two high-level goals, three especially striking causal dimensions of MPWT's institutional success stand out. First, in the broader context of the administrative and economic reforms introduced with NEM, MPWT has skillfully retained sector policy making and planning primacy, while delegating implementation through decentralization to the provincial units of the ministry and commercialization of road construction and maintenance to private sector partners. MPWT has thus evolved from being a direct service provider to an institution that sets policy for and manages service provision but does not implement it directly.

Second, MPWT has astutely managed the high level of donor funding and support in the sector by retaining the driver's seat and ensuring country ownership of policy making, capacity building, and analytical tools and systems. Donors have been essential in the sector for introducing new ideas, models, and skills; they have demonstrated the fruits of a sustained and focused partnership with committed counterparts. The donor-supported Road Maintenance System itself is a major factor in the success of needs analysis and planning in the sector. Most crucially, however, MPWT has experimented with these inputs so as to learn from them and adapt them to the Lao context and to meet Lao administrative and political goals. Partly as a result of its close partnership with donors, MPWT emphasizes evidence-based decision making and sector management, improving its effectiveness in delivering on its mandate and enhancing its legitimacy in the broader institutional and political arena.

Finally, MPWT has astutely implemented creative, bureaucratic modifications that enable it to push against the constraints of the Lao administrative system. Such innovative adaptations include a sophisticated in-house personnel management system, as well as the leadership's and overall ministry's emphasis on learning-by-doing, personal and team initiative and performance measures, and an evidence-based, problem-solving approach to the implementation of sector policy.

Notes

1. Prior to 2006, MPWT was the Ministry of Communication, Transport, Post and Construction (MCTPC). MPWT consists of six departments: the Department of Civil Aviation, Department of Housing and Urban Planning, Department of Inland Waterways, Department of Planning and Cooperation, Department of Roads, and Department of Transport.
2. See Gwilliams (2007), ADB (2010), and SHER Consulting Engineers (2010) for further detail on these challenges and the technical and financial complexities associated with them.
3. Data from National Statistics Center (2008).
4. Road Department Statistics, 2000–10, Ministry of Public Works and Transport.
5. Road Department Statistics, 2000–10, Ministry of Public Works and Transport.
6. Barma (2002) provides details on the Lao road sector in the 1980s and 1990s, along with an assessment of the institutional development impact of International Development Association (IDA) lending in the sector.
7. The other four sectors LPRP viewed as pillars of socialist modernization, to which all villages should have access, were electricity, health, education, and water.
8. MPWT's share of public expenditure peaked in 2005/06 at 48 percent; subsequently, the government set a cap of 35 percent on the MPWT portion.
9. Law on Public Roads (Government of the Lao PDR 1999).
10. RMF was created as an entity within the organizational structure of MPWT. It is supervised and directed by an advisory board, which comprises public and private sector representatives, appointed by the prime minister, from the Ministry of Finance, MPWT, provincial authorities, the Lao National Chamber of Commerce and Industry, private and state-owned road and passenger transport operators, and the general public. RMF coordinates with MPWT's Road Administration Department on financial support for national road maintenance and with the Local Roads Division on local roads (ADB 2010).
11. The share was calculated based on RMF revenue and expenditure summaries from 2002–08. RMF was largely supported by donors in its first year; by 2008, 91 percent of its revenues came from government tax sources. Total revenues tripled from 2002 to 2008.
12. By Decree 09/PM, January 2001.
13. This decentralization initiative was being discussed as early as 1997 but was formalized later by Prime Minister's Decree 01 (2000) and operationalized even later through the 2003 Law on Local Administration (Government of the Lao PDR 2003). In the road sector, the decentralization process preceded countrywide reforms, being implemented through the 1999 Law on Public Roads (Government of the Lao PDR 1999).

14. Gwilliams (2007) provides more details on this delegated implementation system.
15. Each of these companies was originally named after the road they were charged with constructing. Hence, SOE names such as Road Construction Company #8 (designated to build Road 8).
16. This devolution was undertaken under the Law on Public Roads (Government of the Lao PDR 1999).
17. Senior official in Champassak Province (February 1, 2012).
18. It appears that the practice is more common in the richer provinces and those connected with Thailand and Vietnam.
19. In the case of the latter road, Vientiane's 450-Year Road, the government agreed that a private company would provide the financing for road construction. The government, in turn, plans to "convert land assets into capital" by later selling commercially attractive plots on either side of the road for development and to thereby cover the costs of road construction. See http://laovoices.com/new-six-lane-road-gets-green-light/.
20. Interviews with district-level OPWT official and front-line technical staff.
21. Government public expenditure records, 2008/09, and data from Ministry of Planning and Investment, *ODA Annual Reports* (2000, 2007, 2010).
22. World Bank (2010) provides details of Lao PDR's civil service human resource management system, including compensation policies and practices.
23. Earlier assessments (e.g., Barma 2002) were less sanguine on this point.
24. Interview with road construction company representative.
25. Interview with senior MPWT official (February 9, 2012).
26. It was noted that contract staff (nonpermanent civil servants) are essential to getting the work of the ministry done; these contract workers can be later converted to government employment if they are under 35 years of age.
27. World Bank (2012) provides a detailed assessment of these new financing and construction models.

References

Asian Development Bank (ADB). 2010. *Lao People's Democratic Republic: Transport Sector*. Report LAO 2010-44, Sector Assistance Program Evaluation, Independent Evaluation Department.

Barma, Naazneen H. 2002. "Assessing the Institutional Development Impact of IDA Lending: Case Study of the Lao People's Democratic Republic." Unpublished manuscript.

Dennis, John. 2000. *A Review of Social Policies Lao PDR*. GMS Regional Environmental Technical Assistance 5771. Poverty Reduction and Environmental Management in Remote Greater Mekong Subregion Watersheds Project (Phase I).

Government of the Lao PDR. 1999. *Law on Public Roads*. No. 04/99/NA.

———. 2003. *Law on Local Administration of the Lao PDR*. No. 47/NA.

———. 2009. *The Ketsana Typhoon in the Lao People's Democratic Republic*. Vientiane: Government of the Lao PDR.

Gwilliams, Ken. 2007. *Paving the Road for Better Capacity*. Washington, DC: World Bank.

Ministry of Public Works and Transport (MPWT). 2009. *Strategy for Transport Sector Development for the Period 2008–2010 and Direction for 2011–2015*. Vientiane: Government of the Lao PDR.

National Statistics Center. 2008. *Lao Expenditure and Consumption Survey 2007–2008*. Vientiane: Government of the Lao PDR.

Pholsena, Vatthana, and Ruth Banomyong. 2007. *Laos: From Buffer State to Crossroads?* Thailand: Silkworm Books.

Robert Oksen, Stephanie. 2012. "Aide Memoire on The Ministry of Public Works and Transport: ESW Exercise on Institutions Taking Root in Fragile States." Unpublished manuscript.

SHER Consulting Engineers. 2010. "A Long and Winding Road: Evaluation of Lao-Swedish Road Sector Projects 1996–2009." SIDA Evaluation Report. Draft manuscript.

Warr, Peter. 2010. "Roads and Poverty in Rural Laos: An Econometric Analysis." *Pacific Economic Review* 15(1): 152–69.

World Bank. 2010. *Lao PDR: Civil Service Pay and Compensation Review: Attracting and Motivating Civil Servants*. Report 58018-LA. East Asia and Pacific Region Poverty Reduction and Economic Management Unit, World Bank, Washington, DC.

———. 2012. "Off-Budget Road Infrastructure Investments in Lao PDR: How Big, Where and Why?" Draft manuscript. World Bank, Washington, DC.

PART III

SIERRA LEONE

CHAPTER 7

The Institution-Building Context in Sierra Leone

Marco Larizza and Brendan Glynn

The unique provenance of Sierra Leone, combined with its ethnic distribution, has had a determining influence on the country's sociopolitical development. Founded in the late eighteenth century as a safe haven for freed and escaped slaves, the settlement of Freetown and its immediate peninsular area were brought under direct British control in 1808 as the Sierra Leone Colony. The settlers, the Krios, were at first detached from the peoples of the interior, but a trading relationship developed between them and, increasingly, other forms of societal interaction. In 1896, Britain declared a protectorate over the Colony's hinterlands, delineating the greater country's boundaries.

Sierra Leone was dominated by two large ethnic groups, the Temne and the Mende, and two numerous but smaller groups, the Limba and the Kono. With eventual universal suffrage, the relationships between these groups (plus the Krios) would characterize the local political environment.

Throughout the pre-independence period, however, the critical factor was the colonial government's policy of remote, indirect rule of the Protectorate. Paramount chiefs were favored or replaced to contain dissent and maintain allegiance under the watch of district commissioners. The chiefs were generally unimpeded in exercising their traditional writs. Concerted modernization efforts were largely confined to Freetown and the Western Area, where educational development and the establishment of a professional civil service were particularly notable. The stark opportunity and entitlement divide between the old settlement and the hinterland persisted into the modern era.

Since Independence

Political Movements: 1970s

Before and after the country's independence, Dr. Milton Margai's Sierra Leone People's Party (SLPP) was ascendant on the local political scene. Margai became the first prime minister, but he was soon opposed by Siaka Stevens, who formed the All People's Congress (APC). Ethnic fault lines became even more pronounced, with Mendes attaching themselves largely to the SLPP and Temnes and Limbas to the APC.

Army interventions emerged as a regular feature, with coups in 1967 and 1968. The 1968 coup reestablished Stevens in power after his earlier parliamentary victory. In the following decade, Stevens consolidated the APC position but increasingly in the form of personal power and self-aggrandizement. In 1971, Stevens became the executive president the Republic of Sierra Leone. The abolition of local government the following year accentuated the entrenchment of clientelism, as Stevens gave preferential treatment to individual Paramount Chiefs in return for their quiescence at the national level. In 1978, a referendum approved Stevens' proposal for a new, one-party constitution.

Economic Problems: 1980s

Coinciding with this stage of the centralization of power, incremental deterioration of the economy set in. Particularly far-reaching in their effects were the depletion, and regime plunder, of alluvial diamonds and the closure of the iron ore mine in Marampa. The situation was compounded by an accelerated exodus of qualified civil servants and the undermining of the morale of those who stayed in their posts. The regime required that all civil servants be members of the party. The once meritocratic civil service became more and more politicized, and there was an effective exclusion of Mendes in senior posts. Meanwhile, as indirect taxes dropped, expansionary fiscal and monetary policies were used to stimulate economic activity. The widening gap in the budget was financed through the heavy use of short-term debt, which furthered the downward trajectory of economic decline.

The government sought external multilateral support in 1989; resources for economic and administrative reform were mobilized by the World Bank, IMF, and African Development Bank. However, the degradation of the state apparatus had reached crisis proportions, and discontent was mounting, notably in the hinterland, where, after years of central neglect and patrimonial politics, the power elite was about to reap a bitter harvest. In particular, the mood of the rural youth was becoming increasingly volatile. Their dissatisfaction was stoked by their marginalization, and the frequent extraction of their labor by individual paramount chiefs.

Civil War: 1990s

The first incursion of the Revolutionary United Front (RUF) across the border from Liberia took place in March 1991. The incursion sparked the decade-long civil war, which capitalized on the widespread disenchantment in the country. While the insurgents gathered numbers to their ranks and gained territory, Freetown was not directly affected by the violence. But the diminution of the authority of the government was such that an unplanned revolt by junior army officers was able to topple the APC government.

With the continuing relative immunity of the capital and the Western Area from rebel attacks, the newly installed National Provisional Ruling Council (NPRC) junta was able to function in a comparatively authoritative fashion. The position of the NPRC was helped by the presence in Freetown of troops from the Economic Community of West African States Monitoring Group (ECOMOG). In addition, the continuation of external support allowed the maintenance of core services, as did the residual professional loyalty and skills in clusters of the public service, for example at the Ministry of Finance. The junta's internal cohesion remained brittle, however, and in 1996 it ceded the political space to allow for new elections.

At this juncture, APC's reputation was at its lowest, and APC was seen as the party that had caused the breakdown of the state and the coming of the civil war. SLPP, under Ahmad Tejan Kabbah, was able to deliver its traditional southern and eastern vote while benefiting sufficiently from disaffected former APC voters elsewhere in the country. However, when SLPP assumed office, the internal insurgency was still unresolved and disgruntlement continued in the army. Following a coup the next year, a new Armed Forces Revolutionary Council (AFRC) junta was installed. Kabbah retreated to run a parallel government across the Freetown harbor, protected by ECOMOG. In February 1998, Nigerian troops marched into Freetown and expelled the junta. In January 1999, a new incursion into the city environs was launched by AFRC and Revolutionary United Front (RUF) combined forces.

After the Civil War: 2000s

The war was declared over in early 2002. By that time, between 20,000 and 70,000 Sierra Leoneans had been killed and thousands more had been maimed or displaced. The country's infrastructure was devastated and economic activity severely derailed. The SLPP government and the Kabbah presidency were returned again in the same year. They faced not only the challenge of reconstruction, but also the general transformational issue of poverty reduction in of one of the most impoverished countries in the world. Even by 2009, the United Nations Human Development Index ranked Sierra Leone at 180, with only Afghanistan and Niger behind. According to the United Nations Development Programme, in Sierra Leone, life expectancy at birth was 47 years, the adult literacy rate was 38 percent, and the combined primary and secondary school enrollment rate was 45 percent.

The Economy

On the positive side, the country's abundant mineral resources and potential in agriculture and fisheries prefigured considerably increased external earnings. Likewise, donor commitments were rapidly increased, and a skills inflow was presaged by the willingness of members of the diaspora to return or invest in the country. Furthermore, reflecting the traditionally high levels of education and loyalty in professional and technical niches in Sierra Leone, the government had an enduring pool of expertise available to it. This was augmented (for example, in the Ministry of Finance) by specialized technical assistance. On the policy front, the government sought to address the underlying causes of war by focusing on youth dislocation and the reintroduction of elected local government and its integration into decentralized service delivery.

Political Change

Progress was identifiable in the key policy areas, but the government was increasingly regarded as self-serving, complacent, and tolerant of corruption. Remarkably, the northern elite had regrouped around what had been considered the discredited political vehicle of the APC. A new leader, Ernest Koroma, pushed the renewed brand strongly and particularly assailed corruption at high levels. Another factor in the next (2007) election was the emergence of a rival, southern-oriented party, the People's Movement for Democratic Change (PMDC). In a reverse of the situation 11 years earlier,

APC was able to deliver the vote in the northern and western zones (plus in Kono by way of alliances), while SLPP's traditional vote was dissipated or not mobilized. The election marked the first in a post-conflict country in Africa in which an incumbent party was defeated and (prompted by significant external pressure) respected the outcome.

Economic Growth

Sierra Leone's economic growth since the end of the civil war has been impressive. In the early years, there was a surge in economic growth of more than 10 percent, followed by an average annualized rate of 7.3 percent in 2004–06. The growth rate flattened as oil and food prices increased after the 2008 crisis, but it remained above 5 percent. As the 2010 Public Expenditure Review (PER) emphasized, this trend bodes well for the realization of several of the goals of the Poverty Reduction Strategy Paper (PRSP II). The PER also noted that the authorities successfully adjusted their fiscal stance to the reduced levels of net external assistance in the period. What is more, there has been marked progress in public financial management and concerted efforts on reform since 2004 have brought Sierra Leone up to the level of regional averages on respective indicators.

Social Challenges

In the social sphere, however, the sustained growth has not translated effectively into improved indices. The poverty headcount has declined, but it is still around the 60 percent mark (World Bank 2010). Pro-poor spending has continued to increase, but, the Decentralised Service Delivery Project II PAD, 2012, observes the following: "… Human development and service delivery outcomes have shown only modest improvements. In all three sectors, which are of particular concern vis-à-vis HD outcomes, health, education, water and sanitation, Sierra Leone falls significantly short of the Millennium Development Goals."[1] The government's commitment in these areas has remained firm, nonetheless, as does its decentralization policy for service delivery through the community planning, administrative, and monitoring systems of the local councils. As covenanted, the central government is continuing to channel at least 30 percent of its domestic revenues (less wages, interest, and some statutory transfers) to subnational government. In his parliamentary address, following his (and APC's) election victories in December 2012, President Koroma reasserted the government's adherence to these policy commitments.

Political Economy

The 2012 elections were carried out peacefully and with Electoral Commission and international validation. However, although the processes of formal electoral democracy have thus been solidified—representing a significant achievement—a number of substantial negativities remain in the political economy environment. It is characterized by embedded structures of patrimonialism, in which politicians at all levels are involved in private rent-seeking and channeling private goods to support groups or individuals. Such mechanisms, working against any notion of collective public interest, reached their high point under the Stevens regime, followed by that of his nominee, Momoh. The military interregnums did little to change the situation (although the client profile changed). After those regimes, an elected, civilian government returned, but the successive regimes continued the focus on mobilizing their core ethnic support as a first priority.

The corrosive effects of these patrimonial mores are evident. As Robinson (2008) notes:

> [P]roperty rights are insecure. People only have property because patrons allow them to have it, but such rights are always conditional and can be withdrawn....Moreover, laws are selectively applied with no concept of the rule of law or equality before the law which of course are completely inconsistent with how clientelism is dispensed. In a patrimonial regime you have rights if you are a client of the patron and otherwise you do not. Third, ... patrimonial regimes create distortions in market prices to create rents which can then be politically allocated.... Finally, patrimonialism undermines the coherence of the bureaucracy. This is because the bureaucracy represents a potential source of political opposition to patrons.

Major players in the system are the chiefs, particularly the 149 paramount chiefs. Tellingly, in 2002, when their prestige was at a low ebb, the Kabbah government avoided the opportunity of reform of chieftainship and signaled their full reinstallation as the key local power brokers. Land allocation, most critically, has remained their preserve, as has the collection (for supposed later co-sharing with the local councils) of the local development tax. Furthermore, the influence of the paramount chiefs is still situationally important in diamond and mineral rich areas. If anything, the position of the chiefs has been reinforced over time. With the adoption of the National Decentralisation Policy in 2010, the designation of the local councils as the "highest political authorities" in their respective territories contained in the 2004 Local Government Act was adjusted to read the "highest developmental authorities." Clearly, the core chief-ruling party nexus in the system of patrimonialism has an enduring robustness based on mutual interest.

Countertrends

The tendency to tailor measures in line with the pattern of private incentives and to perpetuate the beneficial order is further evidenced by the partial retreat on decentralization represented by the reintroduction of district commissioners; the effective curtailment of parliamentary oversight; and (in the current APC tenure) the continuing domination of the Cabinet by northern personages.

These negative, historical continuities are exposed to countertrends, however, which augur well potentially for a shift in the current and-persistent paradigm. First, there is a voluble, open press and media environment despite ongoing attempts to muzzle journalists and commentators. Second, other channels of social accountability and political expression are opening up, notably as a result of the decentralization process. An aspect of this is that the war, to some degree, promoted greater community consciousness and voice, more so in the worst-affected zones. Third, political allegiances, although largely stereotypical, are not immutable. Importantly, the swing vote can be posited as increasing, including owing to accelerated urbanization in the Freetown area (although this could serve to marginalize the hinterland again). Finally, rapid economic developments—prominently related to the extractive industries in the immediate future—will inevitably reverberate in societal change, which will not be fully amenable to the marshalling of elites for their own interests.

Note

1. http://www-wds.worldbank.org/external/default/WDSContentServer/WDSP
   /IB/2012/08/24/000356161_20120824004236/Rendered/INDEX/720570PJP
   R0v1003550August016020120.txt.

References

Robinson, James. 2008. "Governance and Political Economy Constraints to World Bank CAS Priorities in Sierra Leone." Research Paper, World Bank, Washington, DC.

World Bank. 2010. "Joint Country Assistance Strategy for the Republic of Sierra Leone." World Bank, Washington, DC.

CHAPTER 8

Sierra Leone Case Study: Ministry of Finance and Economic Development

Lorena Viñuela and Ousman Barrie

Sierra Leone is heavily dependent on external assistance. Institutional capacity is generally weak but some pockets of effectiveness do exist. The history of the country has been marked by a steady decline since 1961 and by widening ethnic, regional, and economic cleavages. The country's political economy has been marked by the prevalence of patrimonial politics and conflict. Despite new forces that have emerged and greater political inclusiveness, political competition continues to rely on ethnic-based clientelism.

The stark deterioration of the administrative capacity prior to the conflict and the efforts to sustain the state during the civil war generated consistent (domestic and external) efforts to prioritize the institutional building of the Ministry of Finance and Economic Development (MoFED). Signaling transparency and technical capability in public financial management was the keystone of the government's strategy to attract external support, which has significantly risen since 2000.

Freetown and the Western Peninsula remained relatively isolated from the attacks of the rebels and the core government functions were not at risk, except at the end of the conflict in 1998–99. This made it possible for development partners to maintain their support and assistance to MoFED throughout the war. The financing of external consultants and local technical assistants by development partners enabled MoFED to recruit and retain key personnel. During the conflict and in its aftermath, a critical mass of technical staff stayed with the institution. This continuity contributed to preserve institutional memory and lay the foundations for future reforms, but also increased the institutional capacity and credibility of commitments with external partners.

In recent years, the institution has benefited from increasingly coordinated efforts by donors and the simplification of reporting requirements. For example, the Multi-Donor Trust Fund has financed the Institutional Reform and Capacity Building Project and the Integrated Public Financial Management Reform Program. Another example is the establishment of an annual Performance Assessment Framework to inform and guide budget support. However, the strong influence of donors has at times translated into disruptive isomorphic pressures.

Taking advantage of this context, MoFED has undertaken various structural changes, introduced a new information system, updated processes, and improved communication channels with government clients and partner agencies. Notably, since 2007, the ministry has considerably enhanced its presence in the line ministries through the deployment of budget officers, procurement officers, and internal audit personnel in all ministries, departments, and agencies (MDA) and local councils.

Institutional Success

After emerging from a protracted conflict and decades of state weakness, the MoFED made significant progress in building its institutional capacity, improving results in macroeconomic and public finance management, and increasing its legitimacy. Various reforms have included strengthening existing departments, implementing business process reform, updating legal and regulatory frameworks, and developing new structures and institutions.

Moreover, in the past 15 years, the ministry has proved it has significant resilience in withstanding conflict, coup d'états, a change of ruling party, volatility in official assistance, and a turbulent international financial environment. The ministry has consistently improved its credibility and legitimacy vis-à-vis external and domestic stakeholders, further strengthening its relations with clients and partners.

Results

Since 2002, MoFED has achieved measurable and gradually improving results with respect to a sizeable portion of its core mandate. The ministry has exhibited sustained improvements in key areas, including budget formulation, execution, and accounting; procurement practices; internal and external audits; and coordination with stakeholders and clients. Although tax collection has increased, its comparatively low levels remain a significant problem. Other challenges include improving fiscal discipline and the credibility of budgets. The low credibility of the budgets stems from the fact that official assistance is often unpredictable.

MoFED's performance is comparable to other Sub-Saharan African countries and low-income economies in most indicators (see figure 8.1 and figure 8.2.) Sierra Leone outperforms these countries in terms of budget management and soundness of intergovernmental relations. It lags in terms of internal audit, macroeconomic management, and revenue administration. However, Sierra Leone's scores are markedly higher than those of other post-conflict countries in the region.

Sierra Leone's Country Policy and Institutional Assessment (CPIA) scores show that the country is above the International Development

Figure 8.1. Performance of Key Central Finance Agency Functions in Sierra Leone and Peer Group

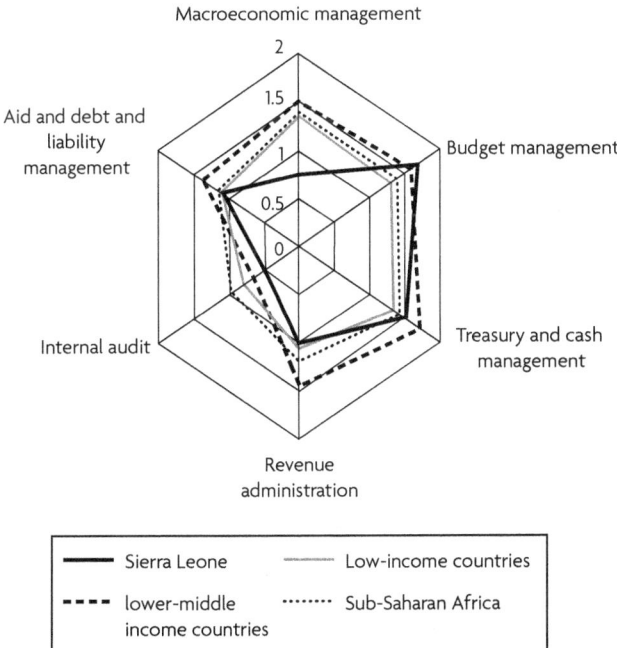

Source: Brumby et al. 2010.
Note: Scores from 0 to 5.

Figure 8.2. PEFA Score in Sierra Leone, Liberia, and Democratic Republic of Congo

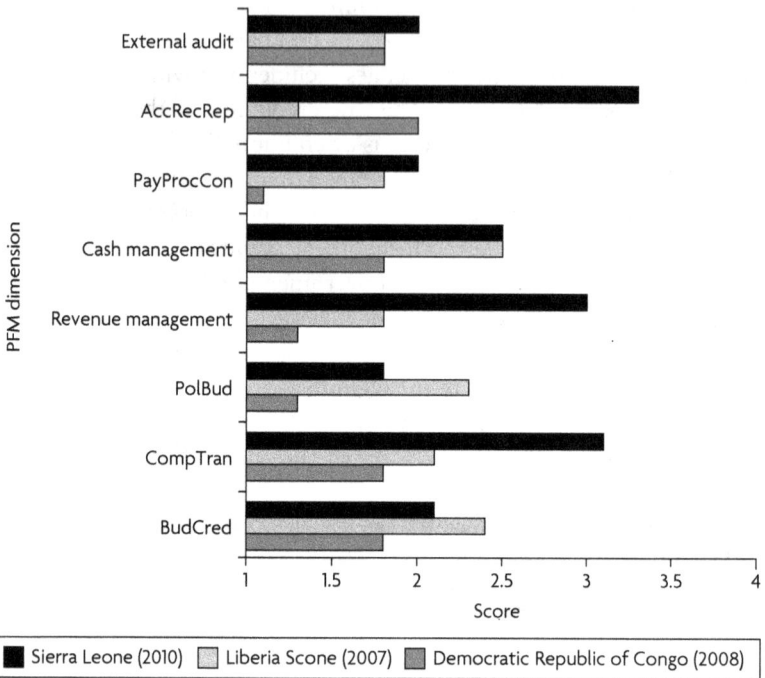

Source: PEFA Secretariat.
Note: PEFA = Public Expenditure and Financial Accountability. Scores from 1 to 4.

Table 8.1. Country Policy and Institutional Assessment Scores, 2005 and 2010

Dimension	Sierra Leone		Average	
	2005	2010	2005	2010
1. Macroeconomic management	4.0	4.0	3.8	3.7
2. Fiscal policy	3.5	3.5	3.4	3.5
3. Debt policy	3.5	3.5	3.4	3.4
13. Quality of budget and financial management	3.5	3.5	3.2	3.3
14. Efficiency of revenue mobilization	3.0	3.0	3.4	3.5
16. Transparency, accountability, and corruption in the public sector	2.5	3.0	2.9	2.9

Source: World Bank (2011).

Association (IDA) average on dimensions such as macroeconomic management, fiscal policy, debt management, quality of budget and financial management, and transparency (table 8.1). The areas in which the country lags are related to the efficiency of revenue mobilization. The quality of public administration is comparable to the average for IDA countries and has not registered any significant improvement since CPIA started being collected.

Importantly, MoFED has increased the transparency of the budget process and revenue allocations. Between 2007 and 2010, 10 scores improved in the Public Expenditure and Financial Accountability (PEFA) indicators and in three areas—comprehensiveness of the information in the budget, transparency of intergovernmental fiscal relations, and availability of information in the service delivery units—received the maximum score (see annex 8A.3). The frequency and accuracy of reporting of government debt, expenditure, and revenues have also improved substantially. There is a new cadre of budget officers in line ministries reporting to the Budget Bureau, the rollout of the Integrated Financial Management Information System (IFMIS) is ongoing (100 percent of national expenditures processed, 65 percent in real time), and the timeliness of financial reporting and audit is increasing. In parallel, new legislation and changes in implementation mechanisms have positively impacted the procurement environment.

The reorganization of revenue administration and the introduction of the goods and services tax have led to a fivefold increase in tax revenues since 2002 (see figure 8.3). Although several challenges related to macroeconomic management remain, the overall deficit excluding grants has decreased from 18 percent of gross domestic product (GDP) in 2001 to 6 percent in 2007. External assistance, in the form of budget support,

Figure 8.3. Tax Revenue, 2000–10

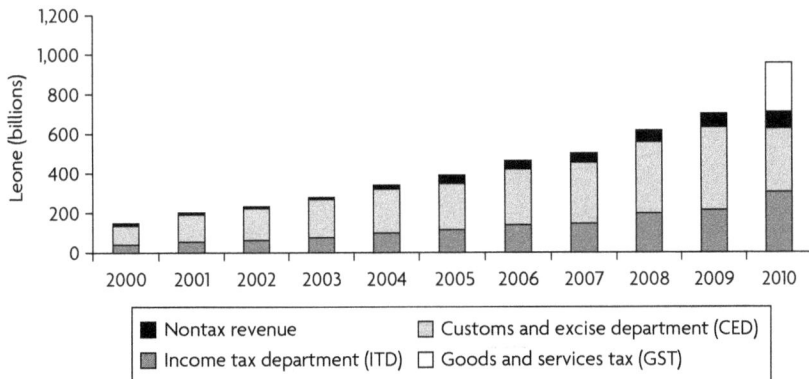

Source: MoFED (2011).

allowed the government to fill the fiscal gap and reduce the deficit to 1 percent of GDP by 2007. In 2008 and 2009, the deficit widened as a result of the food crisis to 3 percent with grants and 10 percent excluding grants. This represented a setback, but performance has bettered since 2010. In addition, figure 8.4 shows that expenditures have stabilized but with a similar setback in the latter part of the 2000s.

Legitimacy

Clients (MDAs and local governments) and external partners largely agree that MoFED is a capable institution. Its relationship with clients and the frequency of communication have greatly improved with the deployment of accountants, budget officers, and internal auditors in all major MDAs and local councils. MoFED clients have highlighted the greater transparency and timeliness in the transfer of resources, although many challenges remain in terms of budget credibility, but they acknowledge that this is largely outside the control of MoFED. The ministry is seen by the majority of its clients as a strategic partner in building relations with development partners. The assurances related to financial management and procurement given by the ministry are generally considered a major contribution to the line ministries' mandate. Donors' willingness to use budget support also reflects the level of trust that exists in the processes put in place during the past decade.

Figure 8.4. Total Expenditure/GDP, 2001–09

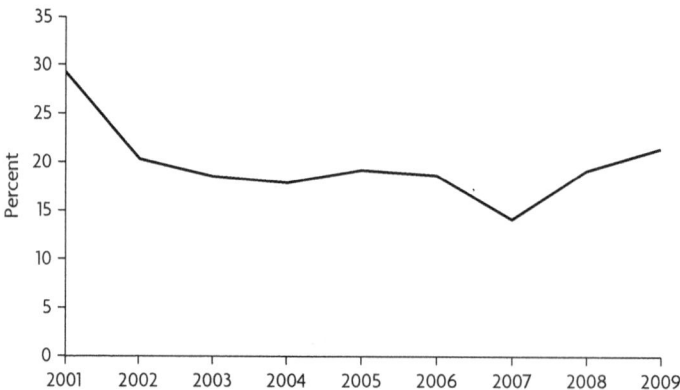

Source: West African Monetary Institute (WAMI), ECOWAS, WAEMU convergence criteria, 2001–09.

Resilience

The integration of local technical assistants (LTAs) into the permanent staff and improving the remuneration and skills of civil servants remain major problems. But the resilience of MoFED is evidenced in the fact that the ministry continued to function even when the government was ousted in 1998 during the attacks on Freetown. The ministry has been able to withstand several changes in political leadership, a change in governing party, and various external shocks. More recently, the ministry has been able to endure exogenous shocks created by the food crisis and the international financial downturn (and its rippling effects for development aid) by adapting to changing circumstances.

Sociopolitical and Historical Context: State Retraction and Conflict

Starting in the late 1970s, an incremental deterioration of the economic and political landscape led to weakened state capacity. The drain of qualified civil servants resulted in a stark weakening of MoFED's functioning. The depletion of alluvial diamonds and the closure of the iron ore mine in Marampa had far-reaching effects on the economy. As indirect taxes dropped, expansionary fiscal and monetary policies were used to stimulate economic activity. The widening gap in the budget was financed

Figure 8.5. GNI per capita, 1980–2010

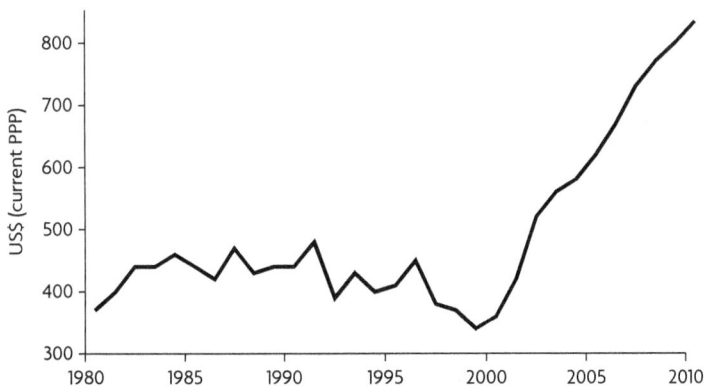

Source: World Bank Indicators, 2011.

through heavy use of short-term debt (World Bank 1979), which set the country on a downward trajectory of economic decline, as shown in figure 8.5.

Unsound economic policies and the widespread corruption and predation of the Stevens government led to a sharp decline in public revenues. Public revenues started to drop circa 1975 and a decade later they represented less than 5 percent of GDP. Figure 8.6 illustrates the negative trend in revenue mobilization that only started to revert in the late 1980s. The precipitous decline in public revenues forced the government to cut back public expenditures to 16 percent of GDP. The adjustment translated into the breakdown of public services during the 1980s and a dwindling social and economic infrastructure, which drastically reduced living standards.

The decline of salaries, amid worsening economic conditions, was the main factor behind the deterioration of the quality of the civil service (Bates 2008). As employees worked fewer hours and resorted to other activities to meet their basic needs, absenteeism was rampant and the level of corruption rose as citizens had to bribe officials to access services (Bates 2008). In the Ministry of Finance and in other central agencies, the drain of professional and technical skills heightened. The limitations of Sierra Leone's labor market at that time and later the uncertainty and instability created by the conflict motivated many qualified individuals to leave the country, resulting in a severe

Figure 8.6. Government Revenues Excluding Grants, 1975–2010

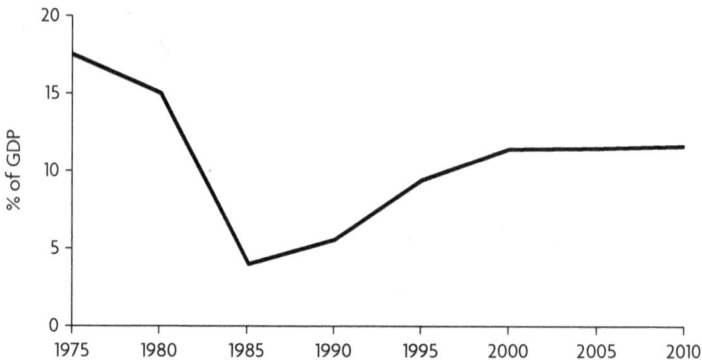

Sources: Adapted from Bates (2008) and World Bank Indicators, 2011.

weakening of the civil service across the board. The wage bill reached its lowest point in 1989, representing 6 percent of recurrent expenditures (World Bank 1993).

President Stevens had introduced a new constitution, transforming Sierra Leone into a one-party state with the All People's Congress (APC) as the sole legal party in 1978. The regime required that all civil servants be members of the party. The once meritocratic civil service became more and more politicized and several senior and experienced staff members were driven away. Given that historically Mendes have not been supporters of APC, the requirement also meant that in practice they were excluded from senior civil service positions from then on.[1]

In 1989, faced with decaying public sector institutions and acute deterioration in the delivery of basic services, the government sought external support. With the restoration of normal financial relations with the donor community, multilateral agencies provided new financing (see figure 8.7 and figure 8.8). The government agreed with the World Bank on a Salary Rationalization Program designed to adjust the real income for civil servants and improve career streams. Between April 1992 and October 1993, the World Bank approved three projects in succession to support the reform program, namely the Reconstruction Import

Figure 8.7. Net ODA as a Share of GNI in Sierra Leone, Sub-Saharan Africa, and Low-Income Countries, 1960–2010

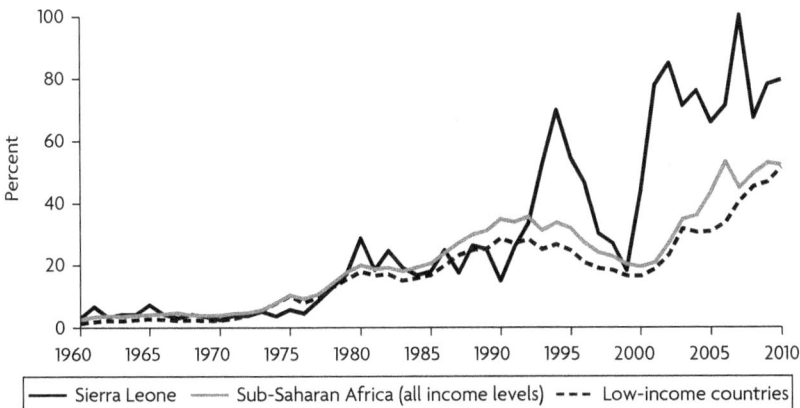

Source: World Development Indicators, 2011.

Figure 8.8. Net ODA and Net ODA per Capita in Sierra Leone, 1960–2010

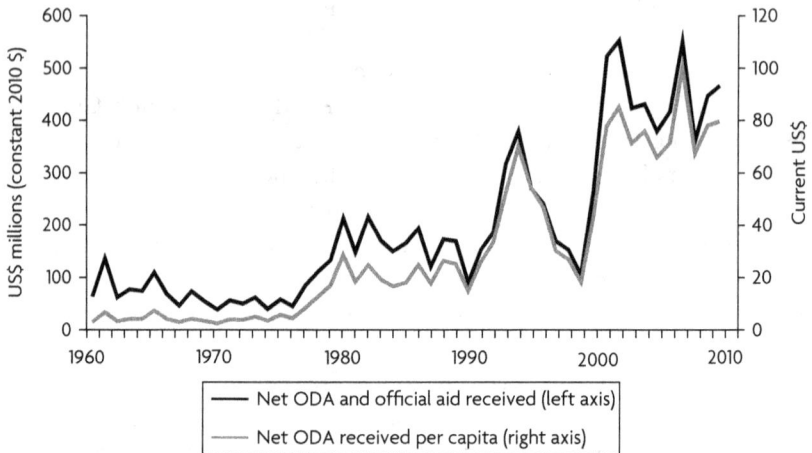

Source: World Development Indicators, 2011.
Note: ODA = official development assistance.

Credit, the Public Sector Management Support Project (PSMSP), and the Structural Adjustment Credit. The International Monetary Fund (IMF) and the African Development Bank also resumed their support and, as a result, concerted and sustained efforts to improve the performance of the Ministry of Finance were initiated.

In the following decade, the government undertook several steps to lay down the foundations of effective public expenditure management (see annexes 8A.1–8A.3). A new budgeting system was adopted in 1994, including unifying recurrent expenditures with development and capital outlays. A computerized accounting system was introduced to improve expenditure control and monitoring of the budget implementation and the allocations of social and economic sectors were improved substantially (World Bank 2002). The projects provided several offices and units with experts, local contract personnel (LTAs), equipment, and training for local staff—including Budget and Expenditure Controls, the Accountant General's Office, Economic Affairs, Procurement Office, and Aid Coordination. PSMSP also provided financing and staff for a new unit—the Economic Policy Research Unit—with the goal of improving macroeconomic analysis and forecasting to provide a stronger foundation for the budget process.[2]

The geography of the war meant that Freetown in the Western Peninsula remained relatively insulated from the attacks of the rebels and the core government functions were at relatively lower risk. This in turn made it possible for development partners to maintain their support and assistance to MoFED throughout the war years. Although there was fighting in the outskirts of the city on several occasions, the capital remained insulated from the violence for the most part.[3]

In May 1997, after the government announced a plan to rationalize the supply of rice to the military, the Armed Forces Revolutionary Council formed a junta led by Major Johnny Paul Koroma and ousted President Kabbah. Kabbah was airlifted to Conakry (Guinea), where he established and ran a parallel government in exile with most of his cabinet. After the coup, there were days of pillaging by soldiers. The Ministry of Finance was looted and torched. The ministry moved to a rented building in a nearby area and continued operating. Nine months later, in February 1998, Nigerian troops marched into Freetown, expelled the junta, and restored order; the Kabbah government was restored about a month later. Then again in January 1999, a combined Armed Forces Revolutionary Council– Revolutionary United Front onslaught seized part of Freetown but was driven out after weeks of bitter fighting. In its wake, there were 5,000 dead and the city was devastated. Fighting continued for months outside Freetown before the conflict was finally declared over in January 2002.

Throughout the conflict, the appointment of consultants and the recruitment of highly qualified nationals allowed the budget process and public expenditures to continue. Despite the setbacks in 1997 and 1999, when valuable personnel were lost and most of the equipment and systems were destroyed, reporting of government expenditure and revenues continued (World Bank 2002). A team of consultants and employees were able to reconstruct the records and databases by comparing and consolidating information sets from hard copies and printouts, backups on floppy disks, and the few laptops that escaped the destruction. It was a prolonged and tedious exercise and continued for several years after the war.

In the aftermath of the war, rapid mobilization of human resources was possible thanks to the human capacity and a diaspora with strong links to the country that provided a pool of skilled individuals who could fill positions in the ministry. Sierra Leone counts with some of the oldest and best regarded higher education institutions of West Africa. Education had been a priority after independence and while fragility and conflict had severely damaged its quality, there are still remnants. Before the war, these institutions attracted students from other former British colonies in the region and were the door for nationals to continue higher education in the foreign institutions with which the university was affiliated. Because of this, Sierra Leone counted with more professionals than other countries in the region.

External Operational Environment: Solving Governance Challenges Through Dialogue and Interagency Coordination

In a context of turbulent socioeconomic conditions and scarce domestic resources, the external operational environment in which MoFED finds itself has been largely marked by significant dependence on the support received by donors prior, during, and after the war. The ongoing and continuous assistance was critical in laying down the foundations for future reforms and increasing the credibility of the ministry to scale up programs. At the same time, large amounts of external resources channeled through the ministry were accompanied by accountability mechanisms and reporting requirements that significantly shaped interactions with other government agencies and branches and, more recently, citizens.

Donor fragmentation in the provision of technical assistance to the ministry was first addressed through informal coordination and later formalized through the use of multi-donor trust funds. The ongoing Integrated Public Financial Management Reform Program, supporting public finance reforms, is the most recent example of how donor coordination has evolved. Other instruments that have improved MoFED's capacity to maximize donor funding include the Development Assistance Coordination Office (DACO), which largely benefited from the provision of additional human resources after the 2007 restructuring, and, more recently, from the establishment of an annual Performance Assessment Framework to inform and guide budget support.

Building External Accountability and Outreach

The connections between citizens and MoFED have changed over time. External audits and anticorruption controls have slowly improved. Citizens have more direct and indirect access to fiscal information, but interactions between civil society and MoFED are still relatively limited. For example, the Government Budgeting and Accountability

Act of 2005 provides for civil society to be part of the District Budget Oversight Committees. However, these committees have not been able to exercise supervision functions effectively because of the delays with which districts share financial information. The vibrancy of the Budget Advocacy Coalition—which brings together all nongovernmental organizations working on public expenditure transparency—is certainly another positive sign. However, civil society organizations still face significant challenges in capacity and technical expertise to engage meaningfully with MoFED and in having timely access to information. Since 2011, MoFED has increased its efforts to improve communication with civil society and used its own resources to provide funding to the coalition for capacity-building activities. Nevertheless, this has been in part done to comply with the requirements of Integrated Public Financial Management Reform Program.

Recently, the Annual Public Accounts by the Accountant General and their audit have been brought up to date, after a delay of several years. A further improvement in transparency and accountability is the publication of unaudited quarterly financial statements by the Accountant General, which has become a regular practice in recent years. A review of the legal provisions on the requirements, timing, and procedures for the submission of accounts to parliament is currently in progress to make them more consistent with international best practice.

Since 1990, MoFED has been monitored by development partners through formal and informal mechanisms. The successive programs, projects, and interventions have included structural benchmarks, prior actions for effectiveness, and tranche disbursement conditions or triggers that had to be met by the government to continue receiving external support. Because of the country's heavy dependence on external assistance, development partners have been influential. It is important to note that many local technical assistants and consultants report directly or indirectly to donors.

Through the merger of the Ministry of Finance and the Ministry of Development and Economic Planning, the subsequent strengthening of the Development Assistance Coordination Office, and the issuing of an Aid Policy, the government has sought to streamline and structure its engagement and interaction with donors. Development partners have informally coordinated since the early 1990s. Yet the introduction of a single institutional structure for the management of disbursements from donor program funds has led to a greater rationalization of technical assistance and support. Regular joint meetings with development partners are held to discuss donor assistance and the achievements and challenges of various programs.

Reestablishing a Relationship with Clients and Partners

Since 2004, MoFED has developed a strategy for outreach to clients. To increase and facilitate day-to-day interactions, the ministry has deployed accountants, budget officers, and internal auditors in all the major MDAs to improve their capacity for public financial management and facilitate information exchange. MoFED's clients are unanimous that this strategy is a positive development. In the words of the permanent secretary of a client ministry: "They are no longer the desk type. They move, they come, the director [of Budget] comes, the budget officer." The clients also stressed that there have been significant improvements in the timeliness of release of funds, processing of transactions, and payments and there is a somewhat improved predictability of the budget that has enhanced their ability to plan and implement their respective programs.

Furthermore, the role of the ministry in facilitating access to donor funding and the support received during the preparation of projects has been identified as an important service. Transparency in public finance management was seen as critical to give assurance to donors and, therefore, increase access to external assistance.

Most of the clients who were consulted expressed trust in the technical capacity of the ministry. However, many stated that the Ministry has not done enough to increase domestic revenues and lamented that their agencies are not given greater priority in budgetary allocations. The acute financial constraints that line ministries face are a source of discontent. In addition, some of the MDAs continue to have to go to the Accountant General's Department to process transactions and payments either because the IFMIS has not yet been rolled out to them or because there are still technical problems in its functioning that are yet to be resolved.

On the macroeconomic side, the creation of additional coordination mechanisms has been seen by counterpart organizations as a positive development. The establishment of the Monetary Policy Committee and an ancillary technical committee in 2008 reportedly increased coordination among the key agencies of monetary policy management. The governor of the Bank of Sierra Leone chairs the Monetary Policy Committee, whose membership includes the Financial Secretary of MoFED, the Commissioner-General of the National Revenue Authority (NRA), and the Statistician General. With a similar arrangement at the technical level, the Net Domestic Financing Committee meets weekly to monitor the Treasury's short-term cash flow situation and the implied domestic borrowing requirements within the macroeconomic framework. A Macroeconomic Forecasting Working Group was established in 2008.

Coping with Isomorphic Influences

The institutional design of MoFED follows a similar model as that found in ministries of finance in the region and across the world. Development partners have played a great part in the ministry's becoming increasingly similar to those of other countries and introducing good practice models for public finance management.

By the accounts of the current and former members of staff of the ministry, the institution's structure has been transformed by various mechanisms. These align closely with the ones described by Dimaggio and Powell (1983), that is, they are coercive, mimetic, or normative isomorphic change. Isomorphism results from formal and informal pressures exerted by entities on which the organization is dependent. For example, the enactment of certain legislation, the creation of specialized units, or the strengthening of existing ones in the ministry have often been linked directly to support programs from Sierra Leone's major bilateral and multilateral budget support partners. Disbursement has often been conditioned on prior actions related to such reforms. The strengthening of the Accountant General's Department; the restructuring of the Economic Policy and Research Unit (EPRU) in the early 1990s; the creation of the Public Debt Unit, the Internal Audit Units, and the Local Government Finance Department; and more recently the merger with the Ministry of Development and Economic Planning have all at one time or the another been included as conditions for various programs.

In addition, many of the changes were the result of supply-driven initiatives by development partners that specialize in certain areas. By imitating others that appear to be successful, the organization has sought to reduce uncertainty and signal credibility to external and domestic actors. One illustration of this is the establishment of a separate Public Debt Management Unit that was largely the result of the Commonwealth Secretariat and African Development Bank program. This division later received support from the Commonwealth Secretariat to improve the recording of debt and coordination with the Bank of Sierra Leone with the introduction of a Debt Recording and Management System in the 1990s. MoFED's internal organization and functions were taken from other countries.

At the same time, personnel rotation; secondments to other institutions, including international financial institutions; and training have contributed to the diffusion of professional norms and beliefs about what the proper structures for a central finance agency are. All these elements have contributed to increase isomorphic pressures.

Internal Institutional Workings: Focusing on Efficiency and Balancing Short-Term Needs with Sustained Development

The ministry has undergone several structural changes since the end of the war, which are summarized in table 8.2. The most recent change is the merger with the Ministry of Development and Economic Planning. The merger is

Table 8.2. Milestones of MoFED

Year	Sociopolitical context	External operating environment	Internal institutional workings
1989	Reestablishment of diplomatic relations		
1990		World Bank–financed Salary Rationalization Program	
1991	Revolutionary United Front began a campaign against the government and civil war New constitution adopting multiparty system		
1992	President Joseph Momoh ousted in military coup led by Captain Valentine Strasser	World Bank–financed Public Sector Management Support Project (PSMSP I)	Introduction of LTAs
1993	ECOMOG established	World Bank–financed Structural Adjustment Credit	
1994			Establishment of Economic Policy Research Unit Computerized accounting system introduced
1996	Strasser ousted in military coup Kabbah elected president		

(continued next page)

Table 8.2. Milestones of MoFED (*continued*)

Year	Sociopolitical context	External operating environment	Internal institutional workings
1997	President Kabbah deposed by army The Commonwealth suspends Sierra Leone and United Nations Security Council imposes sanctions		
1998	Nigerian-led ECOMOG drives rebels from Freetown and restores Kabbah as president	European Union–financed institutional strengthening of the Ministry of Finance	Valuable personnel lost and equipment and systems destroyed
1999	Rebels seize part of Freetown, leaving vast destruction Lome peace agreement ECOMOG fights rebels in the outskirts of Freetown		
2000	Disarmament of rebels begins; army regains control of rebel-held areas		Reconstruction of Treasury Building
2002	Kabbah is reelected and Sierra Leone Peoples Party wins majority in Parliament	World Bank–financed Public Sector Management Support Project (PSMS II) National Revenue Authority Act	Adoption and development of MTEF Reorganization of Central Statistics Office Establishment of National Revenue Authority
2004	First local elections in more than three decades	Multi-donor institutional reform and capacity building Public Procurement Act Local Government Act Audit Service Act	IFMIS implementation begins Preparation of fiscal decentralization
2005	United Nations assistance mission established 90% of the country's $1.6 billion debt written off	Government Budgeting and Accountability Act	Statistics of Sierra Leone, National Authorizing Office, and National Public Procurement Authority established
2006			
2007	Ernest Bai Koroma wins the presidency and All People's Congress wins a majority in Parliament		Debt management unit established Financial management regulations issued
2008	Local elections		Aid policy issued
2009			Merger of planning and finance ministries Integration of DACO, public financial management reform and local government finance department

Sources: Authors' compilation based on World Bank (2002, 2009), Tavakoli (2010), and interviews with MoFED.
Note: ECOMOG = Economic Community of West African States Monitoring Group, LTA = local technical assistant, MTEF = Medium Term Expenditure Framework, DACO = Development Assistance Coordination Office.

the third attempt at bringing the finance and economic planning functions of the public sector together.[4] Whereas structurally the lines of demarcation among the constituent components of the two entities remained unaltered in all three cases, which in turn made it easier to break the two wings, this was the first time that both institutions have been placed under the same roof. An exception is the Development Assistance Coordination Office, which has been unified. A number of challenges remain to integrate planning and finance functions effectively. Since 2007, the ministry has considerably enhanced its presence in the line ministries through the deployment of budget officers, procurement officers, and internal audit personnel, in addition to the traditional presence of the Accountant General's Department staff in all MDAs.

Currently, the ministry has 13 departments, divisions, and units.[5] There are several semi-autonomous agencies, including the National Revenue Administration, the National Public Procurement Authority, Statistics of Sierra Leone, and the National Authorizing Office. The large number of departments and units is the result of the merger and isomorphism. Similarly, the introduction of semi-autonomous agencies has been driven by donor advice and the adoption of best practice models.

The reforms have been the result of bottom-up and top-down changes. On the one hand, some units emerged from the creation of groups that specialized in one function and were later formalized as a separate division. On the other hand, new units were created as a result of provisions in different pieces of legislation.

Benefitting from Continuity in Leadership

Over the years, a critical mass of technical staff stayed in MoFED (or returned to it after significant professional experience abroad). This continuity in human resources not only contributed to preserve institutional memory, but also increased the institutional capacity and, therefore, the credibility of commitments with external partners. Moreover, this factor implied that a strong and effective leadership emerged from the institution itself (more precisely, within the LTA cadre introduced in the ministry). The cases of the former Minister of Finance (former Financial Secretary until his appointment to the IMF) and the current Financial Secretary are only the better-known ones.

Among the staff, there is a strong sense of identity with the ministry and its mission. This sentiment is shared by individuals who used to work at the ministry and are now in other line agencies occupying positions of responsibility, such as permanent secretary. The esprit de corps appears to be stronger among LTAs that share similar professional training and career paths. Thus far, LTAs have had strong incentive to support reform and innovations. Although the sense of belonging and commitment is strong, there are still tensions created by the dual pay system for civil servants and LTAs and in some of the units that formerly belonged to the Ministry of Planning and Economic Development. The latter institution benefitted from capacity-building support but mainly through short-term training and had relied almost exclusively on civil servants, short-term (mostly external) consultants, and one or two longer-term external consultants to carry out its functions.[6] As a result, there is a visible disparity in capacity and in the number of LTAs working in the finance and planning branches of MoFED, which often creates a sense of neglect among the staff of units that have received less additional support.

Using Short-Term Solutions and Parallel Systems to Bridge Capacity Gaps

The role of the ministry as the main government counterpart of development partners meant that it became the pilot for many public sector management reform programs. This created additional space for the institution to design and implement reforms and insulated it to some extent from the prevailing practices or problems of the public sector. Since the mid-1990s, the ministry has strived to improve its information systems on a number of fronts, including macroeconomic modeling; debt recording; and monitoring, budgeting, accounting, and cash management. The early support of the IMF and the World Bank focused on improving the ministry's systems to collect data on national accounts statistics and perform macroeconomic and revenue forecasting. More recently, the ministry has taken steps to integrate information systems and give access to other institutions, such as the Central Bank. Through the rollout of the IFMIS project, the timeliness and accuracy of financial information has improved considerably.

The ministry has introduced several strategies to improve internal communication, including a newsletter for staff. Several divisions issue regular bulletins and other materials. Formal communication has been improved through the simplification and automation of processes. At the same time, the small size of the units makes informal communication easier. Larger departments, such as the Accountant General's Department, have regular town hall meetings, including personnel deployed in line ministries.

The head of the Budget Bureau also holds frequent meetings with the de-concentrated personnel.

One distinctive characteristic of the MoFED is that it has a relatively high number of contract personnel, known as LTAs, in line management positions. The contract staff, representing 39 percent of all staff, provides the bulk of the institution's skilled workforce. The ministry's workforce comprises 49 employees in grades 1–6, 26 in grades 7–13, and 34 LTAs (six of which were formerly contracted by the Department for International Development, DfID) (see figure 8.9). In addition, the Accountant General's Department has 319 staff and nine LTAs, of which the majority are chartered accountants.

The financing of external consultants and local technical assistants by development partners allowed MoFED to recruit and retain critical personnel during the precipitous deterioration of its once-capable civil service. The core elements of the current model and human resource management practices can be traced back to the early 1990s with the second World Bank Public Sector Management Project. Having these personnel in place gave assurance to donors that the ministry was able to absorb funding and put in place the basis for future reforms. In doing so, it ensured the continuity in the flows of external assistance to the government in critical times. The experience of other post-conflict countries that followed a different path might indeed suggest that this model provided an important asset for institutional performance.

Figure 8.9. Staff by Grades and Contractors of the Ministry of Finance and Economic Development

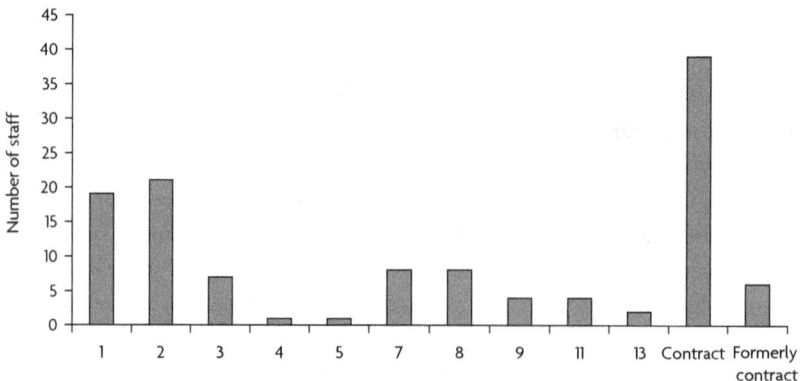

Source: Authors' update based on GHK 2008.

During the 1970s and 1980s, the largest loss was in technical grades 6–10. Rather than trying to address this issue systematically, successive governments and donors tended to adopt ad hoc measures in response to the immediate needs and pressures to enable the ministry to perform its core functions. Sierra Leonean diaspora and skilled personnel available outside the country were attracted to work in the civil service through more competitive donor-supported salaries. Table 8.3 shows that six of the departments and divisions are headed by contracted personnel. Presently, LTAs outnumber professional civil servants. LTAs are on average younger than civil servants in grades 11–13 and are more qualified. Almost all LTAs have a bachelor's degree, a third of contract staff has professional qualifications, and half has postgraduate qualifications (GHK 2008). Moreover, there are considerable disparities in the monthly remuneration between the professional grades in the civil service (US$119 to US$1,391) and contract personnel (US$ 1,744 to US$2,500).

MoFED has resorted to the use of LTA positions as a way of attracting qualified professionals. The ministry faces high competition from the private sector for accountants and economists, especially from the expanding banking sector and the semi-autonomous agencies that offer more competitive salaries. However, the ministry attracts individuals for its access to training, better working hours, exposure to international networking, and professional exchange opportunities. The ministry also offers status and social recognition to its employees. Civil servants seek

Table 8.3. Distribution of Local Technical Assistants in the Ministry of Finance and Economic Development

LTA	AGD	BD	EPRU	IAU	PDU	PFMRU	RT	PIU	Total
Director	0	1	1	1	1	1	0	2	7
Deputy Director	0	0	1	0	0	0	0	0	1
Principal	1	0	1	0	0	0	0	0	2
Senior	0	0	1	0	0	0	0	0	1
Accountants/economists/IT	5	3	3	2	3	7	1	1	25
Technician/assistant accountant	3	0	0	0	0	2	0	0	5
Office assistant	0	0	0	0	0	2	0	2	4
Total	9	4	7	3	4	12	1	5	45

Source: Authors' update based on GHK (2008).
Note: AGD = Accountant General's Department, BD = Budget Department, EPRU = Economic Policy and Research Unit, IAU = Internal Audit Unit, LTA = local technical assistant, PDU = Public Debt Unit, PFMRU = Public Finance Management Reform Unit, RT = Revenue and Tax Policy Unit, PIU = Project Implementation Unit, IT = Information Technology.

to join MoFED and have access to senior positions in other agencies after having gained some experience in the sector.

Being largely funded by donor projects, LTA staff has been subjected to external accountability mechanisms to monitor their performance. For example, LTA staff has to provide monthly progress reports to the relevant project implementation unit (PIU). These accountability mechanisms— relatively strong, especially if compared with endemically weak country performance appraisal systems—might have contributed to the enhanced capacity of MoFED to achieve measurable and gradually improving results toward its core mandate.

The Public Financial Management Reform Unit (PFMRU) has been tasked with coordinating the implementation of institutional and business process reforms in public financial management, including the management and coordination of the Integrated Public Financial Management Reform Program. PFMRU supports reforms in the line ministries and the local councils in the areas of public financial management, which has gone a long way in addressing administrative barriers in the relationship between the ministry and its clients. PFMRU was created in 2004 under the Institutional Reform and Capacity Building Project and was housed with the rest of the project-supported departments (including the Local Government Finance Department) outside of the Ministry of Finance. PFMRU and the Local Government Finance Department have been integrated and moved into the ministry.

In 2010, a quality assurance assessment mechanism was introduced by the Internal Audit Unit. Although this reporting instrument is still in its infancy, its introduction is noteworthy as it has the potential to enforce better monitoring practices within the ministry and provide the foundation for a broader—and still missing—performance assessment process at the unit and ideally the staff level.

Challenges

Since 2009, MoFED has covered the cost of LTAs that were previously financed through projects or direct support from donors. Currently, LTAs account for 85 percent of the ministry's wage bill if the accountant general's department is excluded. This raises questions about the affordability of increasing civil servant wages or expanding the number of LTAs. Although

MoFED's personnel costs amount to less than a percentage point of the total public service wage bill, the absorption of LTAs may set a precedent for other ministries with a large number of contract staff and have unintended consequences for fiscal discipline.

The use of LTAs has been effective in rapidly bringing in skills and experience. LTAs were recruited into different units within MoFED by DfID, the European Union, the African Development Bank, and the World Bank as a short-term solution to address capacity gaps. However, the parallel system has created tensions and has been highly divisive within the staff in an otherwise cohesive culture. Civil servants deplore not only the remuneration gap, but also lesser access to long-term training opportunities and therefore fewer prospects for career advancement. As a result, civil servants are reluctant to contribute in the work and collaborate with LTAs. On the other hand, contract staff has no tenure and have more and more frequent reporting requirements than civil servants.

There have been demonstration effects from the better performing departments to the rest of the ministry. Many old and new units adopted a model centered on the use of LTAs and greater mechanisms to assess performance and recompense personnel. These demonstration effects were stronger in the finance wing. Indeed, finance seems to have benefited from this model much more than the development and planning side, which has been somehow marginalized—according to the staff working in it—or less capable to capture the opportunities when they arose—according to other external observers and colleagues from the finance units.

Despite the merger, a stark difference seems to persist in the level of institutional performance between the financial and planning wings, with the latter clearly lagging behind. It is not clear to what extent this situation is the result of less human capital available in key planning units or rather a consequence of a deliberate choice by the political leadership to prioritize the key objective of macroeconomic stability. Preliminary evidence indicates that turnover rates are higher in the planning units than in the finance units, perhaps suggesting lower retention capacity and relatively less attractive working conditions. The case of the central planning unit, with an average of 10 percent turnover over the past four years, is an interesting example.

The ministry is considering several transitional arrangements to integrate LTAs as permanent staff. There are some additional challenges. Donors have employed LTAs, and their remuneration and benefit packages have varied depending on the development partner that funded them and the timing of the recruitment. In addition, there is a need to consider the reintegration within the grade and pay revisions that the government is undertaking.

Conclusion and Operational Insights

MoFED's institutional development is the result of a mix of short-term and long-term interventions and technical assistance. Although many challenges remain related to the integration of the contract personnel and civil servants, improving procurement practices, and external oversight, the short-term measures allowed Sierra Leone to put in place the minimum components necessary for effective public finance management. At the same time, it ensured the continuation of core functions during the conflict and in the immediate aftermath. Long-term engagement on areas such as budgeting, cash management, fiscal reporting and accounting, and automation of processes has built on those foundations and relied on the human capital and the partnerships created by earlier interventions.

Moving forward, it is important to highlight and consider the elements of the LTA model that should be transferred to a new human resource management system. These include competitive recruitment, competitive remuneration, built-in accountability and reporting systems, and opportunities for training and continuing learning. Providing incentives for performance needs to be accompanied by adequate compensation and systems that continue to attract technically capable staff. Moreover, existing staff must be equipped to respond to new incentives and opportunities.

Increasing donor coordination and reducing reporting mechanisms appears to be another important element from this case. The use of budget support appears to have been effective in further fostering change and providing a clear framework for accountability that allows the ministry to transmit the requirements to other key stakeholders.

Relevant Legislation and Official Documents

Aid Policy, 2008
An Agenda for Change, Second Poverty Reduction Strategy (PRSP-II), 2008-2012
Budget Call Circular, 2011

Budget Speech, 2011

Financial Management Regulations, 1998, 2007

Government Development Grants Program, Revised Operations Manual, August 2006

Local Government Act, 2004

National Revenue Authority Act, 2003

Public Procurement Act, 2004

The Government Budgeting and Accountability Act, 2005

MoFED. Organisational Framework for Effective Functioning of the New Ministry of Finance and Economic Development

MoFED. 2010. Explanatory Notes on the New Organogram

Annex 8A

Figure 8A.1. Organogram of the Ministry of Finance and Economic Development

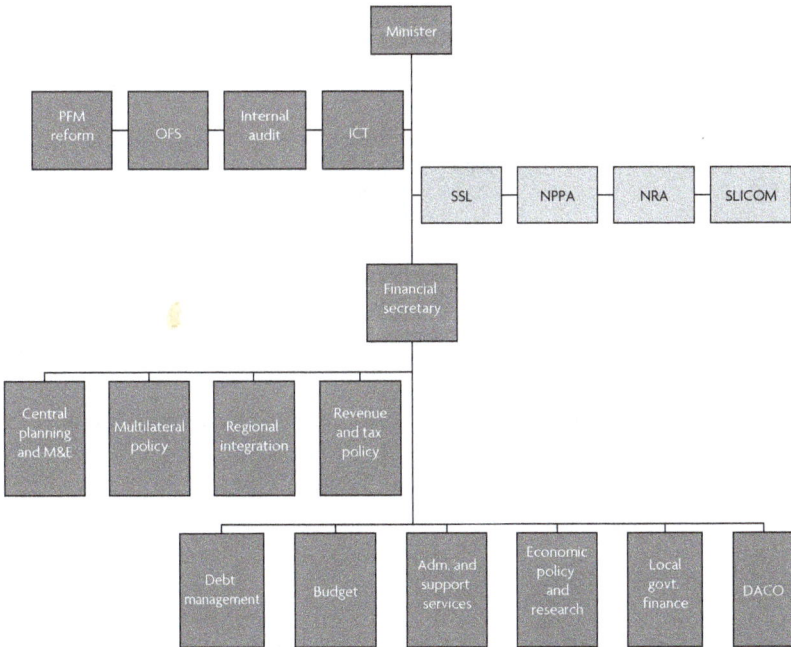

Source: MoFED 2011.
Note: The gray boxes are semi-autonomous agencies. OFS = Office of the Finance Secretary, ICT = Information and Communication Technology, SSL = Statistics of Sierra Leone, NPPA = National Public Procurement Authority, NRA = National Revenue Authority, PFM = Public Financial Management; SLICOM = Sierra Leone Insurance Commission, M&E = Monitoring and Evaluation, DACO = Development Assistance Coordination Office.

Table 8A.2. Development Partner Support to Public Finance Management

Donor	Projects supporting public finance management
African Development Bank	Technical assistance to Accountant General Technical assistance to the Audit Service Technical assistance on Public Financial Management and the Public Debt Management Unit
Commonwealth Secretariat	Technical assistance to the Public Debt Management Unit
International Monetary Fund	Technical assistance Balance of Payment Support under the PRGF Debt Relief
Department for International Development	Support to the Auditor General Technical Assistance to the National Commission for Privatization Technical assistance on records management Technical assistance to Anti-Corruption Commission Technical assistance in the implementation of the National Action Plan and PFM aspects of budget support Support to the National Revenue Authority
World Bank	Public Investment Program 1992/93–1994/9 Reconstruction Import Credit 1992 Public Sector Management Project I and II 1993–2004 Structural Adjustment Credit 1993–1999 Institutional Reform and Capacity Building Project 2004–2011 (supported public financial management reforms, Integrated Financial Management Information System introduction and rollout, and fiscal decentralization)
European Union	Technical assistance to the Accountant General's Department Technical assistance to the Ministry of Finance
Multi-Donor Trust Funds, World Bank, Department for International Development, European Union	Institutional Reform and Capacity Building Project 2004–2011 Budget support
World Bank, Department for International Development, European Union, African Development Bank	Integrated Public Financial Management Reform Program 2009–2013
United Nations Development Programme	Technical assistance to Aid Coordinating Technical assistance to Planning

Table 8A.3. PEFA Scores, 2007 and 2010

Indicator dimension	2007	2010
A. PFM OUT-TURNS: Credibility of the budget		
PI-1 Aggregate expenditure out-turn compared with original approved budget	B	B
PI-2 Composition of expenditure out-turn compared with original approved budget	C	C
PI-3 Aggregate revenue out-turn compared with original approved budget	B	C
PI-4 Stock and monitoring of expenditure payment arrears	0	D+
B. KEY CROSS-CUTTING ISSUES: Comprehensiveness and Transparency		
PI-5 Classification of the budget	A	C
PI-6 Comprehensiveness of information included in budget documentation	C	A
PI-7 Extent of unreported government operations	0	0
PI-8 Transparency of intergovernmental fiscal relations	B	A
PI-9 Oversight of aggregate fiscal risk from other public sector entities	C	C+
PI-10 Public access to key fiscal information	B	B
C. BUDGET CYCLE		
C(i) Policy-Based Budgeting		
PI-11 Orderliness and participation in the annual budget process	C+	D+
PI-12 Multiyear perspective in fiscal planning, expenditure policy, and budgeting	D+	C
C(ii) Predictability and Control in Budget Execution		
PI-13 Transparency of taxpayer obligations and liabilities	C+	B
PI-14 Effectiveness of measures for taxpayer registration and tax assessment	C	B
PI-15 Effectiveness in collection of tax payments	D+	D+
PI-16 Predictability in the availability of funds for commitment of expenditures	C+	C+
PI-17 Recording and management of cash balances, debt, and guarantees	C+	C+↑
PI-18 Effectiveness of payroll controls	D+	D+
PI-19 Competition, value for money, and controls in procurement	C	C+
PI-20 Effectiveness of internal controls for nonsalary expenditure	C+	C+
PI-21 Effectiveness of internal audit	D+	D+↑
C(iii) Accounting, Recording, and Reporting		
PI-22 Timeliness and regularity of accounts reconciliation	C	B
PI-23 Availability of information on resources received by service delivery units	A	A
PI-24 Quality and timeliness of in-year budget reports	C+	B+
PI-25 Quality and timeliness of annual financial statements	D+	C+
C(iv) External Scrutiny and Audit		
PI-26 Scope, nature, and follow-up of external audit	D+	C
PI-27 Legislative scrutiny of the annual budget law	C+	C+
PI-28 Legislative scrutiny of external audit reports	D+	D+↑
D. DONOR PRACTICES		
D-1 Predictability of direct budget support	C+	D
D-2 Financial information provided by donors for budgeting and reporting on project and program aid	D+	D+
D-3 Proportion of aid that is managed by use of national procedures	D	D

Source: PEFA Secretariat, 2010.
Note: 0 = no score.

Notes

1. Section (4) of the 1978 Constitution enumerated the offices for which All People's Congress membership was a prerequisite as being: (a) principal representatives of Sierra Leone abroad, (b) the Commissioner of Police, (c) the commanders of the armed forces, (d) permanent secretaries, (e) the secretaries to the president and the vice president, (f) the secretary to the Cabinet, (g) the Financial Secretary, (h) the secretary to the Foreign Minister, (i) the Establishment Secretary (who is the personnel manager of the government), (j) the Development Secretary, (k) the Director of Public Prosecutions, (l) the Solicitor-General, and (m) the Administrator and Registrar-General.
2. External funding has continued to increase, and in 2009 budget support constituted a third of recurrent expenditures (IMF 2010). In 2010, Sierra Leone received the second largest allocation of official development assistance as a share of GDP in Sub-Saharan Africa (World Bank Indicators, 2011).
3. Liberia offers a relevant comparison. Monrovia was relatively more vulnerable to attack and became the main battleground for most of the war years. Unlike MoFED, the Ministry of Finance of Liberia had to start from almost zero in 2005/2006, relying mostly on the use of international consultants in early post-conflict program implementation.
4. The two attempts took place from 1992 to 1993 and from 1998 to 1999. Under the military junta, the National Provisional Ruling Council created the one-year Department of Finance, Development and Economic Planning on takeover in April 1992. Later, in March 1998, President Kabbah attempted to integrate the two entities. That lasted about 15 months and broke up again in late 1999.
5. These are Administration, Economic Policy and Research, Information and Communications Technology, Accountant General, Central Planning Monitoring and Evaluation, Development Assistance Coordinating, Regional Integration and South-South Cooperation, Budget Bureau, Debt Management, Revenue and Tax Policy, Public Financial Management Reform, the Local Government Finance Department, and Internal Audit.
6. These were the chief technical advisers fielded by the United Nations system at the Central Statistics Office between 1989 and 1992; around the same time, until 1994, there was a chief technical adviser in the Ministry of Development and Economic Planning. Some argued that the counterpart arrangement had limited impact on sustainability and transfer of knowledge. However, several civil servants were trained during that period, including at least four statisticians and two development planning officers. The problem was retaining them; at least two are currently employed in the United Nations system while three are in the United Kingdom and the United States.

References

Bates, Robert. 2008. *When Things Fell Apart; State Failure in Late-Century Africa.* New York: Cambridge University Press.

Brumby, James A., Gibril Sesay, Vanya Pasheva, Nicholas Howard, and Murray Petrie. 2010. "Strengthening Central Finance Functions in Sierra Leone." Unpublished manuscript. World Bank, Washington, DC.

DiMaggio, Paul J. and Walter W. Powell. 1983. "The Iron Cage Revisited: Institutional Isomorphism and Collective Rationality in Organizational Fields." *American Sociological Review* 48(2): 147–60.

GHK. 2008. Design of an exit strategy and arrangements for transitional DP support for remuneration of contract PFM staff. GHK, Freetown.

International Monetary Fund. 2010. "Sierra Leone: Article IV Consultation and First Review Under the Three-Year Arrangement Under the Extended Credit Facility, Request for Modification of Performance Criterion, and Financing Assurances Review." International Monetary Fund, Washington, DC.

Ministry of Finance and Economic Development. 2011. "Public Financial Management Report Update."

Tavakoli, Heidi. 2010. "Public Financial Management Reforms in Fragile and Conflict-Affected States: Providing Operational Guidance for Development Practitioners; Sierra Leone Case Study." Unpublished manuscript. World Bank, Washington, DC.

World Bank. 1979. "Sierra Leone Country Economic Memorandum." Report No. 2153-SL. Western Africa Programs Department I, World Bank, Washington, DC.

———. 1993. "Sierra Leone Country: Policies for Sustained Economic Growth." Report No. 11371-SL. Western Africa Department, Africa Region, World Bank, Washington, DC.

———. 2002. "Implementation Completion Report of the Second Public Sector Management Support Project." Credit 2546-SL. World Bank, Washington, DC.

———. 2009. "Republic of Sierra Leone: PFM Performance Assessment Report." World Bank, Washington, DC.

———. 2009. "Societal Dynamics of Fragility: Improving the World Bank Response to Fragile Situations." Concept note for the Social Development Network Flagship Report. World Bank, Washington, DC.

———. 2011. *World Development Report 2011: Conflict, Security, and Development.* Washington, DC: World Bank.

CHAPTER 9

Sierra Leone Case Study: Local Councils

Marco Larizza and Brendan Glynn

This chapter analyzes the second case study of successful institutions in Sierra Leone: the local councils. This case has been identified on the basis of early consultations and interviews with the Sierra Leone country manager and selected members of the Sierra Leone country team. The ultimate objective of the chapter is to provide context-specific narratives of the paths to institutional development while articulating a compelling investigation and rigorous empirical test of the underlying research hypotheses of the Institutions Taking Root Project. Set against these hypotheses, the case of Sierra Leone is notable and instructive.

Although it was ambitious in its expectations, the reestablishment of local councils had no guaranteed prospects of success. On the one hand, overt and covert opposition could be anticipated from an array of self-interested parties concerned about their potential loss of control of resources. On the other hand, the fragility of the postconflict institutional architecture created additional challenges. First, in 2002, the presence of the state outside Freetown peninsula had collapsed and had to be rebuilt from scratch. Second, the dearth of human capital at the national and local levels was a massive impediment for any large-scale interventions aiming to restore local governance. Third, the institutional and collective memory of the local government system in the country was buried under more than 30 years of hypercentralized rule, further undermining local capacity to implement decentralization reform.

Despite these countervailing forces, the new disposition for local government has taken on a momentum and maturity, cementing its institutional presence in the architecture of the state. The institution of local councils has become embedded in the sociopolitical structure. As reflected in three peaceful rounds of local elections (2004, 2008, and 2012), in the eyes of the population, there is a sense of growing legitimacy of the elected structures and avenues for the expression of development priorities. A frequently expressed view across the focus group discussions was that on matters related to community development, the population automatically refers to the council and places its expectations in it.

Success has been determined within a particular configuration of situational factors. Opportunities that were presented were acted on purposefully but not necessarily with consistent regard to the longer-term strategy. Progress has often been fitful and threats abide, not least in the vagaries of party politics and the broader political sphere.

The chapter is organized as follows: it describes the research design, data sources, and sampling strategy of the study. It then describes the institutional context in Sierra Leone, with a special focus on the contextual factors that bear relevance for the institution-building process of the local councils (including the history of local government). The degree of success is considered across three key dimensions: results, legitimacy, and durability. The chapter then highlights the key factors driving the success and how the process was managed, and it outlines critical, pending challenges. The chapter concludes by considering possible policy implications and key lessons that can be drawn from the Sierra Leone experience for future efforts to support institution-building processes in postconflict and fragile states.

Research Design: Data, Sources, and Sampling Strategy

The subject case study of the chapter represents an effort to document and assess empirically the degree of institutional success achieved by the institution of local councils. The case study takes advantage of a rich set of background studies carried out by researchers and development practitioners in Sierra Leone. These secondary sources are complemented with intensive fieldwork and interviews carried out in the country between June 13 and July 4, 2011.

Semistructured focus group discussions were undertaken in a sample of four local councils (Port Loko District, Bo Town, Bo District, and Kono District). To identify the sample group (from 19 local councils), the team followed a two-stage approach. First, a few situational dimensions were

Table 9.1. Overachiever Local Councils and Their Classification against Contextual Dimension

Local council	Location	Party affiliation	Province	Ethnicity
Port Loko District Council	Rural	APC dominant	Northern	Temne/Limba
Kono District Council	Rural	APC dominant	Eastern	Kono
Bo Town Council	Urban	SLPP dominant	Southern	Mende
Bo District Council	Rural	SLPP dominant	Southern	Mende

Source: Glynn, Larizza, and Viñuela (2011).
Note: APC = All People's Congress; SLPP = Sierra Leone Peoples Party.

taken into consideration. The issue of geographical spread in the Sierra Leonean context is especially important as ethnicity strongly accords (outside the capital) with specific locational zones. In turn, this correlates with dominant political party allegiance, with the exception of a few notable areas, such as the capital city, Freetown. A provincial distribution accordingly provided an appropriate ethnic and party preference representation. In addition, urban and district councils were included in the sample. This approach was considered critical to maximize within-country variation and enhance the analytical leverage.

Second, the criterion of success (durability, results, and legitimacy) was applied by reference to the data available from the National Public Service Survey (NPS, 2005–2008) and combined with the results of the Comprehensive Local Government Performance Assessment System reports (Dec-Sec 2006, 2010, 2012). Although the dimension of durability could not be used as a selection criterion (all the local councils were established at the same time), combined used of NPS and Comprehensive Local Government Performance Assessment System (CLoGPAS) data allowed the team to capture the councils that have been overachievers (i.e., ranked above the median) in capacity to deliver results and legitimacy before the ordinary citizens. Overlaying the success measures on the earlier criteria produced the selection shown in table 9.1.

History and Development of Local Government in Sierra Leone

Local government has been an integral part of governance in Sierra Leone since the colonial era. Under colonial rule, the British authorities established a strong political and administrative divide between the colony (Freetown and the Western Area) and the protectorate (represented by the three modern provinces). The colony was ruled directly by a locally elected council and governor representing the British monarch. The protectorate was designed as a sphere of "indirect rule" in which district commissioners were responsible for the administration of the districts in close collaboration with traditional authorities (paramount chiefs and their networks of subchiefs and chiefdom functionaries).[1]

The symbiotic relationship between the Sierra Leone Peoples Party (SLPP) and the chiefs is crucial to understand why the traditional authorities survived the colonial period (Chaves and Robinson 2011, 5). At independence (1961), SLPP quickly put in place a political strategy deeply rooted in colonial institutions. On the one hand, the modern administrative arrangements established by the British were strengthened by assigning additional tasks to district councils,[2] including development of the respective local communities. On the other hand, the system of indirect rule remained largely intact, meaning the chieftaincy system survived. The conservation of the traditional authority structures in the postcolonial era helped to keep the formal state small and thus amenable to oligarchic control. It also enabled chiefs to accumulate considerable power as political brokers and thus served as a suppressant of mass political mobilization.

In 1972, the district councils were abolished by the president of the All People's Congress (APC), Siaka Stevens, because they were said to be highly corrupt and politicized (Tangri 1978). Their dissolution resulted in the transfer of their infrastructure and staff to the central government's provincial administration under the supervision of the provincial secretary and district officers (Zhou 2009, 29).

Although chiefs became increasingly active in the collection of revenues, basic services at the local level were undersupplied and heavily dependent on the support of international nongovernmental organizations (NGOs) and the rule of paramount chiefs was perceived as being increasingly arbitrary and predatory.[3] Combined with the overcentralization of power in the hands of a single party in Freetown, the APC, the authoritarian tendencies of the chiefs magnified popular discontent, marginalized wide sectors of the population, and provided a ready opening for youth conscription into the fighting rebel factions, eventually bringing the country to civil war (Reno 1995; Richards 1996; Hanlon 2004; Krijn 2011).

The revival of elected local government was a declared (yet unfulfilled) policy of military and civilian governments during the civil war. An early rationale was set out in the consultancy study commissioned by the National Provisional Ruling Council and led by the United Nations Development Programme (UNDP) in 1994 (Zwanikken,

Olowu, and Chiviya 1994). Later, through the enunciation of a strategy on "Good Governance and Public Sector Reform" by the new SLPP government, an agenda for decentralization by devolution was initially designed (Government of Sierra Leone 1996, 1997). However, the escalation of conflict overtook these plans, and the opportunity to implement the policy intent did not materialize until the end of the war in 2002.

The political economy of the civil war—with its deep-rooted urban-rural divide—deeply affected the collective memory of the population. The war generated large, popular demands, and pressures on the postconflict SLPP-led government to defuse social tensions by reestablishing the state presence outside the Western Peninsula. This urgency to deliver a rapid peace dividend throughout the country implied that effective state capacity would have to be built in parallel at the central and local levels.

The view of decentralization as a national priority for Sierra Leone's peace-building efforts was widely shared among the international community. Soon after the Peace Accord, the government's Poverty Reduction Strategy Paper formalized this view by defining decentralization as a key strategy for promoting good governance, consolidating peace, and reducing poverty (Government of Sierra Leone 2005, 81; 2002).

A government Task Force on Decentralisation (nominally chaired by the vice-president) coordinated expert seminars and public consultations on decentralization reforms in late 2003. The Department for International Development (DfID), UNDP, and World Bank provided consultants at this stage to facilitate discussions on a number of key policy issues that thus far had been neglected by the task force. The discussions dealt primarily with intergovernmental fiscal relations and accountability arrangements.

The consultation process led to the drafting of the Local Government Act (LGA), ratified by the parliament in February 2004. The 2004 LGA radically reshaped the administrative, functional, and fiscal intergovernmental relationships between the central government and the subnational authorities. Parallel to the reestablishment of 19 democratically elected local councils, the 2004 LGA put in place a clear sequence of decentralization reforms with a progressive devolution of powers in a four-year transition period.

The reestablishment of local councils in 2004 was combined with a sustained attempt to re-legitimize the institution of the paramount chiefs (Sawyer 2008). The national government and the donors were deeply divided on their understanding of the role that the chieftaincy should play in the postconflict local government system. On the one hand, the SLPP-led government "viewed local councils first and foremost as development agencies. It had no intention of removing the hierarchy of paramount, section and village chiefs from their role as the state's primary agents for maintaining social order in rural areas" (Fanthorpe, Lavali, and Sesay 2011, 53). On the other hand, the donors were convinced that the institution of the chieftaincy was deeply implicated in the governance failings that had led to the war, that it was undergoing a terminal crisis of popular legitimacy, and that a modern and democratic system of local government was urgently needed to ensure that chiefs were not given the opportunity to capture the decentralization process (Jackson 2007).[4]

The 2004 LGA did not fully address the relationships between the local councils and the chieftaincy system. The implicit choice was rather to postpone the resolution of these tensions, under the assumption that doing so would have enabled donors and government to bypass politically sensitive issues and focus instead on the technical modalities of the decentralization implementation process. Although this approach worked for a fast-track and technical reform program, the hybrid arrangements it generated contributed to growing tensions between the two local authorities.

External Operational Environment

Since 2004, the process of formal interactions and negotiations between the institution of local councils and its bureaucratic principal (the central government) has been marked by substantial financial dependence on the center. Given the small revenue base at the local level, the vast majority of funding for local councils comes from central government transfers, in the form of grants tied to specific sector expenditures. Transfers as a share of the central government's nonsalary, noninterest expenditures have steadily increased over time, from 4.9 percent in 2005 to 11.9 percent in 2009 (Srivastava and Larizza 2011, 144–45). Despite this progress, however, evidence from the focus group discussions suggests that transfers to local councils are still often delayed, undermining the local councils' capacity to perform their service delivery functions.[5]

Partially as a consequence of persistent funding gaps from the central government, the historical evolution of the local councils has been shaped by the constant and increasingly coordinated technical and financial support received from the international community, namely from the World Bank, European Commission, and DfID. The Institutional Reform and Capacity Building Project (IRCBP) represented the key instrument of the coordinated donor response to support decentralization and the local council institutional development and capacity-building process.

The main formal rules that define how the institution of local councils interacts with the broader socio-political environment are defined in the 2004 Local Government Act (and its statutory instruments) and, more recently, the National Decentralisation Policy (approved in 2010). These legislative and policy documents establish the mandate and functions of the local councils, defining their powers and responsibilities. The documents also define the obligations of local councils to other governmental agencies and institutions, including the Ministry of Local Government and Rural Development (MLGRD), the Ministry of Finance and Economic Development (MoFED), and the other ministries, departments, and agencies (MDAs).[6] MLGRD is the chief bureaucratic principal charged with policy, monitoring, and inspecting local councils. MoFED is responsible for the intergovernmental fiscal transfer system and the financial probity of local councils.

Another formal channel of accountability is through the parliament. As indicated in figure 9.1, the relationship between the parliament and the local councils is defined as hierarchical because Sierra Leone remains a unitary state and financing is overwhelmingly through the approval and accountability system of the center (therefore also subject to scrutiny of committees and the full parliament). The relationship with individual members of parliament, however, has been characterized by conflict and competition for access to financial resources. According to the focus group discussions, local councils have come under pressure from members of parliament for a share of the political credit for the decentralization program (Fanthorpe, Lavali, and Sesay 2011, 18).

Aside from the formal rules, other laws and informal practices persist that are inconsistent with the provision of the Local Government Acts (or duplicate them) and have not been repealed. This is especially the case of the various laws governing the chieftaincy (box 9.1). The laws and practices reflect the clouded bifurcation of powers that can suit political interests.

The chiefdom councils are required by the 2004 LGA to collect the community levies (fixed by council resolution) and to hand over a precept of 60 percent of the total to the local councils. However, in 2008 the Ministry of Local Government issued a directive stating that no local councils' precept should be collected for 2008. A subsequent directive in 2009 further interfered with the formal revenue-sharing process by imposing a variable rate of transfer between 5 percent and 20 percent. The proceeds

Figure 9.1. Key Stakeholders of Local Councils

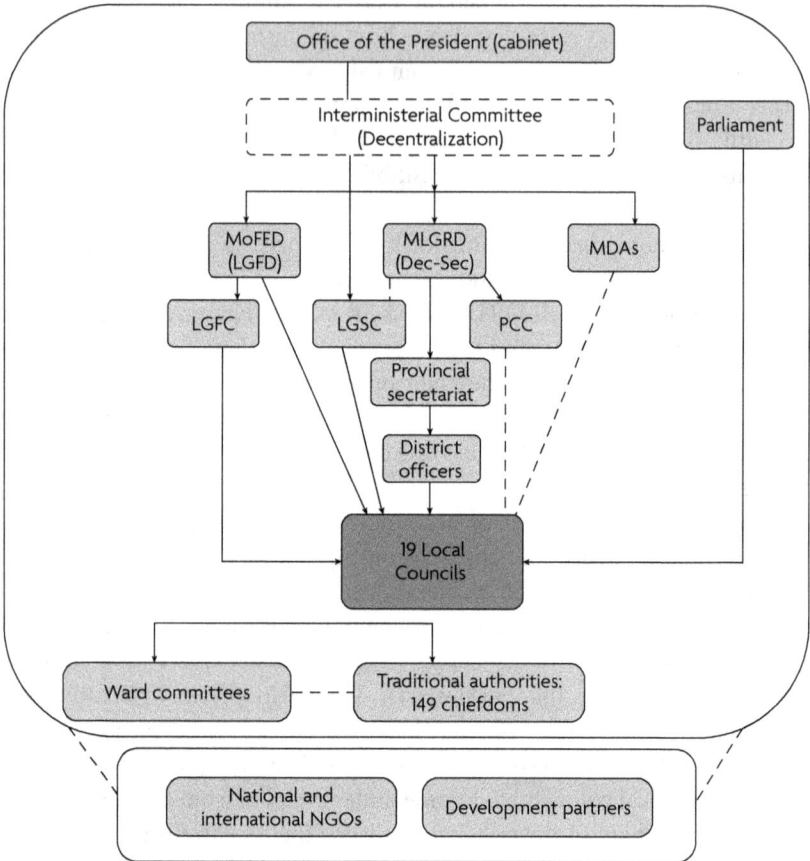

Source: MLGRD; National Decentralization Policy.
Note: The solid arrows indicate relationships legislatively defined as hierarchical; the dotted lines identify relationships between functionally interdependent agencies. Development partners and NGOs are depicted as separate entities as they are outside the government structure. MoFED = Ministry of Finance and Economic Development; LGFD = Local Government Finance Department; MLGRD = Ministry of Local Government and Rural Development; Dec-Sec = Decentralization Secretariat; MDA = ministries, departments, and agencies; LGFC = Local Government Finance Committee; LGSC = Local Government Services Commission; PCC = Provincial Coordinating Committee; NGO = nongovernmental organization.

for councils from this source have been reduced significantly as a result. This has increased tensions between the councils and the chiefdoms, which were already aggravated by the sharing of mineral licensing proceeds and the perspectives on the role of the chiefs vis-à-vis the ward and council elected structures.

BOX 9.1

Mapping the Structure of Local Traditional Authorities

Each of Sierra Leone's 149 chiefdoms is ruled by a single paramount chief who is considered the top authority in his or her chiefdom. The position of paramount chieftaincy and its associated responsibilities are established by law in a series of acts, many of them predating independence, and are enshrined in the 1991 national constitution. The roles of paramount chiefs can be delineated as follows (the last three in consultation with chiefdom committees and chairpersons of local courts): (a) uphold and maintain the traditions, customs, and practices of the chiefdom; (b) serve as the custodians of the land for the people of the chiefdom; (c) settle disputes; (d) maintain law and order; and (e) deal with land and customary and traditional matters in the chiefdom.

In practice, the chief is the primary representative of his or her chiefdom to outsiders having any dealings with the chiefdom, including NGOs and other development agents, government representatives, politicians, and mining companies and other commercial interests. Paramount chiefs also play a major role in resolving disputes. Chiefs no longer have the legal right to operate a court, but they are allowed to mediate or arbitrate and often still adjudicate, despite the legal prohibition.

Paramount chiefs are elected for life by chiefdom councilors, and candidates must come from a ruling family or ruling house. There is no formal or written list of ruling houses—the set of acceptable lineages is entirely local knowledge—and the system has never been institutionalized.

Underneath the paramount chiefs is a structure of subordinate chiefs, village chiefs, and section chiefs, all of which are automatically members of the council, along with a member of parliament who comes from the chieftaincy and other elites. The electorate is extremely elitist (Chaves and Robinson 2011). These functionaries are somewhat less formally mandated than the paramount chief, although many are recognized by legislation, and all are considered official by local community members. Some (specifically chiefdom treasury clerks and court clerks) are employed as civil servants by the central government. Others are paid a salary from the chiefdom coffers.

Town chiefs have the primary responsibility for strangers (nonresidents) who are visiting the community. Customary law dictates that strangers must report to the town chief on arrival in a community and that residents must report any strangers whom they have brought into the town. These reports generally are seen as security measures. Town chiefs sometimes are responsible for collecting tax revenue, which they pass on

(continued next page)

BOX 9.1 (continued)

to section chiefs and the chiefdom treasury clerk, often receiving a rebate equivalent to a percentage of the revenue collected.

Section chiefs, in turn, resolve cases brought to them, but they may hear larger or more important cases—or different types of cases—than their town-level colleagues. For instance, the household survey found that just 17 percent of all cases, but 28 percent of land disputes, were reported first to the section chief. For land disputes, section chiefs were the second most used authority after village chiefs. Section chiefs are usually involved in tax collection and chiefdom decision making.

Sources: Manning (2009); Chavez and Robinson (2011).

Figure 9.2. Timeline of the Decentralization Process in Sierra Leone

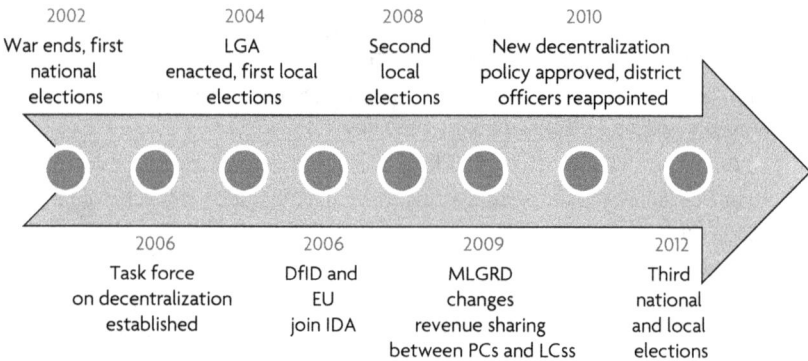

2002	2004	2008	2010
War ends, first national elections	LGA enacted, first local elections	Second local elections	New decentralization policy approved, district officers reappointed

2006	2006	2009	2012
Task force on decentralization established	DfID and EU join IDA	MLGRD changes revenue sharing between PCs and LCss	Third national and local elections

Note: LGA = Local Government Act; DfID = Department of International Development; IDA = International Development Association; MLGRD = Ministry of Local Government and Rural Development.

Figure 9.2 summarizes the major historical landmarks and the time line of key events in the external operational environment that have shaped the institutional development and evolutionary trajectory of local councils.

Internal Institutional Workings

The elected council is the corporate legal authority in its jurisdiction for the establishment of plans and budgets, the transaction of business related to the consequential activities, and the accounting requirements of higher national authorities. Council business is led by the chairperson or mayor and supported by a deputy (both post holders are remunerated). The executive power is shared with local councilors, and all major decisions are subject to the approval of the full council. Moreover, operational committees oversee specific segments of council activity (e.g., finance and administration, development, education, and health).

Ward committees represent an essential channel for upward and downward communication with local residents. However, they are hampered in particular by mobility constraints among their often-scattered communities. Nevertheless, the representation of popular views through the ward committee members, with the ward councilor as chair, to the council itself was characterized as effective. Communities would vote (through a stone game) when priorities on development were being conveyed. However, it was accepted that other political factors and influences also came into play in ultimate decision making. Where it was reported, the practice of rotating council meetings around the districts was aiding more effective communication.

More generally, the focus group discussions reported instances of outreach campaigns with the public in all four cases, with local radio being the premier method. This is consistent with the findings of the NPS surveys, according to which local radio is the greatest single source of information on the development plans of local councils, followed by family members and traditional authorities (IRCBP 2010).

The 2004 LGA established elected local councils as the highest political authorities in their localities (although the 2010 National Decentralisation Policy changed this formulation).[7] Local councils are required to operate under democratic principles, to be open about council business, prudent in financial management, and responsive to citizens' needs. Under the current framework, as defined by the LGA statutory instruments, local councils have responsibility for the delivery of primary and junior secondary education, primary and secondary health care, rural water supply, sanitation, waste management, agriculture, youth services, social assistance, and firefighting services. Central ministries and agencies retain the responsibility for strategic planning, setting of standards, quality control, and monitoring. The central government retains the responsibility for salary payments and human resource management of sector staff seconded to local councils and facility-level staff, as well as procurement of certain priority commodities, such as textbooks and drugs.

Day-to-day council affairs are managed by the chief administrator who is responsible for the necessary technical support in each support (nonsector) area. The chief administrator is currently supported in this manner by the following personnel: deputy, finance officer, accountant, procurement officer, monitoring and evaluation officer, development planner, human resources officer, engineer, and internal auditor.[8] Service delivery is organized around the sector areas related to state responsibilities at the national level.

According to the LGA, all 19 councils are required to set up sector committees to ensure direct oversight of the services as they devolve. There are also provincial coordinating committees for wards, chiefdoms, and districts, led by a central government regional minister. Typically each council area will have a director for agriculture, education, health, and so forth, with dedicated technical staff distributed in accordance with national norms (figure 9.3). Where urban councils are surrounded territorially by district councils, the sector directors provide services for each. In addition, some services are organized on a regional basis (e.g., social welfare, youth, and sports).

Intersector allocations are fixed (tied grants).[9] However, the allocations are subject to the discretionary decisions of local councils on the basis of priorities defined in the development plans. Consequently, the annual

Figure 9.3. Organogram of Local Government Structure

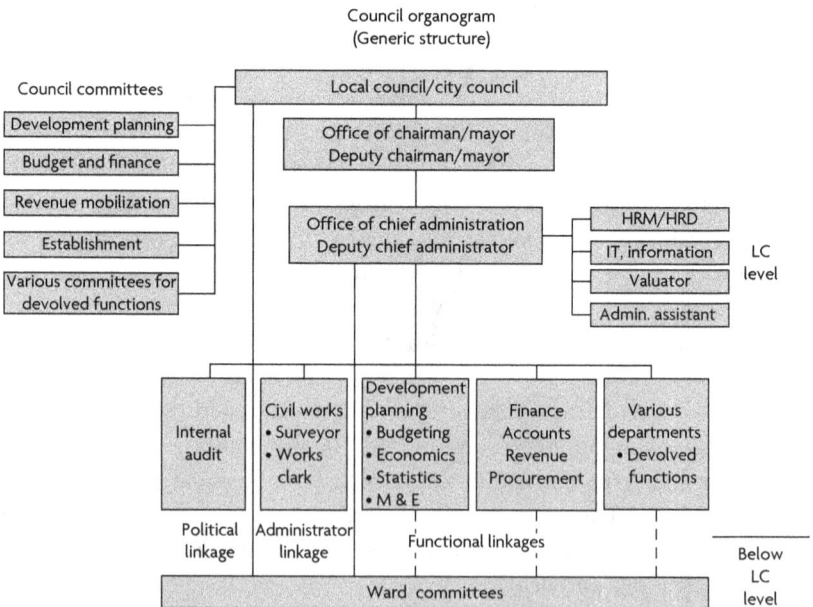

Source: MLGRD.
Note: LC = local council.

council budgeting round becomes the fulcrum for local council discussions of sector priorities. Due weight in this process is accorded to the sector inputs (which are seen as articulating national policy standards and targets), the views of the councilors (reflecting community preferences), and an accepted common view that emerges in the annual budget cycle.

Once the annual budget is approved, an integrated approach to the management of its disbursement similarly applies. Quarterly allocations arrive to the councils' designated accounts. Sectors are informed of available allocations. Public expenditure tracking survey forms are drawn up, accompanied by concept notes, and then scrutinized against internal priorities and the annual budget provisions. Individual sector activities are then funded by cash advances unless a procurement process is involved, followed by the filling of invoices. No subsequent advances are made in the absence of returns. In the event of end-of-year sector balances, however, rollovers are permitted.

Presentation of the consolidated council accounts is the responsibility of the chief administrator and the finance officer under the 2005 Financial Administration Regulations. MoFED requires adequate quarterly returns to be submitted before approval of new flows. Similarly, annual accounts are prepared, submitted, and subsequently audited. A new financial management system utilizing the same codes as the national chart of accounts was introduced in January 2009. Independent budget and finance oversight committees are in place (and legally mandated) and function with variable effectiveness.

Over time, the capacity of local councils to attract skilled staff has improved. According to some observers, the physical presence of decentralized political power (the local council) combined with the direct observation of the growing fiscal and administrative autonomy of the LGA, generated incentives for civil servants to join the local government structure, further strengthening the availability of critical human resource skills at the local level. These incentives complemented other material benefits, such as promotion opportunities and better salary levels (this was especially the case for the appointment of chief administrators).[10]

The Parameters of Institutional Success

Local councils are fully staffed with core skills in the areas of development planning, internal auditing, monitoring, and evaluation and procurement. Local councils hold regular meetings and produce minutes, participatory development planning has taken root, accounts are completed on time and regularly audited, and financial information is disclosed. Figure 9.4 shows the number of councils that met (or partially met) each of the seven minimum conditions captured by the CloGPAS assessment. Between 2006 and 2011, there were significant improvements in all core functions of the local councils, with remarkable achievements in areas such as budget and accounting and functional capacity, where all 19 local councils fully met the minimum conditions. Since 2008, a slight deterioration has been recorded for project implementation and development planning.

Over time, local councils have implemented several rounds of capacity-building activities for local staff in the areas of participatory planning, budgeting, financial management, and project management. This has helped ensure that local governments are staffed with skilled individuals who are able to manage resources in accordance with the new regulations. Significant progress has been made in laying sound foundations of public financial management systems. The latest Public Expenditure and Financial

Figure 9.4. Performance of Local Councils across Critical Functions

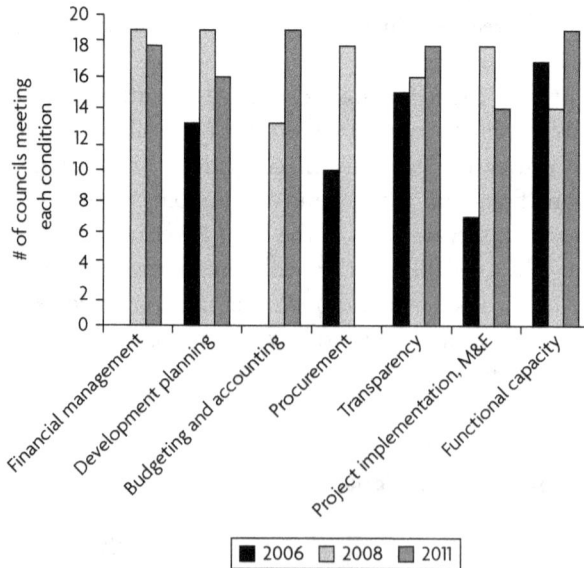

Source: Dec-Sec (2006, 2010, 2012).
Note: Data for procurement were not yet available in 2011.

Accountability (PEFA) report provides evidence consistent with this analysis, showing that in 2010 local councils received the highest scores on key dimensions of budget execution and accounting practices, scoring higher on these dimensions than the national government, as shown in table 9.2 (GoSL 2011). All 19 local councils today use a simplified Petra system that interfaces with the central government's chart of accounts and is managed through an integrated financial management information system. Other notable actions on transparency have been implemented, such as the posting on notice boards at local council offices of relevant financial information on a monthly basis.

Notable improvements were achieved in the availability of basic services between 2005 and 2008 (the period covered by available household survey data). However, the improvements were not consistent across the board, with some sectors making more progress than others. For instance, the number of rural households within 30 minutes of a primary school rose from 68 percent to 74 percent. An even larger improvement was seen in the number of rural households within one hour of a clinic, which rose from 48 percent to 61 percent. The single largest improvement was households with access to water, which increased from 61 percent to about 81 percent (an increase of about 30 percent).[11] Moreover, significant subnational variation across local councils remains (IRCBP 2010).[12] Qualitative evidence from the focus group discussions suggests that variances in LGA performance across service delivery and other critical functions are likely to be a function of organizational factors (including local leadership and availability of qualified personnel) and independent of the devolution of powers and responsibilities per se.

Finally, evidence suggests that traditionally marginalized groups, such as women and ethnic minorities, have been the largest beneficiaries of the new space for political participation guaranteed by the local councils. While in 2004 women occupied 12.7 percent of council seats, in 2008 this increased to 18 percent, a higher rate of representation relative to

Table 9.2. Performance of Local Councils across Critical Functions

Indicator	National	Subnational
Participation in the budget process	D+	C
Effectiveness of payroll controls	D+	C+
Competition and controls in procurement	C+	A
Timeliness and regularity of accounts reconciliation	B	B+
Percentage of aid managed by use of national procedures	D	A

Source: PEFA 2010.

the 12 percent share of women's seats in the national parliament (NEC 2008b). This positive trend is confirmed by the rate of participation of women candidates in local versus national elections: in the national elections in 2007, 11 percent of total candidates running for parliamentary seats were women; this percentage increased to 17 percent in the 2008 local elections (Zhou 2009).

Legitimacy

Over time, the institution of local councils—and their political leadership in particular—has acquired a growing level of influence and legitimacy in the political arena. This is, in part, the product of the increased decision making (devolved functions) and administrative power (local capacity) that the local councils have acquired over time. And in part, it is the consequence of direct accountability channels established with the local communities through three rounds of local elections. In particular, the deselection of inactive former councilors and the increased level of electoral competition from 2004 to 2008 attest to the anchoring of local representational politics. Notably, the second round of elections in 2008 attracted more candidates, which was an indication of greater interest in the local councils, and the number of uncontested wards dropped from 84 to 38 (Zhou 2009).

As a byproduct of these enhanced accountability channels and the increased capacity of local service provisions, local communities now look to the local council as the key actor in the development of their communities. This has been a consistent finding across the sample of local councils. The most frequent illustration in support of this position was the rehabilitation during the past seven years of the physical stock for service delivery (health centers and schools). During the focus group discussions, reference was also made to road improvements and the increased certification of public works by local councils, bringing quality improvement. Diversification in agriculture and support to the business approach in the sector were also cited across the sample of local councils.

A striking point was the case of Kono District Council, where its specific character as among the most heavily damaged and isolated districts during the war seems to have given rise to greater interpersonal trust, social cohesion, and community action. In other words, the fresh memory of violence and brutal devastation left by the war acted as a mobilizing force at the local level, accounting for the increased engagement of citizens in setting development priorities and promoting consensual (rather than confrontational) social attitudes. These results provide additional support to a growing body of field research that consistently shows that exposure to violence and civil war may increase citizens' willingness to engage in collective action and other social activities. For example, Bellows and Miguel (2009, 17–19) find that individuals whose households directly experienced more intense war violence are more likely to attend community meetings, join local political and community groups, and vote. This study suggests that war has had positive, long-lasting effects on citizens' participation in collective action, a greater level of local political mobilization, and greater capacity for collective action. Likewise, Sacks and Larizza (2012) find that in Sierra Leone, respondents who live in areas that were particularly affected by the war are more likely to view their local government councilors as trustworthy.

Evidence from the 2008 National Public Service Household Survey largely confirms the positive trends reported in the focus groups. For example, respondents were asked how they perceived the local councils in terms of honesty and responsiveness to the needs of their community. Overall, 64 percent of respondents in 2008 said they believed the local council cared about the needs of their community—a substantial increase from 37 percent in 2007. As indicated in the NPS household survey, significant subnational variation exists, from 51 percent in Western Area Rural District to 85 percent in Kailahun. When asked if they could trust local councilors, on average 49 percent of respondents in 2008 trusted local councilors, a large increase compared with 26 percent in 2007 (IRCBP 2010). Moreover, local councils made the largest gains among political institutions between 2007 and 2008. As shown in table 9.3, local political authorities are more trusted by citizens than national government officials and are perceived as being more responsive.

Table 9.3. Changes in Relative Rankings of Central and Local Government
Percent

Measure	Local council			Central government		
	2005	2007	2008	2005	2007	2008
Respondents who think government is responsive to their community's needs	52	37	66	39	45	52
Respondents who trust government officials	43	34	49	33	42	44

Source: IRCBP (2011).

The NPS household survey also asked citizens how well they thought the local council would perform if it received a large sum of money (500 million leones or about US$170,000) to complete a project in their area. Remarkably, 75 percent of respondents in 2008 gave a positive response. Kono, Tonkolili, and Bonthe Town scored best on this indicator, with a score of 2.1 on a scale of 0 to 3. Moyamba and Kenema Town scored the worst on this indicator (1.6). These figures represent a substantial improvement compared with 2007 (IRCBP 2010).

However, citizens' trust and support are not unconditional. On the contrary, evidence from a recent study suggests that the quality of basic public services—combined with the administrative competence or perceived honesty of local government—is what really matters to shape citizens' attitudes toward political authorities (Sacks and Larizza 2012). These findings suggest that ordinary citizens can be vigilant in monitoring government performance at the local level, rewarding better performing councilors with a higher level of trustworthiness.

Durability and Resilience

Seven years after the decentralization process was launched, the institution of local councils has arguably taken firm root, leading several observers to suggest that it would be difficult to reverse the process and reconcentrate power at the center. In particular, the active presence of the international community, whose interests are generally aligned in supporting the decentralization process, is perceived as a guarantee against the replication of the prewar political dynamics, such as the dismantling of local councils that took place in 1972. According to Robinson (2010, 17–18), the presence of the international community has substantially constrained the ability of the APC government to engage in the type of overt manipulation of the chieftaincy system it used after 1967. And international presence might have prompted the national elites to adapt to the changed environment by leaving the local councils in place and engaging in divide-and-rule politics.

However, recent developments suggest that pressures might be building to weaken the authority and independence of the local councils, casting some doubt on the long-term resilience of subnational government. The policy environment in which the local councils are embedded might change significantly in the near future, exposing them to potentially destabilizing forces. In particular, the recent reintroduction of the district officers in 2010 (following the approval of the National Decentralisation Policy) and the downgrading of the political status of the local councils provide some evidence of a new containment strategy. This strategy is designed to protect the interests of the national elites and undermine the emerging political power at the subnational level (Srivastava and Larizza 2011).

Drivers of Success and Its Navigation

The drivers of success for the reestablishment of local councils in Sierra Leone start first with managing the legacy of the war. Large demands and pressures were generated in the aftermath of the conflict for a rapid peace dividend in the form of a reestablished state presence and improved access to basic services outside the Western peninsula. These popular demands were common across a broad spectrum of societal groups and prominent civic and official actors.

Moreover, in Sierra Leone, the postconflict environment was more favorable relative to other cases of countries emerging from war, because there was no perceived need to facilitate the peaceful coexistence of former warring factions. As Fanthorpe, Lavali, and Sesay (2011, 52) state, "None of the leading factions in the Sierra Leonean conflict became major players in peacetime politics...." This implied that protracted debates and tense negotiations that delayed the process of institution building in other countries (such as Kosovo or Sudan, for example) were absent in Sierra Leone, making it easier to focus on the technical and policy aspects of the subnational institution-building process. In other words, an authorizing environment emerged that enabled rapid alignment of national and international interests and quickly mobilized donor support.

Since the 2002 elections, the prewar parties (SLPP and APC) have reoccupied the formal political space almost exclusively. Nevertheless, the elites recognized that their legitimacy was tainted. They had an imperative to be seen to be committed to the amelioration of the horrors endured during the abandonment of whole swaths of the population during the war. Decentralization provided a ready political platform to both, meshing with the policy promptings of the international community.

Notwithstanding the continuing governmental deference to the traditional authorities related to securing votes, a window of opportunity existed immediately after the peace settlement to move the new structure of local councils forward.

Navigating the Decentralization Agenda in the External Environment

There was a sequencing of decentralization reforms and devolution of functions. This sequencing approach featured the establishment of democratically elected authorities first, and subsequently the progressive devolution of fiscal and administrative functions. The approach was critical to the success of the local councils because their progressive empowerment—via increased resources and administrative decision-making power—steadily enhanced the accountability relationship with the citizens. It also generated demand for services and thereby shaped the incentives for local authorities to deliver and improve the quality of local services.

Steering the Fast-Track Approach

The approval of critical legislation before the validation of national decentralization policy prevented delays at the implementation stage in two ways: (1) There was de facto blocking of interference by resistance groups (such as line ministries) in the critical start-up period; and (2) The space was minimized for conflicting interpretations (such as the potential conflicts between the chieftaincy system and local councils) that could derail the process. Furthermore, the late elaboration of the National Decentralisation Policy (approved by the cabinet in December 2010) made it possible to benefit from the experience of the early period and quickly identify specific requirements for additional legislative harmonization and change.

Deadlines were set to guide the devolution process. The deadlines were instrumental in keeping up the momentum of the decentralization process and mobilizing demands for sustained capacity-building efforts at the local level.

Quick wins were demonstrated. The Decentralization Secretariat in its early days applied itself to raising the visibility of the decentralization process and linking in the communities. A prominent vehicle for this was the "rapid results initiative," which combined community awareness building with the execution and oversight of prioritized works projects over a 100-day period (Zhou 2009).

The magnitude of donor support was critical to ensure strong resource commitment and support capacity-building initiatives targeting local councils. The modality of donor support was particularly instrumental to achieve rapid results and establish solid foundations for the institutional development of local councils. The modality encompassed the use of highly skilled, donor-funded local technical assistant (LTA) positions within

IRCBP's critical implementing agencies, the Project Coordination Unit, the Local Government Finance Department (LGFD), and the Decentralisation Secretariat (Dec-Sec). In particular, Dec-Sec and LGFD provided the appropriate vanguard organizational structure that, along with strong legislative momentum, acted as a solid catalyst for the institutional reform process. Moreover, because they are funded by donor projects, LTA staffs have been subjected to external accountability mechanisms to monitor their performance.[13] This in turn has facilitated the relationships of the local councils with donors. And it has enabled their support of the institutional development of local councils by channeling large amounts of financial resources (through the Local Government Finance Committee), as well as by providing effective monitoring and an intensive capacity-building program.

Building Matching Dynamics in the Internal Environment

To take firm root, the decentralization project not only had to be sculpted in line with the possibilities presented by the external environment, it also needed a workable and capacitated internal framework. The progressive establishment of the capabilities of the local councils was facilitated by some critical interventions at timely junctures of the decentralization process, which are described in the following:

Clear Articulation of the Formal Mandate of the Local Councils. It was critical to generate over time established, standard operating procedures (particularly in planning, budgeting, and accounting), which in turn have built robustness in institutional management. Moreover, the focus group discussions confirmed that core and sector staff members show a good grasp of the mission and goals of the institution.

Rolling Transfer of Qualified Personnel to Local Councils. Local council staff has been engaged on a staged basis: first chief administrators and finance officers on transfer from the civil service, then procurement and monitoring and evaluation officers, then development planners and internal auditors, then engineers and human resources officers, and so forth. This staged process allowed for the gradual building of capacity at the local level, with observable impacts on institutional performance. The posting of staff outside Freetown raised issues of incentives but (modestly) preferential pay rates helped, as did the appeal of more direct influence on institutional workings.

Mobilization of Advisors at the Council Level. From their inception, the new local councils had available to them the full-time advice of the council coaches (later designated as resident technical facilitators) who were hired directly by Dec-Sec. These in turn were backstopped by regional coordinators and the human resources specialists at Dec-Sec.

Investment in Capacity Building. Sustained capacity building—as described above and through the foregoing and the training and equipping program for staff and elected officials—is reflected in the steady improvement of institutional performance. Not only the council staff, but also the elected officials have benefited from training interventions that further strengthened the identification with emerging council processes.

Presence of Political and Technical Leadership. Combined with the availability of skilled staff, leadership has emerged as a critical driver of performance across the sample of four local councils. Where council chairs or chief administrators have demonstrated clear-cut leadership and where well-skilled staff was available, the effects on performance have been manifest and translated into positive organizational impulses. Bo City provides a good example of the far-reaching impact of leadership on performance, local development outcomes,[14] and effective tax administration (Jibao and Pritchard 2011; Fanthorpe, Lavali, and Sesay 2011).

Objectively-Based Systems Bolstering the Decentralization Process. A strong, early push to the credibility of the decentralization agenda was provided by the design and installation of the intergovernmental financial transfer system. Based on international best practice on criteria and distribution formulas, all parties accepted its objectivity and transparency. Likewise, the installation of CLoGPAS, as an evidence-based tool for local council performance, and the regularized national public service surveys underpin the advancement of decentralization overall. The robust nature of these monitoring systems has obviated the threat of serious contestation and generally insulated Dec-Sec and the involved ministries from dispute.

Communications and Outreach Activities. The focus group participants consistently reported that local council interaction with the local community was at a good level. The growing concentration of outreach activities to the public by the local councils (both legally required and self-generated) has brought positive returns in terms of citizen support to and identification with the local government system.

Party Politics as an Additional Driver of Local Councils' Institutional Performance. In some cases, the informal pressures created by the confrontational and polarized nature of the party system have also created some unexpected outcomes, acting as incentives for local councils to implement critical reforms for the management and collection of local revenues. A recent study, covering four city councils, on the political economy of local tax reforms finds that the perception of fear that central government transfers might have been delayed or withheld for political reasons against opposition-controlled local government has shaped the behavior of local authorities (Jibao and Prichard 2011). This perception has created incentives for enacting tax reforms, with the ultimate goal to enhance financial autonomy and overall institutional performance.

Outstanding Challenges

Local councils remain highly dependent on grants from the national government. Although the volume of these grants has increased over time and a larger proportion of budgeted amounts are now being transferred, the lack of financial autonomy leaves the local councils vulnerable to the whims of the national government. For instance, several of the focus group participants mentioned the late arrival of quarterly transfers from the central government as disruptive to the planned delivery of services. A particular problem arose in the agricultural sector where the flow of funds was significantly out of kilter with the pattern of seasonal needs in the subsectors. Increased property tax revenue (the case of Bo City council is a model in this regard) suggests potential for the future, but the magnitude of the revenue base is insufficient to break the dependence on central transfers (Jibao and Pritchard 2011).

In addition to the problem of local councils' structural dependency on the center, since 2009, the Ministry of Local Government has played a role in altering the share of local tax collected by the paramount chiefs and remitted to the local councils, lowering the amount of local tax precept and laying down a range of 5–20 percent. Despite the government's declared intention to strengthen the institution of chieftaincy by providing additional resources, the focus group discussions consistently reported a sense of frustration among chairpersons and local councilors over a decision they perceived as unjust and contrary to the provision of the law.[15] These election-driven political dynamics have the potential to derail the evolutionary process and represent a serious threat to the survival of the institution, as they are likely to undermine the capacity of local councils to perform their designated functions with sufficient financial autonomy (Srivastava and Larizza 2011).

The relationship between the paramount chiefs and the local councils and their respective domains and functions continues to be marked by tensions. As the chieftaincy retains allegiance and legitimacy (including by way of constitutional provision), however, a modus vivendi needs to apply between all traditional and local modern authorities. Government obfuscation on this issue, in the opinion of Robinson (2010, 5), can be seen as part of a larger political strategy whose ultimate objective was "to create a dysfunctional and quite incoherent set of institutions with local councils under-resourced, dependent on the central state for funding and in conflict with the paramount chiefs or other elements of the chieftaincy institutions." In other words, national elites followed a "divide-and-rule" strategy to ensure that neither the paramount chiefs nor the local councils would have the opportunity to become strong enough to challenge the center's hold on political power.

Relations with MDA and the line ministries vary across the spectrum. In general, cooperation on cross-sector monitoring of outputs is improving, but contradictions between sector and decentralization legislation still need to be resolved by a process of harmonization. Aspects of minimum national standards also need consistent work, sector by sector.

A critical aspect of the interactions between the councils and the MDAs is the prevailing situation of control over locally operational staff and the lack of a clear demarcation of employer and employee relations. This continues to be a source of tensions and frustration and militates against organizational effectiveness, as widely reflected in the focus group discussions. The National Decentralisation Policy (approved in 2010) foresees direct employment and control of all locally based personnel devolved to the councils by 2016,[16] but in the interim, there is clearly an issue of accountability that limits the capacity of local councils to perform their devolved functions. Moreover, even with the handling of human resource matters for the restricted number of core staff (currently fewer than 200), serious incidents have arisen related chiefly to councilor (importantly chairperson) attitudes toward individual staff as well as officer-to-officer tensions. High transfer rates of core staff (notably chief administrators) reflect this trend.

There is a lack of coordination between the respective monitoring and evaluation processes related to service delivery and adherence to and level of completion of council plans. Sector and council monitoring and evaluation—through the appointed officer—appear to be conducted in disconnected channels. Even the intentions behind establishing district monitoring and evaluation committees with formal sector representation (apparently following a directive from the Development Assistance Coordination Office in October 2009) have been frustrated, as meetings are irregularly convened (some actors are not even aware of this proposal). Admittedly, it is not the intention to devolve sector monitoring and evaluation—as in the new center-local disposition, this remains a core function of MDAs—nevertheless, although relevant personnel see the sense and mutual benefit of close coordination, efforts in that direction have been hampered.

In terms of integrating service delivery in an LGA area, difficulties persist with the activities of NGOs (in some sectors, there might be 15–25 agencies working in an area). Although there is always some level of operational contact with these bodies, the sharing of plans is generally unsatisfactory. NGOs are only required to register at the national level with MoFED. They are encouraged to have working agreements with the councils, but in reality, a small minority does. Several participants in the focus groups reported these relationships as depending entirely on the particular organization's willingness to cooperate. Some (e.g., World Vision) were reluctant to do so, while others (e.g., Welthungerhilfe) spontaneously came to the councils on all planning and implementation matters.[17] A similar situation pertains with regard to officially supported national programs, with the United Nations Children's Fund, the Joint United Nations Programme on HIV/AIDS, and the National Commission for Social Action activities all cited during interviews and focus group discussions as operating in some considerable degree of isolation from council annual plans. Expenditure tracking is also problematic. The official national Council Annual Plan may note a commitment from a particular source (e.g., the Food and Agriculture Organization), but there will be no itemization of budgeted expenditure. Financial statements on these programs are not copied to local finance personnel as a rule.

In 2010, the government reintroduced the position of district officers, adding an additional layer of policy oversight and control on the activities of local councils. However, the lack of clarity in the definition of functions and authority of district officers has led several observers to raise concerns that the district officers might abuse their authority over local councils and increase the control of the central government. Even prior to this development, the influence of the three provincial secretariats (where the district officers report) has not been viewed as contributing to local development.

Over time, tensions have developed between the donor-funded contract staff and regular civil servants, hampering organizational effectiveness. This has been especially the case in MLGRD, where Dec-Sec was only formally included in the ministry and instead remained de facto largely autonomous and independent from it. This situation generates the risk that skilled contract staff will not be attracted and retained in the civil service, weakening the process of local councils' institutional development and undermining the long-term sustainability of capacity-building efforts. A similar risk exists at the local level where the local councils have had difficulty in recruiting and retaining capable staff for key positions.

Policy Implications and Conclusions

The reestablishment and institutional development of local councils in Sierra Leone has followed a fast-track approach, similar to the "big bang" decentralization reform program initiative of the World Bank and other donors in 1999 in post-Suharto Indonesia. Like in Indonesia, the objective was to cement institutional reforms while the political climate remained favorable (World Bank 2003). However, the Sierra Leone experience has differed from that in other countries, especially in the following ways:

1. In Sierra Leone, few efforts (if any) were made to reform the institution of the chieftaincy after the introduction of LGA in 2004. This approach was substantially different from the experience of other African countries, where the traditional authorities were the target of legislative initiatives that aimed to reduce their executive and administrative powers and subject them to the authority of "modern" local government systems.[18]

2. The law-based sequencing and time-tabling of devolution gave the process significant impetus, underpinned by early mobilization of personnel capacity. This is a stark difference compared with other decentralized countries in Africa where the resistance to devolution has

been much stronger and no formal deadlines have been established. The case of Burkina Faso and, more generally, the experience of Francophone African states have followed a more gradual and slow process (USAID 2010).

The above analysis suggests that, rather than reflecting other countries' experience (international isomorphism), the design and development of the institution of local councils in Sierra Leone has been largely shaped by the socio-political environment emerging from the war, as well as from the peculiar organizational culture and social norms inherited from the colonial period and the pre-1972 decentralization experience. This "domestic isomorphism" is evident in the similarities between the 2004 LGA and the old District Council Ordinance (of 1950), as well as in the legacies of the "indirect rule" system and the way those legacies shaped the relationship between the district councils and the chiefdoms in the post-conflict context.

Notwithstanding the preceding observations, the successful experience of local councils in Sierra Leone does offer a few interesting lessons that can inform future efforts to build successful institutions in other post-conflict and fragile settings. At the same time, the case of Sierra Leone raises interesting questions on the extent to which this historical experience can be replicated elsewhere. For instance, the creation of donor-funded implementing agencies and the use of LTA staff was a unique approach that facilitated the institutional development of the local councils. The presence of competitively-recruited contract staff acted as a solid catalyst for the decentralization reform process and accounts for the positive results achieved by the local councils over time. However, the long-term sustainability of this approach remains an issue of concern. This requires further reflection on the benefits and potential trade-offs associated with this model of donor intervention and the extent to which the approach followed in Sierra Leone could be replicated in other post-conflict and fragile countries.

The Sierra Leone experience also shows how the historical, social, and political environment provides critical opportunities to support the efforts of local councils to achieve successful outcomes. In particular, the post-conflict environment was conducive to the devolution of power and functions to subnational authorities, given the legacies of the civil war and the quick alignment of international (donor) and national interests. To the extent that other countries do not share a similar enabling environment, it might be difficult to replicate a similar process of institutional transformation and success.

Finally, the experience of the local councils suggests that the trajectory of the institutional reform process is heavily influenced by the degree to which the incentives of various actors play out. In Sierra Leone, the success of the local councils might itself have been responsible for a strong reaction from the central government, whose recent decisions reflect an effort to contain—rather than support—the process of institutional development of the local councils (Srivastava and Larizza 2011). A central lesson emerging from these political economy dynamics refers to the critical role that the international community should play while providing support to local councils. In Sierra Leone, such support has so far been crucial to mitigate the risks for institutional reversals (recentralization of powers and functions) while also helping local authorities in their effort to perform their devolved functions and meet citizens' expectations.

Notes

1. Sierra Leone is divided into 149 chiefdoms, each ruled by a single paramount chief, considered the top authority in his or her chiefdom. Paramount chiefs rule through a network of sub-chiefs and chiefdom functionaries at the chiefdom, section (each chiefdom is divided into 5–15 sections), and town or village level.
2. District councils were categorized in three types: (1) city council (Freetown, the capital); (2) town council (Bo, Kenema, Makeni, Koidu New Sembehun, and Bonthe); and (3) district council (Bombali, Koinadugu, Port Loko, Kambia, Tonkolili, Kono, Kenema, Bo, Pujehun, Bonthe, Moyamba, Kailahun, and Western Area Rural) (Zhou 2009, 29).
3. Much of the exploitation of the people by the chiefs had related to their prerogative to identify those who were indigenous to the chiefdom (indigenes) and guarantee their rights to local residence, land use, and political and legal representation (Fanthorpe and Sesay 2009).
4. In 2002, the Government of Sierra Leone requested financial support from DfID to build houses for the chiefs. Given the earlier poor practices of chiefdom governance and the legitimacy deficit of the chiefs, DfID and other donors pressured the Government of Sierra Leone to initiate chiefdom reforms. Public consultations were held in a dozen localities, reporting strong demand for democratic reform rather than the abolition of the chiefdom system (Fanthorpe 2006). Acting on this basis, DfID provided support for the Chiefdom Governance Reform Programme.

5. Available cross-country data confirm this perception: Sierra Leone continues to lag behind other decentralizing countries in the region, where transfers to subnational governments are about 24 percent of the total revenues collected (see Bahl and Wallace (2004, 5); Searle (2009)). Moreover, in absolute terms, actual transfers remain low and local councils are still underfunded relative to the devolved functions (Srivastava and Larizza 2011).

6. In the case of MLGRD, however, the accountability relationship has been indirect, as the oversight and policy functions have been implemented by the donor-funded Decentralization Secretariat. Despite the fact that this body was conceived as a transitional implementing entity, the persistent delays and failed efforts to mainstream the functions of Dec-Sec staff into the activities of MLGRD continue to create confusion about the central agency to which the local councils are ultimately accountable.

7. According to the Decentralization Policy (Government of Sierra Leone 2010a), the local councils are no longer identified as the highest political authority; instead, they are described as the highest developmental authority.

8. Under LGA, the responsibilities of the local council chief administrator include to "supervise and coordinate the activities of the other staff and Departments of the local council" and to "ensure that staff performance standards are met." In actuality, however, the bulk of staff operating locally is working in the sectors, and their posting is still done by the parent sector ministry directly along with their other personnel management (e.g., recruitment, promotion, disciplining, and so forth). The local council is only a direct employer in the case of the core staff, currently 10 officers (with plans for four more). All the human resources issues pertaining to the core staff are channeled through the human resources officer of the council to the chief administrator on the basis of the provisions of a new manual and under the aegis of the Local Government Services Commission (LGSC).

9. Currently, the vast majority of local councils' funding comes from central government transfers, in the form of grants tied to specific expenditures for devolved functions and administrative costs. The vertical allocation (total funds flowing to local councils) and horizontal distribution arrangements are to reflect capacity considerations and represent the sum of all sector-specific vertical allocations for devolved functions. Each sector allocation is determined through negotiations between LGFD, each line ministry, and the Budget Bureau of the Ministry of Finance. Once the size of the vertical envelope for each sector is established, the horizontal distribution (between local councils) is done on the basis of formulas that take into account equity, simplicity, transparency, stability, and budget autonomy.

10. When the local councils launched the competitive process for hiring core administrative and technical staff, several civil servants—centrally appointed and accountable to the central MDAs—decided to apply and become

locally appointed public servants. Although promotions and salary increases were clearly a driving force, evidence suggests that the perception of being closer to the decision-making authority, and therefore being more able to influence and to some extent scrutinize the decision-making process itself, played a role in the decision to move.

11. It is difficult to establish any stringent causal link between the reestablishment of local councils and general improvement in public services observed in Sierra Leone, if only because there are no equivalent data on the quality of such services before 2004. However, it is worth observing that areas that have had the largest reduction in geographical distance to political power—a direct byproduct of decentralization, measured as the distance to Freetown minus the distance to the council headquarters—have usually experienced the largest gains in service quality. Based on this and other tests, Foster and Glennester conclude that "decentralization has been compatible with consistent improvements in public service delivery" (Foster and Glennester 2009, 83–84).

12. Survey data are available from the authors on request.

13. This included, for example, monthly progress reports to the relevant project implementation unit. These accountability relationships were relatively strong, especially compared with the endemically weak country systems for appraising performance.

14. Bo City Council experienced a significant growth in own source revenues from systemizing the property tax regime (there has been a fourfold increase in annual flows). This in turn has allowed important discretionary spending on health facilities, support for educational improvements, and solid waste management.

15. According to the 2004 LGA, negotiations had to be conducted between paramount chiefs and local councils to define the share of local tax. As a result of these negotiations, a 40/60 rule had become standard practice.

16. This is an expression of assurance on the side of central authority regarding the institutional capability of local councils, but there is no certainty that the staff devolution will be achieved by the target deadline.

17. There are some remarkable successful cases. For example, in Bo District, a project under European Union funding was cited as being designed and run in exemplary fashion.

18. For example, the Constitution of Uganda (adopted in 1995) states explicitly that "a traditional leader or cultural leader shall not have or exercise any administrative, legislative or executive powers of government or local government." In Ghana, successive governments have taken measures to ensure that chieftaincy operates within the confines of the civil society; however, influential chiefs may remain in national politics (Fanthorpe, Lavali, and Sesay 2011, 59).

References

Bahl, Roy W., and Sally Wallace. 2004. "Inter-Governmental Transfers: The Vertical Sharing Dimension." Working Paper 19. International Studies Program, Andrew Young School of Policy Studies (AYSPS), Georgia State University.

Bellows, John, and Edward Miguel. 2009. "War and Local Collective Action in Sierra Leone." *Journal of Public Economics* 93(11–12): 1144–57.

Chaves, I. N., and James Robinson. 2011. "The Architecture of a Fragile State: The Case of Sierra Leone." Unpublished Working Paper. *IFC Growth in Fragile States Workshop.*

Dec-Sec (Decentralisation Secretariat). 2006. *Comprehensive Local Government Performance Assessment System (CLoGPAS): 2006 Summary Report.* Freetown, Sierra Leone.

———. 2010. *Comprehensive Local Government Performance Assessment System (CLoGPAS): 2008 Summary Report.* Freetown, Sierra Leone.

———. 2012. *Comprehensive Local Government Performance Assessment System (CLoGPAS): 2011 Summary Report.* Freetown, Sierra Leone.

Fanthorpe, Richard. 2006. "On the Limits of Liberal Peace: Chiefs and Democratic Decentralization in Sierra Leone." *African Affairs* 105(418): 27–49.

Fanthorpe, Richard, Andrew Lavali, and Mohamed Gibril Sesay. 2011. "Decentralization in Sierra Leone: Impact, Constraints and Prospects." DFID Sierra Leone.

Fanthorpe, Richard, and Mohamed Gibril Sesay. 2009. "Reform Is Not against Tradition: Making Chieftaincy Revelation in 21st Century Sierra Leone." Unpublished, Campaign for Good Governance, Freetown.

Foster, Elizabeth, and Rachel Glennester. 2009. "Impact of Decentralization on Public Services: Evidence to Date." In *Decentralization, Democracy, and Development Recent Experience from Sierra Leone*, edited by Yongmei Zhou, 73–84. Washington, DC: World Bank.

Glynn, Brendan, Marco Larizza, and Lorena Viñuela. 2011. "ITR: Sierra Leone Case Study. Local Councils Focus Groups Synthesis Report." Mimeo. World Bank, Washington, DC.

Government of Sierra Leone. 1996. *Good Governance and Public Sector Reform Strategy.* Freeport, Sierra Leone.

———. 1997. Position Paper on the Reactivation of Local Government and Decentralization, Task Force on Local Government and Decentralization.

———. 2002. "Post-Conflict Development Agenda: Strategies for Growth and Poverty Reduction."

———. 2005. *Poverty Reduction Strategy Paper.* Freeport, Sierra Leone.

———. 2010a. *National Decentralization Policy.* Freetown, Sierra Leone.

———. 2010b. *Public Expenditure and Financial Accountability (PEFA) Sub-National Government Summary Report.* Freetown, Sierra Leone.

————. 2011. Local Council PEFA Summary Report, Freeport, Sierra Leone.

Hanlon, Joseph. 2004 "Is the International Community Helping to Re-create the Preconditions for War in Sierra Leone? *The Round Table*, 94: 459–72.

IRCBP (Institutional Reform and Capacity Building Project) Evaluation. *Report of the IRCBP 2008 National Public Service Survey*. Institutional Reform and Capacity Building Project, Government of Sierra Leone, Freetown, Sierra Leone.

————. 2011. *Report on the IRCBP 2008 Decentralization Stakeholders Survey*. Freetown, Sierra Leone.

Jackson, Paul. 2007. "Reshuffling an Old Deck of Cards? The Politics of Local Government Reform in Sierra Leone." *African Affairs* 106(422): 95–11.

Jibao, Samuel S., and Wilson Prichard. 2011. "The Political Economy of Property Tax Reform in Post-Conflict Sierra Leone." Unpublished draft. Department of Political Science and School of Global Affairs, University of Toronto.

Manning, Ryann Elizabeth. 2009a. "Challenging Generations: Youths and Elders in Rural and Peri-Urban Sierra Leone." Working Paper 49075. World Bank, Washington, DC.

————. 2009b. "The Landscape of Local Authority in Sierra Leone: How 'Traditional' and 'Modern' Justice and Governance Systems Interact." In *Decentralization, Democracy and Development: Recent Experiences from Sierra Leone*, edited by Yongmei Zhou, 110–37. Washington, DC: World Bank.

National Electoral Commission (NEC). 2008a. *Summary of Results of 2008 Local Elections*. Freetown: Sierra Leone. http://www.nec-sierraleone.org/.

————. 2008b. *Final Local Councils Nomination Statistics*. Freetown: Sierra Leone. http://www.nec-sierraleone.org/.

Reno, William. 1995. *Corruption and State Politics in Sierra Leone*. Cambridge University Press.

Richards, Paul. 1996. "Fighting for the Rainforest: War, Youth and Resources in Sierra Leone." International African Institute in association with James Currey.

Robinson, James. 2010. "The Political Economy of Decentralization in Sierra Leone." World Bank, Washington, DC.

Sacks, Audrey, and Marco Larizza. 2012. "Why Quality Matters: Rebuilding Trustworthy Local Government in Post-Conflict Sierra Leone." Policy Research Working Paper 6021. World Bank, Washington, DC.

Sawyer, Edward. 2008. "Remove or Reform? A Case for (Restructuring) Chiefdom Governance in Post-Conflict Sierra Leone." *African Affairs* 107(428): 387–403.

Searle, Bob. 2009. *Sierra Leone: Issues in Fiscal Decentralization*. Washington, DC: AFTPR, World Bank.

Srivastava, Vivek, and Marco Larizza. 2011. "Decentralization in Postconflict Sierra Leone: The Genie Is out of the Bottle." In *Yes Africa Can: Success Stories from a Dynamic Continent*, edited by Punam Chuhan-Pole and Manka Angwafo. Washington, DC: World Bank.

Tangri, Roger. 1978. "Central-Local Politics in Contemporary Sierra Leone." *African Affairs* 77(307): 165–73.

U.S. Agency for International Development (USAID). 2010. *Comparative Assessment of Decentralization in Africa: Final Report and Summary of Findings.* Washington, DC: USAID.

World Bank. 2003. *Sierra Leone: Strategic Options for Public Sector Reform.* Report No. 25110-SL, AFTPR. World Bank, Washington, DC.

Zhou, Yongmei, ed. 2009. *Decentralization, Democracy and Development: Recent Experiences from Sierra Leone.* Washington, DC: World Bank.

Zwanikken, Maria, Dele Olowu, and Esau Chiviya. 1994. "Aide Memoire: Capacity Assessment for Public Sector Management and Decentralization Programming Mission." United Nations.

PART IV

TIMOR-LESTE

CHAPTER 10

The Institution-Building Context in Timor-Leste

Catherine Anderson and Elisabeth Huybens

Occupying the eastern half of the island of Timor, Timor-Leste is a small country with a population of about 1.2 million. Relying heavily on petroleum production, the country achieved lower middle-income status in 2011. Yet poverty remains persistently high, particularly in the rural areas where the majority of the population lives. This chapter provides the background context for three cases of successful institutional development described in the following chapters—the Ministry of Health, the Ministry of Social Solidarity, and the Central Bank.

Tumultuous History

Timor-Leste was a Portuguese colony for 400 years. Following a civil war that was brief but left deep psychological marks, the country declared independence from Portugal in November 1975, only to be invaded within days by neighboring Indonesia. The 24-year occupation that followed is estimated to have caused the deaths of up to one-third of the population. The Timorese maintained a staunch resistance against the occupation through military, civilian, and diaspora diplomatic actions. Following the fall of President Suharto in 1998, Indonesia allowed a referendum in 1999, giving the territory a choice between autonomous status within Indonesia and independence. When the overwhelming majority of the population voted for independence, the outcome was met with a campaign of violence that left more than 1,000 people dead, the majority of the population displaced, and most of the private and public infrastructure in ruins. Nearly all public records were destroyed. Indonesian civil servants fled the territory, leaving the country with few educated professionals.

A multilateral peacekeeping force was deployed, after which the United Nations Transitional Administration in East Timor (UNTAET) was established with supreme executive, judicial, and legislative authority. Timorese leaders guided and informed policy making throughout the UNTAET period, and near the end of UNTAET's mission its cabinet consisted almost entirely of Timorese. The election of a constituent assembly in 2001, the adoption of a constitution that year, and presidential elections in 2002 paved the way for the restoration of Timor-Leste's independence on May 20, 2002. The Constituent Assembly became the National Parliament, and the first constitutional government was sworn in under the leadership of Prime Minister Mari Alkatiri. The United Nations Mission of Support in East Timor was created, and succeeded in 2005 by the United Nations Office in Timor-Leste.

In April 2006, the country was shaken by an eruption of large-scale violence. A third of the army was dismissed amid complaints by the rank and file from the west of the country of discrimination by commanders who hailed mostly from the eastern region. Fighting broke out, followed by widespread violence and looting in the capital, Dili, much of it associated with youth gangs. The police forces essentially imploded, with police officers retreating around geographical and kinship loyalties. Government authority buckled under the pressure of escalating social tensions. Some 40 people lost their lives and more than 100,000 people were displaced. Although the violence was sparked by division within the armed forces, it was fed by a host of complex historical, social, and economic factors. These included decades-old enmities between political elites; disillusionment with the economic constraints at independence, such as widespread poverty and unemployment; disaffection with a government that was led by diaspora figures and appeared distant from the needs of ordinary people; and the surfacing of identities around easterners and westerners and their purported roles in the resistance against the Indonesian occupation.

International troops were called in to restore order, and Prime Minister Alkatiri was forced to resign in June 2006. He was replaced by then Foreign Minister and Nobel Peace laureate Jose Ramos-Horta. Parliamentary and presidential elections were held in 2007. Ramos-Horta was elected president and former president and independence leader Jose Alexandre 'Xanana' Gusmao became prime minister. Insecurity and community-level fighting lasted well into 2007, and there was an attempt to assassinate President Ramos-Horta and Prime Minister Gusmao in 2008. For much of 2006 and 2007, government services were badly disrupted, with the exception of a few agencies, such as the Ministry of Health and the Ministry of Social Solidarity, which responded surprisingly effectively to the crisis.

The country has since credibly emerged from the crisis, reestablished political stability, and generated a new confidence in the state. Largely peaceful democratic elections for president and parliament were held in 2012, followed by an orderly transition to a new government. The United Nations Integrated Mission for Timor-Leste and the International Stabilization Force, both deployed following the 2006 crisis, completed their missions in December 2012.

Contrasting Visions: Building the State versus Building Trust

There is a considerable contrast between the visions embodied by UNTAET and the first government and that of the governments that arose after the 2006 Crisis. Following its deployment in 1999–2000, UNTAET achieved important humanitarian goals, such as the reintegration of more than 200,000 people who had taken refuge in West Timor, as well as reigniting essential financial, economic, and social public services, including education and health. UNTAET also chaperoned the formation of the country's constitutional foundations and organized its first parliamentary and presidential elections.

The first post-independence government was primarily concerned with building the state, and elaborating its legal and administrative architecture at the national and subnational levels. It focused heavily on securing the international agreements underpinning petroleum production in new maritime oil fields. This additional petroleum production generated a considerable increase in public revenues starting in 2005. The government established petroleum revenue management architecture, including a Petroleum Fund that is widely considered international best practice. With a design drawing from the Norwegian experience, the Petroleum Fund is intended to provide transparency and accountability on the use of public revenues, protect public finances from income volatility, and help strike the appropriate balance between current spending and savings for future generations. Withdrawals from the Petroleum Fund are guided by the estimated sustainable income.

However, the effectiveness of the first government was curtailed by low capacity in public financial management and an excruciatingly slow execution of national budgets. The government underestimated the effect on households of the massive economic disruption that followed the withdrawal of the Indonesian administrative and private sector presence and the yo-yo economic effect of the buildup and subsequent draw-down of the United Nations presence. The Alkatiri government had a distinct aversion to social protection programs, considering them a disincentive to productive private initiative and reminiscent of Indonesian rule. By contrast, the Gusmao governments deployed the petroleum-generated public expenditures to secure peace.

From 2007 to 2012, Gusmao's first term, the government concentrated on resolving grievances and rebuilding public trust. It provided payouts to those who registered the original grievances that precipitated the 2006 crisis and to those who had been displaced and lost their homes. It established a generous, if poorly targeted, social protection system, including a system of cash transfers to address the demands of the veterans of the resistance, as well as the needs of the elderly, the disabled, and poor families. It rapidly increased expenditures in highly visible areas, such as power supply, and distributed funds in districts and subdistricts for smaller infrastructure, to create jobs and support the nascent private sector through contracts.

To finance this largesse, the government is drawing double the estimated sustainable income from the Petroleum Fund, with budgets approximately 10 times what they were in 2002 through 2006. This large expansion in public spending has generated jobs and created a visible urban middle class, with increases in living standards slowly becoming apparent in rural areas as well. However, it has led to double-digit inflation and puts fiscal sustainability at risk, especially since the quality of public spending and investments is considered uneven. Rapidly increasing public spending in the face of still weak public institutions also raises concerns over corruption; Timor-Leste's standing in governance rankings has deteriorated. Growth is largely driven by public spending, while agriculture, the primary source of income for most households, remains characterized by low productivity, contributing to persistent poverty and food insecurity in rural areas.

Although Timor-Leste's development path remains complex and uncertain, more than a decade after the restoration of independence, the country can lay claim to several defining accomplishments: at least seven years without a relapse to violence; two free, fair, and democratic national parliamentary elections; a sharp increase in gross domestic product per capita; and improvements in human development. Underlying these achievements are institutional developments that have enabled these gains.

The following chapters track the ingredients of three particular institutional experiences that have contributed to Timor-Leste's transition: the Ministry of Health, the Ministry of Social Solidarity, and the Central Bank. The tracking is done with a pedagogic intent, to unravel the underpinnings of their success. In doing so, two features become particularly clear. First, there is no linear path to success; institutional development is idiosyncratic and full of fits and starts. Second, despite variation in a given macro context, several elements can help in raising or enhancing development prospects and enable institutions to take root in a context in which the odds are against them.

CHAPTER 11

Timor-Leste Case Study: Ministry of Social Solidarity

Catherine Anderson

The experience of the Ministry of Social Solidarity (MSS) is not a case of conventional institutional development. The MSS largely exists to address the country's complex social vulnerabilities,[1] and much of its early success is attributed to its role in guiding the country from crisis to recovery. In delivering on its mandate, the MSS has acted to secure legitimacy in the eyes of its clients and citizenry, building a bridge between government and society and forging the basis of a new social contract.

Tracing the development of the MSS from Timor-Leste's referendum to late 2011, this chapter examines how and why, in an otherwise challenging, low-capacity environment, the MSS was able to deliver on its policy commitments in credible ways (see annex 11A for a timeline of MSS milestones). In doing so, the chapter describes how the core underpinnings of the ministry's success have emerged in the three concentric circles that constitute its operating environment: the sociopolitical context in which it functions, its relationships with its clients and the external environment, and its inner institutional workings. This introduction highlights key

The chapter expands on a mission aide-memoire (December 2012); it is based on the research and interviews drawn from two in-country visits during October 12 to November 4, 2011, and November 15 to 18, 2011, and a series of regional focus groups completed by Josh Trinidad and Fidelis Magalhaes during November 2011 to January 2012. The mission is grateful to Riltom Borges and Sebastião do Rego Guterres for their assistance and to Sofia Cason and Ben Larke for their technical inputs.

elements of that approach and outlines the causal argument that will be elaborated in the sections that follow.

The MSS is essentially a product and an agent of the sociopolitical context in which it functions, and this has substantially contributed to its success. Seizing the opportunities afforded to it, the MSS and its predecessor, the Ministry of Labour and Community Reinsertion (MLCR), responded to the complex social responsibilities attributed to them by directing MSS resources toward three priorities: social reintegration and recovery from crisis, connecting state and society through the engagement of village chiefs (*chefes de suco*) and the adoption of traditional practices, and developing institutional capacity. As a consequence of these actions, the ministry stands out, not only for its social responsiveness in a fraught sociopolitical context, but also for its customized approach and the manner in which it has overcome the constraints of its inner workings.

The MSS has encountered tough and intractable challenges on its path to institutional development. These challenges have involved managing complex client demands and citizen expectations, building trust in fractured and traumatized societal conditions, and expanding embryonic capabilities to deliver results alongside a spike in social spending. Like most institutional development trajectories in fragile and conflict-affected situations (FCS), the MSS's institutional development path has not been linear, and it could well regress. The persistence of chronic poverty, hunger, and malnutrition and the fragility of the country's social conditions are sobering and indicate that much is yet to be done to consolidate early gains and set the ministry on the definitive path of reducing poverty. A large proportion of the population remains susceptible to falling into poverty because of chronic human and administrative vulnerabilities, yet the ministry lacks a coherent poverty reduction strategy. At the same time, the rapid escalation of veterans' pensions threatens to outpace the financial sustainability of MSS programs, and inefficient and poor resource targeting have blunted the engagement of youth and children as vulnerable groups. Absent targeted policy and administrative improvements, these essential challenges suggest that the MSS's initial success could unravel as quickly as it was accomplished.

Mindful of the struggles that lie ahead and taking a longitudinal view of the MSS's development, this chapter describes the distinctive features of its initial success to identify tractable lessons for institutional development practitioners operating in an FCS.

Institutional Success

Widely credited with having guided the country from crisis to recovery, the ministry's initial success is attributed to three factors: its crisis response in 2006, its expanded delivery of social benefits to Timor-Leste's vulnerable and expectant citizenry, and its efforts to connect state and society and to manage the country's social problems through local-level conflict resolution and social dialogue. Recognizing that Timor-Leste has enjoyed just 10 years of independence and that institutional transformation is a generational project (World Bank 2011b), this chapter focuses on the ministry's early accomplishments across three vectors of success—results, legitimacy, and resilience. As it proceeds, this chapter points to the internal and external factors that have contributed to the emergence of these capabilities in the period from the referendum to 2011. At the same time, it reflects on the policy and operational challenges that still lie ahead as the MSS continues on its path of institutional development.

Results

Within two years of the 2006 Crisis and with more than one-tenth of the country's population internally displaced, the ministry's recovery and reintegration program, Hamutuk Hari'i Futuru, decommissioned 65 camps for internally displaced persons (IDPs) and 6 transitional shelters across the country. It built 14,700 homes, and distributed more than US$37.8 million in Phase I and II recovery and reintegration packages to 16,500 families (MSS 2009b). A critical measure of the ministry's success under this reintegration program is that there were no repeat incidents of violence. Complaints regarding eligibility or payments were handled case by case, and decisions were full and final.

The ministry's social transfer programs—including the Mother's Purse (*Bolsa da Mãe*),[2] the Elderly Pension Program, and the Disability Pension Program—have delivered social benefits to an estimated one-third of the population, more than 40 percent of whom constitute Timor-Leste's most poor (see figure 11.1; World Bank 2013, ch. 5).[3] In 2011, social assistance spending prevented a rise in the percentage of households with per capita monthly consumption of only US$32 from 40 to 45 percent,[4] although this came at a disproportionately higher cost compared with the country's regional neighbors and was largely due to the Elderly Pension Program (World Bank 2013).[5] The MSS's social payments are not substantial

Figure 11.1. Social Transfer Beneficiaries, by Program, 2011

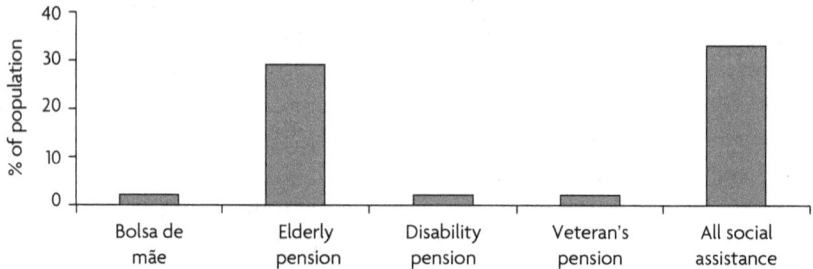

Source: National Statistics Institute 2011b.

Table 11.1. Social Transfer Beneficiaries, by Program, 2009–12

Program	2009	2010	2011	2012
Bolsa de Mãe	8,723	13,458	13,908	15,000
Elderly pension	72,675	83,645	84,623	84,569
Disability pension		4,154	5,539	5,558
Veteran's pension	3,976	9,102	10,953	27,960
Total beneficiaries	89,063	110,146	125,892	142,831

Source: Information provided by the Directorate of Social Assistance, MSS.

monetary sums and, with the exception of the elderly pension, poor targeting blunts the potential poverty impact of these programs. The equity, administrative efficiency, and long-term sustainability of these programs are also uneven and need to be addressed to enhance program performance and impacts in the long run.[6] Yet these programs have injected much-needed financial support into local communities that had not received government assistance before, and urban-rural coverage among beneficiaries is even.

The *Bolsa de Mãe* has expanded incrementally year on year since its introduction (see table 11.1) and in a regionally equitable way although it is only partially pro-poor and payments do not always reach Timor-Leste's most poor. A policy change, introduced in 2011, promises to improve the ability of the program to account for the overall socioeconomic conditions of beneficiaries and their families (for example, number of dependents in the family and family livelihoods). It also aims to improve the accuracy and transparency of the targeting system (World Bank 2013, 66). It is not yet clear whether these policy and administrative changes will have their desired impacts, but they have signaled the MSS's commitment to build on the early gains of its social transfer programs and to examine their performance critically.

It is not possible to gauge the direct impact of MSS social transfers, but the data show some interesting trends. Focus group participants and interviewees almost unanimously reported that the *Bolsa de Mãe* had improved their quality of life and helped them to meet their basic needs. Education-related expenses—shoes, notebooks, pens, uniforms, and school fees—were among the most frequently self-reported expenditures of the *Bolsa de Mãe* payments. There was greater variation in the use of the elderly and disability benefits, and food was the most common expenditure item (table 11.2).[7]

In 2008 the MSS began to pay monthly pensions to veterans and their surviving family members, and in 2011 it honored 236 veterans by awarding them new uniforms and rank badges.[8] By the end of that same year, 10,911 pensions had been paid to veterans and the families of martyrs (see table 11.3). Of the 76,068 former combatants initially registered, 12,540 received pensions and one-off payments in 2008, a further 1,847 in March 2011, and as many as 23,324 in December 2011 (15,502 of these were one-off payments). According to projected estimates, some 22,000 were to receive pensions and one-off benefits in 2012.[9]

Legitimacy

"We have faith in MSS because they help our kids, even if just a little. It counts."

—Focus group discussion with *Bolsa de Mãe* recipients, Oecusse 2011

The ministry has gained substantial legitimacy over the years, and this is largely attributable to its response to the 2006 Crisis and to its role as broker of social stability and a new social contract. Several interviewees observed that the MSS has helped to build a bridge between the government and communities where such ties did not previously exist.

Table 11.2. Primary Use of Social Assistance Benefits as Reported by Households, 2011
Percent of beneficiaries

Program	Food	Health	Education	Purchase of livestock assets	Other
Mother's purse	0.0	6.0	91.1	0	2.9
Elderly pension	88.4	13.4	28.1	6.4	10.7
Disability pension	77.9	7.6	5.0	4.3	5.1

Source: Timor-Leste Social Protection Survey, 2011.

Table 11.3. Beneficiaries of Veterans' Pensions, by Type of Benefit, 2008–12
US$ unless otherwise noted

Type of pension	2008	2009	2010	2011	Projected 2012
Superior pensions					
Number of beneficiaries	7	10	13	14	15
Amount per month	750	750	750	750	750
Special retirements					
Number of beneficiaries	211	235	236	236	735
Roster 1 amount/month	340–550	460–575	460–575	460–575	460–575
Roster 2 amount/month	255–340	345–460	345–460	345–460	345–460
Special subsistence pensions					
Number of beneficiaries	190	269	313	395	7,651
Amount per month	85–120	276–345	276–345	276–345	276–345
Survival pensions					
Number of beneficiaries	1,593	3,455	8,427	10,266	13,801
Amount per month	120–287.50	230–287.50	230–287.50	230–287.50	230–287.50
One-off payments					
Number of beneficiaries	0	0	0	0	15,502
Amount of payment (US$)	0	0	0	0	1,380
Total recipients	2,011	3,969	9,456	10,911	22,202 pensions + 15,502 one-off payments
Total budget (US$, millions)	3.5	15	45.4	37.6	123.1

Source: Information provided by the Secretariat of Veterans Affairs, MSS.

With an initial budget of only US$100,000 in 2002, any early results achieved by the MSS (then the MLCR) were difficult to gauge against the immense needs of the population.[10] Yet the humanitarian emergency created by the events of 2006, together with the spike in government spending that soon followed, created an opportunity for the MSS to demonstrate its capabilities and secure popular trust.

The 2006 Crisis prompted the MSS to strengthen and deepen its inner workings—its leadership and management skills, its shared sense of vision among staff, and its learning and adaptation capabilities. It also sharpened the ministry's responsiveness to its clients and citizenry and improved the quality of its interaction with Timor-Leste's political elites, civil society, and development partners. According to MSS staff, the ministry is now highly regarded, and many had received personal thanks for their work from the relatives of MSS beneficiaries.[11] As one social animator put it, "It is [shown] in the people's behavior toward us. Many appreciate our work."[12]

MSS social transfers benefit 143,000 individuals directly and as much as 33 percent of the population indirectly (World Bank 2013, ch. 5). In a context of severe social instability, the symbolic value of these transfers cannot be overstated—even though many of these benefits constitute a small financial contribution to household spending.[13] MSS payments are often the only form of financial support that beneficiaries receive from government, and this has reinforced popular trust and conveyed the message that the government is considering citizens' interests.

But the MSS's legitimacy is not solely the result of prodigious cash transfers. Its interactions and social connectivity with Timorese communities are more tangible and consistent than those of almost any other government entity, except the Ministry of Health. In particular, the MSS's adoption of customary models of authority, decision making, and dispute resolution has served to embed its programs and presence at a village level, reinforcing its legitimacy in the eyes of the community. A group of *chefes de suco* and subvillage chiefs (*chefes de aldeia*) interviewed for this case study remarked, "The [ministry's] work is to establish the peace, to come and talk about the problems in our community, the unresolved problems."[14]

The MSS has secured credibility despite chronic administrative constraints, which speaks to the strength of its performance. Focus group participants recalled several instances in which irregularities in the data management and verification system had left eligible beneficiaries unpaid. Yet many shared the view expressed by one *chefe de suco*, "Despite all the problems and obstacles, the community trusts the MSS system ... They did a lot of work ... It is not like they are not helping the communities. They deliver a service and look after communities."[15]

Resilience and Durability

An important measure of the ministry's resilience and durability is that it has maintained a consistent institutional development trajectory despite a change of government and minister and national unrest. All of the managers recruited by the United Nations Transitional Administration in East Timor (UNTAET) and by the First Constitutional Government were retained by the MSS through the transition, establishing a baseline of institutional memory.

The ministry's programs have also gained durability over time due to the popular legitimacy that they claim. Echoing what seems to be a broadening consensus, Minister Maria (Micato) Fernandes Alves remarked,[16] "While the structure of the ministry could change with the change of government, its mission is enshrined in the Constitution and it is embedded in popular consciousness and expectation—it will be impossible to change the ministry's program." Representing 8 percent of the overall state budget, it is becoming increasingly clear that social transfers will be the mainstay of a successful social ministry for the foreseeable future, although adjustments will be needed to ensure the fiscal sustainability of veterans' pensions (World Bank 2013).

A final and fitting attribute of the ministry's durability is seen in the institutional integration of its social dialogue and crisis response capability. A recent evaluation of the HHF program found that the ministry's crisis responsiveness and its Social Dialogue Program (SDP) have become an intrinsic part of the ministry's functioning. Previously financed by the United Nations Development Programme (UNDP) and conceived as a tool to facilitate the reintegration of IDPs, the SDP was recently reconstituted as a permanent Peace-Building Unit (PBU) in the MSS to respond to the root causes of conflict that may not have been fully addressed.[17] The government finances the unit, and PBU advisers (previously consultants) have been absorbed into the civil service payroll, pointing to the ministry's continued evolution and contextual fit.

Institutional Context

At its inception, the MSS faced several challenges. Timor-Leste's difficult history had left the country with a population that was highly vulnerable and poor. When East Timor was occupied in 1975, it became Indonesia's 27th province, but it did not enjoy the social benefits afforded to other provinces in the country at the time.[18] Indonesia had invested little in the population's welfare, and any investments tended to be targeted toward sustaining the Indonesian bureaucracy and maintaining its security and control (Knezevic 2005). The province was heavily dependent on external transfers to finance the public sector, and these constituted roughly 85 percent of recurrent and capital expenditures (World Bank 1999, 2). But even with these transfers, by 1999, the poverty rate among Timorese was more than double that of Indonesians, having worsened as a result of the financial crisis and a drought in 1998 (Pedereson and Arneberg 1999). In 1999—the year of the referendum—the situation deteriorated rapidly. Gross domestic product (GDP) had shrunk an estimated 38 percent, unemployment had soared, particularly in the urban areas, and the prices of fuel and other basic goods had risen steeply, partially reflecting the removal of subsidies. With the steep decline in incomes and based on a poverty measure that is highly sensitive to income changes, around half of the population in East Timor was poor (United Nations 2000, para. 24).

Preparations for the transition to independence had begun months prior to the referendum, but the destruction and humanitarian crisis that followed had not been anticipated and consumed the lion's share of social service resources provided by the United Nations. The United Nations organized an interim government, established a Department of Social Affairs, and set about resolving the country's emergency. On independence, a new Secretariat of State for Labour and Community Reinsertion (SSLCR) was formed with responsibility for youth affairs, labor, and vocation training and a small social services portfolio. The SSLCR had few resources or political capital—only 27 staff members, an annual budget of US$100,000, and no authority to vote in the Council of Ministers.

As the euphoria of independence dissipated, social pressure on the Timorese administration mounted, and acted as potential lightning rods for future instability and conflict. Veterans of the resistance were eager for their independence dividend, youth were eager for gainful employment and educational opportunities, and decades of resistance had rendered a large percentage of the population highly vulnerable, widowed, and disabled. IDPs would later join the ranks of those with a social grievance or claim against the state, as they became caught in the crossfire of sharpening perceptions of social inequity.

In 2005, the SSLCR became a ministry (the MLCR), increasing its political leverage. A Secretariat of State for Veterans Affairs was soon added to the ministry's already difficult portfolio,[19] but even then, the ministry's annual operating budget increased only modestly—to US$500,000 annually—and this was needed to finance 100 staff and operational activities.[20] Timor-Leste's simmering social pressures remained unmet.

Prior to 2006, there was no social security system in Timor-Leste, social welfare was left largely to the family, the church, and welfare groups, and poverty was increasing.[21] In 2001, 39.7 percent of the population was affected by poverty, and by 2006 the figure had reached 44 percent.[22] Per capita incomes were about 20 percent lower in real terms than they were in 2002, and unemployment stood at 23 percent overall and 40 percent for youth (58 percent for ages 15–19 years old; National Statistics Institute 2006). Although not the primary driver of the 2006 unrest, Timor-Leste's poor social and human development conditions fueled identity divisions and deepened social grievances.

Timor-Leste had experienced social tensions before—veterans marches in Dili pre-2002, youth riots shortly after independence, and a church-led demonstration in 2005—but not on the scale seen in 2006. That year, the violence quickly escalated. It triggered panic in the population and caused widespread displacement, it paralyzed the government, and it brought the economy to a virtual standstill. To a large extent, these events were rooted in perceived discrimination within the national security forces, but the ensuing instability provided fertile ground to revive historical rivalries. Retribution and political violence spiraled.[23]

Parliamentary elections in 2007 saw a heated political contest. A prominent new opposition, the National Congress for Timorese Reconstruction (CNRT) was established by a former leader of the Timorese resistance, Xanana Gusmão. The CNRT campaigned to restore peace and stability through the reintegration of IDPs and crisis recovery, to alleviate poverty, to pay social transfers (including veterans' pensions), and to adopt more open government. Election results were inconclusive, but the three largest opposition groups came together to form a new coalition government[24]—the Alliance of Parliament.

During this period of transition, the decision was made to have the Ministry of Labour and Community Reinsertion lead the country's social reintegration and recovery, expand its social services, and develop conflict resolution capabilities, under a new mandate as the Ministry of Social Solidarity. The MSS also shed two portfolios—youth affairs and labor—as they were thought to be better served by new entities: the Secretariat of State for Youth and Sport and the Secretariat of State for Professional Training and Employment.

In 2008 the Ministry of Social Solidarity launched its flagship national recovery strategy, the HHF, in an effort to reintegrate the nearly 150,000 individuals who had become internally displaced as a result of the Crisis (IDMC 2009).[25] It also began several direct social transfer programs (the *Bolsa de Mãe,* the Elderly Pension Program, and the Disability Pension Program) and initiated veterans' pensions, enlarging its program of social assistance and targeting key population groups. Later that same year, the MSS extended its reach into local communities through the creation of district and subdistrict posts staffed by child protection officers and social animators. By 2010 the ministry had successfully closed all 65 camps for the internally displaced, and their inhabitants had returned home or relocated to other parts of the country. The HHF had distributed more than US$50 million to 17,000 households, successfully channeling these resources through the state budget (Bulgalski 2010, 20–21). By 2011, MSS social benefits were reaching nearly one-third of the population both directly and indirectly (National Statistics Institute 2011b).

In the sections that follow, this work provides a more granular account of the means by which the MSS has navigated its complex external operating environment and overcome binding internal constraints to achieve results. At the same time, it underlines the very many challenges that still lie ahead if the ministry is to galvanise its initial gains.

Managing Client Demands and Citizen Expectations

The MSS carries hefty social responsibilities and is subject to competing political claims and influence by pressure groups, including from political leaders,[26] veterans and the children of martyrs, current and former IDPs, and community leaders, such as *chefes de suco* and *chefes de aldeia*. Several factors have enabled the MSS to navigate this sensitive terrain: an astute leadership, adherence to legal mandate, efficient use and management of donor inputs, and interactive and communicative engagement with the ministry's clients. The ministry's active solicitation of community feedback has also enabled the MSS to learn by doing and to evolve.

Social and Political Pressure

The ministry's role in guiding the country from crisis to stability has enabled it to secure high-level support for its work, while at the same time shielding it from corrosive political influence. Few political elites wanted responsibility for the difficult task of reintegrating IDPs, managing veterans' affairs, or delivering social assistance in a deeply divided and poor polity. This afforded the MSS the space that it needed to formulate policy and deliver in ways that it deemed equitable and expedient.

Initial attempts by the Fretilin-led government to resolve the country's social and political divisions had proven unsuccessful. The government was reluctant to use cash payments to encourage people to return home and was ideologically opposed to the idea of direct social transfers. By contrast, the new coalition government considered that solving the country's social divisions and reintegrating tens of thousands of IDPs required immediate and durable solutions. Cash transfers were seen as instrumental, and the MSS soon found itself responsible for resolving the country's emerging social and political divisions through direct social transfers, social reintegration, and dialogue. IDP payments, veterans' pensions, the *Bolsa de Mãe*, and the elderly and disability pensions would prove central to this strategy of enabling social stability.

IDPs held particular sway over the government during the period of instability and posed a significant threat to public safety and security. To reduce the threat and facilitate reintegration, the government compensated IDPs for damage to or loss of property and initiated a process of social dialogue.[27] An initial payment of US$4,500 for each family reduced the political leverage of IDPs, although some returned to make further claims on the ministry, arguing that their initial payment was inadequate.[28]

The MSS's initial decision had been full and final, but the prime minister ultimately intervened to call for a second payment of US$500 to compensate former IDPs for the loss of their removable assets.

Shortly after IDP compensation was paid, the MSS initiated a series of additional transfer programs—the *Bolsa de Mãe*, the Elderly Pension Program, and the Disability Pension Program—to begin to address the country's social vulnerabilities. At the time of writing, the MSS was implementing four major cash transfer programs that reached more than one-quarter of the population (both directly and indirectly), financed by a budget that would increase to US$128 million in 2012 (see figure 11.2; World Bank 2013, 30).[29] In 2011 social assistance spending prevented the percentage of households with per capita monthly consumption of US$32 from rising from 40–45 percent (World Bank 2013, ch. 5).

Although the 2006 Crisis has long since passed, the MSS continues to face complex social and political pressures. Veterans arguably constitute the most influential of the MSS's persistent pressure groups;[30] and they exercise their influence through the Secretariat of State for Veterans Affairs, which was constituted to represent their interests. The former commander of the Falintil forces[31] and current prime minister, Xanana Gusmão, has helped to raise the profile of the secretariat and ensure that its activities feature as among the ministry's priorities. According to Secretary Marito dos Reis, "Because of the role of the struggle in history, [the government] always

Figure 11.2. Social Transfer Allocations in the State Budget, 2008–12

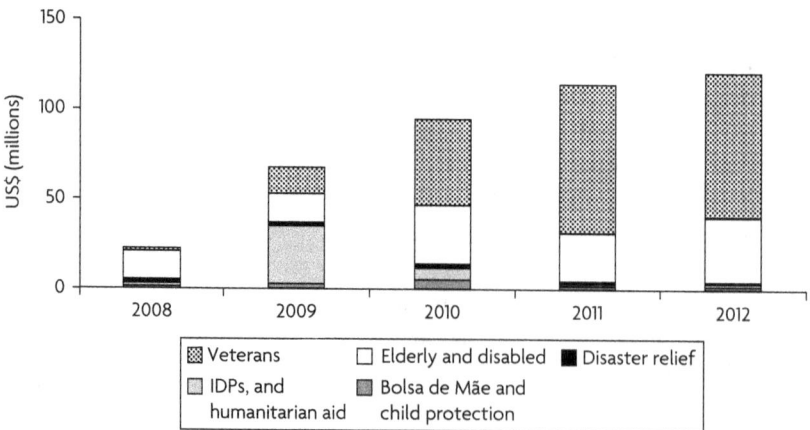

Source: Ministry of Finance 2012.
Note: IDP = Internally Displaced Person.

tries to show tolerance and finds ways to help."[32] This is clearly reflected in the allocation of social transfers, with more than 60 percent of the MSS's total allocation of social transfers directed toward payments to veterans (World Bank 2013, 43). As of 2012, transfers to veterans constituted more than half of all social assistance spending and accounted for 5 percent of the total national budget and 7 percent of non-oil GDP, rendering veterans' pensions a considerable drain on the MSS's budget and a threat to the sustainability of MSS programs (World Bank 2013, 38).

The MSS is developing a reputation for identifying, representing, and responding to the interests of vulnerable and marginalized groups in ways that seek to tackle the underlying causes of their vulnerability, for example, through cash transfers with health and educational conditions. Besides the Ministry of Health, few other ministries represent the interests of vulnerable groups in the way that the MSS does, although the voice and policy influence of these groups remain limited.[33] One civil society group remarked, "Despite a conscious attempt to promote participation and inclusion, an ordinary citizen who is not part of a social pressure group can be left out of the social transfer process." It is also clear that a mismatch exists between results and expectations. The recipients of elderly and disability pensions and *Bolsa de Mãe* benefits who participated in this research welcomed MSS support, although the majority of participants also remarked that the value of MSS benefits—in particular, the elderly pension and the *Bolsa de Mãe* benefits, which are US$30 and US$5 per month, respectively—is inadequate and less than what they need to live.[34] Many of these activities have yet to reach scale in terms of coverage. At the time of writing and in light of mounting evidence that the *Bolsa de Mãe* and other social assistance programs are not meeting poverty or coverage targets (World Bank 2013, 3), the MSS is taking steps to adapt its programs to address the needs of Timor-Leste's most vulnerable and to better contribute to the reduction of poverty.

The Function of Leadership

The MSS has been led by ministers that were committed to delivering and deepening results. Appointed in 2002, the first secretary of state for labor and solidarity, Arsenio Bano, was inexperienced in government but performed well and was politically astute. He communicated well and soon developed the trust and confidence of the prime minister. Initially nonpartisan, Secretary Bano joined the ruling party Fretilin in 2005. Later that same year, the secretariat was renamed the Ministry of Labour and Community

Reinsertion, and Secretary Bano was elevated to the position of minister. When interviewed, the former minister remarked, "In Timor-Leste, if you wanted to be influential, you needed to know where you sit in political terms."

Succeeding Minister Bano, Maria (Micato) Fernandes Alves was appointed minister of a reconfigured Ministry of Social Solidarity under the Fourth Constitutional Government of Timor-Leste. Minister Alves brought much legitimacy to the ministerial office due to her credentials as a member of the clandestine resistance and her leading role in the Timorese women's equality movement as founder of Fokupers.[35] She was also experienced in government, having served as adviser for the promotion of equality to Timor-Leste's first prime minister, and she was known for taking a principled position on matters of policy.[36] Her charismatic legitimacy insulated the ministry from political interference and created space for the MSS to deliver results in a way that was seen as impartial.

The minister had a strong reputation as a technocrat, with a good grasp of policy details. She worked hard to model professionalism and to maintain a nonpartisan ministry, developing strong bonds of trust and confidence with her senior managers and fostering a commitment to social service among staff. Contrary to the experiences in other Timorese ministries, Minister Alves was open to varying political affiliations among staff[37] and reinforced impartiality through a common vision and consistent messaging from the top. A much repeated refrain among staff at the ministry was, "This is the time to liberate our people from poverty" or, to use a football analogy, "We may each wear different jerseys, but in the end we all have a job." This shared purpose and vision motivated staff to transcend party lines and model professionalism.

Priorities and Mandate

The Crisis of 2006 punctuated the MSS's development and sharpened its institutional identity, policies, and mandate. The MSS (then the MLCR) had run some small-scale social assistance programs in the early years of its operations,[38] providing a handful of family subsidies, food packages, and other nonfinancial items to those experiencing the most extreme effects of poverty. But the First Constitutional Government was opposed to making direct cash payments to vulnerable groups, and the ministry focused largely on labor policy and vocational training. When the 2006 Crisis hit, work on less critical aspects of the ministry's mandate (including labor, employment, and vocational training) were temporarily suspended, and all available resources were dedicated to managing the recovery, social reintegration, and security.

Despite volatile sociopolitical conditions, the ministry managed crisis conditions by judiciously mobilizing and deploying resources and learning by doing to deliver results. According to former minister Arsenio Bano, "The activities of the MSS could not wait for the development of the state, the ministry was under urgency to deliver, and we just worked with what was there."[39] Recalling events, the director of social assistance remarked, "*Crise nian kadi ami nia kakutak* [The crisis sharpened our knives]."[40] In 2007, following national elections, the new government formalized and embedded social assistance priorities and made several institutional adjustments. The MSS acquired responsibility for natural disasters from the Ministry of the Interior, and several directorates became secretariats. Youth affairs became an independent secretariat of state, and the MSS also gained a new portfolio of social services to address the issue of contributing and noncontributing pensions for the elderly and veterans.

Although highly susceptible to social and political influence, the MSS acts within the limits of its mandate and uses legal and policy instruments to manage demands from pressure groups. This has strengthened the ministry's internal functioning and its ability to deliver results. It has also enabled the MSS to avoid overloading its operational capabilities. Two particular experiences highlight the kinds of pressure that can be brought to bear on the ministry and the ministry's response.

One involves a community evicted by the Ministry of Justice in 2010 for occupying state-owned land in Aitarak Laran, Dili. The group did not claim title to the land but instead erected an IDP camp in front of the Office of the President, proclaiming themselves to be internally displaced and demanding financial compensation from the ministry. The Ministry of Justice had already paid US$2,000 to each family as compensation for their resettlement, but the community wanted compensation equivalent to that paid to IDPs—that is, US$4,500 per family. Despite overtures to the prime minister and threats that the group would create a disturbance during the national elections, the MSS maintained the position that compensation for eviction and resettlement was the remit of the Ministry of Justice. No further compensation was paid by the MSS, and these IDPs remained in the camp.

A second incident, in early 2011, involved a dispute between youth groups in Zumalai that led to the burning of homes in the village. The ministry was quick to respond by distributing food and nonfood items, but the community felt that the assistance was inadequate. In a letter to Parliament, the disputants requested that the MSS pay an additional US$2,000 to each household as financial compensation. The MSS was steadfast in its refusal to make compensatory payments, in line with its policy of providing only nonfinancial assistance in such cases.

Learning and Adaptation

The MSS has demonstrated an impressive ability to learn, adapt, and respond to client feedback, in line with a building-block approach to institutional development. Learning and adaptation are achieved through program reviews and the direct solicitation of client feedback.

Two particular programs—the Bolsa de Mãe and the Social Dialogue Program—exemplify this approach. The director of social assistance and manager of the Bolsa de Mãe recalled,[41] "Orphanages had grown like mushrooms in the rainy season, not because parents had died, but because some parents were unable to care for their children. A conditional cash transfer was our attempt to provide a solution." The program's eligibility criteria initially targeted individual children within a household, but members of the public complained that the formula was discriminatory and poorly accounted for the circumstances in which people lived and for Timor-Leste's traditional social obligations. The eligibility criteria for the Bolsa de Mãe were subsequently adjusted to account for socio-familial conditions as well as the individual circumstances of the beneficiary. Eligibility is now established through a vulnerability-scoring exercise, and vulnerability is measured against a series of indicators, which include household income, assets, and number of dependents. Households will be resurveyed every two years to identify changes in vulnerability, and those no longer eligible will be phased out (World Bank 2013, 28).

Conceived in 2008, the initial goal of the SDP was to reintegrate IDPs into their respective communities, and this was achieved within the first two years. Riding on its success, social dialogue teams found themselves called on to mediate an increasing range of local grievances ranging from historical revenge killings to land and property disputes and battles between youth and martial arts groups. According to SDP staff, the methodology adopted by the program assists disputants to identify commonalities between them, which helps them to break down inaccurate perceptions and differences. By November 2010, demand for the SDP had broadened so extensively that the program was absorbed into the MSS's permanent institutional structure (see box 11.1).

BOX 11.1

Social Dialogue Program

In July 2008 the Social Dialogue Program was established to assist IDP families to reintegrate into communities where they were no longer welcome or where others had occupied their homes. Initially the SDP was implemented through five MSS/UNDP subdistrict dialogue teams that were regionally located (Same, Suai, Bobonaro, Baucau, and Dili), and it was coordinated by a central team. Two additional teams were established in 2009.

The aim was to replicate the dialogue model adopted during the Truth and Reconciliation Process in Timor-Leste, with some distinctions. The role of the dialogue team was to identify problems between IDPs and receiving communities and to assist in repairing any broken infrastructure. Teams would work with traditional and community leaders and youth representatives and would adopt local traditional practices—*tara bandu, nahe biti bo'ot*, or *lulu biti*—where necessary or practical.

At the time of writing, the SDP had facilitated 770 mediations, including as many as 80 large-scale community dialogue meetings, many of which were attended by high-ranking officials (the president, prime minister, and minister). During the course of these many interactions, disputes mediated by the dialogue teams evolved from those linked to reintegration to more protected historical conflicts and, in some cases, to grievances against the state. According to members of the dialogue team, the MSS's impartial yet participatory approach and its respect for local methods and practices have rendered the SDP a legitimate and credible conflict resolution mechanism in the eyes of community populations. The SDP is now a permanent fixture in the ministry.

The ministry's role in social mediation and dialogue is increasingly highly regarded, in large part because of the success of the SDP. But this success creates more demand for MSS services, which brings with it more responsibility and greater challenges. At the time of writing, the ministry had been designated hefty land dispute resolution functions under the draft land law regime, without prior consultation. The president initially vetoed the regime, and the package of laws went back to Parliament for review. Should it be approved, it will add to the already onerous burden carried by the ministry.

A defining characteristic of the MSS, scarcely practiced elsewhere in Timor-Leste, is the ministry's experience of leading operations with policy as well as law. The ministry has pilot-tested and adopted several policies, including the *Bolsa de Mãe* and its natural disaster management programs, in the absence of a law. This has afforded the MSS the flexibility that it has needed to develop its programs interactively and in response to community feedback, as is particularly evident in the case of the *Bolsa de Mãe* and the SDP. This approach has not been adopted across the ministry writ large,[42] and yet the experience of the MSS suggests that it allows an institution to adapt and adjust its policy or programs to accommodate contextual conditions and to improve program performance.

Building Trust through Social Values and Traditions

"The success of the ministry is predicated on staff who have come to understand that what they do has meaning."
—Minister of Social Solidarity, November 2011

The MSS is not modeled on the social affairs ministry of any other country; it is homegrown.[43] Its mandate is based on Article 56 of the Constitution: "Everyone is entitled to social assistance and security in accordance with the law," and this is further reinforced by a series of complementary provisions.[44] Taken together, the mandate of the ministry is to alleviate the suffering of Timor-Leste's vulnerable population and assist particular interest groups, including veterans of the resistance and their families, youth, the elderly, and the disabled.[45]

Several of the ministry's policies are influenced by policies from elsewhere. The *Bolsa de Mãe* is an adaptation of Brazil's conditional cash transfer programs (the *Bolsa Familia* and the *Bolsa Escola*).[46] The pension schemes are an adaptation of similar pay-as-you-go models found in Portugal and Northern Europe.[47] But policy alignments aside, the MSS is unlike any other institution. Its mandate and programs were created in direct response to Timor-Leste's unique sociopolitical conditions, and this has proven an important attribute of the ministry's development, legitimacy, and resilience. The MSS's mandate is deeply internalized by MSS staff and powerfully resonates with Timor-Leste's citizenry, some of whom feel a sense of entitlement to state support in recognition for their service to the resistance.

In the months and years following the 2006 Crisis, and as part of efforts to break with the past and more directly engage the populous, the ministry extended its subnational capabilities and presence and worked to establish links with Timor-Leste's legitimate traditional leaders.[48] These efforts were intended to facilitate reintegration activities, and to assist with the administration of the *Bolsa de Mãe* and pensions for the elderly and disabled. Expanding the state's reach, these efforts to acknowledge and forge links with local leaders proved to be a crucial first step toward addressing the state-society gap that had persisted for years.

Working with Communities and Reflecting Sociocultural Traditions

Efforts to connect with communities by adopting practices that are consistent with Timor-Leste's strong social traditions are a major source of legitimacy for the MSS. Prior to 2008, despite nearly six years of independence, the government was scarcely present beyond the districts. By 2011, *chefes de suco* and *chefes de aldeia* were playing a prominent role in administering social transfers: facilitating public communications about MSS programs, identifying and registering beneficiaries, and in some cases, assisting with the distribution of cash payments. Traditional leaders have sometimes also worked with the ministry's new subdistrict and community-level representatives—a cadre of social animators and child protection officers—to monitor and manage social grievances.[49] At the same time, the MSS's Social Dialogue Program (box 11.1) has adopted elements of traditional law (*tara bandu*) and practices and procedures for resolving disputes (for example, spreading of the large mat ceremony or *nahe biti bo'ot*).[50] It works with the Timorese traditional elders, the *lia na'in,* in the process.[51] The model of *tara bandu* adopted varies according to the practices or tradition of the community involved, but it is not uncommon for the process to involve the invocation of spirits or cleansing rituals to absolve individuals of wrongdoing and stigma. Several MSS staff (and many focus group participants) said that the ministry's success is largely attributable to the involvement of *chefes de suco* and the regular community dialogues that the ministry has led.

Working with *chefes de suco, chefes de aldeia,* and *lia na'in* has connected the government with local communities, but it also has raised some challenges. A handful of focus group participants complained that *chefes de suco* do not always pass on information and tend to prioritize their relatives in the allocation of MSS benefits. The research team was unable to verify or validate these claims, but a pilot social network analysis conducted as part of a recent World Bank study in the subdistrict of Laleia found that beneficiaries with a kinship relationship to the *chefes de suco* or *chefes de aldeia* were eight times more likely to learn about and register for benefits during the first year than those without kinship ties (World Bank 2011a). In other cases, *chefes de suco* and *chefes de aldeia* were reportedly demanding payments before adding individuals to beneficiary lists.[52] The MSS's relationship with *lia na'in* has encountered fewer difficulties than those with *chefes de suco* or *chefes de aldeia*, as they are not responsible for assessing eligibility for MSS social benefits. Rather, their role is to appraise the dialogue and community engagement procedure adopted to ensure that it is acceptable to the community's ancestors and spirits.[53]

Although *chefes de suco* and *chefes de aldeia* are tasked with implementing government policies and assessing eligibility for social transfers, they are unable to challenge the resulting decisions, which effectively alienates their chiefly problem-solving functions and authority. *Chefes de suco* meet with their subdistrict focal points, but these meetings are irregular, and top-down communication flows render them largely disempowered. One *chefe de suco* complained, "The community is always here protesting that I am not looking after them, and I have told them that if I was the one making the decision, they would have had their money a long time ago. But I have no power over it."[54] Another *chefe de suco* remarked that *chefes de suco* are nonpartisan, and yet their role is increasingly seen as representative of the government, which raises several questions: What will happen if the government changes?[55] What will be the future role of *chefes de suco*?[56] Will they be seen as political?

The MSS's engagement with *chefes de suco* and *chefes de aldeia* is still in its early stages, and the interaction of the state with these local traditional structures raises as many challenges as it does benefits. The graduated reach of the state into domains of community governance is likely to weaken the legitimacy of traditional institutions, which have remained comparably stable since independence, even if they have had limited resources and influence in respect of state authority. Despite these challenges, the MSS's engagement with Timor-Leste's traditional elders and customary decision makers has enhanced the ministry's interaction and connectivity with local communities. It has also instrumentalized the role of *chefes de suco* and *chefes de aldeia* as they begin to act as intermediaries between the community and the government.

Building Communication Links

The ministry lacks a formal communications strategy for many of its programs. Yet it effectively uses the local media and a combination of consultations, public communication, and outreach to engage the public on ministry priorities and programs. Information sharing improved during the events of 2006 as the MSS (then the MLRC) and often the minister himself met with prominent community leaders, interest groups (IDPs, veterans), nongovernmental organizations (NGOs), and partners to coordinate a crisis response, share information, and gather feedback. The MSS retained these coordination and consultation mechanisms. They are still in use today.

Meetings with prominent constituencies such as veterans and IDPs are regularly televised, and MSS directors are expected to convey information on MSS programs through radio broadcasts. Here again, *chefes de suco* act as conduits for public information, although some of them do not play the role well. Bulletins that inform citizens about changes in MSS policies or the outcomes of social benefit applications are posted in local newspapers and on community notice boards, but top-down communication to the village level is still weak, and the *chefes de suco* do not always have access to program information.

Despite variable experiences, community awareness of the ministry's mandate and mission has improved on account of repeat visits by the MSS to local communities. The engagement of *chefes de suco* in the MSS's SDP and in the identification of beneficiaries for the ministry's array of social transfer programs is generating more dynamic communication between the MSS, community leaders, and marginalized and vulnerable groups. The experience has shown that community leaders are engaging more and more with the MSS as they better understand the process, and this contributes to the deepening of MSS policies and programs and institutional legitimacy at the village level. At the same time, the risk of procedural capture is also well known—*chefes de suco* sometimes privilege their own family members—and the MSS is managing their involvement carefully.

Capacity to Deliver

Founded as a secretariat of state, the MSS initially commanded limited political weight and had fewer resources and capacities than other ministries. Yet it soon earned the respect of its peers and, by 2011, was considered among Timor-Leste's leading institutions due to its proven ability to solve social problems.

This section examines the factors that enabled the MSS to overcome the binding constraints of its inner workings and to enhance and expand its capacity to deliver services and achieve positive social outcomes. Four factors stand out as contributing to the ministry's performance and development: an emphasis on bridging gaps in service delivery through effective allocation and use of donor and NGO resources; an emphasis on soft norms as the foundations of internal capacity; a phased and graduated approach to development, even in the context of an influx of resources; and the use of vertical and horizontal accountabilities to discipline performance.

Bridging Service Delivery Gaps

The MSS has forged important links with partners (donors and NGOs) and effectively deployed their skills and resources to bridge service delivery gaps and to respond to crisis. It is mandated by the Constitution to manage and supervise NGOs that work in the public interest (Article 56.3), and it has built long-term partnerships (with the International Labour Organization, the United Nations Children's Fund, and the United Nations Development Fund for Women) in the areas of labor and vocational training and social protection and in the provision of support to vulnerable children and the disabled. Both Ministers Bano and Alves are credited with taking charge of donor and NGO relations, directing partner resources, persuading donors to tow the ministry's policy line, and shielding the ministry from undue donor influence. At no time was this more evident than during the 2006 Crisis, when ministerial leadership was particularly strong. The MSS registers and finances NGOs to deliver public services and administers these arrangements through a system of block grants, which is in line with the approach adopted across government.[57]

The MSS has proven adept at capturing and converting donor resources, deciding who is to do what, and scaling up and coordinating the recovery (including implementation of the HHF), and donors and NGOs have responded well.[58] Mutual trust and confidence run high, except in the area of child protection, where ministry performance lags. Partnerships and coordination are typically managed through specialized working groups, including a Child Protection Network and, since 2006, task forces dedicated to water and sanitation and other activities.

In the context of rapidly accumulating revenues from hydrocarbons, the MSS is becoming less and less dependent on donors for financial aid. As a result, donors and international and national NGOs wield less influence over MSS policies and operations than they do over other line ministries. In 2011, 6.6 percent of the MSS's total budget was provided by donors (compared with 17.6 percent in education and 50 percent in health).[59] The bulk of this money was used to fund humanitarian assistance and peace-building activities, including establishment of the ministry's new Peace-Building Unit. However, despite diminished financial dependence, the MSS will continue to rely on the technical expertise of its partners for some time.[60]

Delegation and Empowerment

The ministry has developed a strident and informed middle management through an iterative approach that has built on existing staff skills (many of which were acquired before independence), and it continues to shape and sharpen those skills through training and the progressive delegation of tasks.[61] The events of 2006 disciplined management skills as they demanded lateral thinking, timely and decisive decision making, integrity, and commitment. During the course of this research, several donors spoke of the tough, disciplined stance of the ministry's directors, particularly in the areas of social security and social assistance. They have grown increasingly confident in making decisions and managing complex programs, such as the *Bolsa de Mãe* and the SDP.

The minister, secretaries of state, and middle management have established and maintain confidence in one another through regular vertical and horizontal communication and strong information flows. Directors remarked that Minister Alves "listens to her staff, technical or otherwise." She also relies on them to issue press releases and make public statements on her behalf and to respond to complex policy and operational matters as they arise. Weekly Consultative Councils are widely attended (by directors, secretaries of state, the director general, and the minister). These provide an opportunity for management to discuss policy issues and to agree on ministry priorities and annual plans of action. They also provide an opportunity for managers to update their colleagues on their respective programs. Free and frank discussion and collaborative problem solving are encouraged.

Authority and Reporting

Reporting lines and authority are strictly enforced within the ministry, which is not always the norm in a Timorese agency. Typically in Timor-Leste, as in other FCSs, ministry advisers (national and international) enjoy privileged access to their respective ministers and function largely on the basis of personalized exchange. In the MSS, advisers are required to follow designated reporting lines. Donors also tend to engage with the MSS at the level of secretariat of state, leaving the minister free from the encumbrances of donor coordination and excessive bureaucracy.

Subnational staff (social animators, child protection officers, and MSS regional coordinators) report to the national center in Dili, copying relevant district administrators. The same staff are also in close contact with *chefes de suco* who, again, are expected to share the information that they receive with their villages. A demand-side accountability mechanism exists through these backward and forward linkages, although, with weak top-down communication and dependence on the commitment and performance of each *chefe de suco*, it does not yet function in the way envisioned. The ministry convenes at least two meetings in Dili each year with all national and subnational staff,[62] and has a system for rotating district staff to Dili for national-level exposure to the ministry and other public agencies.

Adopting a Building-Block Approach

Both ministers have taken a graduated approach to the ministry's development, but in different ways. Minister Bano sought to establish a nucleus of basic institutional and human capacities and a regional presence before developing the ministry's technical expertise. Institutional and skills development continued under the stewardship of Minister Alves, but the 2006 Crisis punctuated this process in important ways, altering the ministry's institutional development priorities. Minister Alves initially set a two-year emergency recovery period and followed this with a three-year consolidation phase that was dedicated to expanding the MSS's pool of social transfer beneficiaries and to enabling systems reform to improve data management and targeting.

Since 2005 and the inception of the MSS, the ministry has sought to develop and expand its frontline services in a graduated way, down to the districts and subdistricts. The recruitment of social animators and child protection officers[63] in the districts and subdistricts in 2008 and the modest yet incremental purchase of operating capital, goods, and services (for example, office space, motorcycles, food, and fuel) enabled the MSS to establish a district and community presence.

Contrasting the ministry's graduated approach to its frontline service delivery, its budget has expanded year on year and by almost 600 percent since 2008. This spike in the ministry's budget has been used to fund crisis management and recovery, veterans' pensions, and direct social transfers. It has also financed the rapid expansion of beneficiaries and payments over the past three years.

The social assistance allocation for 2012 constituted approximately 9 percent of the national budget, more than any other sector besides infrastructure,[64] although this was a relative decline from its peak in 2009, which saw a fivefold increase in the state budget and a tremendous allocation for infrastructure. Of the total budget, 8 percent was allocated to social assistance activities led by the MSS. Indeed, the MSS's social assistance spending has continued to rise in absolute terms, from US$22 million in 2008 to US$121 million in 2012 (World Bank 2013, 37). Recent analysis shows that, when the budget for payments to veterans is excluded, the pattern looks considerably more varied (World Bank 2013, 37); again, payments to veterans constitute a serious fiscal sustainability risk and far outstrip the allocation for other social benefit programs in the MSS. The rapid jump in budgetary resources allocated to the ministry had the potential to paralyze the MSS, given its limited capacity for absorption. Yet the ministry has maintained a strong and consistent track record in cash-based execution, ranking second or third among Timorese ministries, including with spending down to the subdistricts (97 percent execution in 2010).[65] At the same time, the MSS continues to expand its results-based performance.

Despite showing basic capacities to spend, making direct cash payments does not equate with effectively converting revenues into public goods. The MSS's overall track record in planning and budgeting is suboptimal. Planning (particularly bottom-up) and budget links are still weak, as they are across government, and volatility in the government's procurement policy strains the ministry's ability to consolidate its procurement capacity. Directors currently have a US$5,000 limit on procurement, and repeat cycles of devolution and retrenchment in procurement authority have introduced volatility and undermined efficiency in the system, confusing staff and rendering them subject to cycles of re-learning.

Implementing Vertical and Horizontal Accountability

The ministry sees itself as being vertically and horizontally accountable to the political leadership and Timorese citizenry and has adopted several mechanisms to fulfill its fiduciary functions. The minister interacts with the Council of Ministers, reporting on progress in program implementation. The exchange is free and frank, and the minister openly discusses the challenges faced. In line with her principled approach, Minister Alves does not shy away from tough policy debates with political heavyweights in the Council of Ministers.[66]

The ministry conducts independent audits of its programs and accounts (although not all of these are readily available).[67] It also institutes internal disciplinary measures in cases of malfeasance, which is not common practice in a Timorese institution. One director and two senior staff were recently removed, and some 21 staff under temporary contracts with the HHF did not have their contracts renewed due to questionable administrative practices. Two further disciplinary actions were taken against Oecusse-based staff found to be falsifying data and making fraudulent elderly and disabled payments.

In many respects, the MSS is seen as transparent and makes good use of community radio and public notice boards to convey information about public policies and programs. But the ministry lacks a unified database for storing data on MSS programs, and this renders effective case management and monitoring difficult. One *chefe de suco* (Lalawa) complained that the MSS lists of recipients of the *Bolsa de Mãe* and elderly pensions are inaccurate and cited incidents of people actively misleading MSS staff, for example, by taking children from other people's homes to show more dependents or by falsifying dates of birth.[68] The same *chefe de suco* reported that he knew of several cases in which Indonesian citizens had crossed the border from West Timor to Timor-Leste to claim MSS benefits.[69] In other cases, the MSS did not verify the lists of beneficiaries prepared by *chefes de suco* and *chefes de aldeia*, simply taking them on trust. In all, the HHF has encountered several administrative problems, ranging from the falsification and manipulation of data to the preferential and politicized allocation of payments, some of which were either executed or facilitated by MSS staff. The MSS has signaled its intention to tackle these problems by making improvements in several ways—in its verification and data-processing systems, through the development of an integrated database and through the creation of links between accountability and staff performance—but progress is slow (MSS 2009a).[70]

The ministry has taken an impressive stance on handling IDP complaints, adopting case-by-case management and making all decisions public, but the absence of a system for appeals has fragmented the process. Some cases are referred to the Office of the *Provedor* (Ombudsman) for Justice and Human Rights for investigation; some are brought by individuals and community groups directly to members of Parliament and the prime minister, which typically results in the case being referred back to the MSS and, on occasion, to the minister for her response.[71] Ad hoc systems for registering citizen complaints exist in the districts (with social animators), but these are poorly managed, and complaints often go unattended.[72]

Recruiting Locally and Building on Existing Resources

With severely depleted human resources at independence, the MSS was fortunate to recruit several staff with prior social work experience. At the same time, it has taken steps to produce a pipeline of newly qualified recruits. Around 50 percent of MSS respondents for this research had been trained (mostly in Indonesia) and previously worked as social workers, child protection officers, or youth and community liaisons during the occupation and prior to joining the MSS. Similarly, almost all members of the social dialogue teams had experience conducting community dialogues.[73]

In 2002, the MSS introduced a regional recruitment policy to ensure that new recruits (each child protection officer, each social animator, and every member of the social dialogue teams) were recruited from and reside in the regions in which they work. This regional affinity is an important feature of the MSS's conflict prevention and resolution policy and provides a foundation of trust between MSS staff and local communities. Also important is that all of the directors appointed after the referendum and by the First Constitutional Government retained their management position through a change of government and ministry leadership, establishing a foundation of institutional knowledge within the ministry.

The ministry has conducted baseline assessments of staff capacity (self-assessments) and complements these with external assessments of its strengths and weaknesses. South-South exchanges have also helped. The ministry launched a South-South Cooperation Program, sending select SDP staff to Ethiopia to gain experience in a fragile state. Other staff members have been sent to attend conflict and mediation trainings in Oslo and Geneva. The caliber of these training programs is reportedly high, and the conflict resolution approaches that are acquired are adapted and routinely applied in Timor-Leste. The MSS has forged a partnership with the National University of Timor-Leste and is helping it to formulate a social service master's program to generate a domestic supply of social workers.

The ministry is not autonomous in human resource management; the Civil Service Commission is responsible for civil service recruitment and has the final say on staff discipline, but the relationship works well and the ministry can make recommendations on proposed recruitment or dismissal to the commission. MSS staff expressed few of the frustrations expressed by the staff of other ministries about the commission's protracted recruitment procedures. Performance reviews of MSS staff are conducted every six months, in line with the requirements of the civil service regime, and disciplinary actions are taken in cases of underperformance. Improvements in staff performance are slow to materialize due to weak incentives in the Timorese civil service, although again, the 2006 Crisis served to improve staff performance.

Analysis of Causal Factors

To conclude, Timor-Leste is fortunate to have large hydrocarbon reserves, which have afforded the ministry the fiscal reserves it has needed to tackle the country's social divisions through direct social transfers. But the ministry's success is due to more than the prodigious use of cash transfers. The MSS has used the opportunities afforded to it to overcome the binding constraints of its internal and external operating environments to deliver results, gain legitimacy, and build durability and resilience.

The MSS proved capable of tackling three particular challenges that it faced early on: meeting client demand and citizen expectations, responding to a crisis and rebuilding trust between the state and society, and enhancing and expanding its capabilities to deliver results in a highly constrained institutional and operational context. As the preceding schematic and granular analysis has shown, the following factors have contributed to the ministry's initial success in a causal way.

First, the MSS has leveraged its agency as an institution for recovery and change to manage tremendous client demands and citizen expectations in its pathway to development. Charismatic leaders have steered the MSS to deliver what was needed in ways that were nonpartisan and built trust. At the same time, the MSS has judiciously managed competing priorities by adhering to the bounds of its mandate and resisting being drawn into tasks outside of its competence. Equally important ingredients of the ministry's success and its ability to meet client demands are that the ministry has led with policies and not law, enabling incremental policy adjustments; it has embraced innovation and learned by doing, as seen in the SDP and in the *Bolsa de Mãe*; and it has actively solicited and internalized client feedback. This combination of actions and approaches has ensured the relevance, credibility, and durability of MSS programs.

Second, the Crisis of 2006 proved a watershed for the MSS's development, which sharpened the ministry's focus toward addressing the country's social vulnerabilities and securing citizens' trust. It also produced a ministry capable of leading the country from crisis to recovery through a combination of social dialogue, direct social transfers, and community engagement.

The content of its programs—the HHF, the Veterans' Pension Program, *Bolsa de Mãe*, the Elderly Pension Program, and the Disability Pension Program—were a direct response to Timor-Leste's distinct social conditions and deeply resonated with Timorese concerns. The Crisis disciplined internal management capacities and improved performance, particularly in those instances where there was a high risk of a return to violence, as was the case with reintegrating IDPs. The MSS collaborated with local leaders (*chefes de suco, chefes de aldeia*, and traditional elders) to socialize MSS programs; combined outreach, consultation, and public communications; and adopted local traditional practices (*tara bandu and nahe biti bo'ot*) to extend the ministry's reach and resolve local conflicts. These efforts secured MSS legitimacy and ensured that MSS programs are socially embedded at the community level. In this light, the Crisis shaped the ministry's ability to deliver results and triggered citizen-state connectivity—which was built on the MSS's legitimacy—where it had previously not existed.

As perhaps best put by the minister, "The success of the ministry is not simply down to the end result; it is a process, built on those who laid the foundation in the past."[74] The ministry's approach to enhancing and expanding its service delivery capacities was phased and adaptive, providing the basis for a sustained development trajectory, even as the ministry's responsibilities and resources increased tenfold. Here again, this case study presents further evidence that the supplementary ingredients of institutional success are the manner in which the MSS effectively commanded the resources and capabilities of its partners, emphasized soft norms (leadership and management, shared vision, and integrity), and empowered managers to make tough decisions.

Challenges

The MSS's overall performance is impressive, but challenges persist. Left unaddressed, these risk eroding the ministry's capacity to deliver results and its hard-earned legitimacy and resilience.

Although leading the country's stabilization and recovery, the essential challenge facing the MSS is that its current social assistance programs are not well targeted to addressing poverty. Recent analysis shows that, despite a rapid escalation of social assistance spending, the benefits of the MSS's cash transfer programs are not reaching the majority of Timor-Leste's poor. Its social transfers are largely categorical—that is, they are targeted to specific groups (elderly and disabled, war veterans, and vulnerable households)—and this does not correspond with the country's poverty profile across the board.[75] Benefits are skewed: while 60 percent of the poor and 56 percent of the extreme poor are not receiving any assistance from the MSS's four primary cash transfer programs, 23 percent of the population in the wealthiest quintile are benefiting (World Bank 2013, 50–53).[76]

For Timor-Leste, expanding the pool of eligible beneficiaries in a pro-poor way and making payments at scale and to all eligible beneficiaries are necessary to realize measurable welfare and poverty impacts at levels commensurate with the MSS's current level of social spending. This requires policy reforms and improved systems and administration. Program monitoring tools exist—databases, verification systems, monitoring and evaluation, grievance redress mechanisms, and operational reviews—but these are ad hoc and performance is uneven (World Bank 2013, 57).[77] The government has signaled its commitment to reform, but real improvements have been limited.[78]

Veterans' pensions also present a particularly bifurcating challenge for the MSS. Verification and payment of veterans' pensions lag,[79] but these pensions could quickly become unsustainable if they continue to expand. As the country's future revenues come under increasing strain—which may happen in the near term given current rates of spending and delays in the development of Greater Sunrise[80]—difficult choices will need to be made about the MSS's social priorities (World Bank 2013).

The relative success of the MSS's social transfer regime was unexpected, given systemic administrative weaknesses across government at the time and the risks of political capture. But MSS performance in other areas, particularly in the delivery of social services (for example, child protection) and in the management of domestic violence cases, lags behind its performance in cash payments. Ministry resources are stretched and thinning; social transfers increased 600 percent between 2008 and 2011, but staffing levels remained flat, and resource budgets did not expand as quickly as the decentralization of functions. District and subdistrict staff carry hefty responsibilities and are overextended.[81]

Managing the country's social problems will continue to be difficult. Part of this involves mediating historical conflicts while avoiding the pitfalls of becoming the go-to ministry for all of the country's social grievances. Popular and political expectations of the ministry have increased along with its initial success; the downside risk is that the responsibilities of the ministry will continue to expand despite the thinness of its human resources.[82]

Particularly worrying is the wide perception that the MSS compensates grievances with cash, and this view will be difficult to stem.

In the end, managing the surge of popular and political expectations of the ministry requires strong political leadership from the prime minister, the minister, and partner ministries. Yet the designation of more and more complex tasks to the MSS, including management of land disputes, suggests that this need is not yet well understood, and there is much to be said for efforts to twin national priorities and public messaging with the ministry's existing capabilities to allow the MSS to continue to manage and meet popular demand.

Annex 11A Ministry of Social Solidarity Milestones

1975	Indonesian occupation
1976	Timor-Leste officially annexed as 27th province of Indonesia
1999	Referendum for independence, widespread destruction at hands of Indonesian militia
	United Nations Transitional Administration in East Timor (UNTAET) and Department of Social Affairs created
	50 percent of population under poverty line
2002	Timor-Leste gains independence
	Secretariat of State for Labor and Solidarity created Arsenio Bano appointed secretary
2005	Secretariat of State for Labor and Solidarity becomes a ministry
	Secretariat of State for Veterans Affairs created in Secretariat of State for Labor and Solidarity
2006	Timor-Leste social and political crisis, 130,000 displaced
2007	First parliamentary elections in Timor-Leste since independence and new coalition government formed
	Ministry of Social Solidarity established, and Dona Micato appointed minister
2008	Together Building the Future (*Hamutuk Hari'i Futuru*, HHF), the Mother's Purse Program (*Bolsa da Mãe*), the Elderly (*Idosos*) Pension Program, and the Disability (*Invalidos*) Pension Program launched
2009	Payment of veterans' pensions begins
	Last internally displaced persons camp closes
2010	Review of *Bolsa de Mãe*, in collaboration with the Bureau for Conflict Prevention and Recovery, the UNDP, and the World Bank to improve targeting and management information systems
2011	Social Security Law approved in the Council of Ministers
2012	Meeting "MSS 10-Year Review: Looking Back; 10 Years since Independence"

Notes

1. The Department of Social Affairs, established under the United Nations Transitional Administration in East Timor, had focused principally on providing humanitarian assistance, but the department was disbanded on independence, and two independent social ministries (health and education) and a Secretariat of State for Labor and Solidarity (SSLS) were created. The SSLS was given responsibility for youth affairs, labor, and vocational training and acquired a small social services portfolio. In 2005, the secretariat of state became a ministry, and the veteran's affairs portfolio was placed under a new Secretariat of State for Veterans Affairs. The SSLS mandate was broad, and yet it emphasized labor and vocational training. Constrained by scarce resources, social services tended to lag, except in the areas of child protection and humanitarian assistance, where donors were particularly active.

2. The *Bolsa de Mãe* is a cash transfer program established in 2008 that pays benefits to female-headed households to address hardship. The payment of benefits is conditional on enrollment in and completion of each level of schooling.

3. This figure includes direct and indirect beneficiaries—that is, individuals living in a household in which at least one member is receiving a benefit.

4. At the time of report preparation, an updated poverty estimate and profile for Timor-Leste were not available. In order to conduct impact analysis of social assistance, it was therefore necessary to select an alternative subset of the population. The alternative subset selected was the poorest 40 percent of the population in terms of total per capita expenditure. This threshold is designed exclusively to identify key poverty characteristics and to estimate the extent of poverty reduction from the main cash transfer programs and should not be confused with the official poverty line used for the statistical purposes of counting the poor. In the absence of an official poverty estimate for 2011, the underlying indicator of living standards is total per capita expenditure derived from total household expenditure reported in the most recent Household Income and Expenditure Survey (National Statistics Institute 2011a).

5. In Timor-Leste, 15 percent of GDP secured a 5 percent poverty reduction, while an average of 1 percent of GDP achieved a poverty reduction of 3.0, 0.9, and 0.1 percent in the Philippines, Malaysia, and Cambodia, respectively.

6. For example, 60 percent of the total social assistance budget is consumed by payments to veterans. This assistance is overly generous toward too few beneficiaries to have a sizable impact on poverty. At the same time, 86 percent of the elderly are receiving elderly benefits. It is thought that the 5 percentage point reduction in poverty is almost entirely a result of elderly benefits, as only 14 percent of the disabled are receiving their disability entitlement.

7. Although education is free in Timor-Leste, there are fees for exams in addition to costs for transportation and school-related activities.

8. It was further said, "A remarkable delegation of 70 Indonesian officials attended, led by the serving defense minister, armed forces chief, and former vice president, Try Sutrisno, who had been head of the military when Xanana Gusmão had been captured." See International Crisis Group (2011, 13).

9. *Superior pensions* are payable to a small number of veterans distinguished for their outstanding contribution to the struggle, including the president and prime minister, among others. *Special retirement pensions* are payable to veterans who served 8–14 years full-time in the struggle for national independence and to veterans incapable of working due to physical or mental disabilities resulting from their participation in the struggle. *Subsistence pensions* are payable to veterans with at least 15 years of full-time participation in the struggle for national independence, with Roster 1 allocated to those with 20 or more years of service and Roster II to those with 15–20 years of service. *Survival pensions* are payable to the surviving spouse, orphans (regardless of age), parents, or siblings of National Liberation veteran combatants who died as a result of their participation in the struggle or who were beneficiaries of either the special subsistence or special retirement pensions and have since died.

10. MSS advisers tasked with reintegrating IDPs after the 2006 Crisis cited several obstacles, including the security threat posed by rebel leader Alfredo Reinado and his men. The killing of Alfredo Reinado helped to restore security and stability in the country, while the benefits provided under the MSS reintegration program provided the means for people to get on with life.

11. Interview with Silvia Cardosos, MSS social animator for Cristo Rei, Dili, October 28, 2011. She had helped to secure the school fee for a young girl whose father subsequently thanked her for her work. In another example, the social animator in Same reported that the family of a young girl who had been sexually abused had offered their thanks for his efforts to engage child protection. Other family members were less pleased.

12. Interview with MSS social animator, Dili, October 28, 2011.

13. The share of assistance relative to household expenditure varies considerably across programs. In the case of *Bolsa de Mãe*, the value of the benefit relative to household expenditure is low and represents only 2.7 percent of the total household budget for households in the bottom 20 percent. By contrast, veterans' pensions are the most generous benefits, representing 152 percent of the total household budget (World Bank 2013, 53).

14. Focus group discussion with *chefes de suco* and *chefes de aldeia*, Bidau Santana, December 15, 2011.

15. Interview with the *chefes de suco*, Kosta Village, Oecusse, 2011.

16. At the time of writing, Maria (Micato) Fernandes Alves was incumbent minister, and all references to the minister in this study refer to her.
17. Interview, UNDP, Dili, October 12, 2011. At the time of writing, the 2012 Annual Action Plan for the ministry committed a substantial pillar of its work to preventing and minimizing up to 90 conflicts at the community level, including through understanding the root causes of conflict and mediation and dialogue to resolve identified conflicts.
18. See http://geosite.jankrogh.com/borders/other/timor—leste.htm.
19. The ministry became responsible for the Commission for Tribute to Ex-Combatants of National Liberation.
20. Interview with former minister of labor and community reinsertion, October 21, 2011.
21. Poverty was then defined by the capacity to buy food and nonfood items to meet consumption requirements, which was equivalent to earnings of less than US$0.55 per day. The 2006–07 budget foreshadowed specific benefits to veterans who fought in the resistance; basic housing was offered to veterans (US$1 million allocated), and pension payments (US$2 million allocated) were to start in August 2006. But social assistance was still limited and provided only palliative relief to those few most acutely in need (Ministry of Planning and Finance 2006).
22. In the *Timor-Leste Human Development Report* (UNDP 2006), poverty is defined as living on less than US$1 per day.
23. Remarkably, and in a context of considerable threats to public safety and security, the Ministry of Health and Ministry of Labour and Community Reconciliation were among the few ministries that continued operating, indicating their strength.
24. The new coalition involved the National Congress for Timorese Reconstruction, the Democratic Party, the Social Democratic Party, and the Timorese Democratic Social Association.
25. The HHF did more than propose the reintegration of IDPs; several components aimed to address the underlying determinants of vulnerability—that is, security, livelihoods, and social protection—and included a conflict prevention and dialogue program to facilitate IDP reintegration and rebuild trust within communities and between communities and the government. The transitional budget for October–December 2007 allocated US$2 million to support the displaced, and this was spent mainly on replacement tents and tarpaulins, health, drainage, and preparations for the wet season. A further US$15 million was allocated in 2008, but only for reintegration, and this proved inadequate. In the end, the HHF was unable to deliver the comprehensive solution that it had presented, and important elements of the plan were dropped, including the option to resettle in another location, owing to a failure on the part of the Ministry of Justice to make state land available.

Political will to deliver a whole-of-government response apparently dwindled as the complex reality of a comprehensive solution sank in. Leadership by the vice prime minister was weak, and several of the key ministries designated responsibilities under the recovery strategy failed to deliver on their designated tasks.

26. The prime minister has had a particular interest in seeing his electoral commitments met and in satiating the demands of veterans. Other political elites—for example, the president, other ministers, and parliamentarians—have made political commitments, including, in the case of the president and vice prime minister, promises to the poor. Focus group participants spoke repeatedly of the president, vice prime minister (as responsible for social affairs across government), and other senior political leaders passing through villages promising assistance.

27. Focus group discussion with IDPs in Bidau Santana, December 15, 2011. When they were asked if they thought the MSS did a good job, participants responded, "They did a good job, 100 percent."

28. The one-off payments had been intended as full and final and were several times more than the annual per capita income in the country at the time paid. The MSS managed IDP complaints on a case-by-case basis, but, at some point, the prime minister intervened and committed the ministry to making a second one-off payment to compensate the same IDPs for the loss of their removable assets.

29. Although the MSS is the government's primary social assistance provider, it is by no means the only one. Several additional funds established in other parts of the government provide social assistance, including a Food Security Fund run by the Ministry of Tourism and Commerce, a School Feeding Program in the Ministry of Education, and a labor-based Public Works Program under the Secretariat of State for Vocational Training and Employment. However, approximately three-quarters of all social assistance spending is concentrated in MSS programs.

30. Veterans' primary interests are in recognizing their service to the resistance, which is done through medal ceremonies and monetary awards.

31. Falintil was the military front of the resistance.

32. Interview November 2011.

33. Vulnerable groups, as reflected in the focus groups, want to be relieved from the rigors of poverty. They look to the government for the provision of basic necessities and for support to recover from natural disasters when these occur. Focus group discussion with MSS dialogue participants, Babulo Village, Aliambata, November 24, 2011.

34. Focus group participant views in Bairro Pité Village, Dili, October 31, 2011, and Oesono Sub-village, Oecusse, December 22, 2011. Recent World Bank data confirm that the *Bolsa de Mãe* is not having an appreciable impact on

poverty (World Bank 2013, 3), although the same research also shows that the elderly and disability pensions do reflect international standards.

35. Established in 1997, Fokupers investigates women's human rights violations and provides support, including counseling, to women political prisoners, wives of political prisoners, war widows, and survivors of violence against women.

36. Minister Alves was a founding member of Fokupers, while the former minister was a former director of an NGO consortium, the NGO Forum. In 2006, the minister, who was then adviser to the prime minister on the promotion of equality, resigned from the government to protest its poor crisis management. She was then entrusted by the former president (now prime minister) to coordinate the Simu Malu—a National Dialogue for Reconciliation. Simu Malu was initially intended to restore security and trust at the community level to create an enabling environment for return, including through the use of customary peace-building activities. See Trinidad and Castro (2007, 34). The national dialogue met with limited success, largely because there was a lack of resources and unclear division of roles and responsibilities, yet it almost certainly contributed to the minister's appointment in 2007.

37. The minister and many directors are opposition Fretilin party members, while several secretaries of state and mid-level staff are drawn from other prominent political parties or associations, including Fretilin Mudança, Alliance of Parliament, and Resistencia Nacional dos Estudantes de Timor-Leste.

38. Ministerio do Trabalho e Reinserção Comunidade.

39. Interview 2011.

40. Interview of the Director of Social Assistance, Carmen da Cruz, November 2011.

41. Interview 2011.

42. At the time of writing, the social security scheme in the Directorate of Social Security was awaiting passage of a law.

43. The MSS's predecessor, the MLCR, was similar to a ministry in Mozambique.

44. The Constitution of the Democractic Republic of Timor-Leste provides for the establishment of a social security system (Section 56) and support for veterans of the resistance and their survivor families (Section 11), children, youth, the elderly, and the disabled (Sections 18–21, respectively).

45. Section 11, para. 18–21, of the Constitution of the Democratic Republic of Timor-Leste.

46. The Brazilian Poverty Center on Cash Transfers provides advice and guidance to the MSS to improve the calculations and implementation of the Bolsa de Mãe program.

47. In social security, there are two principal types of systems: capitalization and pay-as-you-go. The minister and MSS management decided that pay-as-you-go (as in Portugal and Northern Europe) was best suited to the Timorese context.

48. Including *chefes de suco, chefes de aldeia*, and traditional elders (*lia na'in*).

49. Recruited in 2008, MSS social animators are community-level representatives principally tasked with managing payments to veterans and to the families of martyrs, cases of child abuse, and administration of *Bolsa de Mãe*.

50. *Tara bandu* are traditional laws used by communities in Timor-Leste to regulate relations between people and groups as well as between people and the environment. In the *Tara Bandu* process, communities set out the procedures and methods allowed when using or harvesting natural resources and the penalties for those who violate them.

51. *Lia na'in* are literally the "keepers or masters of words." They are traditional elders or spiritual leaders who come to the office by lineage or heritage. The methods used to resolve disputes vary depending on the nature of the problem. Compensation and the use of traditional procedures for resolving disputes are common. The traditional procedures tend to be used where there are ongoing family relations. The mediation process secures agreement to use the traditional process. It is said that social dialogue works well in Timor-Leste because of the social and cultural context. These mechanisms are familiar to and used by many.

52. Focus group participants in Suco Costa reported, "In Situa Sae people must give money to the *chefes de suco* or *chefes de aldeia* to register their names," and there were similar allegations in other villages.

53. Traditional elders in Timor-Leste are seen as ancestral custodians and conduits of the spirit world.

54. Interview, *chefe de suco*, Costa Village, December 2011.

55. According to Timor-Leste's 2009 Law on Community Authorities, the *suco* is a "community organization," and *suco* leaders, although publicly elected, are not part of the government structure. They consult with the Ministry of State Administration and Territorial Management on all activities specifically falling within its mandate; social protection is not among these activities.

56. *Chefe de suco* from Lalawa.

57. The MSS signs individual memorandums of understanding with each NGO. According to MSS staff, the ministry conducts rigorous monitoring and evaluation exercises every three months to assess NGO results, although at least one MSS adviser suggested that these exercises are of questionable quality.

58. The ministry has been known to undertake policy research and invite donors to share policy options through multi-donor working groups. For example, the World Bank, International Labour Organization, and the Australian Agency for International Development have been invited to give presentations on various social security models.

59. The MSS received 3.5 percent of the total share of development partner support, compared with 8.7 and 5.6 percent for health and education, respectively.

This comprised 19 development partner projects with a combined value of US$6.9 million out of an overall MSS budget of US$104,678 million (that is, 6.6 percent; Ministry of Finance 2011, 29).

60. The law requires the MSS to work with other government agencies in the execution of some of its tasks, such as the Ministry of Justice for data verification; the National Police (*Policia National Timor-Leste*) for reintegration and community-level security; and the ministries of infrastructure, health, and finance for support for disaster and crisis recovery and the allocation of financial resources. The strength of these relationships varies and is not seen as decisive in the ministry's overall performance. Coordination has not always worked well and depends heavily on the leadership and resources of the partner ministry. MSS staff complain that some ministries see social issues as the responsibility of the MSS alone and disregard obvious interagency links. The HHF suffered from the informal nature of its coordination mechanisms and the ad hoc manner in which messages were communicated to lower-level civil servants across government. However, the Ministry of Health and the Ministry of Education impressively mobilized lower-level civil servants to provide in-camp education and health facilities following the Crisis of 2006 (MSS 2009a, 8). However, the *Bolsa de Mãe*, Elderly Pension Program, and Disability Pension Program each encountered problems verifying data held by other government ministries. A more positive experience is seen in the SDP, which has worked well with the Land and Property Directorate of the Ministry of Justice and the National Police, but not so well with others.

61. This was particularly true under the leadership of Minister Bano, where the early foundations of the MSS's middle-management capacities were laid. Minister Micato has continued and deepened this approach.

62. Ministry staff report that these are typically well attended; staff in the field report that they have easy access to the leadership in Dili. Summary of focus group discussions, January 2012.

63. To give an example of MSS resourcing, the Manufahi region has three child protection officers and seven social animators.

64. Approximately three-quarters of social assistance spending is concentrated in MSS-delivered programs. In 2012, the MSS was allocated 8 percent of the total budget, compared with 6 percent for the Ministry of Education, 3 percent for the Ministry of Health, and 1 percent for the Ministry of Agriculture and Fisheries (World Bank 2013, 37).

65. The remaining 3 percent was attributed to data inconsistencies.

66. A popular anecdote circulating in Timor-Leste is that the minister successfully pushed back on political pressure from the prime minister and other senior ministers to expedite IDP removal and close the camps, successfully advocating for a phased and more carefully managed approach.

67. A handful of audit reports are publicly available on the government's new transparency portal, in line with the commitment of the Ministry of Finance to make government data more readily available, although not all MSS audits are public. See http://www.transparency.gov.tl/english.html. The government's transparency portal provides real-time information on budget execution, together with data on aid assistance, government procurements, and government results, although the latter are less regularly updated.

68. Interview with the *chefe de suco*, Lalawa.

69. This particular *chefe de suco* has since taken the initiative to develop his own lists to cross-reference MSS registrants with those receiving payments, to counter the trend in falsifying claims, and to assist MSS in resolving data discrepancies.

70. Although still at a nascent stage, the ministry is in the process of instituting important internal controls, which it is hoped will reduce the incidence of problem cases. Internal audit, the integration of intra- and inter-ministry databases, and building individual accountability into staff performance results are among the measures to try to achieve this.

71. Interview with the International Organisation for Migration country representative, October 14, 2011.

72. Interview with the social animator from the subdistrict of Lautem, October 2011.

73. Among members of the Ermera social dialogue team, one had been the coordinator of a youth group, while another had worked with the Fundação Alola and had a sound basis of experience in dealing with sexual assault and domestic violence cases in local communities.

74. Interview November 2011.

75. The programs for the elderly and disabled are designed as social security to provide a basic subsistence income. By contrast, *Bolsa de Mãe* aims to alleviate poverty and create opportunities for upward mobility for its beneficiaries, focusing specifically on families in need. See World Bank (2013, 66).

76. A recent analysis of expenditure suggests three reasons why the MSS's existing social transfers have not better targeted poverty (World Bank 2013, 57). First, 71 percent of MSS transfers are consumed by payments to veterans, which are overly generous toward too few beneficiaries to have a sizable impact on poverty. Second, categorical targeting overlaps with the incidence of poverty but leaves out a large proportion of the population, particularly youth. Third, although MSS programs, especially *Bolsa de Mãe*, could reduce poverty, they are too small in coverage and in the size of the benefit relative to the poverty gap to affect poverty status.

77. At the time of writing, the MSS was in the process of creating a unified management information system and databases (excluding the database on veterans) and was exploring options to improve targeting, payment reconciliation, and information management.

78. The MSS's administrative capabilities and its inner workings are nascent and fragile, despite early signs of functionality. Improved communications (between central and subnational levels of the MSS, between villages and the ministry, and within communities), together with improved inter-government planning and integrity in fiscal management, will be needed to expand and deepen the MSS's presence and performance. As it is, information goes up but rarely trickles down, and social transfer applicants are often ill-informed about the outcome of their claims.

79. Some 200,000 veterans, *clandestinos*, and their surviving family members are now registered, but only 12,540 are receiving benefits. This has caused disappointment for many veterans and a sense that government policy is inconsistent and opaque. *Clandestinos* refer to members of the unarmed civilian resistance.

80. Greater Sunrise is Timor-Leste's largest hydrocarbon reserve, which sits across two territorial boundaries—that of Timor-Leste and that of Australia. Greater Sunrise is not yet under development.

81. Several of the social animators interviewed were overwhelmed by the sensitivity, complexity, and sheer number of complaints or incidents emerging. Child protection officers are responsible for managing sensitive social issues, including violence (gender-based violence), abuse, and exploitation, and they monitor cases and accompany clients to the courts and through the questioning process. They also monitor shelters and child welfare institutions, participate in subdistrict working groups for women and children, and provide emergency assistance as needed, as in the case of Zumalai Village. Similarly, social animators respond to cases of child abuse and administer *Bolsa de Mãe* and veteran's payments. They are not responsible for resolving individual cases, but they are responsible for monitoring, reporting, and referring cases, and the quality and depth of their qualifications and experience vary hugely. They also have limited resources for shuttling between dispersed communities to solve problems.

82. The ministry was designated hefty dispute resolution functions under the draft land law regime, without being consulted. The president initially vetoed the regime, and the package of laws went back to Parliament for review. Should it be approved, it will add to the already onerous burden carried by the ministry.

References

Bulgalski, Natalie. 2010. "Post Conflict Housing Reconstruction and the Right to Adequate Housing in Timor-Leste." Background paper for 16th session on post-disaster and post-conflict situations, Human Rights Council, Geneva.

International Crisis Group. 2011. "Timor-Leste's Veterans: An Unfinished Struggle." Asia Briefing 129, International Crisis Group, Brussels, November 18.

Knezevic, Neven. 2005. *Timor-Leste: Background Paper on Human Rights, Refugees, and Asylum Seekers*. Report commissioned by the High Commissioner for Refugees, Protection Information Section, Geneva.

IDMC (Internal Displacement Monitoring Centre). 2009. "IDPS Have Returned Home, but the Challenge of Reintegration Is Just Beginning." Norwegian Refugee Council, Dili.

Ministry of Finance. 2011. *Development Partners Book 5: Goodbye Conflict, Welcome Development*. Dili: Government of Timor-Leste.

———. 2012. *Combined Sources Budget 2012*. Books I–V. Dili: Government of Timor-Leste.

Ministry of Planning and Finance. 2006. *Minimum Wages, Job Guarantees, Social Welfare Payments, or Basic Income*. Report MPFDRT-L. Dili: Government of Timor-Leste.

MSS (Ministry of Social Solidarity). 2009a. "Internal Evaluation of Hamutuk Hari'i Futuru: Lessons Learned and Recommendations." Government of Timor-Leste, Dili.

———. 2009b. "Minister of Social Solidarity Provides an Update on Work of MSS during 2009." MSS press release, Government of Timor-Leste, Dili, December 17.

National Statistics Institute (Dirrecão Nacional de Estatistica [DNE]). 2006. "Timor-Leste Census of Population and Housing, 2004." DNE, Dili, Timor-Leste.

———. 2011a. "Timor-Leste Household Income and Expenditure Survey 2011 [HIES]." DNE, Dili, Timor-Leste.

———. 2011b. "Timor-Leste Social Protection Survey [TLSPS]." DNE, Dili, Timor-Leste.

Pedereson, Jon, and Marie Arneberg, eds. 1999. "Social and Economic Conditions in East Timor." Columbia University, School of International and Public Affairs, International Conflict Resolution Program.

Trinidad, Jose, and Briant Castro. 2007. "Rethinking Timorese Identity as a Peacebuilding Strategy: The Lorosa'e-Loromono Conflict from a Traditional Perspective." Dili, June 6.

UNDP (United Nations Development Programme). 2006. *Timor-Leste Human Development Report*. New York: UNDP.

United Nations. 2000. *Report of the Secretary General on the Transitional Administration in Timor-Leste*. S/2000/738. New York: United Nations Security Council.

World Bank. 1999. *Report of the Joint Assessment Mission to East Timor*. World Bank, Darwin, Australia.

———. 2011a. "Protection in Practice: Experience with Cash Transfers at the Sub-National Level in Timor-Leste." World Bank, Dili.

————. 2011b. *World Development Report 2011: Conflict, Security, and Development*. Washington, DC: World Bank.

————. 2013. "Timor-Leste Social Assistance Public Expenditure and Program Performance Report." World Bank, Social Protection and Labor, Human Development Sector Unit, Washington, DC.

CHAPTER 12

Timor-Leste Case Study: Ministry of Health

Catherine Anderson

The Timorese Ministry of Health (MoH) is a frontline health service institution that has shown credible results in a fraught and fragile country context. The ministry (formerly the Interim Health Authority or IHA) faced acute and particular challenges to begin. Yet it made good on the opportunities afforded to it to avert excess mortality, reduce high rates of infant and maternal mortality, halve the incidence of malaria, and provide basic health services at the village level. Through these and later achievements, the ministry gained the trust of a previously disenfranchised population and galvanized its durability and resilience.

In contributing to a volume examining positive institutional experiences, this chapter examines how and why, in an otherwise low-capacity, low-income country, the MoH has maintained and deepened its positive development trajectory over time. As in the other cases, this chapter describes how the core underpinnings of its success are found in the three concentric circles that constitute its operating environment: the sociopolitical context in which it emerged and continues to function, its interaction with clients and external relationships, and its inner institutional workings

The chapter expands on a mission aide-memoire (December 2012) and is based on the research and interviews drawn from two in-country visits during October 12 to November 4, 2011, and November 15 to 18, 2011. A series of regional focus groups, completed by Josh Trinidad and Fidelis Magalhaes during November 2011 to January 2012, provided contributory inputs. The mission is grateful to Riltom Borges for administrative assistance and to the World Bank East Asia Pacific health sector team and Tanya Wells-Brown for their review and inputs.

(World Bank 2011a). Unlike the Ministry of Social Solidarity (MSS), which took root in its response to the 2006 Crisis, the MoH's early success is a product of steady and consistent development and an ability to stay the course through periods of social dislocation, tension, and conflict.

From its inception at independence, the ministry's role and functions were clear, but it had to make difficult choices to begin to address its health sector priorities, and to decide the sequencing of activities and resourcing. Among those decisions, health officials grappled with questions of how to build the foundations for health sector recovery, while at the same time responding to the humanitarian emergency and chronic health conditions that were unfolding across the country. To a large extent, it is the trade-offs and policy choices made by health administrators during this period and up to independence that determined the agency's future success.[1] From the early years of the MoH's functioning and through deliberate efforts to deepen and expand its institutional performance, the ministry has maintained a steady path toward creating an integrated, results-oriented institution that is led by and for Timorese and responds to the unique and difficult conditions facing the country.

The MoH has long stood out as an institution that other Timorese ministries have wanted to emulate, in large part due to its early accomplishments. Yet there was no watershed for the MoH, and its future success remains uncertain. It exhibited strong performance in planning and management in the period from the referendum to 2006, and many of its early efforts have yielded visible dividends. But its performance has fluctuated in recent years. Persistently high rates of malnutrition and maternal mortality are worrying, and the ministry's positive institutional trajectory is setback by deteriorating planning and budget links, volatility in procurement, human resource constraints, and political interference. Under these conditions, the future test for the ministry will be its resilience and durability in the context of increasingly politicized budgeting and administrative uncertainty. Despite this uncertainty, looking back at the sector's initial recovery, several features stand out as having contributed to the MoH's early ability to deliver results and secure legitimacy where there was previously popular mistrust. Many of these achievements are rooted in the ministry's policy priorities and in its social and human capital and warrant deliberate attention, but before highlighting the MoH's developmental attributes, this chapter examines the ministry's record and situates its development in context.

Institutional Success

The Timorese Ministry of Health has produced impressive health status results and expanded health service coverage in the past 10 years. There is considerable rural-urban and inter-district variation, and the ministry's performance has slowed in recent years,[2] yet early Timorization and the delivery of impartial and expanded health services have raised popular confidence that the system essentially works, despite its dysfunctions. Timorese see the system as their own. This section examines the MoH's results and the depth of its credibility and resilience.

Results

Several of Timor-Leste's health indicators had already begun to improve before independence. Communicable diseases had risen following referendum violence, but excess mortality due to chronic health conditions had been avoided. There was a reduction in infant mortality and in maternal mortality also, though to a lesser extent (figures 12.1 and 12.2). Infant mortality declined from 126 infant deaths per 1,000 live births in 1989–90 to 60 in 1999–2003. There were similar improvements in the rate of under-five mortality, which declined from 165 to 83 deaths per 1,000 live births in the same period. This trajectory apparently continued after independence, although the quality and content of the data are subject to considerable variation across sources.

A recent Timor-Leste Demographic Health Survey (TLDHS) shows dramatic improvements in health indicators in the eight-year period to 2009/10, particularly in child health and immunization coverage, although there is variation among districts. Under-five child mortality declined from 83 deaths per 1,000 live births in 1999–2003 to 64 in 2005–09, the largest reduction in under-five mortality by a country worldwide at any time in the period between 1990 and 2010.[3] This improvement was driven largely by a decline in the infant mortality rate, which fell from 60 to 45 deaths per 1,000 live births between 2005 and 2009/10.

Maternal mortality declined steadily from 880 maternal deaths per 100,000 live births in 2003 to 557 in 2009/10, although again the data are subject to large confidence intervals and Timor-Leste's maternal mortality rate still ranks among the highest in the world.[4] Vaccination coverage improved significantly; the percentage of children who are vaccinated nearly tripled, from 18 percent in 2003 to approximately 53 percent in

Figure 12.1. Infant Mortality Rates, 2003–10

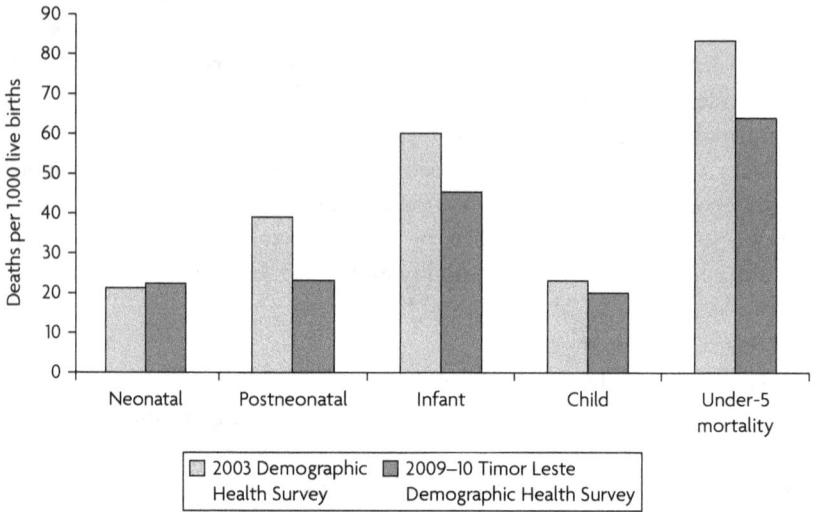

Source: National Statistics Institute 2010.

Figure 12.2. Infant Mortality Rates, by District, 2010

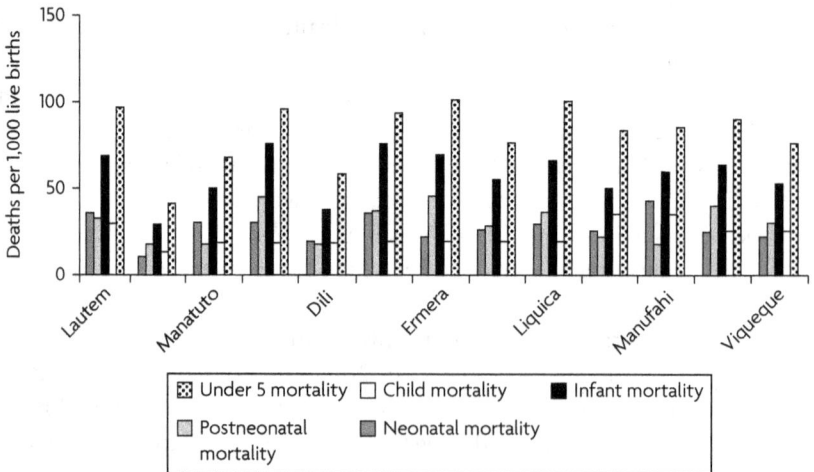

Source: National Statistics Institute 2010.

2009/10,[5] and the World Health Organization (WHO) cites a more than 75 percent decrease in the incidence of malaria in 2000–11.[6]

Access to health services has improved significantly since the Indonesian occupation. Before the referendum, Timorese were typically obliged to pay for health services. Today, health services are free of charge, except after hours, and coverage has expanded, with temporary clinics now providing services at the village level where they had previously only operated in subdistricts. Rosser (2007, 132) reports, "From a state of utter devastation in late 1999, by mid-2004 an estimated 87 percent of the population had a health facility within two hours walking distance from home, and these facilities were within two hours driving time of a hospital in 10 out of 12 districts." As of 2010, there were 193 health posts, 66 community health centers in the subdistricts (an additional 26 in the nongovernment sector), and 442 Integrated Community Health System (SISCA) village posts operational throughout the country (World Bank 2013,5; Ministry of Health 2010a). Five regional referral hospitals (in Baucau, Maliana, Maubisse, Oecusse, and Suai[7]) and the Guido Valadares National Hospital in Dili were also providing specialized care and referral services, lessening the need to transfer patients to Dili.

Timor-Leste has seen improved family planning and birth spacing practices, which may be attributable in part to health promotion and awareness-raising activities. The government has carefully navigated relations with the Church, which was previously opposed to public campaigns on family planning practices, and reached an important compromise that has allowed for targeted advice on birth spacing practices. A fall in the estimated total fertility rate from 7.8 children per woman in 2003 to 5.7 in 2009 is consistent with a reported increase in the use of modern contraceptive methods from 7 to 21 percent (Ministry of Health 2010a), although these reported improvements should be read with some caution as the data are not directly comparable across years. In 2003, interviewees were defined as "ever married women" while, in 2009, interviewees were drawn from a pool of women of reproductive age. There is also considerable variation by district.

Legitimacy

Strong results are the primary source of the ministry's legitimacy. There are no formal public opinion polls of the health sector in Timor-Leste, but it is said that "by 2006, wherever one would travel in Timor-Leste to ask people which public service had become most effective, the answer was unanimously, health" (World Bank 2008). The initial mandate of the United Nations Transitional Administration in East Timor (UNTAET) was to administer the country, and this involved monitoring the performance of Timorese health workers and nongovernmental organizations (NGOs) that were providing emergency relief services. UNTAET carried out its mandate, often at great personal risk of violence. These actions conferred considerable legitimacy on the IHA from the start (Tulloch et al. 2003, 22). The IHA's legitimacy deepened as public health services became more visible through the introduction of mobile services and the reopening of clinics and referral hospitals. That health services are free and people do not to have to travel far to receive attention for minor illnesses has accentuated positive perceptions of the MoH. Focus group participants expressed their broad satisfaction with the MoH despite the fact that some clinics are not functioning, and the stock of medicinal supplies is low and irregular. Focus group participants remarked, "We are happy with the services. We get better after the treatment, and they treat us well."[8] Several participants ranked the MoH highly for its performance.

Timorese poorly trusted and underutilized health services during the Indonesian occupation, but utilization rates increased steadily after independence. The World Bank reports that total outpatient visits increased from 1.4 per capita in 2006 to 2.0 in 2010 and inpatient admissions increased from 1.4 per capita in 2008 to 2.1 in 2010 (World Bank 2011b). Requests for birth attendants have also risen. According to the 2009/10 TLDHS, 30 percent of births were attended by a skilled health professional, up from 19 percent in 2003, while 22 percent of deliveries occurred in a health care facility, up from 10 percent in 2003, although a large disparity exists between rural (12 percent) and urban (53 percent) areas. The proportion of women receiving antenatal care from a skilled provider rose from 61 percent in 2003 to 86 percent in 2010 (National Statistics Institute 2006, 2010; World Bank 2013).

Increased utilization could be attributed to improved access to health services, although the remarks of some focus group participants suggest that it may also reflect increased trust in public health providers. The data are equivocal, and it is difficult to establish clear links between citizen trust and increased utilization rates. In drawing on a subsample of the Timor-Leste Standards of Living Survey 2007, Zwi et al. (2009) observe,

"The primary reason for not seeking treatment was ascertained, and two reasons emerged as most important: not serious enough (45.6 percent) and health facility too far (36.7 percent). Other reasons, such as a health worker not being present (3.1 percent) or the lack of transport (2.6 percent), were less frequently cited." By contrast, according to the 2010 Demographic Health Survey, 96 percent of women reported one or more problems in accessing services, and the non-availability of drugs (87 percent) or a health care provider (82 percent) featured as among priority concerns (National Statistics Institute 2010). Women also expressed concern about obtaining permission to go for treatment (23 percent) or securing money for treatment (35 percent). At the same time, an inverse correlation exists between popular trust and the use of public health services and the use of traditional health practices. Where access to public health services and trust improve, people reduce their use of traditional health practices. Data collected during focus group discussions suggest that increasing numbers of people are visiting qualified health workers (midwives and nurses) and birth attendants and are coming to the hospital instead of using Sharman or traditional methods.[9]

Timorese believe that health workers and the health system should operate in the interests of the entire community; they expect professionalism, commitment, and equal access to services, and the ministry is meeting these expectations (Ministry of Health 2007, 3). According to focus group participants, "Health workers respond swiftly to calls from the community. They come to the village even at night when there is an emergency."[10] Health outcomes show high levels of regional variation, and a handful of anecdotal reports suggest that some health workers are providing family members with privileged access to health services, but there is no evidence of regional bias or prejudice. The professionalism, neutrality, and service orientation of ministry staff during the 2006 Crisis and their determination to avoid being drawn into the conflict have further reinforced the population's trust. The continuity of health support during punctuated periods of violence and humanitarian emergency, together with the incremental and socially connective nature of health sector development, not only assisted Timor-Leste to avert a deeper health crisis, but also elevated the ministry's legitimacy in the eyes of its constituency. In the words of a focus group participant, "People respect [public health professionals]; they really respect them ... People see them as a second God for us."

Resilience

"During the political crisis of 2006, amid spikes of violence and enduring displacement of people, the Ministry of Health continued to deliver critical services and demonstrated that the Government was 'in charge' by managing inputs from external partners and promoting health sector neutrality in ways that helped mitigate the conflict and its consequences."

—Asante et al. 2011

Given Timor-Leste's precarious health conditions and the devastation wrought on its health system following the 1999 referendum, its initial recovery is in some respects extraordinary. The MoH's continued functioning throughout the 2006 Crisis and in the wake of a change of minister and government in 2007 is further evidence of its durability and resilience. According to one senior health specialist, staff gained confidence following the 2006 Crisis. No major outbreaks of disease occurred, and the ministry has largely managed small malaria epidemics and outbreaks of dengue ever since. Ironically, for many internally displaced persons (IDPs) residing in camps across Dili, food, water and sanitation, and essential health services proved more accessible in the camps than they had been in the communities before the 2006 Crisis,[11] and the ministry found itself trying to encourage people to use the routine services provided through community health centers as an alternative (Zwi et al. 2007, 8). By all accounts, the 2006 Crisis sharpened the ministry's emergency and disaster responsiveness and its ability to deliver basic health services, while at the same time reinforcing its professionalism, impartiality, and service orientation.

The ministry has increased its overall budget and readied a pipeline of qualified human resources to expand and deepen its capabilities as a healthcare provider—all of which speaks to its increased durability. At independence, the Interim Health Authority had a budget of US$5 million per year, financed by Official Development Assistance (ODA). By 2009, the government financed 60 percent of health expenditure, and donors financed 40 percent. Between 2005 and 2012, the health budget increased more than threefold from US$14 million to US$51 million in real terms (including the budget for autonomous health agencies), although the health sector allocation as a share of the budget consistently declined from 10.8 percent in 2005 to 3.7 percent in fiscal 2011 during the same period, and is projected to drop to 2.5 percent in 2012. In parallel with fiscal expansion, the MoH has trained and is preparing to absorb a large supply of health specialists to support Timor-Leste's increasingly complex health needs (Ministry of Health 2010b).

Institutional and Sector Context

According to the World Bank–United Nations Joint Assessment Mission (JAM), East Timor was among the poorest regions in the archipelago, with health conditions in 1997–98 similar to those in other developing countries (World Bank 1999). The primary causes of death (pneumonia, malaria, diarrhea, and associated malnutrition) were endemic, and the incidence of tuberculosis was very high. Life expectancy was low, at 55–58 years. Infant and under-five mortality was high compared with Indonesian averages at that time, at 85 and 124 deaths per 1,000 births, respectively (World Bank 1999). A skilled birth attendant (doctor or midwife) attended less than a quarter of all births, contributing to high rates of maternal mortality (Rosser 2007, 123).

The Indonesians had constructed an extensive system of government hospitals, clinics, and health posts, staffed by about 160 doctors and 2,000 nurses and midwives (World Bank 2002). The majority of managers within the system were Indonesian; Timorese tended to provide nursing services. The focal point of the system was the community health center (*puskesmas*). Located in each of the subdistricts, community health centers provided curative, preventative, and promotional services and coordinated outreach activities through health subcenters, mobile clinics, and village midwives. These activities included national programs in maternal and child health, family planning activities, and campaigns against malaria and tuberculosis. Tertiary care was provided through eight small district hospitals, a central referral hospital in Dili, and the Central Health Laboratory. The provincial health department was responsible for oversight, but most key policy and programmatic decisions were made in Jakarta (World Bank 1999; Morris 2001).

According to Rosser (2007, 123),

Although the Indonesian Government financed the development of the health system during its 24-year occupation, the system did not perform well. It was chronically underfunded compared with other provinces, public subsidies were not allocated in a pro-poor way, and health services were of poor quality and unresponsive to the needs and demands of the population. Quality assurance systems and the regulatory framework were inadequate, and it did not produce adequate information for planning and evaluation purposes. [Health services were underutilized] with just over one outpatient visit per capita per year, and the number of outpatient visits per staff member per day employed in the health system was less than five, both figures low by international standards

(World Bank 2000, 2002). The low rate of utilization suggests that the East Timorese either lacked confidence in the health system or faced serious barriers to accessing health services. Some have argued that the fact that the vast majority of doctors and senior health officials in the territory were non-Timorese engendered a lack of trust in the system among the East Timorese.

Already precarious, health conditions deteriorated rapidly during the referendum violence of 1999 and the social emergency that followed. Some 610,000 people, constituting nearly two-thirds of the population, were displaced, and the health system effectively collapsed. Estimates suggest that 75 percent of the health infrastructure was destroyed (World Bank 2009, 1), and whatever remained was looted or seriously damaged, including most equipment and supplies. It was three weeks before health services were reinstated.[12] Few doctors remained in Timor-Leste after the referendum—many had fled to Indonesia—and the Timorese public health system retained fewer than 30 doctors and 1 specialist surgeon (Tulloch et al. 2003, 1–2). The remaining clinicians and nurses collaborated with international emergency relief NGOs and faith-based organizations to provide basic and emergency care.

In October 1999, a World Bank–United Nations Joint Assessment Mission (JAM) reported that only 18 percent of children aged 12–23 months were fully immunized against the six major childhood diseases: tuberculosis, diphtheria, pertussis, polio, tetanus, and measles. Childhood malnutrition was severe, with 44 percent of children under age five underweight (14 percent severely) and 48 percent stunted (27 percent severely), putting the country at considerable risk of health crises. With 52 percent of the population under 15 years of age and a fertility rate as high as 7.8 children per woman, user demands on Timor-Leste's public health system were set to expand dramatically.

Timor-Leste's IHA was created in February 2000, six months after the referendum. The IHA brought together 16 Timorese health professionals at the national level, together with another 13 in the districts and 6 UNTAET health staff.[13] A new Department of Social Affairs and Division of Health Services later replaced the IHA and continued functioning until the Ministry of Health was established under the second transition administration in September 2001. By the end of 2001, the MoH had recruited more than 800 staff and established district health management teams across the country to lead public health services delivery and ensure that government health facilities were adequately staffed. By independence in

2002, Timor-Leste's health sector was functioning at close to 80 percent of what it had been under the Indonesian administration.

Overcoming Systems Constraints

Timor-Leste's tough external conditions are characterized by inhospitable physical and spatial terrain, isolated mountainous regions, and widely scattered populations that are often inaccessible during the rains. The humanitarian emergency, which was triggered by the events of 1999, caused extensive damage to physical infrastructure and saw the exodus of health professionals across the border into West Timor. Facing chronic health conditions and severe systems constraints, difficult choices had to be made about health sector priorities and prospective sites for delivering health services. Three decisions would prove particularly crucial to the MoH's recovery and resilience down the line: building back and innovating from the bottom up, leveraging partnerships to provide service delivery functions, and developing the ministry's policy and institutional framework while delivering emergency services. This section examines the quality and content of those decisions and reflects on the lessons learned from the ministry's approach.

Rebuilding from the Bottom up and Deconcentration

Rosser (2007, 128) remarks, "In the weeks following the referendum, as the emergency was unfolding in Dili and in the country's regions, emergency health service delivery and the resumption of basic health services began locally, in communities, through a network of mobile clinics and the revival of community health posts." The introduction of the SISCA in 2008 continued to build on this bottom-up approach (box 12.1).

UNTAET's initial task had been to conduct a headcount of frontline health workers and a health survey. It did this through a Joint Health Working Group, which was created to tackle health sector priorities and to bring together United Nations agencies, the NGO community, and Timorese health professionals (Tulloch et al. 2003). The health practitioners who had remained in Timor-Leste through the violence continued to work in local communities, without pay, until UNTAET began recruiting staff in August 2001.[14] These clinicians, including many who were nurses during the Indonesian administration, documented their daily activities, and the data (together with the results of an initial health survey) were used to inform the development of future MoH protocols. Informed by

---

BOX 12.1

SISCA: An Integrated Community Health System

In 2008, an Integrated Community Health System (*Sistema Integrado de Saúde Comunitaria* or SISCA) was instituted by the MoH to deliver health services to remote populations. SISCA is a nationwide program, which consists of monthly outreach visits and an integrated service delivery platform designed to promote health awareness and deliver a wide range of basic health services and immunization programs to communities. Some 442 SISCAs currently operate across the country and are run by subdistrict health staff and a cadre of volunteers. The SISCA is typically well regarded by local communities, although the rapid expansion of health posts and services has outstripped the ministry's human, physical (especially pharmaceutical), and financial capacities, compromising the ministry's ability to ensure that these service posts are functioning well.

---

the priorities identified in the health survey, emphasis was also given to the delivery of high-priority programs—immunization, tuberculosis, and nutrition and health promotion campaigns (Rosser 2007).

Timor-Leste's IHA was the first of Timor-Leste's public agencies to deconcentrate its activities and collect data from the bottom-up data collection and planning, and this contributed to the early expansion of health sector coverage. The IHA was quick to establish district health management teams and district health boards to enable community participation in decisions, to respond to the humanitarian emergency, and to renew the delivery of basic health services at a regional level. The IHA created a small grants facility to disburse funds to district health posts and clinics and, where it lacked the capabilities to provide services, it innovated and contracted them out. A decision to contract out medical procurement to a private firm, Crown Agents, proved highly successful and salvaged a badly compromised medical supply chain, although subsequent incarnations of this semi-autonomous agency would later raise some problems.

Leveraging Partnerships and Early Timorization

The IHA's partnership with NGOs and faith-based and humanitarian organizations, together with its strong relationships with donors, was a hallmark of the sector early on and strengthened the IHA's (and the ministry's) crisis response capacity. According to Rosser (2007, 136–37), several benefits flowed from the ministry's partnerships, not least of which was the shared understanding of the health problems facing the territory, which followed the extensive data collected for the JAM and the establishment of baselines in 1999 and 2000. The public health system experienced temporary paralysis following the referendum and prior to the arrival of UNTAET, yet more than 100 international NGOs (including faith-based and humanitarian organizations) responded to the emergency, reestablishing essential services and curbing further loss of life (Roland and Cliffe 2002, 12). Mindful of its limited ability to deliver services, the IHA (then administered by the United Nations) was quick to formalize this arrangement, signing several memoranda of understanding to ensure that each district would benefit from the health services of at least one NGO. These emergency health service providers proved to be a huge asset to the IHA; they employed local staff, mostly nurses who had worked under the Indonesian administration, and bridged the gaps in basic, emergency, and hospital health care services. With these partners actively providing health services locally, the IHA could focus on building the health sector framework and systems. The strengths of health service providers lay in their commitment and willingness to work in remote areas under tough conditions, their operational self-sufficiency, and their ability to respond rapidly. According to Tulloch et al. (2003, 26), "Their contribution to saving lives and to preventing suffering in East Timor was substantial."

The IHA's strategy of leveraging the skills and resources of international NGOs to fill service delivery gaps was not without challenges. The high turnover of staff and the relative lack of experience of some individuals made things difficult (Tulloch et al. 2003, 26). Several years later, during the 2006 crisis, the experience of the MoH was again similar. As in 1999, the rapid and coordinated response of emergency health service providers to the 2006 Crisis bolstered the government's ability to avoid the outbreak of disease and in some cases enhanced the quality of health services available to these same communities.[15] Many IDPs experienced better water and sanitation and improved access to health services during the 2006 Crisis than they had during periods of stability in their own communities. In both 1999 and 2006, donors (largely the European Union) financed health service providers and acted under the leadership and direction of the IHA and later the ministry. This proved essential to the partnership's effective functioning.

The decision to collaborate with non-state health service providers and the continuity of health service delivery in the weeks and months following the referendum prevented the deterioration of already desperate health conditions and bolstered popular perceptions of the IHA. The collaboration also provided an opportunity for the ministry to deepen its performance and legitimacy, on the basis of gains made through this partnership. But the arrangement proved too costly for donors and, foreshadowing a transition, the interim head of the IHA called on Timorese practitioners to take charge of health service delivery themselves. Practitioners responded well, and, by December 2001, a phase-out strategy for NGOs was established.

The decision to terminate emergency NGO services and Timorize management of the health sector was highly controversial. NGOs protested, and the United Nations was initially concerned that the IHA would prove ill-equipped to deliver, but in the end United Nations administrators supported the decision and the phase-out proceeded. According to then minister Dr. Rui Maria de Araujo, services did not falter. Indeed, services improved as staff and clinicians rose to the challenge.[16]

Today the MoH has its own service delivery model and crisis response strategy, but NGOs continue to play an important role in three areas: promoting health behavior change, promoting community use of public health services, and providing logistical support for effective delivery of the Integrated Community Health System (SISCA). MoH–NGO relations are managed through the Department of Partnership Management at the ministry. Building on an earlier precedent, NGOs are required to sign a memorandum of understanding with the ministry to define the district in which they will work and the scope of their activities. A total of 56 NGOs are registered. They tend to work either in health promotion or on specific projects—such as HIV/AIDS (human immunodeficiency virus/acquired immunodeficiency syndrome) or family planning.[17] The principal challenge for the ministry lies in effectively monitoring their activities, a task that is proving difficult because of their increasing numbers (Da Silva 2010, 18).

The generous and coordinated support of donors is an equally prominent feature of Timor-Leste's health sector recovery. Donors financed 100 percent of the health sector budget from 1999 until 2002.[18] An initial outlay of US$10 million helped to rebuild core health infrastructure. And although external financing for the health sector has declined quite rapidly, from 52.5 percent of total health expenditures in 2005 to only 28 percent in 2008 (WHO 2010) and 22 percent (US$13.2 million) in 2012, donors are still important partners to the MoH. The substantial and consistent stream of ODA over the years has buoyed Timor-Leste's health sector responsiveness and resourced the ministry's institutional development. An effort was made to ensure coordination through a sectorwide approach (SWAp), although the merits and constraints of Timor-Leste's SWAp remain somewhat contested. Several respondents observed that the SWAp did not prevent donors from pursuing their own interests and that efficacy has deteriorated over the years. The contrasting view is that it reduced the duplication of donor activities and focused donor attention on an agreed set of priorities and performance indicators.

Balancing Policy Priorities

A particular feature of health sector administration in the early years was its dual-track approach. One focus was on operations and efforts to avert the escalation of a health crisis and resume basic health services locally while rehabilitating service delivery capacity; the other was on national policy, planning, and institutional development, including the creation of a medium-term expenditure framework. In practical terms, striking this balance meant managing a tricky combination of emergency and basic health services delivery, with preventive care and informed health sector development, by creating a system and service that could evolve, adapt, and adjust. This dual-track approach—building short-term confidence while striving for medium-term development—was reproduced as policy guidance in the *World Development Report 2011* (World Bank 2011c).

Against considerable odds, and under assertive foreign and Timorese leadership, Timor-Leste's health system successfully averted a national health crisis and extensive loss of life following the referendum. At the same time, it laid the foundations for the sector's coherent national and subnational development (United Nations 2000, 60). The IHA's performance in the period to independence was thus marked by several important achievements. Access to basic services was restored, immunization programs were renewed, a tuberculosis program was started, and a basic health services package was drafted to provide for the delivery of health services through newly rehabilitated and equipped health centers. Several institutional plans—for example, for human resource development, capacity building, and health training—were also crafted. A civil works program was launched to construct more clinics, and a central medical store and a consultancy for managing an autonomous medical supply system were initiated (Tulloch et al. 2003, 2). This would ensure that drug supplies were reasonably well secured and based on an approved drug list.

Having successfully recovered from a health emergency and having launched a coordinated strategy for health sector development, the ministry shifted its efforts toward consolidating these initial gains by improving the quality and coverage of health services and developing referral and specialized services. More recently, the MoH's development is reaching still further by deepening the efficient and effective public financial management and decentralized service delivery.

Timorese took charge of service delivery in the ministry early on; they developed administrative systems and focused on strategic policy development, including in the areas of health service delivery and human resources development. These efforts would pay important dividends. The health policy framework introduced in June 2002 enabled the MoH to lead the formation of policy in a context of international crowding. It also gave the ministry the space that it needed to define sectoral priorities and shift emphasis toward medium-term institutional development goals as the emergency period came to a close. The ministry's phased and iterative approach would prove central to its initial performance, recovery, and subsequent institutional development.

Confronting Historical Legacies and "Building Back Better"

Building an efficient and effective public health system has required contending with several historical legacies. Particularly challenging was the culture of centralized and personalized administration, popular distrust of health services, and poor health behavior. The ministry has employed a range of tools and acted to mediate and manage these pressures.

Social and Political Interests

The MoH is subject to external pressures and has typically managed them through a combination of leadership and negotiation. As a frontline service provider, it is accountable to an extensive network of primary and secondary health care beneficiaries who want health services that are accessible (within walking distance) and free of charge.[19] Respondents also expressed a rising demand for improved quality of care and medicines that are better tailored to needs.[20]

Remarkably, in a highly personalized culture of public administration, the MoH was initially insulated from the country's prevailing political economy, largely due to the actions of its first minister, Rui Maria de Araujo. Minister Araujo was a highly experienced clinician with robust public health qualifications. His vision was to create an integrated, evidence-based, and performance-oriented health system.[21] He worked well with international donors and made good use of ODA, which earned him respect among his peers. His successor, Minister Martins, hailed from the ranks of a local NGO, but he was also an experienced clinician with a good reputation for his efforts in the struggle against tuberculosis. Both ministers were nonpartisan and held resistance credentials, having practiced either as a surgeon or as a clinician during the Indonesian occupation. However, they held different standings within Timor-Leste's sociopolitical hierarchy, which had implications for the MoH.

During his term in office, Minister Araujo was politically independent and sought assurance from the prime minister that the ministry would not be subject to political interference. This insulated the ministry from corrosive political forces and afforded the minister the autonomy he needed to establish an impartial and functioning agency. Following his departure in 2007, the MoH was increasingly subject to political influence and lacked the political capital needed in the Council of Ministers to influence budgetary allocations. The MoH's budget declined, from an average of 10–12 percent of the state budget under the first constitutional government to 3.7 percent in 2011 and a projected 2.5 percent in 2012.

Among other influential pressure groups, the Church and NGOs are prominent in the ministry's functioning. The Church played an important historical role in health service delivery during the occupation and during Timor-Leste's health and humanitarian emergencies. The MoH manages its relationship with the Church very carefully, mindful that it has a broad constituency of support. In the early years after independence, the Church took a strong pro-life stance on health sector policy, refusing to condone sex education or family planning (including the use of contraception). This opposition undermined government efforts to stem the country's high birth rates. A breakthrough occurred in 2007 when the Church and the government finally agreed on a family planning policy centered on "birth spacing" practices.[22] Birth rates dropped from 7.7 children per woman in 2003 to 5.7 in 2009/10, although it is difficult to draw direct comparisons as the data sets differ.[23] Health promotion campaigns and other factors may have contributed to declining birth rates. Nonetheless, the government-Church relationship and the policy dialogue that stems from it have allowed the MoH to do its job (National Statistics Institute 2010).

Two recent developments—the elaboration of an Overseas Referral Program and the National Priority Program (NPP)—have heightened political pressures on the ministry and are proving a challenge. The NPP is a dual-accountability instrument that was adopted by the government of Timor-Leste in 2008 and serves as a coordinating and reporting instrument. To the extent that it brings government and donors to the table to examine progress in health sector development, the NPP has some relevance, although there are questions about the extent to which it produces results or contributes to improved MoH performance. The MoH is a partner to priority number five—social services and localized service delivery—and has used the NPP to track implementation and sharpen reporting.[24] The ministry's apparent ability to withstand the policy and political influence that can accompany dual-accountability instruments imported by donors further suggests that it is less permeable than it once was.

Vision and Esprit de Corps

Together with a constitutional right to health, the Timor-Leste Strategic Development Plan 2011–2030 speaks of "transitioning Timor-Leste from a low-income to an upper-middle-income country, with a healthy, well-educated, and safe population by 2030." The aim is to have a doctor for every 1,000 inhabitants by 2020, including a doctor in each subdistrict and potentially in each *suco* by 2012. This strategy aligns with the Millennium Development Goals (MDGs)[25] and prioritizes public health as the basis on which to build the country's social capital. Yet the Strategic Development Plan is a small part of what drives the ministry.

The ministry's mission is deeply internalized by staff who convey a strong *esprit de corps* and service orientation. Like the MSS, this is the result of targeted and consistent messaging by senior management and among colleagues at various levels (national, district, and subdistrict). More interesting, however, is that this mission is built on an existing code of ethics among Timorese health workers, which demands that public health services be delivered with impartiality and professionalism. One staff member remarked that MoH staff see their country as being in a stage of rebuilding and are proud to be making a contribution, despite low salaries.[26] The recent spike in government spending and increasingly uneven trend in the payment of salaries and consultant fees, which sees some consultants earn vastly more than others, could soon alter that ethos, and not all accounts of staff performance are positive. A handful of focus group participants spoke of rude MoH staff and commented on the lack of empathy for patients among hospital nurses and birthing attendants.[27] According to Zwi et al. (2009), the anger and blame exhibited by health workers discourage people from visiting clinics, and this has contributed to low utilization rates among women.

Isomorphism and Building Back Better

The MoH has not adopted the institutional development model of another health agency, but it does aspire to meet international standards in primary health care, preventive and curative medicine, and health education. Partners to the ministry have introduced WHO evidenced-based and guiding protocols, such as those for the integrated management of childhood illness and the emergency management of obstetric care, and MoH programs do exhibit a degree of isomorphism. The SISCA is similar to the Indonesian system of health posts—the *Posyandu*—albeit with some distinctions. The SISCA delivers primary health care services (curative and preventive) and conducts health promotion activities across the community as a whole, while the *Posyandu* focuses more closely on child and maternal health.[28] Clinicians have also tended to revert to Indonesian and Portuguese protocols for guidance when they need it.

Although several features of MoH policy and practice are isomorphic, the architects of Timor-Leste's Ministry of Health made a conscious decision not to recreate the project-based, vertical health system constructed by the Indonesians. Rather, the goal was to create an integrated, evidence-based, performance-oriented system,[29] and this contributed to the MoH's coherence and results orientation that would later develop. Targets were set, and staff focused their energies on meeting those goals. It also enabled Timorese to see the health sector as their own. Removal of the Indonesian user-pays requirement was just one measure of that result. One focus group participant remarked, "During Indonesian times, it was all about money. If you pay well, you get a good service. Now we do not have to pay for the medicines. We do not have to pay for anything."[30]

Timorese Ownership and Local Engagement

Timor-Leste's various public health entities have long enjoyed good working relations with donors and non-state health service providers, particularly in times of crisis, and they collaborate in all stages of health sector development. Initially this was achieved through a Joint Health Working Group, which set the minimum standards for the IHA and the sector. Successive ministers have also reinforced Timorese ownership. Minister Araujo was determined to put Timorese staff in charge, and Minister Martins took this approach still further.

In January 2007, Minister Martins reclaimed responsibility for health sector coordination, a role previously played by the World Bank, and took an increasingly arm's-length approach to working with donors, in line with an overall trend in government-donor relations that had accompanied diminished reliance on ODA. As a result, few donors saw the new Health Sector Strategic Plan at its inception, and many find it difficult to meet with the minister, fueling perceptions that he is aloof toward development partners. According to some donors, the change in roles weakened coordination, yet internal accounts suggest that this decision was taken in response to the donor's top-down, supply-driven approach and persistent critique of ministry performance.[31] In the minister's words, "The Ministry of Health is like a child learning to walk—we are fed up of constantly being scolded every time we do something wrong—you would not do that to a child."[32] To a large extent, the early and progressive deepening of Timorese ownership of health sector development, despite heavy external influence from donors, could be attributed to the ministry's growing institutional strength and resilience.

The MoH recognizes that engaging local communities is central to effective health service delivery. It has consistently expanded its presence in local communities and works more and more closely with *chefes de sucos* and *chefes de aldeia* (village and sub-village chiefs, respectively), engaging them as health intermediaries. *Chefes de suco* and *chefes de aldeia* are involved in strengthening community health practices, promoting participation in SISCA, and validating child vaccination programs for the *Bolsa de Mae* (Mother's Purse Program).[33] The MoH also recruits locally, as did the IHA before it. MoH staff are recruited from the districts in which they work and are known to host communities, which has served to restore trust between the community and health workers. Although this was not an official policy at the outset, it proved a practical solution to a logistical problem and was adopted as formal UNTAET policy in 2002.

Chefes de suco and *chefes de aldeia* are purveyors of health information, although some neglect to share that information with their communities, and the quality and effectiveness of community access to health information widely varies. MoH–community engagement through *chefe de sucos* and *chefe de aldeias* is a relatively new phenomenon, and *chefes* are still developing an understanding of the health system and adjusting to their new role. One director of a district health center reported, "When the time has come for implementation at the grassroots, without the assistance and participation of community leaders, implementation is not really good, the community does not come; or if they [communities] do come, this is not due to the participation from leaders, but as a result of health workers going there to mobilize communities."[34]

Community health volunteers (PSFs) support the local implementation of SISCA, extending the MoH's reach. Modeled on a similar experience from Thailand, PSFs play an important role in administering vaccines, weighing children, and supporting clinicians. They are paid a small stipend (US$5 per month). The original concept was that voluntary staff would be identified in an open application process and then interviewed and chosen for the role. But in practice, there is no formal recruitment mechanism, and volunteers are typically selected by *chefes de suco* or *chefes de aldeia*. The experience with PSFs is double-edged, they may be an important contribution to community health service provision, yet the stipends paid to them are inadequate and sometimes do not even reach them, resulting in a high turnover of volunteers.

Poor health practices are significant constraints on the effective delivery of health services in Timor-Leste, and traditional health practices (*matandok*) are an enduring feature of health culture. The ministry has taken the difficult step of reconciling parallel health systems by validating the role of traditional health practices and treatments. In one popular case, the ministry issued a formal certificate of recognition and provided a small grant to a traditional healer for his bone treatment center in Alas, Same.[35] Traditional birth attendants still play a role in birthing, but formal health service utilization rates are rising, albeit slowly—from 1.4 total outpatient visits per capita in 2006 to 2.0 in 2010 and from 1.4 inpatient admissions per 100 in the population in 2008 and 2.1 in 2010 (World Bank 2011b). Requests for nontraditional birth attendants have increased, and focus group participants reported that the use of traditional health practices is declining. According to the 2009/10 TLDHS, 30 percent of births were attended by a skilled health professional, up from 18 percent in 2003.

Deepening Performance and Quality

"What is the reason behind the success of the ministry? Good staff, good planning, great commitment, and a lot of money."
—Celestina da Costa Alves, director, Viqueque District Health Center

Highly educated, experienced clinicians have led Timor-Leste's MoH, and the IHA before it, carefully articulating a sector vision. Yet poorly functioning systems have hampered the MoH's performance and remain a challenge. Benefiting from strong leadership and a vision, ministers and staff have sought to overcome the binding constraints of the ministry's internal systems through the empowerment of middle managers, results-oriented performance, and fiscal innovation. Partnerships and training as well as incremental improvements in data collection and information management have accompanied the ministry's development. This section examines the manner in which the ministry has used the opportunities and resources afforded to it to overcome the constraints of its inner workings. At the same time, it reflects on future challenges.

Managing Leadership Change

Timor-Leste's IHA and ministry have experienced varying styles of leadership, and these have contributed to the ministry's results and functioning in different ways. Before independence, Jim Tulloch led the IHA, taking difficult yet practical decisions to guide health sector recovery in crisis conditions.[36] Minister Araujo and Minister Martins differed in their focus and approach. Minister Araujo focused on delivering primary and secondary health services and establishing the ministry's operating frameworks and planning system, relying heavily on the performance of his managers. By contrast, Minister Martins focused on rolling out the SISCA and research and development, often bypassing systems and giving limited direction to staff on how best to operationalize ministry programs. Even so, he built on the initial foundations of the ministry, expanded basic services coverage, deepened Timorese ownership, and made use of the pipeline of human resources offered by the professional development program in Cuba. Minister Martins largely retained the staff he had inherited and secured their trust, bolstering the ministry's institutional memory, although he did reshuffle his cadre of managers (figure 12.3).[37] Ministry staff have remained loyal to both ministers despite the change in leadership style and focus.

Figure 12.3. Organization Chart of the Ministry of Health

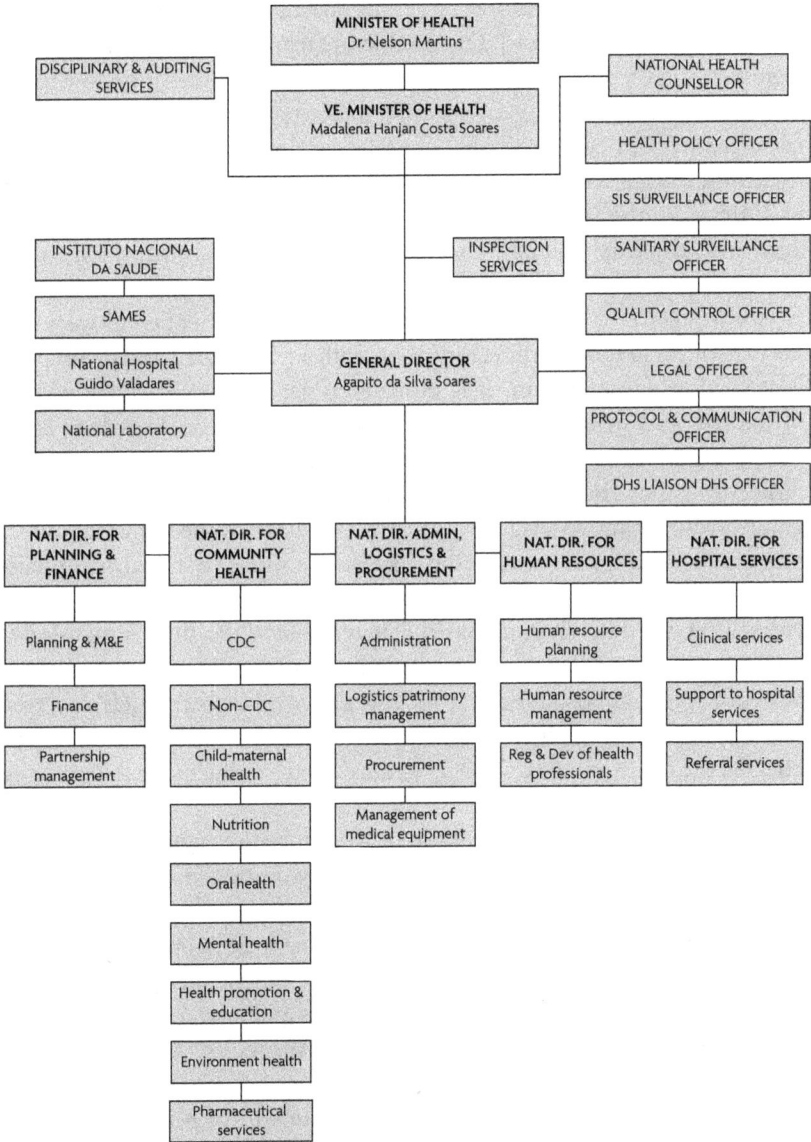

Source: Ministry of Health, http://www.moh.gov.tl.

Building a Health Sector Workforce

The health sector workforce was decimated by the withdrawal of Indonesian health personnel. Of 135 doctors who had been working in the region during the Indonesian occupation, only 30 remained, and low levels of qualified human resources are still a major constraint on the ministry's performance. The rapid response of emergency health workers and NGOs to the referendum violence, together with the arrival of 230 Cuban doctors in 2004, gave the sector a critically needed boost. The MoH's early and aggressive capacity building also made an important contribution to the MoH's future development.

According to the MoH, there are now 1,400 permanent employees and 300 vacancies in the health sector.[38] But, with a fragmented and incomplete health information system, it is difficult to get a comprehensive picture of the size and structure of the health sector workforce (Dewdney et al. 2009). As of 2007, there were some 50 senior managers or directors (grade-level 6 or above) and at least 130 middle-management personnel at grade-level 5 or above (Asante et al. 2011, 3). Each of the ministry's directors interviewed for this case study had been a nurse or a health administrator during the occupation, although management capacities were still weak after the referendum. Basic management skills further developed through steady and consistent empowerment and under crisis conditions. Several MoH and hospital directors, together with district chiefs, received training to sharpen their management capabilities, although funding gaps affected the functioning of these programs[39] and management skills remain highly uneven.

District health centers are still run by district health management teams, and these tend to be well resourced, but the staff often lack suitable skills. Resourcing subdistrict health posts and clinics and staffing the SISCA are particularly difficult, and many services continue to be supported by NGOs and the Cuban Medical Brigade (see box 12.2). District health centers propose candidates for recruitment to health posts and take recommendations from *chefes de suco*, but it is difficult to fill vacancies. The ministry has adopted a top-up policy to incentivize health professionals to work in more remote regions. The policy provides an additional 40 percent allowance for staff working in extremely remote regions, 25 percent for those in very remote regions, and 15 percent for those in remote regions—but the policy is failing to have a major impact.[40] There are simply too few health professionals left in Timor-Leste to recruit, and when staff are sent abroad to study, their posts often remain unfilled.

BOX 12.2

Cuban Medical Brigade

Launched in 2004, the Cuban Scholarship Program affords Timorese the opportunity to study medicine and allied health at the undergraduate or postgraduate level in Cuba. Selected candidates are required to study Spanish prior to commencing the course. More than 700 Timorese students have attended the program. The first cohort of 18 fully qualified doctors returned to Timor-Leste in 2010; they are working in the public health system. By November 2011, in just one district, a further 69 Timorese medical students had returned from Cuba and were studying at Suai Hospital, with another 130 students scheduled to arrive in 2012. Returning students complete their final year of studies in Timor-Leste, through the National University of Timor-Leste, and undertake internships at the referral hospitals to expose them to Timorese conditions.

Source: http://www.moh.gov.tl.

MoH partners have financed extensive professional development schemes, and these have produced mixed results but important lessons. The biggest complaints are that there is no follow-through, training is not linked to the allocation of posts or assignments, and there is no on-the-job mentoring. Emergency management of obstetric care, for example— a model rolled out by the United Nations Population Fund—trains midwives to perform normal deliveries and to recognize complications and the need for back-up or referral. But many deliveries are in private homes, and midwives rarely feel competent or confident to practice these skills in the absence of supervision or while working alone. Supervision is needed but, again, finding health workers willing to spend long periods of time working in remote locations is difficult, and the MoH is poorly equipped to support health supervisors on lengthy regional visits.[41]

With tight human resource constraints, the ministry has found a significant source of strength in its overseas professional development partnerships. In the early recovery period, while the European Commission and World Bank were revitalizing Timor-Leste's critical health infrastructure, Australia, Cuba, and China sponsored their own health specialists to work in Timor-Leste. Australia and Cuba further financed two long-term overseas professional development programs to train cadres of skilled and specialized Timorese physicians. The Australian program was financed by the Australian Agency for International Development (AusAID). It was embedded in the National Hospital—Guido Valadares National Hospital—and staffed by the Royal Australian College of Surgeons. Based on a capacity substitution model, the initiative placed Timorese specialists in overseas training programs, while a rotating cadre of Australian surgeons provided specialized clinical services in Timor-Leste. According to respondents, the program did not follow conventional capacity development models, and yet it has proven vastly more successful than the conventional one-on-one adviser models adopted elsewhere in the health sector.

Since 2004, Cuba has also deployed more than 200 doctors known as the Cuban Medical Brigade to deliver frontline health services in the subdistricts of Timor-Leste. Rotated every two years, these doctors have boosted health service delivery—including in the most remote parts of the country—and delivered in practicum training[42] to returning Timorese doctors and nurses. The Cuban Medical Brigade was key to service delivery during the 2006 Crisis and is the product of a long and productive partnership forged between the governments of Timor-Leste and Cuba on Timorese independence.

The Cuban and Australian professional development programs constitute an important and timely pipeline of skilled resources for the ministry, yet the deployment of new doctors and health professionals across the country will continue to test human resource management capacities for some time. (World Bank 2013, 3).

Managing Performance

For the Ministry of Health, as with any agency in an FCS, it is difficult to recruit and motivate competent staff when salaries are not competitive and systems are dysfunctional. Despite these powerful disincentives, in the early years after independence, the MoH had a strong reputation for open and constructive internal communication, effective delegation of tasks, and productive training. Professional development, performance, and integrity were important tenets of the ministry's human resource management. "Good people were hired and bad people were fired,"[43] irrespective of dysfunctional administrative systems, and this largely remains the case, although weaknesses are emerging.

Staff performance is reportedly assessed against six monthly targets, in line with a government-wide performance monitoring and management framework. Similarly district and subdistrict staff report monthly and each trimester, although it is not clear whether these reports constitute performance assessments, data collection exercises, or methods to track and analyze service targets and impacts.[44] The ministry is collecting data and monitoring and evaluating its programs, although performance tends to be uneven. A local data implementation plan exists, but it is not utilized, and MoH programs—for example, the SISCAs—are sometimes run without data being captured, weakening the ministry's ability to monitor and measure performance results. The case study team was unable to verify the quality of the ministry's monitoring and evaluation model.

The Civil Service Commission leads personnel administration across government, although MoH supervisors meet regularly with their staff and review staff performance.[45] Like the MSS, several disciplinary cases generated by the Office of Internal Audit and Discipline (an internal unit within the MoH)[46] suggest that the MoH is serious about performance management.

Improving Internal and External Communication

The MoH has a mixed record on public information and communication systems. It has sponsored extensive health promotion and behavior change campaigns over the years, including for example, on the importance of immunization and the merits of using treated bed nets to prevent malaria, and the MoH has actively solicited the support of NGOs as campaign partners. Health promotion campaigns are often conducted door-to-door or through national television and radio broadcasts, and some say that these have led to increased use of health services,[47] although few clients have knowledge of the way in which the health system functions. It was not commonly known, for example, that clinics provide primary health care services, while hospitals tackle secondary and more complex health issues.

Basic internal information systems and verbal communications are used to align policy and planning, although the results tend to be uneven. The minister holds monthly meetings with all management staff (including district chiefs) to elaborate joint plans, report back on policy and program implementation, and solve problems. Similarly weekly board meetings involving the minister, vice minister, director general, and directors offer a regular opportunity for management to raise and resolve operational concerns. Overall, however, poor communication flows between directorates within the ministry hinder the implementation of health policy, and the role of the director general and health management information systems are underutilized.[48]

Communications between health posts, health centers, and referral hospitals are weak. In 2001, regular contact with field staff was enabled through a radio network. This health information system was credited with containing an outbreak of measles in the Ermera District in mid-2002, but several informants remarked that two-way communication links, particularly with the subdistricts, have weakened in recent years. District and community health centers report upward to the national and district centers, yet information and communications rarely flow back,[49] and while the ministry also meets regularly (bimonthly) with hospital staff and the autonomous institutions, referral hospitals do not interact or communicate well with district and subdistrict health posts. In the process of conducting this research, it became evident that hospital staff consider primary and secondary health care facilities to be distinct parts of the system.

Specializing through Autonomous Service Units and Referrals

Timor-Leste established several autonomous institutions and a system of referrals to deepen its capacity to provide specialized health services. This network of autonomous institutions includes five regional hospitals (in Dili, Maliana, Baucau, Suai, and Maubisse), a semi-autonomous pharmaceutical supply agency (SAMES),[50] the National Laboratory, and the Institute of Health Sciences and has deepened the ministry's capacity for evidence-based policy and programming as well as service delivery.[51] Several of these institutions have received a sizable funding pledge from donors, enabling them to operate with some independence.[52] Although their relations with the MoH vary (the MoH–SAMES relationship has proven particularly difficult), the autonomous regional hospitals reportedly interact well with the MoH.

The proliferation of autonomous and semi-autonomous institutions is not of itself a panacea for specialized service delivery in Timor-Leste. The form and functioning of many of these institutions are still in flux, and many retain limited budgetary autonomy and rely on the ministry's resources and priorities, which constrains their development.[53] This is particularly true of the referral hospitals. Yet the creation and functioning of specialized clinical services and a system of referrals—to which was recently added the Institute of Health Sciences—have enhanced health sector efficiency and specialization.

Adapting Financial Management

The Ministry of Health was long regarded as effective in planning and budgeting, although there were some early challenges. Initial delays in budgetary decisions kept funds from reaching the districts, and this constrained the implementation of work programs in district health centers. Donors filled the gap, but the delays strained the system and diminished user confidence. In later years, public finance management in the MoH saw some innovations, including the *Pasta Mutin*, which is discussed in the section that follows. Overall, however, and particularly in recent years, MoH performance in public finance management has been uneven. Planning dysfunctions (the lack of national-subnational links), increased politicization of the budget, and fluctuations in the national procurement policy (including debilitating disconnects between the systems of donors and the MoH) have heightened the ministry's administrative dysfunctions.

Building on the MoH's early experience with the use of block grants to finance basic service delivery, in 2008 the ministry introduced the White Pouch Program (*Pasta Mutin*) to ease the flow of funds from the center to the districts. The program provides a monthly allocation, which allows districts to make small health sector investments and to undertake communication and outreach programs. Several subnational health officials remarked that the *Pasta Mutin* has given them financial and operational independence. So its purpose is instrumental, but it also has its drawbacks. The funding does not correlate with identified needs and is not tied to the delivery of specific activities or results (World Bank 2011b). Funds are apportioned evenly between clinics and health posts, even though they serve different demographics.[54] Consistent with reports of increased politicization of the ministry's budget,[55] allocations have also become increasingly unpredictable in recent months, stunting service delivery capacities and leaving clinicians and administrative staff with inadequate resources to do their jobs. Lags in expenditure reconciliation have further caused the Ministry of Finance to withhold advances to clinics.

Despite enviable bottom-up planning and prioritization and fiscal transfer innovations early on, the links between planning and budgeting are unraveling, straining health sector performance. The disconnect between national and subnational systems is deepening, resulting in poorly costed, ineffective local plans and severe budget shortfalls. In 2010 and 2011, district health budgets were spent by September, crippling health service delivery.[56] Budgetary shortfalls also affect autonomous health entities, where the ministry still retains planning control.[57] Hospital staff contribute to ministry plans, but the resulting budget rarely correlates with their inputs, in either recurrent or minor capital allocations.[58] This compromises hospital management, frequently leaves them short on basic operating costs (for fuel, transportation, and medical supplies), and renders the new and "state of the art" hospital facilities difficult to maintain.[59]

Between 2005 and 2010, the MoH's budget increased 150 percent in real terms, from US$14 million to US$35.6 million (see figure 12.4), but shrank as an overall share of the state budget (see figure 12.5; World Bank 2011b). Under the first constitutional government, health sector budgetary allocations were consistently 10–12 percent of the total state budget, but the budgetary allocation for the health sector decreased to 3.7 percent in 2011 and is expected to drop further to just 2.5 percent in 2012, leaving the districts and subdistricts particularly hard hit. According to the director general of the MoH, "In terms of the national budget, we feel that we are an orphan."[60]

Budgetary allocations for logistical and medical supplies, especially transportation, fuel, and pharmaceuticals, are increasingly subject to political intervention and tend to be substantially lower than what is

Figure 12.4. MoH Budget Allocations, 2005–10

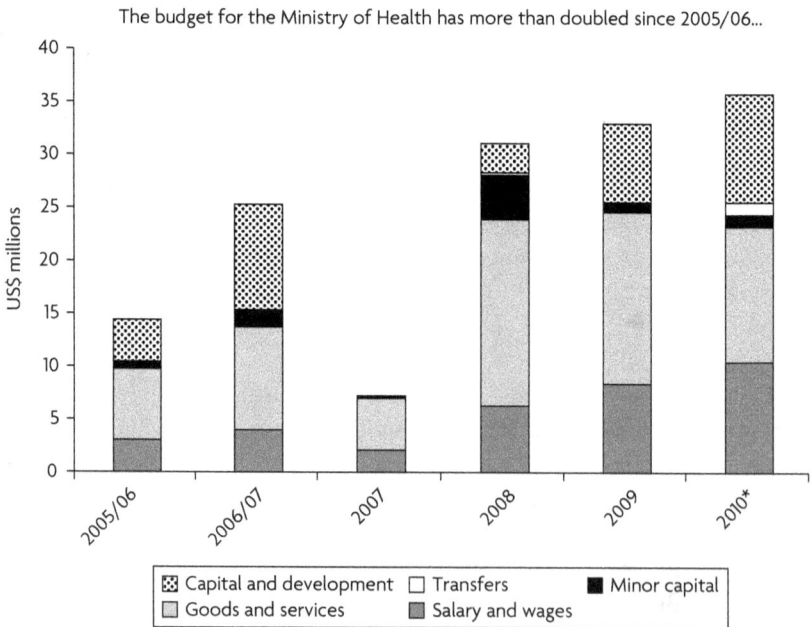

The budget for the Ministry of Health has more than doubled since 2005/06...

Source: World Bank 2011b.
* Current estimate.

Figure 12.5. MoH Allocation as a Share of the Overall State Budget, 2005–10

...but has almost been halved as a percentage of central government funding

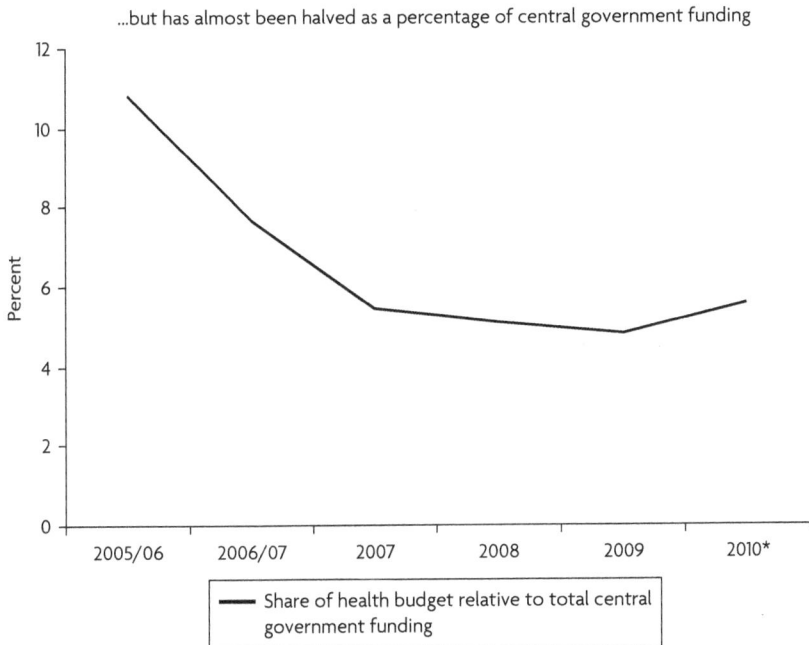

Source: World Bank 2011b.
* Current estimate.

anticipated and needed. Budgetary allocations for goods and services decreased from about 59 percent of the overall health sector allocation in 2008 to 30 percent in 2012 (World Bank 2013), while salary and wages increased as a result of hiring additional staff in 2010 to fill vacancies in the districts and hospitals (World Bank 2013). This has led to a shortage of basic medicines in the districts and villages and has inhibited the ability of health services to reach more isolated communities. Focus group participants complained that the SISCA only distributes three kinds of medicines—Paracetamol, Cotri, and Cloroquim[61]—and that these are used to treat all kinds of illnesses. According to MoH clients, "We have many well-trained medics but not enough medication,"[62] and the range of medicines distributed is limited.

The budget is based on input, and this served the IHA well during the emergency period and during the implementation of the Basic Services Package, which required budgetary flexibility. But it has constrained the ministry's development ever since. Funds do not follow the ministry's

Health Sector Plan and inadequately track program developments, weakening accountability for results. Innovating to manage constraints, the Directorate of Finance and Planning developed a hybrid budget model that was part program and part input based to overcome the constraints of existing budgetary practices. The model was a results-based system that allowed staff to simulate program components of the budget, but after responsible staff moved, the model was no longer used.

In 2006 the procurement threshold for the MoH was between US$50,000 and US$100,000. As with other line ministries, including the MSS, this increased to US$1 million just prior to 2010, but has been repeatedly changed since, devolving and retrenching authority in a cyclical fashion, each time requiring procedural changes.[63] Procurement challenges are exacerbated by the fact that different donors adopt different procurement models and the ministry is highly permeable to procurement influence. The United Nations uses a single-envelope model, as does the MoH, while SAMES has adopted the World Bank's two-envelope bidding system.[64] This dual system has caused significant procurement delays for the government, as donors challenge the use of different envelopes. The impasse reached the point at which the MoH asked its donor—in this instance the World Bank—not to interfere with the ministry's administrative practice.[65]

Causal Factors

The Ministry of Health faced considerable challenges on inception: chronic health conditions and system constraints; an Indonesian legacy, which had corroded popular trust in public services and projectized health services delivery; and a health service that lacked staff and had a history of underperforming. The physical and human destruction wrought on Timor-Leste in 1999 had not been anticipated. Yet the policy decisions made during this emergency period shaped the institution's capacity to deliver results and determined its successful development trajectory.

Heavily influenced by deplorable health conditions and a deepening humanitarian crisis, foreign and Timorese administrators took several defining decisions early on—to leverage a large body of NGO and donor resources to bridge service delivery gaps, to prioritize emergency and basic health service delivery locally, and to build an institutional and policy framework around these efforts. The vision to create an integrated performance- and results-oriented ministry from the ground up, using Timorese capacities and resources, provided the foundation for the ministry's coherent health sector development and established a basis of trust. Timorese communities saw and felt the impact of these decisions, and this buoyed the ministry's legitimacy early on. The dual effect of balancing emergency and basic health service delivery with preventive care and long-term sector development provided immediate relief to the population (Tulloch et al. 2003).[66] At the same time, it informed the development of a health sector framework, creating space for the strategy to evolve, adapt, and adjust.

With the immediate humanitarian and health crisis averted, future health ministers could prioritize the expansion of health service coverage and the development of specialist and referral services. At the same time, the ministry doubled-down to overcome internal constraints and deepen the ministry's performance by fostering an already strong *esprit de corps* among staff, reinforcing that mission through consistent messaging from the top and the empowerment of middle managers. Partnerships between Timor-Leste, Cuba, and Australia (through AusAID) brought a large cadre of qualified Cuban doctors and a rotating pool of Australian surgeons to Timor-Leste. The Cuban and Australian doctors provided primary and specialized health services, while enabling scores of Timorese clinicians to be trained to meet future health sector demands.

Besides these programmatic and technocratic advances, perhaps the most striking aspect of Timor-Leste's health sector development is the credibility and trust that have been built with the population over time and through various strategies. Ministry staff and clinicians have fostered local trust by making themselves visible locally and by working in difficult and isolated conditions, even during violent historical junctures and often in the context of direct personal threats to the safety and security of attending clinicians.[67] Similarly, the decision to rebuild the health sector from the ground up and to strengthen the delivery of health services by recruiting and empowering local Timorese staff, almost from the start, enabled the ministry to connect with local communities. The presence of SISCA at the subdistrict and village levels in recent years has heightened the ministry's profile and deepened its legitimacy further among village populations. Through the engagement of *chefes de suco* and *chefes de aldeia* in the organization and administration of SISCA, the MoH has been able to extend its operations and enhance its interaction with previously underserviced constituencies, working with intermediaries that communities largely understand and trust.[68]

Challenges

Despite the impressive renewal of a previously distrusted and dysfunctional health system, challenges in health services coverage, the quality of those services, and administrative functioning persist and threaten to weaken the ministry's future performance and prospects.

The ministry has been particularly successful in executing primary technical functions—that is, in treating serious illnesses and preventing and managing communicable diseases through vaccinations and primary health care in the districts.[69] These are fields in which Timorese clinicians have historically also exceled. By contrast, however, "soft functions"— such as the development of middle-management capacities, monitoring and supervision, health management information, and efforts to change health behaviors—are taking longer to develop, although they are gaining ground. Soft functions are intrinsically more difficult to tackle, particularly in environments where performance incentives are weak.[70]

Gaps in the supply of qualified human resources constitute the single biggest binding constraint on consistent and effective health sector delivery. The MoH's strategic vision is highly ambitious, all existing human resources are committed, and these are still inadequate. Mechanisms such as training programs that are established in the referral hospitals and that are financed by donors and supported by the National University of Timor-Leste promise a pipeline of skilled human resources in the future, but human resource needs are immediate. A cadre of returning doctors could see the ratio of doctors to population increase, but not enough to achieve the ministry's target of 1 doctor per 10,000 persons (World Bank 2011b, 3). There are also concerns about the sector's near-term capacity to absorb a new stream of doctors, who are likely to place a considerable strain on already limited financial and pharmaceutical resources.

Predictable, well-resourced health service delivery that is spatially distributed is needed in the villages. SISCA is the basis for the ministry's expanded health service delivery, but it has several weaknesses. The program was planned and resourced according to density and not spatial distribution, and the end result is that more remote communities still suffer from a lack of access to basic health services. Focus group participants complained that SISCA operations are inconsistent and not always delivered on schedule; when the rains come, the SISCA simply stops visiting the more isolated regions.[71]

Yet perhaps the most salient challenge facing the ministry is found in the arteries of the institutional system—planning and budgeting. Increasingly poor links between plans and budgets are corroding national-subnational ties, weakening procurement and service delivery capacities, and resulting in uneven health services performance. The same problems are also stunting the functioning of the sector's autonomous institutions, such as the district health centers, the community health centers, and the referral hospitals.

Not discounting measurable and marked achievements, weak links between plans and budgets, human resource constraints, and inconsistent or unreliable frontline service delivery at the village level each need to be tackled for the ministry to continue to move forward.

Annex 12A Ministry of Health Milestones

1975	Indonesian occupation
1976	Timor-Leste officially annexed as 27th province of Indonesia
1999	Referendum for independence
	Widespread destruction and humanitarian crisis: 610,000 displaced, 75 percent of health system destroyed, 30 doctors and specialists remain
	UNTAET and Department of Social Affairs created
	50 percent of population under poverty line
2000	Interim Health Authority established, 16 national health staff and 13 district health professionals recruited
2001	Ministry of Health created, 800 staff and district health management teams appointed
	NGO emergency health care strategy phase-out concluded
2002	Timor-Leste gains independence
	Dr. Rui Maria de Araujo appointed minister
	New heath policy framework established
2006	Timor-Leste social and political crisis: 130,000 displaced
2007	First parliamentary elections in Timor-Leste since independence
	New coalition government formed
	Dr. Nelson Martins appointed minister of health
2008	Integrated Community Health System (*Sistema Integrado de Saúde Comunitaria*, SISCA) initiated
	Health Sector Strategic Plan–Support Project (HSSP-SP) launched
2009	IDP reintegration complete, health crisis averted
2010	Cuban-trained Timorese doctors start returning
2011	Health Sector Strategy 2010–30 produced
	New HSSP adopted
2012	HSSP–SP Phase II launched

Notes

1. Focus group discussion, Fatuberliu.
2. For example, the under-five mortality rate is higher in rural areas than in urban areas: 87 deaths per 1,000 live births in rural areas compared with 61 in urban areas. (National Statistics Institute 2010).
3. As reported by the Child Health Epidemiology Reference Group; http://www .unicef.org/media/files/Child_Mortality_Report_2011_Final.pdf.
4. WHO data, which are based on interagency estimates for the period 1990–2008, indicate that the maternal mortality rate has declined in Timor-Leste (from 650 deaths per 100,000 live births in 1990 to 370 in 2008).
5. The proportion of children aged 12–23 months who have received DPT3 increased from 56 percent in 2003 to 66 percent in 2009/10 and measles vaccination increased from 47 percent in 2003 to 68 percent in 2009/10 (World Bank 2013, 4).
6. http://www.who.int/malaria/publications/country-profiles/profile_tls_en.pdf.
7. The hospitals in Maubisse, Maliana, and Oecusse were financed under European Commission grants, Suai and Baucau were government financed, and Dili was financed jointly.
8. Focus group discussion (three women and three men 35–60 years old), Umaberloi Village, November 24, 2011.
9. Summary of key findings from the focus groups.
10. Focus group discussion, Beacu, Viqueque, November 22, 2011.
11. Focus group discussion, Beacu, Viqueque, November 22, 2011.
12. Interview with the former minister of health, Dr. Rui Maria de Araujo, October 25, 2011.
13. The IHA comprised 16 senior Timorese health professionals in Dili and 1 in each district, along with a small number of international experts (Roland and Cliffe 2002; Tulloch et al. 2003).
14. Former district-level health practitioners report that, between 1999 and 2001, staff at the health posts in the subdistricts were given three kilos of rice each month as compensation for service rendered and that, whenever they had more critical patients, they called the International Force for East Timor.
15. One public health sector specialist observed that donors often channel money to health during an emergency, as it is the easiest and quickest route. If donors had been able to channel money through the MoH, health service providers would have been able to respond without NGO support.
16. Interview with the former minister of health, Dr. Rui Araujo, October 25, 2011.
17. The MoH recently signed five memoranda of understanding with Care International, Oxfam UK, Child Fund, Healthnet, and Medico do Mundos to support nutrition and SISCA implementation in Timor-Leste (Ministry of Health 2010a).

18. The European Commission, World Bank, Australian Agency for International Development, U.S. Agency for International Development, Portugal, Cuba, China, and United Nations agencies (World Health Organization, United Nations Children's Fund, United Nations Population Fund, and the Global Fund).

19. Community representatives (village chiefs and sub-village chiefs) strongly endorse the views of their constituencies and have a role in disseminating public health information and mobilizing their communities to use public health systems. However, as with the MSS, their performance as health care intermediaries varies widely because of inexperience or lack of commitment.

20. Focus group discussions, Beacu and Fatuberliu.

21. Interview with former minister of health, Dr. Rui Araujo, October 25, 2011.

22. Birth spacing is a natural method of family planning that encourages women to defer having their first child and to allow more than two years space between children.

23. Data for 2003 are drawn from ever-married women, while data for 2009 are drawn from all women over the age of 15 years.

24. According to the MoH and adviser informants, MoH attendance at the joint quarterly meetings of the NPP was patchy. The MoH had already established planning and coordination structures (including a health sector plan, a medium-term expenditure framework, and a sector-wide approach) and saw the NPP as duplicative. But as the NPP gained legitimacy and permanence, the MoH scaled up its engagement.

25. The health MDGs include combating malaria, tuberculosis, and other diseases (MDG 6); reducing child mortality (MDG 4); improving maternal health (MDG 5); expanding access to safe water and sanitation to half the population (MDG 7); halving the proportion of people suffering from hunger (MDG 1); and improving access to essential medicines (MDG 8).

26. Interview 2011.

27. Interview with Dr. Bourdaloue F. Moniz, director general of the Referral Hospital Maliana, and focus group discussion, Memo Subdistrict, Maliana, November 9, 2011.

28. The *posyandu* targets pregnant mothers and mothers with preschool children.

29. Tulloch et al. (2003) and interview with the former minister of health, Dr. Rui Araujo, October 25, 2011.

30. Interview with the director general of the district hospital in Maliana, November 9, 2011.

31. Tensions were particularly heightened with the change of government in 2007 because of the perception that development partners tended to pursue their own agendas and did not listen to the changing needs of the ministry. At the time, the government was fighting fires on several fronts, with people in camps, a pharmaceutical emergency, and ministries still trying to reorganize following the elections.

32. Timor-Leste development partners meeting.
33. Interviews with Ministry of Finance staff, October 2011.
34. Interview with Celestina da Costa Alves, director of the Viqueque Health Center.
35. Focus group discussion, Caicassa Subdistrict, Fatuberliu, Same, November 17, 2011.
36. Mr. Tulloch worked with Dr. Sergio Lobo, an experienced surgeon, who was then reengaged to prepare the national Health Sector Strategic Plan and, in late 2012, was himself appointed minister.
37. An overwhelming majority of management staff informants were outwardly loyal to both ministers, while at the same time acknowledging the differences in their leadership styles.
38. Interview with the director of human resources, MoH, October 20, 2011. According to the World Bank human development team, there are some 3,000 clinical and nonclinical health workers, including permanent and nonpermanent staff (or contractors).
39. Interview with MoH staff, October–November 2011.
40. When interviewed, Same district health staff suggested that more appropriate incentives and three-year bonds for new staff recruited locally to health posts were needed to try to address existing human resource gaps.
41. USAID is exploring options to establish regional health support centers.
42. "*In practicum*" training means practical or on-the-job training in house or in residence.
43. Interview with former minister of health, Dr. Rui Araujo, October 25, 2011.
44. The case study team noted public performance targets and tracking in each of the district and subdistrict health posts visited.
45. Compared with the MSS, MoH staff consider themselves somewhat constrained by delays in Public Services Commission processes.
46. Interviews with the director general and director of community health services, December 2011.
47. Most focus group participants had been exposed to MoH and NGO health promotion campaigns, particularly related to child and maternal health, HIV/AIDS, and basic sanitation.
48. Interview, November 2011.
49. Interview in the community health center, Laleia.
50. An autonomous procurement agency, it has five directors and a director general and reports to a fiscal board (two members of which are appointed by the MoH and one by the Ministry of Finance). The director general reports to the minister of health and is appointed by the Council of Ministers. It is a political appointment.
51. An Institute of Health Sciences is tasked with ensuring that programming research, baseline surveys, and evaluations are vetted through an ethics committee consisting of academics, Church officials, and medical doctors. It was

initially difficult to secure donor funding for the office, but AusAID, WHO, and the World Bank each provide contributory financing. This research cabinet is an example of a technically sound, semi-autonomous institution embedded in the MoH that complements health sector developments (Martins and Hawkins 2012).

52. This is particularly true of SAMES, the creation of which was successfully contracted out, and the regional hospitals, which were constructed largely by donors.

53. The National Laboratory and Institute of Health Sciences have particularly good interaction with the MoH, likely because of the minister's research orientation. By contrast, the relationship between the ministry and SAMES has long been difficult, as SAMES wants more autonomy from MoH influence over its policies, program, and budget. The same holds true between the MoH and the referral hospitals. Again, these institutions regularly interact and seem to enjoy positive relations, yet senior management staff at the hospitals were clearly frustrated and felt operationally constrained by the financial control retained by the ministry (interview with Dr. Horacio Sarmento da Costa, director of Maubisse Referral Hospital, November 15, 2011).

54. The same is not true of referral hospitals, which are allocated budgets according to population size.

55. Initially, district health centers received US$15,000 per month, and community health centers received US$1,500 per month. Community health centers now receive US$1,000 every quarter, while district fiscal envelopes oscillate wildly, with districts often receiving much less than the US$15,000 monthly stipend they once received.

56. Interview with former head of planning, now portfolio manager of Global Fund, November 18, 2011.

57. The regional hospitals are supervised by regional supervisors who visit from time to time.

58. At the time of the interview, funding constraints at Suai Hospital were severe, with only US$32,000 remaining in the budget allocation for July to December 2011. Added to that, the region was desperately short on water, and there was a view that a special source of water needed to be safeguard to ensure the continued functioning of the hospital.

59. The hospital has surgery, radiology, pharmacy, and emergency laboratory capacity.

60. Interview, November 2011.

61. One commentator noted that this may be a result of the protocols of the Cubans, rather than the availability of stock, as the Cubans are known to overprescribe and not follow treatment protocols, which contributes to stock-outs.

62. Focus group discussion, Beacu, Viqueque, November 22, 2011.

63. In 2010, a Central Procurement Hub was created to procure all items above US$3 million; anything below that threshold was to be procured by the ministry. The Central Procurement Hub functioned for three months before procurement reverted to the ministries, and a Procurement Commission was then given responsibility for all procurements above US$1 million.

64. The World Bank typically adopts the two-envelope bidding system, in which technical qualifications are specified in one and costs in the other. The United Nations uses a one-envelope system, subsuming both requirements into one package. MoH procurement staff are aware of the difficulties inherent in the two-envelope system, as it indirectly precludes small firms, and talks are under way to adopt single-envelope bidding, but there is variation across health sector institutions, and it will take time to adopt a single-envelope system.

65. The country's underdeveloped procurement regime has invited the proliferation of donor procurement systems, leading to confusion and favoritism of some methods. The procurement law was generated by the Ministry of Finance, which procures very little and did not consider the needs of line ministries that procure large quantities of goods and equipment. Future efforts should focus on strengthening line ministries alongside the Ministry of Finance in basic public financial management.

66. This approach is in line with notions of building short-term capacity together with medium-term development.

67. This has had important impacts for the ministry's performance, resilience, and social credibility down the line.

68. Although shortcomings in how SISCA was planned have raised implementation difficulties and although the real results of community-level service delivery are not yet clear, focus group participants and community informants vigorously advocated the merits of SISCA. This suggests that SISCA plays an important role in building confidence between citizens and the MoH.

69. Suai Hospital has existed since the Indonesia era, although it was formerly an internment clinic and did not do operations. Following the referendum, the clinic provided emergency operations (Cesarean sections) with help from Medecins San Frontiéres SF, and then the New Zealand and Slovakian military hospitals were mostly used. Mobile clinics were used to serve the subdistricts. Suai Hospital was established in 2003.

70. Most district-level managers interviewed as part of this lessons-learned review are qualified and practicing health clinicians, but few were qualified in management, leaving subnational health centers short on management skills. One of the proposals put forward in the National Health Workforce Plan 2007–2015 is that district health managers and their

deputies have both a clinical background and suitable management credentials (Heldel et al. 2007).
71. This was the experience of the subdistrict of Bobonaro, which the research team visited.

References

Asante, A., et al. 2011. "A Review of Health Leadership and Management Capacity in Timor-Leste." University of New South Wales, Human Resources for Health Knowledge Hub, Sydney.

Da Silva, João Olivio. 2010. "Mid-Term Review: Health Sector Performance 2008–2010." Ministry of Health, Government of Timor-Leste, Dili.

Dewdney, J., J. Martins, A. Asante, and A. Zwi. 2009. *Strengthening Human Resources for Health in Timor-Leste: Progress, Challenges, and Ways Forward.* Sydney: University of New South Wales.

Heldel, Einar, Rui Maria de Araujo, Nelson Martins, Jaime Sarmento, and Constantino Lopez. 2007. "The Case of the Democratic Republic of Timor-Leste." World Health Organization, Geneva.

Martins, Nelson, and Zoe Hawkins. 2012. "Striving for Better Health through Health Research in Post-Conflict Timor-Leste." *Health Research Policy and Systems* 10 (April): 13.

Ministry of Finance. 2011. *Combined Sources Budget 2011: Books I–V.* Dili: Government of Timor-Leste.

———. 2012. *Combined Sources Budget 2012: Books I–V.* Dili: Government of Timor-Leste.

Ministry of Health. 2007. "Timor-Leste: Health Sector Resilience and Performance in a Time of Instability." Collaborative project with Australian National University, University of New South Wales, Menzies School of Research, and the Australian Government.

———. 2010a. *Health Sector Mid-Term Review.* Dili: Government of Timor-Leste.

———. 2010b. *National Health Plan: 2010–2030.* Dili: Government of Timor-Leste.

Morris, K. 2001. "Growing Pains of East Timor: Health of an Infant Nation." *The Lancet* 357 (9259): 873–77.

National Statistics Institute (Dirrecão Nacional de Estatistica [DNE]). 2006. "Timor-Leste Census of Population and Housing 2004." DNE, Dili, Timor-Leste.

———. 2010. "Timor-Leste Demographic and Health Survey 2009–10." DNE, Dili, Timor-Leste.

Roland, K., and S. Cliffe 2002. "The East Timor Reconstruction Program: Successes, Problems, Trade-offs." Working Paper 2, World Bank, Conflict Prevention and Reconstruction Unit, Washington, DC, November.

Rosser, Andrew. 2007. "The First and Second Health Sector Rehabilitation and Development Projects in Timor-Leste." In *Aid That Works: Successful Development in Fragile States*. Directions in Development. Washington, DC: World Bank.

Tulloch, Jim, et al. 2003. *Initial Steps in Rebuilding the Health Sector in East Timor*. National Research Council, Roundtable on the Demography of Forced Migration, School of Public Health, Columbia University. Washington, DC: National Academies Press.

United Nations. 2000. *Report of the Secretary-General on the United Nations Transitional Administration in East Timor*. S/2000/53. Geneva: United Nations.

———. 2006. *Report of the United Nations Independent Special Commission of Inquiry for Timor-Leste*. Geneva: United Nations.

WHO (World Health Organization). 2010. *World Health Statistics*. Geneva: World Health Organization.

World Bank. 1999. *Report of the Joint Assessment Mission to East Timor*. World Bank, Dili, East Timor.

———. 2000. "Project Appraisal Document on a Proposed Grant in the Amount of $12.7 Million Equivalent to East Timor for a Health Sector Rehabilitation and Development Project." World Bank, East Asia and the Pacific Region, Human Development Sector Unit, Washington, DC, May 24.

———. 2001. "Project Appraisal Document on a Proposed Grant in the Amount of $12.6 Million Equivalent to East Timor for a Second Health Sector Rehabilitation and Development Project." World Bank, East Asia and the Pacific Region, Human Development Sector Unit, Washington, DC.

———. 2002. "East Timor: Policy Challenges for a New Nation." World Bank, East Asia and the Pacific Region, Poverty Reduction and Economic Management Sector Unit and East Timor Country Unit, Washington, DC.

———. 2008. "State (Trans-) Formation in Timor-Leste: Building Institutions that Contribute to Peace." Occasional Note 3, World Bank, Fragile and Conflict-Affected Countries Group (OPCFC), Washington DC.

———. 2009. "Second Health Sector Rehabilitation and Development Project." World Bank, Washington, DC.

———. 2011a. "Institutions Taking Root: Building State Capacity in Challenging Contexts; Project Description and Case Study Guide." World Bank, Washington, DC.

———. 2011b. "Timor-Leste: Health Sector Financing Note." World Bank, East Asia and Pacific Region, Human Development Sector Unit, Washington, DC.

———. 2011c. *World Development Report 2011: Conflict, Security, and Development*. Washington, DC: World Bank.

———. 2013. "The Health Sector Strategic Support Plan: Support Project." World Bank, East Asia and Pacific Region, Human Development Sector Unit, Washington, DC.

Zwi, A. B., I. Blignault, D. Glazebrook, V. Correia, C. R. Bateman Steel, E. Ferreira, and B. M. Pinto. 2009. "Timor-Leste Health Care Seeking Behaviour Study." University of New South Wales, Sydney.

Zwi, A. B., J. Martins, N. J. Grove, K. Wayte, N. Martins, and P. Kelly. 2007. "Timor-Leste Health Sector Resilience and Performance in a Time of Instability." University of New South Wales, Sydney.

CHAPTER 13

Timor-Leste Case Study: The Central Bank of Timor-Leste

Lorena Viñuela

Emerging from a 24-year struggle and the widespread violence and destruction that followed the 1999 referendum, Timor-Leste's economic challenges were daunting. A decade later, the young nation has made important strides toward reconstructing its economy and physical infrastructure. The Banking and Payments Authority (BPA) played a critical role in the transition to independent economic management.

The institution, formally transformed into the Central Bank in September 2011, is responsible for holding government accounts, making payments, licensing banks and insurance companies, compiling and publishing monetary and banking statistics and other economic information, managing the operations of the Petroleum Fund, and issuing *centavo* coins. These functions were previously carried out by BPA (2001–11) and the Central Payments Office (CPO) (2000–01), which had been created by the United Nations Transitional Administration of East Timor (UNTAET) in 1999 and administered the country until 2002.

Having recorded important successes along its development, the organization stands out in a context in which most public agencies are weak. Among other achievements, BPA was the first public agency to staff all middle and senior management positions with nationals, a process known also as "Timorization." When the country adopted the U.S. dollar as the national currency, it took BPA less than a year to replace the many currencies that were being used. More important, BPA, and later the Central Bank, has managed with good results the high-profile Petroleum Fund and the banking system through turbulent economic and political conditions.

The organization has supported the rapid adoption of international standards in the banking sector and the dissemination of technology to support them.

The key elements driving success have been early and uninterrupted assistance from development partners, a simple institutional and legal framework, reliance on a building-block approach for organizational development, sustained emphasis on improving the capacity of national staff and organizational learning, and stability of middle and senior management. The consistent financial and technical support from donors and the government has given the institution the space and resources to pursue capacity building at a steady pace. At the same time, senior and middle management have strongly supported the institutional development roadmap and kept a consistent focus on reaching milestones and, ultimately, the goal of becoming a fully independent central bank. Early successes have contributed to creating a strong organizational identity and culture, including demonstrating the importance and benefits of transparency and reaching out to stakeholders.

The early development of the institution was the result of the temporary alignment of the priorities between the transitional government and those of the agency. During the first years of independent life, the Timorese government prioritized the adoption of international best practices and creating a lean public sector. This approach, favored by the transitional administration and shaped by the experiences of the returning diaspora, placed an important emphasis in laying the foundations for an independent central bank and the transparent management of revenues from the then nascent oil sector. For the governing elite, having an independent central bank had important symbolic implications for the nation-building project. This ensured the support of all political camps. BPA was fully capitalized in July 2005, demonstrating the government's strong commitment to the institutional development roadmap.

Despite its many achievements, however, the Central Bank continues to face important challenges in managing rising inflation. In the absence of monetary policy, its role remains limited. Rising public revenue, driven by increases in oil production and prices, has created strong political pressures to expand spending and led to the revision of the architecture of the Petroleum Fund. The planned, large-scale public investments and the ever-increasing withdrawals from the Petroleum Fund add to these challenges. In addition, the financial services sector remains underdeveloped, and there is little credit culture or access in the country.

Institutional Success

When the Central Payments Office (later converted into the Banking and Payments Authority) was created in 2000 to act as a quasi-central bank, UNTAET confronted daunting difficulties. In addition to the complete destruction of physical infrastructure and reliable means of communication, there were almost no locals with the required skills or experience in banking. Multiple currencies were circulating in the country (Australian dollar, Indonesian rupiah, Portuguese escudo, American dollar) and being exchanged in informal markets. There was a small nascent banking sector, but its costs and risks were high. In that setting, most payments were, and still are, made in cash and to individuals. A few years later, when the country established the Petroleum Fund, there was considerable uncertainty about the capacity of the organization to manage it. The institution tackled these challenges and built its credibility in a relatively short period of time. This section discusses some of the main achievements of the organization related to results and legitimacy as well as how it has forged resilience in the face of a rapidly changing political environment.

Results

The main areas in which the organization has exhibited sustained improvements are currency management, legal and organizational infrastructure for the supervision of the banking and insurance sectors, and the performance of the Petroleum Fund. One of the first achievements of BPA was the introduction of the U.S. dollar as the only currency with legal status in Timor-Leste. The task required personnel to visit all districts and villages. The BPA launched a wide-reaching but low-cost sensitization campaign that took place between August 2001 and April 2002. The U.S. dollar had been selected by the transitional government because it was expected to support low inflation and low interest rates. The staff member that led this process described it as being "a success well beyond our original expectations" (interview with senior staff, November 2011). In approximately eight months, the use of the U.S. dollar was general and almost the exclusive means of payment in the country, as it is today. According to senior staff members, this experience decisively shaped the manner in which the institution approached the public and its communication strategy, inculcating the importance of reaching the population beyond Dili. The dollarization program also contributed to building a lasting sense of achievement.

Shortly after, BPA started producing Timorese coins. Despite its limited economic implications, this event constituted a symbolic milestone for the organization and the government. The 2002–03 annual report refers to this event as an "excellent reason to feel proud, having contributed, albeit on a small scale, to the history of Timor-Leste, because the first emission of currency in a newly independent country is a unique occurrence that cannot be repeated" (BPA 2002–03 Annual Report).

The organization worked closely with the government and parliament to develop policy and legislation on the areas of the treasury, payment transactions, insurance, licensing, and anti–money laundering, which are important pillars for the development of the financial sector of a country. The then-BPA was actively involved in setting up the resource wealth management framework.

While building the legal framework for its operation, the organization developed systems and put together teams and divisions in charge of their implementation. In 2008, an automated credit registry was introduced with the goal of improving the quality of credit assessments and reducing risks in lending. New rules on the settlement of large-value transactions (Clearing and Settlement of Interbank Card Transactions) were implemented through the establishment of a clearing house, enabling the processing of payments in the same day starting in 2004. According to client banks, this innovation has allowed them to prevent fraud and deal with difficult cases in a timely manner.

Despite the remaining challenges in extending access to finance and improving financial literacy, the Timorese banking system has grown (table 13.1). Credit to the private sector has increased in areas such as construction, trade, finance, and individual loans (Central Bank 2011). The existing foreign bank branches belong to profitable parent banks, some of the key indicators are presented in table 13.2. Foreign ownership

Table 13.1. Financial Soundness Indicators, 2009–11

Percent

Indicator	2009	2010	2011
Return on assets	1.73	0.31	0.58
NPLs/total loans	32.1	41.7	39.1
Total provisions/NPLs	162.6	131.7	125.4
Loans/deposits	38.4	36.5	43.0

Sources: Central Bank 2011; IMF 2012a.
Note: NPL = nonperforming loan.

of the banks has contributed to a more rapid adoption of international standards in the services provided and the dissemination of technology to support them in collaboration with BPA.

The overall condition of the banking system is positive and considered "healthy" (IMF 2012a). By 2012, foreign assets (mostly in the Petroleum Fund) have risen to US$500 million, which is equivalent to 170 months of imports (see figure 13.1). The amount of deposits in commercial banks grew from US$58.5 million in 2002 to US$344.4 million in 2012, mainly driven by rising public receipts from the oil sector. Credit to the private sector is slowly increasing, currently representing 13 percent of non-oil gross domestic product (GDP) (IMF 2012a) (table 13.2). The volume of credit in the first quarter of 2012 was US$133.3 million, which is more than ten times that of 2002 (see figure 13.2). The rate of nonperforming

Table 13.2. Parent Bank Financial Soundness Indicators, 2011

Capital adequacy ratio	ANZ	Bank Mandiri	Caixa Geral de Depositos
Total	12.1	13.4	12.3
Return on equity	15.3	24.4	4.1
Return on assets	1.0	3.4	0.3

Source: IMF (2012a).

Figure 13.1. Total Assets, 2004–12

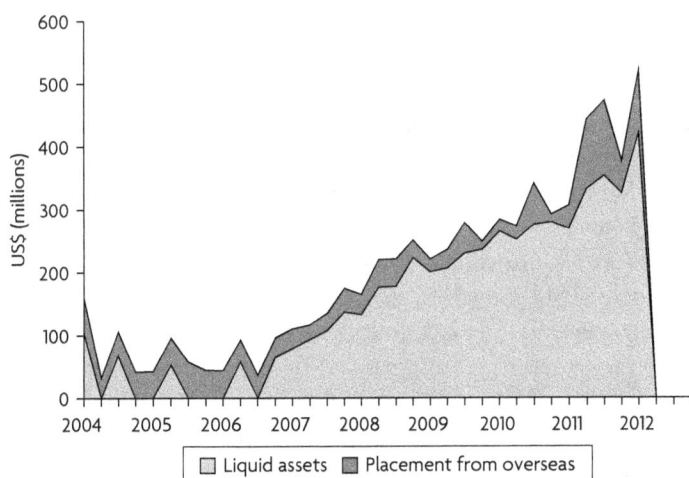

Source: Central Bank 2012.

Figure 13.2. Loan Performance, 2004–12

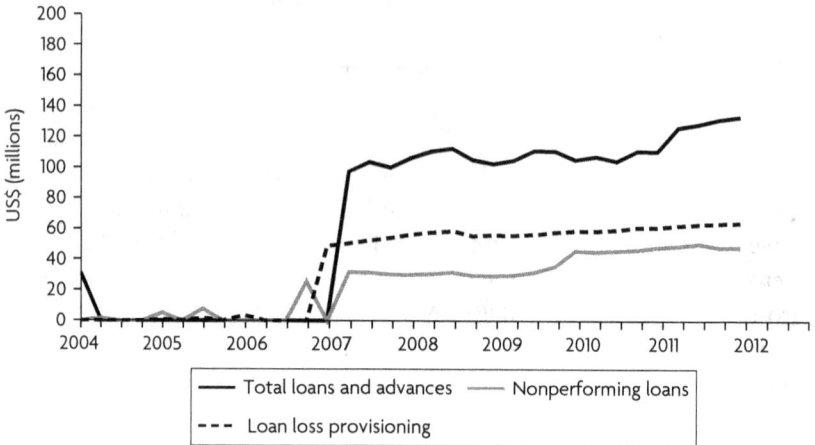

Source: Central Bank 2012.

loans is relatively high, but they are fully covered by provisions against potential losses (Central Bank/BPA 2011). Concurrently, the percentage of money that banks are placing abroad has decreased as a consequence of the higher number of domestic loans. See also tables 13A.1 and 13A.2 in the annex.

According to the Petroleum Law, all the taxes and revenues from the oil industry are deposited in the Petroleum Fund and channeled through the budget. Since its inception in 2005, the Petroleum Fund's holdings have grown geometrically. New projects coming online in the Timor Sea and high international oil prices have led to a steady increase in revenues. Starting with a balance of US$250 million dollars, the Petroleum Fund had reached more than US$10.3 billion by the first quarter of 2012. BPA was directly involved in the process of limited diversification of the investment strategy for the Petroleum Fund and in selecting its managers.[1]

Annual withdrawals are subject to a ceiling based on the Estimated Sustainable Income (ESI). However, since 2008 the government, with the approval of parliament, has made withdrawals exceeding the ESI.[2] Budget execution has accelerated in recent years, with expenditures going from US$65 million in 2005 to US$1.2 billion in 2011 (see figures 13.3 and 13.4). Since then, the government has pursued an aggressive policy to increase budget execution and capital investment, while strengthening basic financial management and delegating procurement authority to line ministries.

Figure 13.3. Government Capital and Current Expenditures, 2005–12

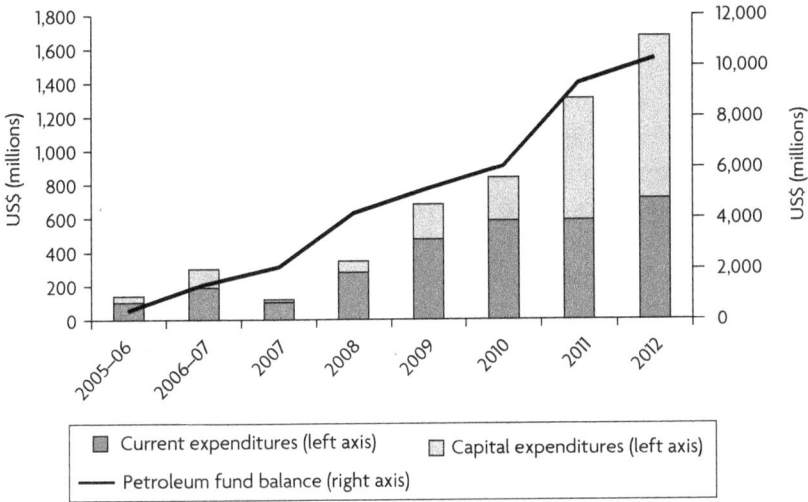

Source: Based on data from the Ministry of Finance of Timor-Leste.

Figure 13.4. Government Revenue and Expenditure, 2000–11

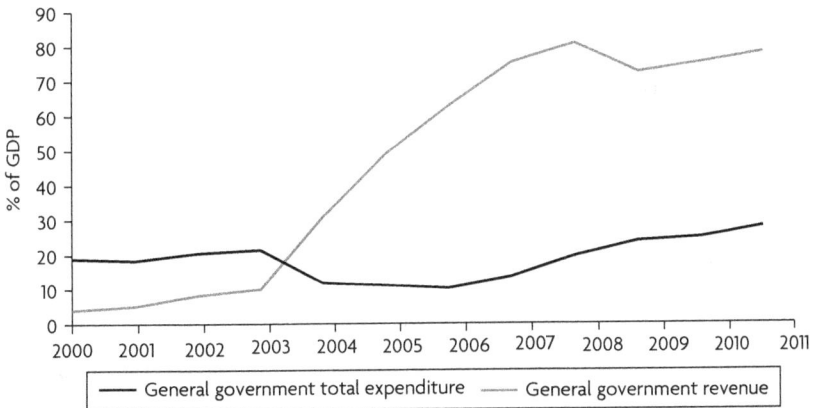

Source: IMF 2012b.

Importantly, the institution has managed and adapted to an ever-growing volume of operations ranging from processing and clearing checks and interbank payment orders, the execution of domestic and international payments related to government activities, payments to civil servants, and importing and distributing currency. Almost from the beginning, the agency used real-time accounting, and developed information management systems that have allowed it to closely control its transactions. This was achieved despite the difficulties arising from the changing characteristics from CPO to BPA and the constraints in the environment. In addition, the institution has made considerable progress in areas that are still not fully developed in most government agencies, such as statistics, internal audit, and procurement.

The Central Bank has successfully handled the drastic increase in government transactions and has maintained transparent reporting on all aspects of the management of the Petroleum Fund. In fact, in 2010 Timor-Leste was declared compliant with the terms of the Extractive Industries Transparency Initiative, which aims to increase the accountability of governments and companies in resource management throughout the world. Timor-Leste was the third country in the world to achieve that status.

Another dimension in which the organization has been successful is in collecting data, completing balance of payments and annual reports on time, and sharing all publications publicly. BPA started collecting economic statistics and publishing them in various formats, including the *Economics Bulletin*. Most of the publications are available in multiple languages. Importantly, since 2008 the institution has been in compliance with the International Monetary Fund's (IMF's) standard report forms, and national statistics are now published regularly in the International Financial Statistics database.

Legitimacy

The Central Bank's legitimacy is crystallized in the positive reputation that it enjoys among domestic and international stakeholders and partners alike. The fact that the institution acts within a delimited and clear legal framework provides it with an important source of procedural legitimacy. The institution is governed by a board that represents all major stakeholders. Its legitimacy also derives from the active outreach campaigns that the organization carries out to engage the public, members of parliament, and civil society about its role. The institution has made efforts to be transparent to the public, publishing its monetary statistics in local newspapers and through its quarterly bulletin, which is available in all official languages.

In the face of prohibitive interest rates, the Central Bank is looking to expand microlending programs in rural areas, which could be a future source of local legitimacy.

The institution has contributed to reaching a wider swath of the population across various regional and socioeconomic divides by expanding financial services. Banks and microfinance institutions have been licensed to operate in nine districts (of 13). Public education about dollarization has been an effective means of bringing the institution closer to citizens, as the 2009 BPA report describes.[3]

International legitimacy is reflected in investments by several international banks that have set up operations in the country. The Central Bank's increasing capacity and its compliance with international norms have earned recognition from the IMF. Two years after its establishment, the Petroleum Fund was ranked the third most transparent and sound sovereign wealth fund in the world (Truman 2008). Although the current rating has dropped because of concerns about the lack of enforcement of the ESI, the Petroleum Fund is still considered among the most transparent in the world.

Resilience

BPA has withstood significant challenges in the past decade. The institution went through a leadership transition in 2004 with the first Timorese assuming the top management role. BPA was the first organization in the country to have all senior management positions filled with nationals. Initially funded by donors, through UNTAET, the institution is now fully capitalized by the government and independent from external financial assistance. Importantly, the institution has continued to make progress amid economic and political instability.

The organization was able to anticipate risks associated with the international financial crisis and effectively protect the domestic financial system. The 2008–09 Annual Report describes this:

The financial year of 2008/09 has been a year of opportunity as well as challenges for the BPA as a juvenile institution which is trying to learn from the experiences and addressed the challenges ahead. The ... financial crisis has given BPA the opportunity to learn from its peers on how to address the distress. The lessons learnt have been enormous not only in relation to the areas where a central bank has to deal with but the most important things are a proper institutional setting to deal with the distress.

(BPA Annual Report 2008/2009)

Sociopolitical and Historical Context: Locking in a Roadmap for Autonomy

In its short life, the Central Bank has continued to expand and adapt its mandate and strategies to the evolving political-economic context and the overall institutional evolution of the government. Building on the credibility and capacity generated by early achievements, the institution has been able to safeguard its autonomy and gain standing as a technically competent organization.

Timor-Leste is undergoing a simultaneous process of nation building and transition to democracy. The consolidation of a democratic regime confronts important problems, including divisions among the elite on what the national development project should be and how to achieve it. The Office of the Prime Minister has concentrated more power, with a strong role in the allocation of public funds. The Parliament remains relatively weak and marginalized in the policy-making process. The general lack of capability of state institutions and their vulnerability to partisan manipulation serve to feed grievances and create windows for opportunistic behavior. After an intense process of capacity building in the early post-independence period, institutional capacity appears to have stabilized at a fairly low level. The country's score for quality of public administration in the World Bank's Country Policy and Institutional Assessment has remained unchanged since 2006. Some progress has been made on the side of macroeconomic management and fiscal policy, especially in relation to capacity building on public financial management.

Against this backdrop, the Central Bank stands out as an institution that has achieved steady development and displayed consistent results in its performance. The organization has continued to stress its political and economic independence and carefully positioned itself vis-à-vis the changing government policy on the Petroleum Fund.

Early in 2000, UNTAET laid the technical foundations of a macroeconomic management framework, establishing the Central Fiscal Authority (CFA) to act as the treasury, collecting revenues from customs and tax, and developing a first budget covering all state expenditures. UNTAET created the Central Payments Office to handle payments for the administration. The bases of a regulatory framework for the supervision of a banking system were also introduced. CPO was the nucleus of what would become the Banking and Payments Authority and later the Central Bank. During the transition to an independent government, BPA led the process of dollarization and issuing of the Timorese coins.

The establishment of the Petroleum Fund in 2005 gave BPA a more central role in the economic management of the country. The Petroleum Fund was created to manage the considerable revenues that the country receives from the extraction of oil and gas in the Joint Petroleum Development Area that Australia and Timor-Leste share. The main objectives were to smooth public expenditures to mitigate negative economic impacts and ensure intergenerational equity in the use of the resources. Following the Norwegian model, the Petroleum Fund was designed to ensure transparency and discourage off-budget spending. According the Petroleum Law, all withdrawals from the fund are to be transferred directly to the national budget, and the amount should be determined by a formula that estimates the sustainable level of consumption. Managing the fund has since been one of the main activities of BPA.

Initially, the country faced important challenges in building the credibility of the Petroleum Fund. The 2006 Crisis cast additional doubt on the economic prospects of the country. Nonetheless, a year later, the Peterson Institute ranked Timor-Leste's sovereign wealth fund as the third best in the world in terms of governance and management performance. During 2006 and 2007, the institution continued to invest in capacity in collaboration with the IMF and the Bank of Portugal and Bank Indonesia. It worked with the government to pass important pieces of legislation, including regulations on banking and insurance. In the words of the then-General Manager, referring to the crisis, "Despite the storm the boat was taken to harbor safe" (interview with senior staff, November 2011).

Concerned with maintaining political stability and building citizen support for state institutions, the Gusmão administration has considerably scaled up public spending and prioritized investment in infrastructure and social sectors. In particular, there have been considerable efforts to assist internally displaced persons by providing them with cash settlements and other forms of aid. In 2009, a referendum package was approved to promote small infrastructure projects in all districts and to promote the local private sector and short-term employment. The government also introduced several cash transfer programs and pensions for elderly and disabled persons. And it has taken several steps to revise the architecture of wealth management introduced in 2005 by the Petroleum Law and launched a strategic plan to diversify the economy. The 2012 budget included capital investment to total US$958 million, representing 45 percent of the 2011 spending and twice the level of ESI established by the Petroleum Law.

The institution has played a crucial role the identification of potential external managers and the definition of the terms of reference and transparency requirements. In 2009, the Bank of International Settlements (BIS) was entrusted to manage a fifth of the balance of the Petroleum Fund to invest it in sovereign and supranational bonds in euros, U.S. dollars, Australian dollars, British pounds, and Japanese yen. In 2010, Schroeder Investment Management was selected as the first equity manager to invest 4 percent of the Petroleum Fund in global stocks. The rest of the funds continue to be managed internally by the Central Bank. In March 2012, the Ministry of Finance and the Central Bank announced that up to 20 percent of the fund will be progressively invested in equity.

In September 2011, BPA became the Central Bank of Timor-Leste. The new organic law (No. 5/2011) gave broader powers and autonomy to the new central bank. The entity is to be managed by a governor supported by two deputy governors and a board of directors. Abraão Vasconselos, who previously was general manager of BPA since 2004, was appointed as the first governor. The transformation of BPA into the Central Bank of Timor-Leste was seen as an important step in the completion of the macroeconomic management architecture of the country.

BPA and its successor have been important advocates of the Petroleum Fund's architecture and the need to protect it from individual or group political and economic interests. The institution uses its regular press releases and press conferences, as well as its communications with the government, as a means to stress its position regarding macroeconomic management. For example, at the inaugural ceremony of the Central Bank, the governor underscored the need "to advance Accountability and Transparency, defining the powers conferred by its functions as Central Bank and allowing the process of supervision by the Public" (Governor's Speech at the Inaugural Ceremony, September 2011).

The unique circumstances under which the organization was established and the fact that, for many years, external partners had significant influence, created an environment that was conducive for its development. The visibility of the Petroleum Fund has guaranteed the continuing support and interest of international finance institutions and bilateral donors. In addition, having an independent central bank is an important marker in the process of state building and, therefore, consistent with the goals of the elites and the government. However, the new resource wealth management structure could have negative consequences in the long term and limit the role of the Central Bank in economic policy.

External Operational Environment: Securing Autonomy and Building Relationships with Stakeholders

Whereas the operating environment of public administration in Timor-Leste has been turbulent and marked with change, BPA and the central bank have been largely sheltered from it. The institutional setup insulates the agency from the political economy context and grants it considerable independence. The institution has the strong backing of international stakeholders and banks.

Isomorphic influences are visible. CPO closely followed the model of the public financial management system implemented in Kosovo by the United Nations and the IMF, whereas the design of the Petroleum Fund mirrored Norway's sovereign wealth fund and international best practice. At the same time, clear international standards for banking supervision and other functions performed by central banks have allowed the institution to devise a long-term development plan and assess its progress against the various accepted benchmarks.

Considering the Timorese context, the Central Bank adapted some of its services and acted as a bank and a tax collection agent and, on occasion, mounted mobile payment units to reach districts. The institution opened a branch in Oecusse, which is physically separated from the rest of the territory.

Using Partnerships to Deliver on the Organizational Mandate

The organization has strong relations with external partners that have been instrumental in creating the existing capacity. These include the IMF, the World Bank, and the central banks of Portugal, Malaysia, and Indonesia, among others. Over 85 percent of the technical staff has received training abroad or participated in secondment programs. Through these exchanges, the staff has been introduced to professional networks and the institution now participates in regional forums for central bankers. They share the goal of sustaining technical gains as a means to maintain macroeconomic stability and long-term policy development. In the management of the Petroleum Fund, the institution works in partnership with JP Morgan, the BIS, and Schroeder Management.

Use of the U.S. dollar as national currency has contributed to the credibility of the country, while relieving the Central Bank from pressures to use monetary policy in the short term. At the same time, the original framework of wealth management protected the Central Bank from external pressures by defining a clear division of responsibilities.

At present, there are three commercial banks in Timor-Leste, all of which are branches of foreign-owned banks, including ANZ, CGD (Caixa Geral do Depósitos), and Bank Mandizi. ANZ is not a lending institution, but provides financial services in the Dili area. CGD has branches in six districts (Bacau, Gleno, Maliana, Oecusse, Viqueque, and Suai), and offers a variety of products targeted to the informal sector and rural areas. Bank Mandizi mainly serves Indonesian businesses in Timor-Leste and commercial enterprises. ANZ and CGD started their operations in 2000 and Bank Mandini in 2003. Although the financial sector is still small and developing, the low financial literacy among the majority of the population translates into little demand.

The microfinance sector is also small. The main institutions providing this type of services include IMFTL (Instituição de Microfinanças de Timor-Leste), three nongovernmental organizations (CASHPOR, Moris Rasik, and Tuba Rai Metin), and a credit union established by the Asian Development Bank. These are members of the Association for Microfinance in Timor-Leste. Although the Central Bank does not regulate them, it grants them a limited license with caps on the microcredit loan portfolio, the amount of deposits maintained, and the liquidity ratio.

Placing Transparency at the Center of Stakeholder Engagement

BPA has stressed the importance of transparency, and it actively engages external stakeholders and civil society. As part of its communication strategy, the institution regularly publishes quarterly publications on statistics, monthly reports on the performance of the Petroleum Fund, and the minutes of the committee meetings. BPA conducted a broad public outreach campaign to educate the public about the adoption of the dollar as a single currency. Following these practices, the Central Bank holds regular media conferences, and it was one of the first institutions to have a working website, with most materials available in Tetum, Portuguese, and English.

The Central Bank has since its early days strategically used the speeches of the governor and the communiqués of the board to introduce and highlight topics of the public agenda related to the institutional mandate as defined by the incorporation law. This aspect has been highlighted as very positive by civil society representatives and development partners alike. In its July 2011 submission to the parliament on the proposed amendments to the Petroleum Law that would be passed later that year, BPA expressed its concerns about the implications of the changes in the following manner (July 2011 Submission to Parliament):

> The BPA notes that the proposed amendments to the law have the poten-
> tial to significantly increase the influence and authority of the Ministry
> of Finance over the management of the Petroleum Fund at the expense
> of the institutional checks and balances built into the existing law. In
> particular, the Minister of Finance will have the power to determine
> (with the approval of parliament) who the operational manager shall
> be. Furthermore, the proposed amendments transfer significant responsi-
> bilities from the Investment Advisory Board to the Ministry of Finance,
> while at the same time disenfranchising the Central Bank and Treasurer
> from their ex officio positions in the Investment Advisory Board, poten-
> tially separating the investment and management of the Petroleum Fund
> from the nation's fiscal and monetary functions.
>
> In 2004/5 BPA officials actively worked with the Ministry of Finance
> throughout the legal drafting of the Petroleum Fund law as it stands
> today. However during the 2010/11 review, the Ministry of Finance
> has not involved the Banking and Payments Authority in the develop-
> ment of the proposed amendments, except to the extent of giving the
> BPA an opportunity to make a written submission on an earlier draft of
> the amendments during the brief period of public consultations in late
> October 2010, at which time the Minister gave the BPA an even shorter
> period. . . .

The institution works closely with counterparts such as JP Morgan, which is the custodian of the Petroleum Fund and manages passive invest-ments, and with BIS and Schroeder who handle active investments. The Central Bank diligently supervises three banking institutions and has fre-quent communications with them in addition to regular supervision visits. The clients describe the staff as "a competent team with a good organiza-tion and division of labor" and as "paying great attention to details." The clients in the interviews for this study provided many examples in which the close collaboration with the Central Bank has allowed them to solve problems and avert risks. Similarly, they unanimously recognize the signifi-cant gains in capacity made by the institution in a relatively short period of time and the professionalism and work ethic of its staff, which in their view are not as common in the public sector.

Another important client of the Central Bank is the Ministry of Finance and in particular the Director-General for Treasury. The advisors and staff members interviewed agreed that the institution has steadily improved its capacity and "supported the ministry in the rapid scaling up of payments and transactions since 2007." The Central Bank has helped the ministry to improve its own technical capacity in areas such as economic modeling and statistics. The interviewees appreciated that the institution has resisted external pressures, including from donors, to keep expatriates in management and consistently followed a policy of merit-based appointments and Timorization.

Incorporating the Lessons from Other Postconflict Experiences

The design of the Central Payments Office and the decision to implement a quasi-central bank model were directly informed and influenced by the experience of the United Nations, the IMF, and the World Bank in the Balkans and particularly in Kosovo. This model emphasized the introduction of a simple structure and set of regulations, on the basis of which more complex tasks and structures could be built as the government and the domestic financial sector developed. Similarly, the institutional structure for managing oil and gas, as well as the revenues resulting from its exploitation, closely replicates that of Norway. The fact that Australia shares the rights to the Joint Development Area also has influenced the design of the petroleum regime and the features of the natural resource management architecture.

Another factor that has contributed to normative isomorphism is that central bankers and bank supervising agencies form one of the strongest transnational networks of government officials (Slaughter 2004).[4] There is strong consensus among experts and practitioners on the principles and structures that would achieve the best results. These are crystallized for example in the Core Principles for Effective Banking Supervision.[5] Yet, the concept of an autonomous central bank, stressing the importance of taking politics out of the economy to ensure fiscal discipline and monetary stability, is relatively new (Polillo and Guillén 2005); it spread during the 1990s (Keefer and Stasavage 1998).

The staff was introduced to these concepts and the professional network through training and exchange programs early in the development of the organization.[6] Most of the staff were recruited and trained by the IMF and the World Bank. They were subsequently divided into two groups, one for CPO and one for CFA. Many of the staff members have spent time abroad in development assignments and working for peer organizations. Moreover, the returned diaspora, many of whom went on to occupy positions of leadership in the transitional government and in the economic sector, had been exposed to these ideas in the countries where they were educated and began their professional careers, such as Australia, Indonesia, and Portugal.

In addition, there have been other elements that have enforced this approach. The strong influence of donors for most of the independent history of the country has been a driver of the adoption of the current economic management structure. In many instances, funding and technical assistance were made conditional on the country introducing specific institutional reforms. At the same time, having an independent institution managing monetary policy and supervising banks constitutes an important signal to foreign investors that the government is committed to macroeconomic prudence. Thus, it was required for attracting the banks and investors necessary to achieve the economic diversification that the government sees as an important pillar of national development.

Benefitting from Effective Donor Coordination

Close donor coordination has been in place from the outset of the peacekeeping operation and during the international administration. This coordination effort covered not only United Nations agencies, but also nongovernmental organizations and bilateral assistance. A Joint Assessment Mission conducted in October 1999 resulted in a common diagnosis of needs and a division of labor among development partners. The strong multilateral coordination was reflected in the establishment of two trust funds, an IDA-administered Trust Fund for East Timor administered by the International Development Association (IDA), amounting to US$170 million, and a smaller UNTAET Trust Fund to cover recurrent expenditures and capital expenditures of the civil administration and justice sectors.[7] A coordination unit at UNTAET facilitated the work of bilateral donors. The simple macroeconomic framework established ensured transparency in the financial management of these resources and laid the foundations for the new government (World Bank 2006). In the specific context of CPO and CFA, the main donors working with the institution were the IMF, World Bank, and Asian Development Bank.

Internal Institutional Workings: Building-Block Approach and Organizational Learning

Strong donor coordination, an initial consensus between domestic and external stakeholders on a blueprint for organizational development, consistent resourcing and technical assistance, and enough political space to guard the independence of the institution were some of the most relevant factors of the external operating environment that explain the early success. At the same time, these elements have been reflected in how the institution developed internally (see table 13.3). The mandate has grown since the

Table 13.3. Milestones of the Central Bank

Year	Sociopolitical context	External operating environment	Internal institutional workings
1999	Referendum and ensuing violence INTERFET deployment		
2000	UNTAET became responsible for the country's administration Australia signed memorandum of understanding over revenues from oil fields in Timor Sea, giving Timor-Leste 90% of revenues		Creation of the Central Payments Office
2001	Election of 88-member Constituent Assembly, Fretilin party gained majority		Transition to the Bank and Payment Authority
2002	Independence declared Political mission, UNMISET, replaced UNTAET Constitution approved		Dollarization and issuing of Timorese coins
2004	Production at offshore gas field began at Bay Undan	Introduction of own terms of payment Petroleum Law passed	Completion of Timorization Creation of Petroleum Fund Division
2005	Remaining Australian peacekeepers left	Capitalization Memorandum of understanding with the government on Petroleum Fund management	Petroleum Fund commenced operations Credit Registry Information Systems and Large Value Transfer Systems operational

(continued next page)

Table 13.3. Milestones of the Central Bank (*continued*)

Year	Sociopolitical context	External operating environment	Internal institutional workings
2006	Factional violence left 25 dead and thousands internally displaced Foreign troops returned to Dili Prime Minister Alkatiri resigned UNMIT set up		
2007	Elections resulted in a coalition-led government with Xanana Gusmao as Prime Minister, prompting violent protests	Timor-Leste EITI candidate	
2008		Scaling-up of public spending	
2009	International crisis Food crisis		Appointment of the Bank for International Settlements as external manager of 20% of the Petroleum Fund
2010			Appointment of Schroder Investment Management Limited as manager of 4% of the Petroleum Fund (to be invested in global stocks)
2011		Central Bank Organic Law passed Timor-Leste EITI compliant	Incorporation of the Central Bank of Timor-Leste

Source: Banking and Payments Authority and Central Bank Annual Reports, 2003–11.
Note: EITI = Extractive Industries Transparency Initiative, INTERFET = United Nations International Force for East Timor, UNMISET = United Nations Mission in East Timor, UNMIT = United Nations Integrated Mission in Timor-Leste, UNTAET = United Nations Transitional Administration of East Timor.

creation of the Central Payments Office, but initially it was quite succinct. Building on early achievements, the mandate was expanded considerably in the past decade, going from an office exclusively dedicated to making the government's payments to handling a multibillion dollar Petroleum Fund. Each new task has been accompanied with the addition of a specialized department, following a building-block approach to institution building from less to more complex activities.

Shielded from the political cycle, the institution has enjoyed stability in its top leadership and in middle management. Senior management has emphasized professionalism and the strict adherence to the formal mandate of the institution as a means of defending its independence, as well as converging with international standards. These values are manifest in the activities and culture of the organization.

The organization has gone a long way in terms of building capacity and actively promoting learning. CPO was initially staffed by international experts. A cohort of Timorese staff were recruited in the early days of independence, trained and paired with an international staff until they were ready to take over the tasks. However, the staff was told that they needed to be ready to take over functions if expatriates were to leave at any time. Beyond the initial training and mentoring, the organization continued to invest in building the capacity needed to carry out the functions and acquire experience as central bankers. The introduction of the 2004–07 Corporate Plan stated, "The intellectual capital of the BPA is in many ways more important than its financial capital, and the emphasis on this aspect of our development is so that we can continue to respond to the changing environment..." (BPA Corporate Plan 2004). This strategy has been facilitated by the autonomy that the institution has over human resource management decisions and by a more competitive pay scale.

The structure was designed to address core functions and in such manner that departments would be added as these expanded. There are four departments and four divisions (see figure 13A.1). The institutional structure has not significantly changed since its inception, except for the addition of the Petroleum Department and the personnel and specialized investment and risk management divisions.

Developing Timorese Leadership and Corporate Identity

The institution has focused on generating human capital to fill top positions and on maintaining stability. At the early stage of its establishment, the organization was managed by international expatriates under the technical assistance program of the IMF. Since August 2004, all line management positions have been Timorized, with a small number of expatriates remaining as advisors in key areas. The Central Bank has consistently invested in human capital through long- and short-term training, secondments (in the Bank of Portugal, Bank Indonesia, Bank Negara Malaysia, Indonesian Banking Institute, South East Asian Central Banks (SEACEN), and the IMF Institute in Singapore) and more recently the establishment of a training center. The Central Bank is exploring the possibility of sending personnel to train in other entities with which it has links, such as JP Morgan, Mercer, BIS, KPMG, and Deloitte.

In the first 10 years of the organization's history, there have been only two general managers, Luis Quintaneiro, 2002–04, and Abraão Vasconcelos, since 2004. All the department heads have been with the institution since the creation of CPO. Only one left to spend some time in the private sector and then returned after a year. Both general managers have emphasized accountability and transparency as central values that should guide the institution's daily work. In the speech for the inauguration of the Central Bank in 2011, Mr. Vasconcelos stated, "The creation of the Timor-Leste Central Bank is an initiative to control the activities carried out by private banks scattered across the territory, and thus can advance with Accountability and Transparency, defining the powers conferred by its functions as Central Bank," as well as that the institution "aspires to the highest standards of Stability, Transparency and Prosperity." The emblem of a buffalo was chosen as the institutional logo because it represents "the Timor-Leste property and symbolizes the concept of stability and transparency in the Timorese financial system," in Mr. Vasconselos' words (Governor's Speech at the Inaugural Ceremony, September 2011).

There is a strong emphasis on professionalism and work ethic, as well as a merit culture that is promoted at all levels of leadership. Employees refer to these values as the features that distinguish the Central Bank from the rest of public administration. They consider themselves "lucky that after being recruited they were assigned to CPO instead of CFA" (interview with senior staff, 2011). To them, their professional standing results from their belonging to the organization.

The Central Bank adopted a code of conduct in 2011 that stresses that in their conduct staff members should act to preserve the independence and credibility of the agency and be mindful of their legal obligations and what is proper. Other values that are stressed include honesty and diligence, as well as promoting equality in the workplace.

Laying the Building Blocks for Organizational Development

The building-block approach has been translated in successive changes and improvements to the structure and management of the institution. Various tools and organizational innovations have been introduced, with the financial and technical assistance of external partners, to respond to the expanding mandate and new demands from clients. The consistency of government supports the goal of creating an independent central bank, even in times of turmoil. Consistency has translated into a fairly predictable external operating environment that in turn has allowed the institution to focus on and deploy resources to improve its management practices. Buy-in from staff to these efforts has been critical.

The organization has introduced various information management systems, such as the Credit Registry Information Systems and the Large Value Transfer Systems, statistical packages, and accounting and human resource management utility programs. Most of the documentation produced by the Central Bank is posted monthly and quarterly on the website, including calls for bids and job openings (and updates on various processes) since its early days.

Since 2004, the organization has had its own remuneration system. In 2006, remuneration conditions were revised and a plan to attract qualified human resources developed. In 2009, with technical support from the Bank of Portugal, the institution underwent a complete review of its human resource policy, resulting in the implementation of a new Human Resource Management Integrated System, named SIGRH, and a new salary structure and bonus system. A key goal of the system has been to focus human resources management and rewards on merit rather than seniority and to promote a culture that is aligned with the institution's mission and strategy.

The SIGRH was designed as a communication tool to reinforce the corporate identity and assess performance according to the importance of the position in the institution's hierarchy, skills, knowledge, and attitudes required by each job definition. Furthermore, in the new career system, individuals who achieve certain goals or skills can be promoted faster without going through all the steps. The Performance Improvement System was designed to measure performance in a more transparent manner, while providing rewards, including an annual bonus, to those employees that meet their expected objectives. The institution has improved its recruitment and selection processes and implemented a new training policy that created opportunities for in-house training and increased transparency in the allocation of scholarships for study abroad. As part of its three-year corporate plan, the organization regularly assesses the staffing needs to accommodate possible expansion of activities and operations.

Challenges

After emerging from a long struggle for independence and internal conflicts in 1999 and 2006, Timor-Leste has made substantial progress in setting up a sound architecture for the management of its economy. Yet, many challenges lie ahead, including the need to extend financial service access, control double-digit inflation, decide whether the country should adopt a national currency different from the U.S. dollar, and what the mechanisms for managing its oil wealth should be.

In the absence of monetary policy to fulfill the objective of containing inflation, the Central Bank would need to persuade the government to change or phase spending and only increase government expenditures gradually. Rising government spending has helped spur short-term economic growth (figure 13.5), but has increased price pressures and imposed costs on the poor (IMF 2012a). The previous spikes in inflation were associated with the social unrest of 2006–07 and high food prices in 2008 (see figure 13.6). Many experts have pointed out that the actual rate of inflation may be higher. In addition, Timor-Leste is affected indirectly by the appreciation of its neighbors' currencies vis-á-vis the U.S. dollar.

Although Timor-Leste has been relatively insulated from the global financial crisis, the internal downturn has meant that the investments of the Petroleum Fund have not produced the expected returns. The low interest rates set by the U.S. Federal Reserve has decreased the return on U.S. government securities, which make up the majority of the portfolio.

Figure 13.5. Gross Domestic Product in Constant Prices, 2000–11

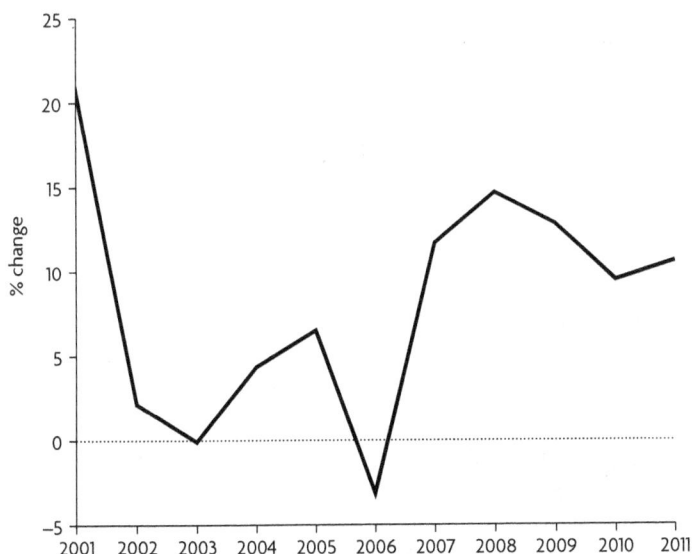

Source: IMF 2012b.

Figure 13.6. Inflation, End-of-Period Consumer Prices, 2000–11

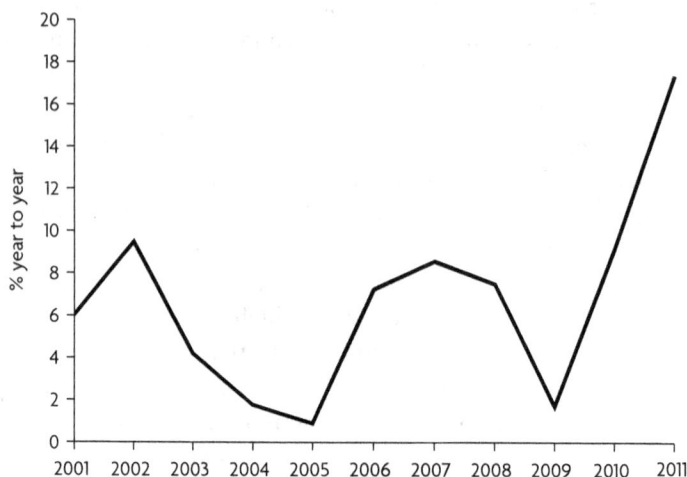

Source: IMF 2012b.

At the same time, if the Petroleum Fund had invested in stocks, there could have been capital losses. Thus, the more conservative strategy proved sound in light of the losses suffered by other sovereign wealth funds, such as Norway's sovereign wealth fund, which lost US$15 billion in 2011 as equities slumped due to concerns about Europe's debt crisis.

However, the architecture of the Petroleum Fund has been increasingly challenged. The main changes proposed to the Petroleum Law included diversification of investment and risk management, the possibility of assigning the administration of the Petroleum Fund to an entity other than the Central Bank, and the government's use of the fund for temporary appropriations that do not require parliamentary approval. The main argument used to support these changes is that because Timor-Leste has little domestic capital and extensive infrastructure needs, frontloading capital investments would have greater economic and social returns than investments in foreign securities. At the same time, there are concerns around the quality of spending and how allocation decisions are being made to ensure that the expected returns materialize.

The fact that the large majority of Timorese remains unbanked and with limited access to credit is another important challenge that the Central Bank and the government have not yet tackled. The interest rates remain high as a result of the business risk and the relative fragility of the economy. Most of the potential borrowers do not have collateral, and there are significant issues around land titling in urban and rural areas, as well as problems related to the regulation of commercial activity. Simultaneously, the owners of saving deposits are receiving negative interest because the interest rates are very low.

Conclusions

The key elements driving success have been the deployment of a simple legal framework, a progressive approach to institutional development, a sustained emphasis on improving the capacity of national staff and organizational learning, and the stability in middle and senior management. At the same time, there has been strong buy-in from senior and middle management to the institutional development roadmap and a consistent focus on reaching milestones. Early successes have contributed to shaping the organizational identity and culture, including demonstrating the importance of communication with stakeholders and transparency.

The external support from donors and the Timorese government has given the institution the space and resources to pursue capacity building at a steady pace. There have also been consistency and continuity in technical support and a conscious choice to use country systems (as opposed to creating parallel structures staffed with consultants) and phase out expatriates. Having an independent central bank has had important symbolic implications for the nation-building project. This has ensured the support of all political camps. At the same time, the high profile and visibility of the Petroleum Fund ensured that developing the institution remained a high priority in the public agenda. The increasing degree of political and financial autonomy has allowed the institution to increase the remuneration of employees and introduce an innovative performance management system. Nonetheless, these elements came later on and are the result rather than the cause of success.

The trajectory of this institution, culminating with the incorporation of the Central Bank, demonstrates the benefits of following a building-block approach in postconflict settings that need to build capacity from a very low level or zero. Starting with a simple structural design and setting modest goals on the basis of which more complex functions and structures could be added has been a critical element behind the success of the Central Bank.

This case demonstrates that when factors such as a broad and sustained commitment by all camps of the elite are coupled with sufficient resources, access to specialized technical assistance, and strong buy-in of the institution's leadership and staff to the organizational development roadmap, state capacity can be built in a relatively short period of time and in a cost-effective manner.

Introducing transparency and communication strategies to reach a wide audience early on not only helped the institution to build its credibility, but also demonstrated the benefits of transparency to internal and external stakeholders. To some extent, openness became the default way of operating and deviating from it became more difficult and increasingly costly.

Annex 13A

Table 13A.1. Monetary Developments, 2006–11
Percent, unless otherwise indicated

	2006	2007	2008	2009	2010	2011
Banking system[a]						
Net foreign assets[b]	113	318	393	443	622	558
Gross reserves	84	230	210	250	406	368
Other foreign assets	61	126	211	219	244	368
Foreign liabilities	31	38	29	26	28	178
Net domestic assets	−13	−174	−200	−174	−327	−210
Net credit to central government	−83	−219	−230	−206	−331	−248
Net credit to state and local government	0	0	0	0	0	0
Net credit to public nonfinancial corporations	0	0	0	0	0	0
Credit to private sector	111	101	102	104	110	136
Other items (net)	−42	−56	−73	−72	−105	−97
Broad money	100	144	193	268	295	348
Narrow money	54	75	104	157	141	167
Currency in circulation	2	2	2	3	3	4
Transferable deposits	52	73	102	155	138	163
Other deposits	46	68	88	111	154	181
Central Bank						
Net foreign assets[b]	84	230	210	238	394	356
Gross reserves	84	230	210	250	406	368
Foreign liabilities	0	0	0	12	12	12
Net domestic assets	−76	−210	−185	−182	−340	−293
Net credit to central government	−56	−190	−196	−163	−318	−240
Net credit to other depository corporations	1	1	42	2	24	8
Other items (net)	−20	−20	−31	−21	−45	−61
Monetary base		20	26	56	55	63
Currency in circulation[c]	2	2	2	3	3	4
Other liabilities to depositary corporations	6	18	23	53	51	59
Memorandum items						
Annual broad money growth	28.2	43.9	34.1	39.3	9.9	18
Annual reserve money growth	30	147	25.9	120.4	−2.7	15
Annual credit to the private sector growth	5.2	−9.8	1.9	1.1	5.9	23.6
Credit/non-oil GDP	25.6	20.3	16.1	13.1	12.5	12.9
Broad money/non-oil GDP	22.9	29.1	30.4	34	33.7	33.1
Credit/deposits	113.6	71.1	53.9	39	37.6	39.4
Nonperforming loans/total loans	27.8	30.2	28.2	32.1	41.7	—
Amount of nonperforming	25.6	30.3	29.7	35.6	46.3	—
Loan[d]	16.6	15	12.3	10.8	11.1	—
Deposit[e]	1	1	1.1	1.1	1.1	—

Sources: Central Bank of Timor-Leste; IMF staff estimates.

Note: — = not available.

a. Includes the Central Bank, three commercial banks (branches of foreign banks), and a microfinance institution.

b. An oil fund was created in September 2005, and the deposits were moved off-shore and onto the government balance sheet.

c. Includes only coinage issued by the Central Bank. No data are available for notes because of the dollarization of the financial system.

d. Rate offered by other depository corporations on three-month time deposits in U.S. dollars. The rate is weighted by deposit amounts.

e. Rate charged by other depository corporations on loans in U.S. dollars. The rate is weighted by loan amounts.

Table 13A.2. Timor-Leste: Summary Operations of the Central Government, 2008–16

	Budget			Budget 2011	Proj. 2011	Budget 2012	Proj.ª 2012	Projectionsª 2013	Projectionsª 2014	Projectionsª 2015	Projectionsª 2016
	2008	2009	2010	2011	2011	2012	2012	2013	2014	2015	2016
Revenue	2453	1910.5	2407.2	2940	3372.3	2225.9	2957.4	2832.8	2608.4	2748.2	2771.7
Petroleum revenue	2400.2	1844.7	2323.4	2829.5	3261.5	2089.9	2821.3	2674.1	2422.9	2530.3	2515.3
Domestic revenue	52.8	65.8	83.7	110.4	110.8	136.1	136.1	158.7	185.5	217.9	256.3
Expenditure	594.2	627	794.2	1307.9	1206.4	1763.4	1415.6	1538.9	1646.6	1753.6	1858.8
Expense	409.8	405.4	526.5	588.4	559	679	679	710	741.9	775	804.3
Net acquisition of nonfinancial assets	184.4	221.7	267.7	719.5	647.4	1084.4	736.6	828.9	904.7	978.6	1054.5
Overall balance (net lending [+]/ borrowing [-])	1858.8	1283.4	1612.9	1632.1	2165.9	462.6	1541.8	1293.9	961.8	994.6	912.9
Non-oil overall balance	–541.4	–561.2	–710.5	–1197.5	–1095.6	–1627.3	–1279.5	–1380.2	–1461.1	–1535.8	–1602.5
Cash flows from financing activities (% of GDP)											
Net acquisition of financial assets	2026.5	1298.9	1658.5	1632.1	2165.9	495.7	1584.9	1374.1	1042.9	1097.4	1092.9
Net incurrence of liabilities	0	0	0	0	0	33.1	43.1	80.2	81.1	102.8	180
Revenue	80.8	72.5	75.2	68.1	78.1	54.6	72.6	68.1	62.3	59.4	55.3
Taxes	1.3	1.8	1.6	1.5	1.4	2.3	2.3	2.6	2.9	2.9	3
Taxes on income, profits, and capital gains	0.6	0.6	0.6	0.5	0.5	1	1	1	1.1	1.1	1.1
Taxes on goods and services	0.5	0.9	0.8	0.8	0.7	1.1	1.1	1.2	1.4	1.5	1.5
Taxes on international trade and transactions	0.1	0.2	0.2	0.2	0.2	0.3	0.3	0.3	0.4	0.4	0.4
Petroleum revenue	79.1	70	72.6	65.6	75.6	51.3	69.3	64.3	57.8	54.7	50.2
Other revenue	0.5	0.7	1	1.1	1.1	1	1	1.2	1.5	1.8	2.1
Expenditure	19.6	23.8	24.8	30.3	28	43.3	34.8	37	39.3	37.9	37.1
Expense	13.5	15.4	16.5	13.6	13	16.7	16.7	17.1	17.7	16.7	16.1
Compensation of employees	1.7	3.3	2.9	2.7	2.6	3.4	3.4	3.5	3.6	3.4	3.3
Purchases of goods and services	7	8.1	7.6	6.8	6.5	8.5	8.5	8.7	9.1	8.6	8.2

(continued next page)

Table 13A.2. Timor-Leste: Summary Operations of the Central Government, 2008–16 (continued)

	Budget				Proj.	Budget	Proj.[a]	Projections[a]			
	2008	2009	2010	2011	2011	2012	2012	2013	2014	2015	2016
Subsidies/Social Benefits	4.8	4	6	4.1	3.9	4.8	4.8	4.9	5	4.7	4.5
Net acquisition of nonfinancial assets	6.1	8.4	8.4	16.7	15	26.6	18.1	19.9	21.6	21.1	21.1
Gross operating balance	67.3	57.1	58.8	54.5	65.2	38	55.9	51	44.5	42.6	39.3
Net lending / borrowing	61.2	48.7	50.4	37.8	50.2	11.4	37.9	31.1	23	21.5	18.2
Cash flows from financing activities											
Net acquisition of financial assets	66.8	49.3	51.8	37.8	50.2	12.2	38.9	33	24.9	23.7	21.8
Net incurrence of liabilities	0	0	0	0	0	0.8	1.1	1.9	1.9	2.2	3.6
Revenue	386.5	241.9	274.9	279	320	177.8	236.2	190.5	147.6	130.9	111.1
o/w Petroleum revenue	378.2	233.6	265.3	268.5	309.5	166.9	225.3	179.8	137.1	120.5	100.9
Expenditure	93.6	79.4	90.7	124.1	114.5	140.8	113.1	103.5	93.2	83.5	74.5
Expense (recurrent expenditure)	64.6	51.3	60.1	55.8	53	54.2	54.2	47.7	42	36.9	32.3
Net acquisition of nonfinancial assets (Capital expenditure)	29.1	28.1	30.6	68.3	61.4	86.6	58.8	55.7	51.2	46.6	42.3
Non-oil overall balance	-85.3	-71.1	-81.1	-113.6	-104	-130	-102.2	-92.8	-82.7	-73.2	-64.3
Memorandum items											
Development Partner Commitments (in millions of US $, grants)	184.4	215.6	263.9	272.8	245.5	188.9	188.9	128.8	72	63.7	0
Rice operations (in millions of US $)											
Sales	16.8	20.4	12.6	10	10	0.8	0.8	0.9	1.1	1.2	1.3
Purchases	77.8	31.8	35	0	0	0	0	0	0	0	0
Education (millions of US $)	45.9	61.7	68.8	85	111.1	—	—	—	—	—	—
Education (percent of non-oil GDP)	7.2	7.8	7.9	8.1	8.9	—	—	—	—	—	—
Health (millions of US $)	27.6	28.9	34.6	40.5	51.1	—	—	—	—	—	—
Health (percent of non-oil GDP)	4.3	3.7	4	3.8	4.1	—	—	—	—	—	—
ESI (percent of non-oil GDP)	62.4	51.7	57.3	69.6	73.3	52.9	61.4	52	44.1	37.3	31.6

(continued next page)

Table 13A.2. Timor-Leste: Summary Operations of the Central Government, 2008–16 (*continued*)

	Budget				Proj.	Budget	Proj.ᵃ	Projectionsᵃ			
	2008	2009	2010	2011	2011	2012	2012	2013	2014	2015	2016
Withdrawals above ESI (percent of non-oil GDP)	0	13.2	35.3	18.6	5.2	74.5	37.3	35.4	34	30.9	25.4
Petroleum fund balance	138.3	204.1	215.8	204	216.4	228.2	268.2	295.5	318.4	311.8	310
Crude oil price (US $ per barrel)ᵇ	87.7	73.7	75.7	78.6	81.6	84.7	—	—	—	—	—
Crude oil price (US $ per barrel, WEO)ᶜ	97	61.8	79	104.2	100	99.5	97.5	96.5	95.5	—	—
Non-oil GDP at current prices (in millions of US $)	635	790	876	1054	1054	1252	1252	1487	1767	2099	2494
GDP at current prices (in millions of US $)	3035	2634	3199	4315	4315	4073	4073	4161	4190	4630	5009

Sources: Timor-Leste authorities; IMF staff estimates.

a. IMF staff proposals.

b. Simple average of EIA's low case and reference prices.

c. September 2011 World Economic Outlook assumptions.

— = Not available.

Figure 13A.1. Organogram

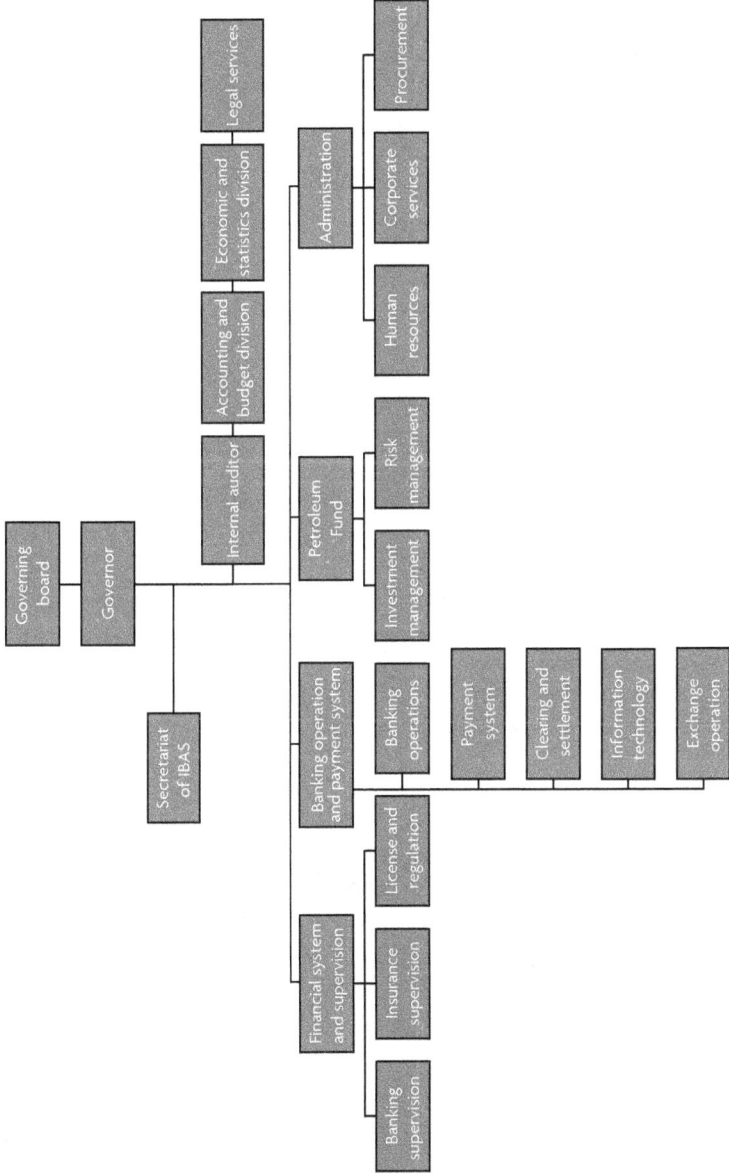

- Governing board
- Governor
  - Secretariat of IBAS
  - Internal auditor
    - Accounting and budget division
    - Economic and statistics division
    - Legal services
  - Petroleum Fund
    - Investment management
    - Risk management
  - Administration
    - Human resources
    - Corporate services
    - Procurement
  - Financial system and supervision
    - Banking supervision
    - Insurance supervision
    - License and regulation
  - Banking operation and payment system
    - Banking operations
    - Payment system
    - Clearing and settlement
    - Information technology
    - Exchange operation

Source: Central Bank of Timor-Leste.

Notes

1. Currently, the assets in the Petroleum Fund are allocated in the following manner: 4 percent in U.S. foreign government and supranational bonds, 4 percent in other government bonds, 4 percent in global equity, and the rest in U.S. bonds.

2. Notwithstanding the rapid increase in oil revenues, spending plans implied that ESI would be exceeded by a significant amount in 2012. The projections on the performance of the Petroleum Fund are contingent on the level of the withdrawals in the next few years and the prospects of developing new fields.

3. "Over the last years the BPA continue to play important roles in educating the community and businesses on the use of the official currency. Various programs have been introduced through public education campaign using different means that cover all territory of Timor-Leste. During the year the BPA focused its program to educate the population to differentiate the counterfeit notes. The program was conducted through staff visit to each district and sub districts, TV and radio programs, distributions of brochures and posters as well as training to relevant entity such as the national police including National Investigation Unit." (BPA/Central Bank 2009)

4. The process by which organizations such as firms or states adopt similar structural forms or practices takes place as a result of normative, mimetic, or coercive pressures (Meyer and Rowan 1977; DiMaggio and Powell 1983).

5. The document has been prepared by a group that includes representatives from the Basle Committee and from Chile; China; the Czech Republic; Hong Kong SAR, China; Mexico; Russia; and Thailand. Nine other countries (Argentina, Brazil, Hungary, India, Indonesia, the Republic of Korea, Malaysia, Poland, and Singapore) have adopted it. The Basle Committee on Banking Supervision brings together banking supervisors. It was established by the central bank governors of the Group of Ten countries in 1975. It consists of senior representatives of banking supervisory authorities and central banks from Belgium, Canada, France, Germany, Italy, Japan, Luxembourg, the Netherlands, Sweden, Switzerland, the United Kingdom, and the United States. It usually meets at the Bank for International Settlements in Basle, where its permanent Secretariat is located.

6. As early as in 2002, the senior staff of BPA took part in conferences and congresses such as the 12th Lisbon Meetings for central banks in countries having Portuguese as the official language; the conference The Challenge of Sustainable Outreach, organized by the Asia-Pacific Rural and Agricultural Credit Association with GTZ (German Agency for Cooperation) in Sri Lanka;

and the Spring Meetings of the IMF and World Bank in Washington (BPA/ Central Bank 2002–03).

7. As Posner (2007) explains: "The TSP [Transition Support Program] has also provided a mechanism for development planning. The two-week joint missions for the TSP that have been held every six months since it began have been crucial in this respect. These missions have involved a series of meetings and discussions among government officials, representatives from bilateral and multilateral donors, and the members of the TSP mission team. These missions have provided a forum in which the government and donors have been able to discuss policy issues, resolve donor coordination problems, review the government's progress in implementing an array of measures and activities agreed on with donors during earlier TSP missions, and formulate a new set of measures and activities for the coming year."

References

BPA/Central Bank. Various years. *Petroleum Fund Annual Reports*. 2005–2011. Central Bank of Timor-Leste, Dili.

DiMaggio, Paul J., and Walter W. Powell. 1983. "The Iron Cage Revisited: Institutional Isomorphism and Collective Rationality in Organizational Fields." *American Sociological Review* 48(2): 147–60.

International Monetary Fund (IMF). 2012a. "Democratic Republic of Timor-Leste: 2011 Article IV Consultation." Country Report No. 12/24. IMF, Washington, DC.

———. 2012b. *World Economic Outlook: Growth Resuming, Dangers Remain*. Washington, DC: International Monetary Fund.

Keefer, Philip, and David Stasavage. 1998. "When Does Delegation Improve Credibility? Central Bank Independence and the Separation of Powers." Working Paper WPS/98/18. Centre for the Study of African Economies, Oxford.

Meyer, John W., and Brian Rowan. 1977. "Institutionalized Organizations: Formal Structure as Myth and Ceremony." *American Journal of Sociology* 83(2): 340–63.

Polillo, Simone, and Mauro F. Guillén. 2005. "Globalization Pressures and the State: The Worldwide Spread of Central Bank Independence." *American Journal of Sociology* 110(6): 1764–1802.

Posner, Daniel N. 2007. "Regime Change and Ethnic Cleavages in Africa." *Comparative Political Studies* 40(11): 1302–27.

Slaughter, Anne Marie. 2004. *New World Order*. Princeton, NJ: Princeton University Press.

Truman, Edwin M. 2008. "Blueprint for Sovereign Wealth Fund Best Practices."
Policy Brief No. PB08-3. Peterson Institute for International Economics,
Washington, DC.
World Bank. 2006. "Strengthening the Institutions of Governance in Timor-Leste."
World Bank, Washington, DC.

ECO-AUDIT
Environmental Benefits Statement

The World Bank is committed to preserving endangered forests and natural resources. The Office of the Publisher has chosen to print *Institutions Taking Root* on recycled paper with 100 percent postconsumer fiber in accordance with the recommended standards for paper usage set by the Green Press Initiative, a nonprofit program supporting publishers in using fiber that is not sourced from endangered forests. For more information, visit www.greenpressinitiative.org.

Saved:
- 32 trees
- 15 million BTUs of total energy
- 2,801 lbs. CO_2 equivalent of greenhouse gases
- 15,190 gallons of waste water
- 1,017 lbs. of solid waste

green
press
INITIATIVE

www.ingramcontent.com/pod-product-compliance
Lightning Source LLC
Chambersburg PA
CBHW071829270326
41929CB00013B/1937